Teaching 21 Thinking Skills for the 21st Century

The MiCOSA Model

CAROL ROBINSON-ZAÑARTU
PATRICIA DOERR
JACQUELINE PORTMAN

PEARSON

Boston • Columbus • Indianapolis • New York • San Francisco • Upper Saddle River
Amsterdam • CapeTown • Dubai • London • Madrid • Milan • Munich • Paris • Montreal • Toronto
Delhi • Mexico City • São Paulo • Sydney • Hong Kong • Seoul • Singapore • Taipei • Tokyo

Senior Acquisitions Editor: Meredith D. Fossel
Executive Development Editor: Linda Bishop
Marketing Director: Bridget Hadley
Editorial Assistant: Laura Marenghi
Marketing Manager: Krista Clark
Production Editor: Mary Beth Finch
Editorial Production Service: S4Carlisle Publishing Services
Manufacturing Buyer: Linda Sager
Electronic Composition: S4Carlisle Publishing Services
Cover Designer: Diane Lorenzo
Cover Photos: Background, Leonello Calvetti/Shutterstock. Clockwise from top: Tyler Olson/Shutterstock; Monkey Business Images/Shutterstock; Monkey Business Images/Fotolia; Minerva Studio/Shutterstock; Monkey Business Images/Fotolia; Hasloo Group Production Studio/Shutterstock; Michaeljung/Shutterstock; Wavebreakmedia/Shutterstock; Monkey Business Images/Shutterstock.

Credits and acknowledgments borrowed from other sources and reproduced, with permission, in this textbook appear on the appropriate page within text.

Microsoft® and Windows® are registered trademarks of the Microsoft Corporation in the U.S.A. and other countries. Screen shots and icons reprinted with permission from the Microsoft Corporation. This book is not sponsored or endorsed by or affiliated with the Microsoft Corporation.

Library of Congress Cataloging-in-Publication Data

Robinson-Zañartu, Carol.
Teaching 21 thinking skills for the 21st century: the MiCOSA model/Carol Robinson-Zañartu,
San Diego State University, Patricia Doerr, Conejo Valley Unified School District, Jacqueline Portman, San Marcos Unified School District, Paloma Elementary School.—First edition.
  pages cm
 ISBN-13: 978-0-13-269844-3
 ISBN-10: 0-13-269844-7
 1. Thought and thinking—Study and teaching. 2. Critical thinking—Study and teaching.
 3. Learning, Psychology of. I. Title.
 LB1590.3.Z36 2015
 370.15'2—dc23

2013033984

10 9 8 7 6 5 4 3 2 1

ISBN-10:   0-13-269844-7
ISBN-13: 978-0-13-269844-3

About the Authors

Carol Robinson-Zañartu (Ph.D., University of Pittsburgh) has authored or co-authored over 50 professional publications largely devoted to issues of educational equity. She has written and directed over $11 million in federal grants to prepare graduate students to work with underserved students, especially Native American and bilingual Spanish-speaking youth. She has worked as a teacher, school psychologist, school principal, and university professor. Until recently, she served as chair of the Department of Counseling and School Psychology at San Diego State University. She has trained both teachers and school psychologists to assess for and create interventions in the classroom to help students develop thinking skills while considering their cultural background as well as content standards. Active in multiple professional associations, she currently serves on the Executive Board of the International Association for Cognitive Education and Psychology, and as a lead reviewer for NASP/NCATE. She is a former president of the California Association for Mediated Learning; consulted broadly across school districts and universities, and made close to 100 presentations to state, national, or international professional associations. At the university level, she teaches graduate courses in the dynamic assessment of cognitive skills and in developing classroom interventions to enhance student thinking.

Patricia (Trish) Doerr (M.S., California Lutheran University) holds her master's degree in special education and a Diploma in Education of Handicapped Children (London University). She has taught special and general education from elementary through secondary levels both in England and the United States, and was a university lecturer in reading. She has served as a district mentor in both special education and language arts, a county teacher-on-leave specialist in language arts, curriculum, and assessment; served as an educational therapist in private practice; and written numerous manuals in the area of language arts. She received the Amgen Award for Teacher Excellence. She has been a trainer for the California Reading and Literature Projects RESULTS and A Focused Approach to Frontloading EL Instruction; a presenter for and fellow of the South Coast Writing Project; a district level Trainer of Trainers for writing across the grade levels; and a consultant to the MindLadder Project. She was a member of the Board of the California Association for Mediated Learning, has studied a variety of models of thinking skill development, and has made numerous professional presentations on their usefulness in the classroom for professional associations, schools, and universities.

Jacqueline (Jackie) Portman (BA Spanish, Nazareth College of Rochester) is a former National Board Certified bilingual teacher, and holds teaching credentials in multiple subjects with a bilingual emphasis in Spanish (San Diego State University). She has taught elementary grades 1–6, ELD/bilingual, and been a university lecturer in the mediation of thinking in the classroom. She has served as a district elementary curriculum specialist, providing district-wide staff development and coaching. She was a mentor teacher for international children's literature in Spanish; initiated a Spanish as a Second Language Program; co-authored district writing curricula in English and Spanish; revised and translated district math curriculum; and presented bilingual workshops in language arts. She served as a consultant to the MindLadder Project, and as a member of the Board of the California Association for Mediated Learning. Over the past 15 years, she has made presentations on classroom and parent applications of cognitive education programs to state and national conferences and school districts. She currently teaches fifth grade and works at the district level to help integrate technology and assessment into the Common Core Standards. For the last decade, her classroom has become a practical laboratory for graduate students at San Diego State University to practice and apply their knowledge of the thinking skills.

Contents

Preface

Have you ever met colleagues who share your excitement about an idea, and then found that their work so complemented your own that the synergy of ideas moved you to a new creation? Several years ago, such a synergy emerged among the three of us. We authors had come from very different experiences in education, yet found ourselves on a common quest to help students develop thinking and learning skills in meaningful contexts. Influenced by impressive researchers and clinicians, each of us had had our own powerful successes in the classroom. Each of us was sharing and presenting our work, yet stumbling with the many requests for the best book for follow-up reading and study. We had found no book that was both practical and highly accessible that showed educators how to skillfully structure and scaffold their language and instruction to really help students develop and apply their thinking. We had found no teaching resource that linked this "mediation" of thinking skills in the classroom with curriculum and standards, built on students' cultures, and helped students learn to transfer their learning. We decided that this story needed to be told, and that we would do our best to tell it. To capture the key ideas of our model, we used the acronym MiCOSA, which stands for **M**ediation **i**n the **C**lassroom: An **O**pen **S**ystems **A**pproach to critical thinking and learning.

Several questions compelled and guided our work in developing *Teaching 21 Thinking Skills for the 21st Century: The MiCOSA Model*: How can you best help students to engage and excel in an era of rapid and dramatic change? How do students best develop the skills needed to thoughtfully access the Common Core State Standards, and become the critical thinkers and collaborators needed to successfully compete in tomorrow's marketplace? How can we assure that MiCOSA's methods also build on and illustrate respect for students' diverse cultural and linguistic backgrounds and ways of learning? These were key questions we strove to answer, drawing on extensive research on how people learn and building on our many combined years of classroom and university experience.

Many of today's educational materials feature critical thinking opportunities. However, the teacher is often faced with the dilemma of how to facilitate the *development* of those critical thinking skills. This is part of the power of MiCOSA. *Teaching 21 Thinking Skills for the 21st Century: The MiCOSA Model* shows teachers how to use a mediating framework—a set of deliberately scaffolded conversations—designed to help students *develop, take ownership of,* and *use* twenty-one carefully selected thinking skills essential to fully access their critical thinking, and to do so within their lesson plans. Using the same framework of mediation, teachers can then help their students learn to *transfer* thinking skills across contexts, bridging from home to school and beyond. Students begin to respond to critical questions and explore problems in new ways and to think more deeply, more clearly, and more precisely about what teachers ask them to consider or do.

The MiCOSA Model builds on teachers' prior knowledge by providing a new lens through which to see several familiar ideas. For example, MiCOSA links the familiar idea of building on prior student knowledge with building on the cultural knowledge and thinking that emerges from their home contexts. MiCOSA links the familiar idea of integrating lessons with strong content and attention to standards with how to find thinking skills within those standards and redesign powerful lessons to capitalize on that thinking. MiCOSA links the use of varied and responsive assessments with introducing assessments to evaluate thinking and transfer. Beyond this, MiCOSA attends to contexts critical to the 21st century: developing critical thinking habits, respecting and responding to our students' diversity, supporting their competence as individuals and as collaborators, and helping them learn to create and express their ideas using innovative experiences and projects. One teacher colleague previewing the book remarked, "All these years we've been told to teach students how to think, but we've not been taught *how* to teach thinking. We haven't really even been taught how to analyze our own thinking. I'm weeping with gratitude that you wrote this book." Augmenting the content, we use the mediating framework to help students build affective resilience as well.

Key Features of the Book

We created this model to guide our fellow educators—from new and seasoned teachers to administrators, teacher educators, and school support personnel—toward understanding their teaching at deeper and richer levels, while supporting their students to become critical and creative thinkers. The book is designed to provide a timely, user-friendly, research-based, and highly applicable set of ideas, skills, processes, and examples. We wanted to assure that teachers could access and use the concepts; we also wanted to ensure that they were realistic and teacher-tested. To support these goals, we included the following pedagogical features:

- *21st Century Demands and Skills* contextualize the work and are referenced throughout the book through MiCOSA's concepts, case scenarios, and strategies.
- *21 Thinking Skills* are thoroughly explained and illustrated. They enable students to successfully access content and standards, and to develop critical thinking needed in the 21st century. We have teacher-tested each skill, individually and often in combination, in real classrooms.
- *The Mediation Framework* provides the teacher with dialogues and interactions that help students develop depth in and ownership of the thinking skills, and then use or transfer them from one context to another.
- *The Common Core State Standards* are integrated throughout—in classroom examples, through finding thinking skills in standards, by understanding Big Ideas

and essential questions, and of course in lesson planning. Teachers are able to see how MiCOSA's 21 thinking skills connect to and support those standards.

- *Over 200 Classroom Strategies* support the integration of thinking skills into lessons and activities. Multiple suggestions to support each thinking skill make it easier for teachers across content and grade levels to select helpful ideas for their own classrooms. Strategies build on familiar techniques and introduce many new ones, supporting gradual integration into the classroom. They are found in the book as well as in PDToolkit.

- *21 MiCOSA Thinking Skill Cards and Posters* each provide a graphic representation to support understanding. The cards provide sentence starters to help students begin to bridge and transfer the thinking skill. They can be downloaded from PDToolkit to support, reinforce, and bridge student learning across content areas. The posters can be placed around the classroom to remind students of the thinking skills they may be using or may want to access in any lesson or project.

- *Case Examples from Real Classrooms* illustrate and help teachers relate to the concepts. All student examples are drawn from real classroom experiences.

- *Video Clips* show classroom examples of teachers using many of the concepts discussed. Throughout the text, icons direct the reader to specific video examples that are available on PDToolkit. Video examples help "make it real," allowing teachers to picture how someone else does it, and then envision how they themselves might mediate or introduce a given skill into their own lessons.

- *Ideas for Working Effectively with Culturally Diverse Students* are central to the model, as well as to 21st century skills of multicultural competence and global awareness.

- *Up-to-Date Assessment Ideas* are integrated into and complement the model. In addition, MiCOSA includes *unique* assessments to support both the teacher and students in evaluating student strengths and challenges with each of the thinking skills.

- *The MiCOSA Lesson Planning Guides,* both short and long versions, help teachers integrate thinking skills, standards, assessment, attention to diversity, and strong content. Lesson planning draws the map for the teacher, and helps teachers incorporate and track all the key components of the model.

- *Teacher Reflection During Reading.* As each thinking skill is introduced and illustrated, teachers are asked to think of a student who might perform better if he or she was more efficient with that skill: "My example: Think of a student who is inefficient with _____." Then, following a discussion of various ways to mediate that skill or issue, we ask the teacher to reflect, "How might I mediate _____ [the student they named above] ."

- *A Scaffolded Guide to Getting Acquainted with MiCOSA* outlines a process for teachers using the book to learn and practice the model. It can be used individually, in teams, or as a whole school across the year, and provides supporting materials.

PDToolkit for Teaching 21 Thinking Skills for the 21st Century: The MiCOSA Model

Purchase of Teaching 21 Thinking Skills for the 21st Century: The MiCOSA Model includes access to PDToolkit, a website with media resources that, together with this text, provides the tools you need to fully explore and implement the concepts presented in the book. The PDToolkit for Teaching 21 Thinking Skills for the 21st Century: The MiCOSA Model is available free for 12 months after you register using the access code that comes with this book. After that, it is available by subscription for a yearly fee. Be sure to explore the following resources:

- 34 Video Clips Support Implementation
- Over 120 Additional Strategies and Activities
- 21 Thinking Skill Cards and Posters (downloadable)
- Thinking Skill Assessment Questionnaires and Interview Forms
- Sample Lesson Plans and Downloadable Forms
- Administrative Leaders and Facilitators' Support Materials

Overview and Organization of the Book

The book is organized around four thematic sections: Contextual and Conceptual Frameworks; Critical Components of the Model; Implementing MiCOSA; and Motivating Tomorrow's Learning. Together, they address, in depth, what is needed to help your students emerge as critical thinkers in the 21st century, why that is so important, and how to bring this to life in your classroom.

Part I: Contextual and Conceptual Frameworks (Chapter 1)

The first section of the book shares foundational ideas behind the work. In Chapter 1, we discuss what new student skills will be needed in the 21st century, as well as what we know about creating change in student thinking. Three core components of the MiCOSA Model are highlighted: (1) building on prior knowledge and cultural grounding; (2) using mediating conversations to bring change to the learner; and (3) developing 21 critical thinking skills. These components influence and empower one another, and thus are treated as parts of a system.

Part II: Critical Components of the MiCOSA Model (Chapters 2–6)

Part II provides detailed descriptions, classroom examples and support strategies for each of MiCOSA's core components: prior knowledge and cultural grounding, 21 thinking skills, and mediating conversations. In Chapter 2, we explore what culture, language, and community have to do with learning, and how MiCOSA helps you link your students' cultural backgrounds, knowledge, and embedded thinking to their newer learning. Chapter 3 provides a framework for mediation used throughout the book. We discuss and illustrate each type of mediating conversation that helps students acquire and use thinking skills with independence, flexibility, and autonomy: (1) establishing intent and reciprocity, (2) mediating meaning, (3) bridging thinking, (4) guiding self-regulation, and (5) building competence.

Chapters 4, 5, and 6 elaborate and illustrate MiCOSA's 21 thinking skills, chosen for their direct relationship to classroom content and for their responsiveness to change. We organize them into a three-phased framework: thinking skills for *gathering* information (Chapter 4); thinking skills for *transforming* information, which includes skills often referred to as critical thinking, higher order, or executive skills (Chapter 5); and thinking skills for *communicating* information (Chapter 6). In each of these chapters, we define the thinking skill and then use case scenarios to demonstrate examples of students efficient and inefficient in its use. Next, we provide a section on how to mediate or support change in those students' thinking skills within the classroom. Finally, for each thinking skill we provide multiple strategies that support its development.

Part III: Implementing MiCOSA (Chapters 7–10)

In Chapter 7, you learn to integrate the thinking skills into your work with standards and objectives. Because students need skills that will go beyond immediate assignments or projects, and which support their future learning, we devote Chapter 8 to bridging, providing a structure to help students deliberately engage in transfer. In addition, we outline how to develop and use both Content Big Ideas (CBIs) and Broader Big Ideas (BBIs) as bridges to guide instruction. Chapter 9 introduces the assessment of thinking skills from independent student development of skills to assessing critical thinking within your lessons. It interweaves formative assessments guided by essential questions, and is structured to lead students to understanding Big Ideas. Chapter 10 introduces you to *MiCOSA's Teacher's Guide to Planning Instruction* and to the *Lesson Planning Guides* that help you integrate all parts of the model.

Part IV: Motivating Tomorrow's Learning (Chapter 11)

When students develop the thinking skills to succeed in the face of challenge, that success motivates them to continue to think critically in the future. In addition, assuring their resilience in the face of challenge and difficulty is a second key to motivation. In Chapter 11, we draw on research that points to teachers' positive relationships with students as among the most powerful influences in supporting student resilience. Using the MiCOSA mediating framework, you will learn specific ways teachers can help students develop the protective factors that support student resilience, using a format parallel to that in the thinking skills chapters.

Getting Acquainted with MiCOSA: A Scaffolded Approach

There are many ways to use the resources in this book; however, scaffolding your learning with team discussions and activities is extremely helpful. The following figure, *Getting Acquainted with MiCOSA: A Scaffolded Guide* (Figure P.1), supports teachers and schools in getting started with implementing MiCOSA. It's two-phased graduated approach can support small groups of teachers at their own pace, or can guide whole-school implementation over a two year period. This figure outlines a sequence of reading and activities to support, reflect on, and connect each chapter to your classroom. Activity organizer handouts accompany most chapters, which you can download from the online PDToolkit. A more detailed description of the context is found in PDToolkit within the *Administrator and Facilitator's Guide*.

Phase I lays out a sequence of reading and activities that supports teachers in learning, chapter by chapter. Within each chapter there are opportunities for teachers to reflect on their own classrooms, or on identified students within their classrooms. Teachers use the suggested activity organizers from the previous Figure P.1 to mold their team discussions of each chapter. Activity organizers indicated in each area are provided in downloadable form with PDToolkit. By the end, teachers will be creating and delivering whole integrated lessons.

 PD TOOLKIT™

FIGURE P.1

Getting Acquainted with MiCOSA: A Scaffolded Guide

PHASE I: Getting Started with MiCOSA: One Chapter at a Time

	Chapter Title	**Activity Handouts*** **Use after you read each chapter to support your learning. Share your results with colleagues in PLC**
Ch. 1	The MiCOSA Model and its 21st Century Contexts	Read, discuss and raise questions.
Ch. 2	Prior Knowledge and Cultural Grounding	Send a letter home to your students' parents to elicit student strengths learned in the context of their home and cultures. (*Sample Letter)
Ch. 3	Mediating Conversations for Enhancing Thinking	Look at tomorrow's lesson. Find opportunities to establish each of five conversations. (*Organizer)
Ch. 4	Thinking Skills for Gathering Information	Look at this week's lessons. Can you identify one of these thinking skills you might infuse each day? Create a bridging principle for each thinking skill you identify. (*Organizer)
Ch. 5	Thinking Skills for Transforming Information	Look at this week's lessons. Can you identify one of these thinking skills you might infuse each day? Create a bridging principle for each thinking skill you identify. (*Organizer)

(Continued)

FIGURE P.1 (Continued)

PHASE I: Getting Started with MiCOSA: One Chapter at a Time

	Chapter Title	**Activity Handouts*** **Use after you read each chapter to support your learning. Share your results with colleagues in PLC**
Ch. 6	Thinking Skills for Communicating Information	Look at this week's lessons. Can you identify one of these thinking skills you might infuse each day? Create a bridging principle for each thinking skill you identify. (*Organizer)
Ch. 7	Content, Curriculum and Standards: Finding the Thinking Skills and Writing Objectives	Using the models from Chap. 7, work from a standard you identify and then write one content objective and one thinking skill objective. You may also write one that connects content and thinking. Do this for four days this week. (*Organizer)
Ch. 8	Teaching for Transfer: Getting to the Big Ideas	This week, create a Content Big Idea (CBI), a Broader Big Ideas (BBI), and bridging principle to go with one lesson on at least three days. (*Organizer)
Ch. 9	The Power of Assessment	Begin with a standard, then identify the core concept and content objective. Develop Essential Questions, design one post-assessment, one pre-assessment, and one formative assessment centered around the content and thinking skill objectives. Try using the MiCOSA Student Thinking Skills Survey. (PDToolkit) (*Organizer)
Ch. 10	Lesson Planning: Pulling it all Together	Create your first full Level I lesson. Write as much dialogue as you can, using the long form of the MiCOSA Lesson Planning Guide. (*MiCOSA Lesson Planning Guide–PDToolkit)
Ch. 11	Engaging Expectations and Promoting Resilience	Identify a student who could benefit from building more resilience. Choose a protective factor of focus and try one of the strategies from Chapter 11 or the PD Toolkit for the next four days. (*Organizer)

*Activity organizers to support discussion are found in PDToolkit.

Since teachers will have created a whole lesson in Phase I, they will expand their repertoires, take some risks, and share their work in Phase II! The first month of this second phase, or year, allows for a slower start, assuring teachers time to develop, review, and revise before implementing processes, and time to debrief following delivery of the teachers' first lessons. During the first lesson, teachers will "post" the icon for the thinking skill (on a website,

PHASE II: Launching Level 1 Lessons with MiCOSA: Working in Teams

Month 1: **Plan and try one lesson together with team support.**	Week 1. Grade level or subject matter teams review standards and select one new thinking skill to focus on every two weeks of the school year. Use the MiCOSA Thinking Skills Assessments to determine your class strengths and weaknesses and target your skill development.

	Week 2. Take a previously developed lesson and reformat it to work within the MiCOSA framework, adding in the thinking skill, mediating conversations, and a bridging principle. Try out some running dialogues and prompting questions with your team as you are learning. Be sure to include CBIs, BBIs (with corresponding Essential Questions), as well as pre-, post-, and formative assessments.
	Week 3. Share the lesson draft with your team and collaborate, giving feedback and ideas to improve, while celebrating the strong, creative ideas.
	Week 4. Deliver your first MiCOSA lesson. Post the icon for the thinking skill alongside the Essential Questions (on website; classroom wall). As students develop bridging principles, post those too. Report back to colleagues in a team meeting or on a blog or discussion board. Discuss feedback you received from the different assessment skills you gave, what went well, and what you'd like input on. Share a success.
***Month 2:* Plan and Deliver two lessons. Provide team support and feedback**	**Week 1.** Develop your second MiCOSA lesson with input from your team.
	Week 2. Deliver your second MiCOSA lesson. Post the icon for the thinking skill alongside your Essential Questions (on website; classroom wall). As students develop bridging principles, post those too. Where possible, integrate this thinking skill where it fits in other lessons that week. Through the use of the bridging principles, ask students how thinking skills they have learned will help with new assignments.
	Week 3. In your grade level (or subject matter) meetings, discuss your successes, share your lesson plans, and brainstorm ideas to improve. Begin planning your third MiCOSA lesson. Finish the design that week.
	Week 4. Deliver your third MiCOSA Lesson. Post thinking skills, essential questions, and bridging principles as they are developed. Share (give and get) ideas with colleagues on your team, and discuss powerful feedback you received from the assessments you gave.
***Months 3–8:* Develop and deliver two lessons with team support; extend student learning with bridges.**	**Week 1.** Develop your next MiCOSA Lesson with input from your team.
	Week 2. Deliver the MiCOSA lesson. Post the icon for the thinking skill alongside your Essential Questions (on website; classroom wall). As students develop bridging principles, post those, too. Integrate the new skill into other lessons as it occurs to you. Continue to ask students how thinking skills they have learned will help with new assignments (linked to the bridging principles they have developed). Ask also how they have used each one outside of school. Encourage students to assess how input from assessments supported their learning.
	Week 3. In your grade level (or subject matter) meetings, discuss your successes with the lesson plan implemented. Share ideas for your next lessons plans, and brainstorm ideas to improve where you have questions. Make sure you discuss the feedback from your assessments. Begin design of your next MiCOSA lesson, including ideas for progress charts and assessment rubrics to support the learning.
	Week 4. Deliver your next MiCOSA lesson. Post thinking skills, essential questions and bridging principles as they are developed. Share (give and get) ideas with colleagues on your team.

(Continued)

Months 9 and 10	**Grade-Level Teams.** Meet with teams above and below your level, sharing your annual plan, and the lessons each of you has developed during the year. Discuss students' current growth. Reassess with the MiCOSA Student Thinking Skills Questionnaire, in addition to school and classroom assessment results, so that you can pass this information on to your students' next teacher(s). Share and celebrate exemplary classroom experiences and work samples. This provides an idea of what your incoming students may come with, as well as ideas to build on. **Subject Matter Teams.** Meet with two other subject matter teams and share your annual plans, along with one lesson each of you has developed during the year. This gives you an idea of what your incoming students may be getting from other teachers in your grade level, as well as what younger ones will come with. Sharing this bridging will enrich your own bridging and ideas in your classes.

bulletin board, or classroom wall). Following student development of bridging principles, those are posted as well (along with content and thinking skill objectives and essential questions). Each month following that, teachers develop and try out two new MiCOSA lessons (or revise prior lesson plans into a MiCOSA format), as do the other team members. With each lesson, the icon for the thinking skill goes "up" beside the first one (on a website, bulletin board, or classroom wall), along with bridging principles as students develop them. Many teachers will also find themselves integrating the thinking skill where it fits in other lessons that week. Now they can begin asking students if there are thinking skills they have learned that will help with new assignments. Teachers will be amazed at what students come up with—they become pretty natural at bridging relatively soon.

In six months, each teacher will cover each thinking skill at least once, and have the opportunity to review most of them. By week 24, classes will be using multiple thinking skills. Even if teachers allow up to four weeks for assemblies, testing, and other odds and ends, that leaves almost two months for integrating and reviewing multiple thinking skills, as well as revising those that students may not be mentioning because they did not fully understand them. At the end of the year, each teacher will have *his or her* 21 lessons, along with 21 *additional* lessons from however many colleagues are working in the same grade level (or subject matter at higher grades).

The 21st century demands for students to become innovators, active problem-solvers, collaborators, and leaders lend a critical context to this work at a critical time in our history. We look forward to having you join us on this journey to further empower those who will become our future!

Carol Robinson-Zañartu
Patricia Doerr
Jacqueline Portman

Acknowledgments

We would like to express our deep appreciation to those who inspired our work with MiCOSA through their teaching, modeling, and visions:

- Dr. Reuven Feuerstein for his passion for the work of seeing capable, competent, and engaged learning emerge where sorrow or doubt had gone before; for his theories and lessons, on which we have built on our own work.

- Dr. Mogens Jensen, master clinician, for his lessons and patience, his theoretical musings and brilliance, his creativity, and his belief in possibilities for all children.

- Dr. Tre Jensen for modeling the "translation" of hard-to-understand concepts into comprehensible and doable strategies that parents and children could accomplish together through daily life activities.

- Dr. Larry Emerson for his lessons on indigenous worldview and the mediation of learning through culture; his guidance and modeling, and his work to demonstrate the transformation of angry young men to engaging young men, filled with ideas and prepared to make a difference.

- Dr. Asa Hilliard for his passion and his friendship, for his acknowledgement and belief in the power of mediation to support student potential, for his leadership on culturally affirmative teaching, and for his modeling as a brilliant African American scholar.

- Dr. Lois Campbell for her loving and enthusiastic "Pied Piper" ability to inspire educators and bring them together to conceptualize and implement mediating cognition in the school setting.

- Dr. Carol Genrich, for her mentoring and guidance in understanding cognition, and for providing a lens to educators through which to see the thinking behind their instruction and their students' learning.

In addition, we deeply appreciate the support of a multitude of family members, friends, and colleagues, without whom this work would not have come to fruition:

- Each of our children who has been "mediated" from an early age, and who now mediates others around them, in home, school, and business settings: Brandon, Freddie, Felipe, Dan, Nick, and Carla. To partners Hans and Bill, and to our good friends and colleagues for their unwavering support and belief in the project.

- The many graduate students at San Diego State University, now professional educators, who have piloted the ideas in this book, and made a tremendous difference in the lives of the children they have worked with.

  Krystle Aguilar, Noe Alvarado, Marlene Armenta, Tania Arriaga, Alyssa Ashley, Yolanda Barba, Christine Benton, Diandra Benton, Natalia Cardoso, Tania Castro, Amy Clarey, Angelica Contreras, Amanda Estrada, Catherine Galvan, Armando Godinez, Lissette Gomez, Liliana Gonzalez, Oyuki Gonzalez, Oscar Grajeda, Jessica Gutierrez, Aamna Hassan, Cuong Hoang, Jennifer Inaba, Ayako Ikeda, Chelsay Jimmie, Andy Kim, Marisa Lopez, Nicholas McIntosh, Sherrell McClain, Derek Moehlenbruck, Michelle Morrison, Vi Nguyen, Cristina Nojara, Karen Nunes, Evelyn Ontiveros, Sarah Overton, Natalie Pontino, Jacob Price, Mallory Rachel, Monica Rohloff, Deidra Smith, Yasaman Taleghani, Kieu Tang, Rochelle Telebrico, Janice Tso, Boa Xiong.

- The children of Paloma Elementary School in the San Marcos School District, as well as administrators Eric Forseth, Dan Trujillo, Elizabeth O'Toole, Tracy Garcia, and Anthony Barela, who partnered with us over the years to test out ideas and support the children.

- Conejo Valley Unified School District administrators, past and present: Dr. Tim Stevens, Dr. Elly Love, and Dr. Antonio Castro for their early enthusiastic support and belief in this work. The students of Meadows Elementary and Los Cerritos Middle School who helped pilot MiCOSA's ideas and strategies.

- Our colleagues for their valuable feedback, especially Saskia Maria Boom, Mariko Cavey, Elly Love, and Kasjia Butcher.

- Rudy Vaca for his film expertise and many trips to Paloma Elementary School.

- Hans Doerr for his support in filming the students at Los Cerritos Middle School.

- Felipe Zañartu for his amazing video and video editing support, his technology expertise, his mediation of our learning, and his support throughout the entire project.

- Dr. James Bylund, for his clever suggestion of the title.

- Appreciation to Pearson's many editorial and support staff members and reviewers who made the production of this book possible. Finally, we have the deepest gratitude for our remarkable executive development editor from Pearson, Linda Bishop. We especially appreciate Linda's keen eye, detailed ideas for change and clarification, persistent and deep enthusiasm for the potential of our work, and spirit of hope.

Chapter One

The MiCOSA Model and Its 21st Century Contexts

The MiCOSA Model helps assure that your students have the foundational and advanced thinking skills needed to fully engage in critical thinking essential for the 21st century. The acronym MiCOSA stands for Mediation in the Classroom: An Open Systems Approach.

The room buzzes with activity as students work in small groups to study immigration issues. One group shares information to support their ideas on why immigrants to the United States left their homelands; a second group researches the devastating effect this migration had on the Native Americans. A third group accesses first-hand accounts from immigrants and tribal leaders, comparing their points of view, while a fourth makes a Skype call to hear from family members about why and how they came to America. The teacher, hard to spot at first, sits among the groups, listening intently to explanations of their presentation plans—and every now and then asks thought-provoking mediating questions to guide their development to think more critically.

In the 21st century, students are accessing information generated at a laser-like pace, and doing so from a variety of sources. However, those sources vary widely, from the expert to the novice, and from original and reliable sources to mere hearsay. Students who are able to distinguish relevant from irrelevant and valid from invalid information, as well as sort through and select, combine, and create information in meaningful ways, will have a strong advantage over those who use information arbitrarily.

Teaching the thinking skills needed to do this represents a shift away from the major focus on content, toward an equal focus on the processes of acquiring, using, and creating content. To learn how to teach and integrate thinking skills into rich lessons and content, teachers need a framework. The MiCOSA Model provides that pedagogical framework.

21st Century Contexts

Teaching for the 21st century shifts your role as a teacher. Because idea generation far outpaces textbook publication, you must prepare students to create solutions for problems not yet conceptualized (Darling-Hammond, 2010), to use technologies not yet invented, and work with concepts yet to be developed. You must ask your students to engage in critical thinking, to collaborate across diverse groups, and to generate innovative ideas. To tackle these issues, leaders in business and in education (Partnership for 21st Century Skills, 2009; The New Commission on the Skills of the American Workforce, 2007) have identified a number of 21st century "literacies" and skills your students will need, including:

- Critical thinking and problem solving
- Creative thinking
- Technology as a tool
- Collaboration, teamwork, and leadership
- Multicultural competence, communication, and global awareness

Using the MiCOSA Model, you will interweave these 21st century skills and literacies into a framework in which students think actively about what they are doing, as well as how they can transfer their learning beyond the project or lesson. You will help them develop new thinking skills that support stronger problem solving and greater autonomy and creativity.

21st Century Learning

In the 21st century, well-developed understanding of concepts in English, mathematics, and science, as well as literature, history, and the arts, will remain central to schooling; however, they will now be connected to such 21st century skills as critical thinking and collaboration. For example, instead of having students read a text and respond to questions about the information they read, you might have them work together to analyze several sources of information—ranging from text-based to electronic, video or interview—on the same topic. They can then use this information to compare and contrast key points, debating and then summarizing a rationale for their selection. This might include examples of how the information might be used in "real world" problem solving. Integrating 21st century skills into learning enhances student engagement, memory, and transfer. If you review the Common Core State Standards, you will find that they incorporate many of these skills. The MiCOSA Model will illustrate how to weave them together.

Critical Thinking and Problem Solving

Critical thinking involves applying a number of thinking skills when making carefully reasoned judgments. When students think critically, they raise questions, gather relevant information, seek evidence, suspend judgment while considering a variety of possibilities, hypothesize and test out those hypotheses, analyze, and synthesize. Critical thinking occurs when students think and engage deeply in finding answers to questions, or when they exchange and debate ideas while collaborating to solve a problem or create a project. It can occur when they write essays or read with complex goals in mind. These skills can be learned. Thus, critical thinking is central in the MiCOSA Model.

Assignments that require critical thinking set the stage for teaching MiCOSA's 21 thinking skills and mediating them so that your students will personalize, internalize, hypothesize, and use those skills. Your role as mediator will support you in personalizing those thinking skills across your students' backgrounds and cultures, making connections to their prior knowledge and that of other students, as well as with information gathered from relevant sources. You become a facilitator of their thinking. Some thinking skills, such as *systematic search* and using *multiple sources* of information, help students effectively choose and gather information they need to start critical thinking. Others, such as *finding connections and relationships*, address critical thinking directly.

Lantos (2006) suggests teaching critical thinking by creating environments in which students can sift through a mass of facts being "thrown" at them, and then begin to identify pathways of interconnectedness. There's no guarantee, however, that setting up the problem alone will help them do this "sifting through." Negotiating and selecting information requires a number of thinking skills. For example, students must first gather and hold *multiple sources* of information, learn to sustain *focus and attention*, and select useful information with *precision and accuracy*. Then they use critical thinking skills such as *finding connections and relationships, comparing,* and *hypothesizing* as they look for the most relevant or innovative connections.

The MiCOSA Model explains what skills, both critical and creative, are important to teach and how to teach them.

Creative Thinking

In addition to critical analysis and selection of relevant and valid information, you want your students to construct or *create* new knowledge. You will want them to engage in *creative* thinking, coming up with something new or original. Creative thinking taps into some of the same skills used in critical thinking, such as *seeking relationships* and *hypothesizing,* but also engages "flexibility, originality, fluency, elaboration, brainstorming, modification, imagery, associative and metaphorical thinking" (Teacher Tap, 2010). Creativity can be relative; that is, students may devise something absolutely new to them, although another person may have had the same idea earlier. Does that show true creativity or innovation? In the context of developing 21st century thinkers, it certainly does. Learning to be innovative, and the excitement that comes with it, sparks further innovation.

In the MiCOSA Model, critical and creative thinking go hand in hand, informing one another. You will learn how to use MiCOSA's 21 thinking skills in meaningful contexts to support critical and creative thinking.

Technology as a Tool

Technology can support students' development of thinking skills as well as critical thinking and knowledge creation. By implementing the MiCOSA Model, you will help students use a variety of technologies as they put thinking skills into practice to gather, transform, and use information, as well as communicate their findings. A wide range of strategies is offered for using innovative technologies to develop thinking skills, ranging from ideas for using electronic "smart boards," iPads, and *wikis* to the more conventional whiteboards and pocket charts.

Collaboration, Teaming, and Developing Leadership

Collaboration often enhances the development of thinking processes. For example, Rogoff (1998) discusses how collaborative cognition enhances thinking when parents, children, and their peers think and work together to develop expertise in culturally relevant activities and practices. Meaningful problems, whether situated in cultural contexts from students' backgrounds or in compelling current events, can become the basis of team projects that motivate student investment. Making projects meaningful also leads to useful rather than just intellectual conclusions (Trilling & Fadel, 2009). MiCOSA classrooms thrive on collaborative work at all levels of the thinking process. Leaders emerge because they have been empowered by the process.

By using the MiCOSA Model offered in this text, students develop eager attitudes toward learning, a belief in their ability to take on and solve problems, and the skills to develop meaningful and creative solutions. They develop confident mindsets about their ability to interact collaboratively and effectively with others in the world. As a teacher, your faith in their potential to do this is significant; your communication of that faith offered in an authentic and believable way is vital to their success. When your students leave the classroom empowered, creative, and productive, their successes become your successes. Even more powerfully, they become family and community successes.

Introducing the MiCOSA Model

The MiCOSA Model provides a pedagogical framework that responds to 21st century mandates with new targets for learning and ways to bring them about. Belief in student openness to change and knowledge of specific processes that help mediate that change underlie the 21 thinking skills central to the model.

As noted earlier, MiCOSA is an acronym for **M**ediation **i**n the **C**lassroom: An **O**pen **S**ystems **A**pproach to critical thinking and learning.

M Is for Mediation

MiCOSA's "M" is for mediation. As mediators of thinking and learning, teachers are "go betweens," great listeners and helpers, translators and facilitators who look for opportunities to "make learning happen." For instance, you may "go between" a child's fear and her potential, making a safe space for trying something new; you may listen very carefully for thinking skills already developed in the home cultural experience and bring that familiarity to new learning experiences. As a mediator, you may help translate seemingly complex assignments into manageable components and processes, and you may facilitate a child's empowerment by helping her experience something new and different. You will help her personally "own" the thinking strengths she practices as she goes on to solve a new and challenging problem.

iC Is for in the Classroom

The MiCOSA Model is for teachers. Therefore, MiCOSA's iC, **i**n the **C**lassroom, recognizes the critical relationship between teacher and student in the learning process. Although the "classroom" may spill into the community or occur at parks, museums, or online, the classroom represents the "place" where you design and provide strong contexts for your students to learn and practice 21st century thinking skills.

Classroom learning contexts may range from cultural activities to science and technology projects. When you deliberately link the use of thinking skills to accessing and transforming information within those contexts, it leads to a deeper understanding and engagement. For example, you bring the thinking and learning skills to the "forefront" of your students' attention in context—from making *masa* or chocolate chip cookies to learning to ski or perform algebraic equations. In the following example, the teacher connects the thinking skill of planning that a student used at home to an upcoming school activity:

> "Cheryl, thanks so much for the cookies you baked for the fund-raiser and let us sample! Let's talk a little about what thinking skills you used when making your cookies. It looks like you needed a well thought-out sequence of steps—you read the recipe, gathered all the ingredients, combined them in the right order, baked them just the right amount of time and at the correct temperature, then cooled them just enough for us to enjoy a sample while they were still warm. They were delicious. I am impressed with your cookies and by your use of thinking skills. You set goals, planned well, sequenced what needed to happen, and followed through. How could you use those same planning skills to figure out what your group will need to do on this project? What goal, plan, steps, and sequences will your group need?"

In future lessons and contexts, Cheryl's teacher helps her and others in the class "bridge" that thinking skill of *planning* to new areas of learning. In doing so, students strengthen their "ownership" of the thinking skill and use it more frequently and more flexibly.

OSA Is for Open Systems Approach

MiCOSA's "OSA," the **O**pen **S**ystems **A**pproach, refers to a belief system underlying the model's framework. The open system implies that your students' thinking is still malleable and open to change (Jensen, 2012). As a teacher, you will influence the development of each of MiCOSA's 21 thinking skills. Because thinking skills are not isolated actions, but influence one another, that complex relationship is referred to as a thinking system.

Consider what happens in your classroom when one key person is absent, or another key person comes into the room. The dynamics of your classroom system change. New elements introduced into a system influence the others. Similarly, the dynamics of your students' thinking systems change with the "entrance" of a new thinking skill or two. Things start to click. When students gain one or two new thinking skills, additional ones may be influenced, or even emerge in response. Because thinking systems are open systems, you will be able to help your students shape new habits of thinking.

In contrast, "closed" system approaches assume that thinking skills (or cognitive functions) either exist or do not exist, and that measured abilities virtually never change. In a closed system, you rely on tests to define your students' abilities and upper limits, "protecting" them from things that are too difficult. Your influence is minimized.

Learning is not just an isolated activity of the brain. Environmental factors, history, culture, affect, and teaching actually modify the brain. Each student's "system" is unique. Thus, you will not treat Jane and Jared as though they were exactly the same, nor expect each to flourish in the same way.

Core Components of the MiCOSA Model

The MiCOSA Model builds on known best practices in learning and combines familiar educational concepts with new ones. For instance, most of you will be familiar with the idea of building on prior knowledge. Other familiar concepts include supporting student resilience, using research or evidence-based curriculum to access content and standards, and developing assessment useful for feedback. The MiCOSA Model builds on these familiar concepts, adds in mediating conversations, and supports the development of 21 specific thinking skills essential to meet the demands of the 21st century.

The MiCOSA Model has three interlocking core components that, when integrated, provide the foundation of the teaching framework. This core is then incorporated into identifying standards, writing objectives, getting to the bigger ideas, and using assessment for feedback as you develop full lesson plans. Other elements of MiCOSA motivate learners and support the transfer of learning from one content area to another.

The three key components that lie at the heart or center of the MiCOSA Model are: (1) Prior Knowledge and Cultural Grounding, (2) Mediating Conversations, and (3) the 21 Thinking Skills. Figure 1.1 illustrates their interconnectedness. In studying the components of the MiCOSA Model, you will learn to:

- Link the prior knowledge and cultural grounding your students bring into the classroom with the 21 thinking skills
- Engage in mediating conversations to help bring the 21 thinking skills to life for your students
- Teach the 21 thinking skills so students can learn to gather information, transfer the information they gather, and communicate about what they learn.

Prior Knowledge and Cultural Grounding

The MiCOSA Model begins by connecting and building new knowledge and thinking skills on the rich foundation of students' prior understanding of the world, learned through their homes and communities. They come with beliefs about content as well, some of which may differ from what is taught in schools. With MiCOSA, you will be encouraged to acknowledge these different perspectives, using them as learning opportunities. When teachers introduce new concepts while building positively on prior knowledge, students demonstrate greater understanding (Bransford, Brown, & Cocking, 2000; Lehrer & Chazan, 1998; Shepard, 2000).

All learners try to connect new information to something they already know, thereby developing more complex understandings of the old information as well as patterns of connectedness with the new. Therefore, when you access prior knowledge in the classroom, you go beyond simply asking students what they know about certain content. You design questions and listen for how they have understood that content area in the past, maybe within a cultural context. In addition, you listen for cues to help you access and

FIGURE 1.1

The MiCOSA Model

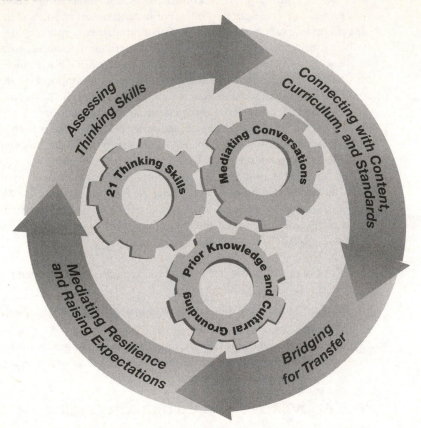

verbally recognize their strengths. In this way, you help them build resilience and also strengthen the connections of your learning community. Acknowledging the power of individual student "prior knowledge and cultural grounding" enriches the base of learning for your entire class, group, or team.

Mediating Conversations

Mediating conversations are both deliberate and powerful. They help students carry a rich understanding of prior knowledge into current projects, as well as help them link thinking skills to content and change behavior to enhance relationships. You might say, for instance, "Jamal, I was impressed to see how thoughtfully

you collected and integrated *multiple sources* of information on this project. Your rich description reflects how well you have learned to do that." These guided conversations help connect the parts. Rather than giving students direct answers, you help them to connect current knowledge to past experiences, make meaning, and discover solutions themselves. For example, "Class, each of your teams has just shared examples from home of *finding relationships* between the natural world and how your families work to accomplish what is needed. How will you use that information as you *seek relationships* between the natural world and laws of physics?" Through repeated opportunities, successes, and applications, you can learn to consciously help students develop new thinking skills into new habits of thinking.

Where did this concept of using mediating conversations originate? One strong influence was the work of Vygotsky (1962, 1978), who proposed that intellectual growth occurs through sociocultural mediation in combination with the child's personal experiences. Both Feuerstein (1979) and Jensen (2003) proposed and researched specific processes of mediation. Their work produced clinical evidence of helping facilitate change in thinking and learning skills. Based on their work, and after trying these in our own classrooms, we developed five sets of intentional mediating conversations for use in the classroom:

1. Intent and Reciprocity
2. Mediating Meaning
3. Bridging Thinking
4. Guiding Self-Regulation
5. Building Competence

When you use the mediating conversations, students become self-aware of their own thinking, and begin to "self-regulate" their behaviors and learning process. This improves their academic outcomes. Across culturally diverse populations, from students in general education to those identified as gifted and talented, and those struggling with ADHD and learning disabilities, research supports the idea of helping students attain self-regulation through mediation (Lane, Harris, Graham, Weisenbach, Brindle, & Morphy, 2008; Perin & Graham, 2006).

21 Thinking Skills

Students need thinking skills to access and strengthen knowledge. Individual thinking skills network together and draw sustenance from prior knowledge and culture. Within their home culture, for example, students may have already learned to use the thinking skills of *compare* and *categorize* as they differentiate right from wrong, see *connections and relationships* among the roles of different family members, and *hypothesize* a reaction to a decision they

FIGURE 1.2

FIGURE 1.2

MiCOSA's 21 Thinking Skills for the 21st Century

Thinking Skills for Gathering Information	Thinking Skills for Transforming Information	Thinking Skills for Communicating Information
Systematic Search	Goal Setting	Labels, Words, and Concepts
Focus and Attention	Planning	Precision and Accuracy
Labels, Words, and Concepts	Comparing	Appropriate Pragmatics
Multiple Sources	Ordering, Grouping, and Categorizing	Feedback for Self-Regulation
Position in Space	Finding Connections and Relationships	Collaboration
Position in Time	Visualizing	
Precision and Accuracy	Inferring	
	Cause and Effect— Hypothesizing	
	Summarizing	

may make. Your students bring these prior thinking skill experiences to the classroom. When they build overt awareness of thinking skill processes, they can then transfer those processes into new and appropriate settings (Bransford, Brown, & Cocking, 2000; Jensen, 2004). Engagement and comprehension increase.

Figure 1.2 lists MiCOSA's 21 thinking skills in three categories:

1. Thinking skills used to gather information
2. Thinking skills used to transform information once it has been gathered
3. Thinking skills used to communicate information.

Several criteria were used to select each of the thinking skills: first, each is amenable to change and can be enhanced with mediation; second, each is fairly easy to connect with the curriculum and standards, with a special emphasis on the Common Core State Standards; and finally, each plays a role in the critical thinking students need. Critical thinking skills like *goal setting, planning, hypothesizing, comparing,* and *seeking relationships*, obviously linked with curricula, are core among MiCOSA's 21 skills. These critical thinking skills help students *transform* information.

However, in order to think critically, whether hypothesizing or drawing complex relationships, students must first adequately *gather* sufficient and relevant information to work with. Think of the student who does not read all the directions before he begins a project, or the one who lacks certain words and concepts to the extent that it interrupts her moving forward. Additional thinking skills, such as gathering and using several sources of information simultaneously *(multiple sources)*, beginning with key academic language *(words, labels,* and *concepts)*, and using *precision* and *accuracy*, help students *gather* information.

In addition, some students may do a good job of putting together concepts to create new ideas in their heads, but not be adept at *communicating* them. For instance, *collaboration*, considering audience *(appropriate pragmatics)*, and *using feedback for self-regulation* are skills that support the communication of ideas. Thus, these additional skills make up MiCOSA's full 21 thinking skills. You will often use MiCOSA's thinking skills in combination with one another; however, as you learn about each one, you will find the categories helpful.

Subsequent chapters on thinking skills within each of the three broad areas give you detailed definitions, examples of how they look in the classroom, and an array of strategies to help you help your students improve them. Appendix A provides a listing of over 200 strategies and activities that support your work with MiCOSA, and their location in the chapters or in the online PDToolkit.

PD **pd** TOOLKIT™

PDToolkit: In Video Clip 1.1 Trish uses the *Reading the Walls* (TCI) reading fluency and comprehension strategy to develop multiple thinking skills.

Extending MiCOSA's Core Components into the Classroom

Once you are familiar with MiCOSA's core components, you will be ready to extend this knowledge, allowing you to:

- *Find thinking skills in standards, and write objectives that integrate those thinking skills with content.* Students still need a rich foundation of factual knowledge to become competent thinkers (Bransford, Brown, & Cocking, 2000). However, to build real depth, students must also intertwine their developing knowledge with critical thinking skills. Once they begin using critical thinking, and start to see connections, patterns, and relationships, they can then explore even more depth and build expertise (Boshuizen, 2009; Rikers, Van Gerven, & Schmidt, 2004). The thinking skills taught through the MiCOSA Model fit naturally into the content, curriculum, and standards you teach, including the Common Core State Standards. By identifying thinking skills within standards, you will learn to develop objectives that foster thinking skill development and critical thought alongside your objectives that foster deep understanding.

- *Transfer learning and thinking processes across content, locating and using the content big ideas in the standards, and reaching for broader big ideas in life.* You want students to have rich depth of content; however, you also want them to be able to use that content, to transform and apply it. This requires them, consciously or intuitively, to abstract the bigger ideas behind the instruction, and then use them again in a new place. This is called transfer of learning. To help students learn to transfer their learning, MiCOSA builds on what Wiggins and McTighe (1998, 2008) and Ainsworth (2003) call Big Ideas. Combined with the transfer of thinking skills, Big

Ideas help students understand the enduring lessons they will take with them into the world.

- *Use assessment (pre-, formative, and summative) to evaluate and focus your thinking skills work, and to gain feedback about student learning over time.* Assessment designed and used as a dynamic process motivates and supports learning. It helps teachers pinpoint instructional needs through useful feedback, and motivates students to take on new challenges, make new connections, and experience their own creativity. Because MiCOSA integrates thinking skills into content and standards, MiCOSA's assessments address both content and thinking skill objectives. In addition, three unique assessments of students' thinking skills will help you assess for either formative or summative purposes.

- *Develop positive affect and resilience in students.* The affective side of learning gives students the passion, motivation, confidence, and stamina to hold out in the face of difficulty and complete the challenging tasks that confront them. This confidence and ability to solve problems as they arise—*resilience*—contributes strongly to whether or not students experience success. It directly enhances academic engagement and achievement (Arkansas Department of Education, 2009; Zins, Weissberg, Wang, & Walberg, 2004). Using the MiCOSA Model, you will build on what you learn about mediating the student's learning to engage a triad of positive expectations (student, teacher, parent) that help your students develop and sustain resilience.

- *Build lessons that integrate all components of the MiCOSA Model.* A teacher's guide walks you through how to put all the pieces together as you design full lessons that integrate the core components with depth of content. Multiple examples support your learning.

PD **TOOLKIT**™

PDToolkit: In Video Clip 1.2 a teacher reflects on the richness of his team's lesson plan and its connection to 21st Century skills.

You are about to embark on a journey that will have your students thinking deeply and engaging enthusiastically in their work. Use this book like a workshop or series of workshops as you develop skills and gradually augment your current work with critical thinking and cultural connectedness. You will find examples and strategies that support the work throughout the book, and also in the online PDToolkit. If your school or a team within your school is using the book together, you might set out a plan such as that found in the Guide to Implementing MiCOSA (see Preface). Your journey will be worth the investment because you will be giving your students the ability to access and use information both effectively and efficiently. Through mediation, you will help them identify and use the 21 thinking skills that are the foundation of their critical thought.

SUMMARY

- Educators and business leaders across the nation have shared an urgent need for a workforce that has 21st century skills. This need is driving a change in the focus of education, requiring teachers to shift from focusing on a content orientation to placing an emphasis on the processes of learning within 21st century contexts, moving students from being passive to active learners who engage in critical thinking, collaboration, teaming, creativity, and innovation.

- The MiCOSA Model, a framework for teaching critical thinking skills through an Open Systems Approach, emphasizes three core components, including the accessing of students' prior learning grounded in cultural perspectives. Mediating conversations guide students to access, use, and adopt 21 thinking skills selected for their relevance to accessing core standards and to critical thinking essential for 21st century learning.

- The core components of the MiCOSA Model—prior knowledge and cultural grounding, mediating conversations, and 21 thinking skills—inform lesson objectives built from Common Core State Standards and a comprehensive lesson planning process. Principles to bridge thinking skills across content areas facilitate student development of big ideas and the transfer of learning. Essential questions lead assessment, which is augmented with MiCOSA's thinking skill assessments. The components of the MiCOSA Model are supported by scaffolding the transfer of learning and engaging expectations for students that will lead to academic success.

REFERENCES

Ainsworth, L. (2003). *Unwrapping the standards*. Lead + Learn Press. Retrieved from www.leadandlearnpress.com

Arkansas Department of Education, State Personnel Development Grant. (2009, October). *School-wide discipline, behavior management, and student self-management: Focusing on social skills instruction and selecting an evidence-based social skills program*. Little Rock, AR: Author.

Boshuizen, E. (2009). Teaching for expertise: Problem-based methods in medicine and other professional domains. In K. A. Ericsson (Ed.), *The development of professional performance: Approaches to objective measurement and designed learning environments* (pp. 379–404). UK: Cambridge University Press.

Bransford, J. D., Brown, A. L., & Cocking, R. R. (Eds.). (2000). *How people learn: Brain, mind, experience and school: Expanded version*. Washington, DC: National Academy Press.

Darling-Hammond, L. (2010). *The flat world and education: How America's commitment to equity will determine our future*. New York, NY: Teachers College Press.

Feuerstein, R. (1979). Ontogeny of learning. In M. T. Brazier (Ed.), *Brain mechanisms in memory and learning*. New York: Raven Press.

Jensen, J. (2004). *Principles of generative phonology*. Amsterdam, The Netherlands: John Benjamins Publishing Company.

Jensen, M. R. (2003). Mediating knowledge construction: Towards a dynamic model of assessment and learning. Part II: Applied programs and research. *Educational and Child Psychology, 20*(2), 118–142.

Jensen, M. R. (2012). *The mind's ladder: Empowering students in the knowledge economy—Dynamic assessment and classroom learning guidebook 3.0*. Roswell, GA: Cognitive Education Systems.

Lane, K. L., Harris, K. R., Graham, S., Weisenbach, J. L., Brindle, M., & Morphy, P. (2008). The effects of self-regulated strategy development on the writing performance of second-grade students with behavioral and writing difficulties. *Journal of Special Education, 41*, 234–253.

Lantos, J. (2006, September). Critical thinking is critical. *Los Angeles Times*. Retrieved from http:// articles.latimes.com/2006/sep/16/opinion/oe-lantos16

Lehrer, R., & Chazan, D. (1998). *Designing learning environments for developing understanding of space and geometry*. Mahwah, NJ: Lawrence Erlbaum Associates.

Partnership for 21st Century Skills. (2009). *P21 framework definitions*. Retrieved from www.p21.org/ documents/P21_Framework_Definitions.pdf

Perin, D., & Graham, S. (2006). Teaching writing skills to adolescents: Evidence-based practices. *Perspectives on Language and Literacy* [Special issue], *32*, 10–14.

Rikers, R. M. J. P., Van Gerven, P. W. M., & Schmidt, H. G. (2004). Cognitive load theory as a tool for expertise development. *Instructional Science, 32*, 173–182.

Rogoff, B. (1998). *Cognition as a collaborative process*. In D. Kuhn & R. S. Siegler (Eds.), *Cognition, perception and language,* Vol. 2, *Handbook of child psychology* (5th ed., W. Damon [Ed.], pp. 679–744). New York: Wiley.

Shepard, L. A. (2000). The role of assessment in a learning culture. *Educational Researcher, 29*, 4–14.

Teacher Tap: Professional Development Resources for Teachers and Librarians. (2010). *Critical and creative thinking*. Retrieved from http://eduscapes.com/tap/

The New Commission on the Skills of the American Workforce. (2007). *Tough choice or tough times*. National Center on Education and the Economy (executive summary). Washington, DC. Author. Retrieved from www.skillscommission.org/pdf/exec_sum/ToughChoices_EXECSUM.pdf

Trilling, B., & Fadel, C. (2009). *21st century skills: Learning for life in our times*. San Francisco, CA: Jossey-Bass.

Vygotsky, L. S. (1962). *Thought and language*. Cambridge, MA: MIT Press.

Vygotsky, L. S. (1978). *Mind in society: The development of higher psychological processes* (M. Cole, V. John-Steiner, S. Scribner, & E. Souberman, Eds. and Trans.). Cambridge, MA: Harvard University Press (Original work published 1935).

Wiggins, G., & McTighe, J. (1998). What is backward design? In *Understanding by design* (1st ed., pp. 7–19). Upper Saddle River, NJ: Merrill Prentice Hall. Retrieved from http://nhlrc.ucla.edu/ events/startalkworkshop/readings/backward-design.pdf

Wiggins, G., & McTighe, J. (2008). Put understanding first. *Educational Leadership, 65*(8), 36–41.

Zins, J. E., Weissberg, R. P., Wang, M. C., & Walberg, H. J. (Eds.). (2004). *Building academic success on social and emotional learning: What does the research say?* New York: Teachers College Press.

Chapter Two

Prior Knowledge and Cultural Grounding

Students' prior knowledge and cultural backgrounds provide both a socio-emotional and cognitive grounding—rich resources from which to draw in school as well as throughout their lives.

Each student enters your classroom carrying a story about who he or she is in the world, and who he or she is as a learner. Although these stories likely sit at the back of their consciousness, they influence student behavior, attitudes, aspirations, and motivations. These stories emerge over time, developing with contributions from the students' homes, cultures, communities, and schools.

Your students' stories will influence their interactions with you and with others. Each student has taken in bits and pieces from an array of experiences, constructing or co-constructing this personal life narrative (Winslade & Monk, 2000, 2007). Some of these stories portray schools as places of nurture or excitement; others hold pictures of classrooms as places with the potential to shame them. You see their stories acted out in their physical bearing, their voices, and their ease or caution with others.

Perhaps because students carry these powerful personal narratives below the surface of awareness, they play a profound role in shaping beliefs about themselves—whether they are capable or not capable, likeable or not likeable, or have a real and valued place in the world and in your classroom (Gay, 2000; Rosaldo, 1989).

The Power of Personal Narrative

As a teacher, you play a part in the co-construction of these stories. Your contributions to the stories come from you as an individual, as part of the school system, and as a member of your socioeconomic and/or cultural group. If the student's story does not include capability and cooperation, then you want to help contribute to co-constructing an alternative story (White & Morgan, 2006)—one that portrays hope and personal effectiveness, and results in behavior that reflects those beliefs.

Stories can also heal and empower. This is part of why your students' personal life narratives are so powerful. For example, one school district in southern California uses a leadership program called *Encuentros* (Reveles, 2000) with their Latino middle and high school males. *Encuentros* engages the students with rich stories of Latino men overcoming obstacles, facing tough questions, and building on the assets of their cultural heritage. The story-based "encounters" range from history and culture to mental, economic, and social realities. They bridge ideas about overcoming obstacles in life to those in school and learning. The young men in the program show steady and impressive gains in grades and attendance, and decreased behavioral referrals (Aganza, 2011; Aganza & Cline, 2009). When the Latino students were asked what difference the program made to them, hands shot up. Student after student related that they were proud to be Latino, and intended to go to college and be leaders. They volunteered that they were learning to learn better, to study, and to succeed in school and in life.

Encuentros is but one example of building the "alternative narrative," a story your students can carry that inspires and supports, freeing them to reach for their potential. For many of these young men, these "encounters" became part of their new personal narratives, replacing old "story lines" that had fed a negative image with a new image of hope.

Dip into the well of your students' potential assets to support them in building a culturally rich and healthy personal narrative within your classroom. All students come to you with some notions about how the world works. Begin by asking them to share their ideas. Based on what they have learned at home, through their communities and cultural contexts, they also have a sense of how "things" should be done—from how to greet someone, what constitutes respect, or whether it is smart or shameful to speak out as an individual. Much of this rich prior knowledge occurs within cultural or community contexts, from Latino and Native American to African American, Euro-American, or Asian. You can capture this same power using the MiCOSA Model, which supports you in linking prior knowledge and cultural grounding and building on them.

Activating and Using Prior Knowledge and Cultural Grounding

Activating prior knowledge and cultural grounding helps students become active rather than passive learners. Brazilian education philosopher Paulo Freire (1972, 1995) wrote about the passivity that results from what he called a "banking" system of education. In this analogy, he points out that the system sees students as "empty bank accounts," and teachers as the depositors of knowledge and information. Although most teachers seek more meaningful engagement with their students, the sense of urgency to get all the students to "know" all the standards in some classrooms has led to a resurgence of this banking system. This one-way "teaching" leaves students in the role of passive "recipients"; as Freire observed, that passivity then leads to student disengagement and disempowerment. In contrast, referring to the engagement and empowerment you want your students to experience, William Butler Yeats wrote, "Education is not the filling of a pail, but the lighting of a fire."

Lisa Delpit (2008) provides a wonderful example of "lighting those fires" and building on students' cultures to do so. Spending time in an African American–dominant middle school, she noticed far too many of the girls were distracted from their lessons by concerns about their hair and looks. Surmising that most African American girls would have a bottle of "Luster's Pink Oil Lotion Moisturizer" in their backpacks, she consulted with the science teacher to develop a unit on its chemical content and that of other cosmetic products. From this unit, students became engaged in learning the names, properties, and purposes of the chemicals, as well as their effects on people. She located the work of an ethnomathematician, who created a unit on patterns and tessellations based on studying African braiding. She developed classroom activities that included drawing tessellations and holding a hairstyle show featuring different tessellations. Since most braiders are from Africa, she had the students interview braiders about their home countries, identify why they left, and then create a linguistic map of Africa based on the interviews. Weaving these lessons into the curriculum created a level of engagement and "belonging" with the subject matter.

Bransford, Brown, and Cocking (2000) make three important points about working with students' prior experience and knowledge that you can apply to teaching within the MiCOSA Model.

- Prior knowledge relevant to a topic can and should be used as a strength.
- Prior knowledge that is actually misinformation causes students to struggle.
- School teaching practices that conflict with practices in students' communities can result in students having great difficulty applying what they know.

In MiCOSA, you will learn to apply three actions to these concerns as you work with students from a variety of backgrounds in the classroom:

I. *Activate Relevant Student Knowledge.* Using MiCOSA, you will "activate" students' content and thinking skill knowledge relevant to a learning situation, building on their backgrounds in both areas.

II. *Reframe Misinformation from Prior Knowledge.* When a student's prior beliefs have led to misinterpretation of new information, you will help them re-frame that prior knowledge, uncover the misunderstanding, and get back on track.

III. *Mediate Conflicts Between Cultural and School Practices.* When a student's community or cultural practices conflict with particular school teaching practices, you can help students by varying teaching practices and helping translate between the two environments.

Examining these three concepts in depth will provide you with ideas and strategies to help you put them into practice. In addition, you will explore just what culture has to do with learning, and how prior knowledge and cultural grounding can enhance 21st century global citizenship.

I. Activate Relevant Student Knowledge

When you incorporate the diversity of your students' prior knowledge and cultural backgrounds into the curriculum, and link classroom *content* to it, school achievement improves (Gay, 2010; Nieto & Bode, 2008). Cognitively, this awakens existing neurological pathways that provide a foundation on which students can build. Emotionally, it values students' experiences, their homes, and their communities, which enhances motivation.

Consider the breadth of what your students already know and how it relates to your lessons. Their "relevant knowledge" may be *content* information about the topic you are studying, but also may be about the *processes* or *thinking skills* used to understand and work within that context. You will tap prior knowledge and cultural grounding in both areas.

For instance, if you are studying natural sciences, and you plan to have your students compare the life cycle of snakes with that of bears, you will want to evaluate two levels of content background: First, what do students already think they know from their own knowledge and experiences with snakes and bears? Second, what do they know about life cycles? Their personal stories of seeing snakeskins or bear tracks support rich discussions. Ask students what they may have heard at home and in their communities, so that the class can benefit from the richness of diverse experiences. Ask a community leader or elder to come share an experience or perspective from time to time. This goes beyond the cursory "hook" to gain attention, and literally provides the opportunity for students to see and hear what they are bringing to the topic or the process as strengths, and then to build on their culturally grounded knowledge.

Comparing life cycles involves *making connections* with and understanding the relationship of survival with the seasons, climate, and specific environments. Therefore, after your students gather information, you will ask them to compare, seek relationships, and perhaps make inferences. This will require them to use critical thinking skills such as *comparing* and *finding connections and relationships*. For some this will be new and challenging. However, you will want all your students to develop an easy familiarity with the thinking skills and to feel competent in knowing how, when, and why to use them. To facilitate this, you will introduce key thinking skills prior to requiring their use. Similar to seeking prior knowledge with content, you will build on students' prior knowledge and cultural grounding in using the thinking skill.

In order to activate prior knowledge about using a thinking skill, you often begin by having students relate to the thinking skill within areas of personal prior knowledge or experience. This builds their familiarity with the skill and their knowledge that the skill can be used in multiple situations, from home and cultural contexts to science and school. This will also support you when helping students transfer and use the skill again later in new contexts.

For example, you might ask what they already know about thinking skills such as *comparing*: "Let's start with what you already know about using this thinking skill of comparing, so we can establish what it really means and how you will use it. Think of something you did at home this week where you had to compare something. It could be comparing ideas, reasons, prices, ingredients . . . whatever relates to your experience." Then, using student-generated ideas, move into extracting definitions of the thinking skill from the examples. Further, ask them how using that thinking skill is helpful. This prepares the foundation of your bridge into natural science, where students will apply their knowledge of the thinking skill to your life cycle project.

Whether activating prior knowledge about content or process, you should build on the prior knowledge and cultural grounding as a student strength. You will likely do this intuitively, weaving student stories and ideas into your introduction, or into your explanation or clarification of a topic. However, a process such as the three-step Elicit–Validate–Incorporate process may also prove helpful.

Elicit Student Response   There are many ways to elicit a student's prior knowledge. Some teachers ask outright, "What do you already know about [bears]?" or the relevant topic. You may use what is known as a "KWL" (or KWHL) chart, recording responses as you elicit what students think they already know (K); what they want to know (W); how they will find out (H); and what they learned (L). You might display a "mind map" on your classroom screen or smart board, and gradually fill it with ideas from the class. Some teachers use Web-based versions of the KWL chart, such as those available on *Inspiration*, or they have individual students generate and track ideas on their own computers.

To help your students generate ideas, develop a series of open-ended questions or prompts. For example, in eliciting knowledge about *comparing* as a thinking skill, you might ask: "How do you think that you have used the thinking skill of comparing in your everyday life? Think about when you go shopping, when you are preparing for your day, or when you are making decisions that involve your family." This allows students to share a variety of ideas and backgrounds.

Add breadth and depth to eliciting prior knowledge by asking students to think more critically. For example, suppose you are studying rock formations in your local area. Rather than listing what students say they already know, ask, "How do you believe these formations came to be the way they are? What might you have heard in your family or community? What is the relationship between history, weather, and these formations? What other factors might be involved?" Bring in some samples and photos or ask students to do so.

Tap into the 21st century skills of collaboration, developing multicultural competence, and the use of technology. Go beyond individual responses and facilitate contributions that promote the use of collaborative skills. Rather than emphasizing the success of one individual or competition among teams, ask students to think of the welfare of the group, and encourage them to learn from and to help one another. Make this a more typical instructional approach to developing collaborative skills, along with engaging them in critical thinking. You may think of other methods, but here are two ideas for starters.

- Pose an open-ended question to the class, and have the students work together in small groups. First, one person in the group responds to the prompt: "Share your initial thoughts on the topic." Person two acknowledges what he or she heard (e.g., "I heard you say. . ."), then adds, "and I would add or clarify with (their ideas)." A third person may use the same format as the second to add his or her thinking; then, each group member attempts to summarize the thinking. After everyone has spoken, the group selects the best summary to contribute back to the class. You may find it helpful to have the process modeled first in front of the class, emphasizing appropriate responses to one another.

- Overtly teach that collaborative thinking can change and enrich your own thinking, and ask students to experiment and share what they find. Again, pose an open-ended question. In groups of five, (a) the first person shares an idea; (b) the second person builds on the idea and shares how it influenced his or her own; (c) the third person builds on the first two, and shares how his or her own thinking was influenced by the others; (d) the fourth person summarizes the content response; (e) the fifth person summarizes how collaborative thinking influenced the process.

As you move from hearing students' ideas to using their ideas as strengths in the learning process, your second step is to validate the ideas.

Validate Student Ideas

Some of the experiences students share will be familiar to you and your students. Others may be unusual or unknown to you or to some of your class. You can ensure students believe that what they "bring into the classroom" truly matters by validating their contributions. Repeating and validating the student idea in front of others often works well in mainstream groups. Here is one method: Using two sentences, first repeat or reframe what your student said and then add at least one sentence about why his or her contribution matters. For instance, "Robbie has actually lived in an area where snakes hibernate in the winter. He learned how to walk more cautiously in the woods during the non-hibernating times." By using the information that students share, which connects personal experiences with topics such as the life cycle of snakes, and pointing out the connections and relationships between the seasons and elements of the life cycle, you validate students' relevancy to the topic and enrich the discussion. This often leads to deeper study.

Remember too that your students' diversity and differences may cause some students to feel hesitant or even embarrassed by being called on or pointed out individually in public, because culturally it is not seen as appropriate to stand out as an individual (e.g., some traditional Native American or Asian students). Therefore, calling on these students or pointing to their responses may cause disengagement rather than greater engagement. Be sensitive to these cultural differences. Rather than ask for individual sharing, consider having small groups report their collective ideas. Support them with a range of methods, from group discussions to *wikis* or blogs. In that way, you validate the ideas from the group rather than point out students as individuals. Displaying ideas in a variety of modalities (e.g., artistic, verbal, musical) also supports access.

Incorporate Student Responses   In the third step, incorporate students' contributions and experiences so that they become strength-based beginnings to new learning. Be sure to keep track of them and incorporate one or two contributions into any one phase of your work. Have small groups include one another's background ideas in quick writes, goal setting, or small projects. Three factors help explain the importance of including all your students' ideas: (1) brain connections, (2) motivation, and (3) engagement.

- *Brain connections.* Building on prior knowledge as an asset actually helps activate the mind's readiness to take in new learning and supports memory. Linking to existing neurological connections facilitates building more complexity in the network, so students begin with some element of familiarity.

- *Motivation.* Personally and culturally meaningful contexts enhance motivation. Too often, schools do not provide students from diverse backgrounds with faces that "look like them," or interactive styles similar to those they know from home. This can lead to alienation and feeling unwelcome. By eliciting, validating, and then incorporating student experiences, you begin to bridge this gulf. Building on specific and culturally grounded prior knowledge, you establish an emotional comfort zone— a kind of belonging in the classroom and welcoming to the topic for new learners.

- *Engagement.* Similarly, when students know they already have something to build on that relates to them, it not only supports motivation, but also leads to active engagement.

Here are a few additional ideas of how you might help students make this "bridge" from their prior knowledge to new knowledge:

- Display their ideas around the room and refer to them as you introduce content.
- Use their examples as a springboard to create class projects related to the work.
- Use graphic organizers to categorize the kinds of information they bring into the topic of the lesson.
- Ask them to consciously describe how their earlier knowledge helped them understand new information or how older knowledge sets might have changed.

II. Reframing Misinformation from Prior Knowledge

Sometimes misinformation is embedded within student reports of prior knowledge. Scan and listen for this so that you can correct the misinformation tactfully. Understanding the source helps. Often, two culprits cause student misinformation: (a) Students may hold only superficial knowledge and incorrectly infer based on their preliminary understanding; or (b) they may tend to be inflexible, not having the skills needed to shift their thinking. A third source concerns teacher responses to relational thinking styles, and has interesting cultural components.

Reframing Superficial Knowledge and Incorrect Inference   When students begin with only superficial levels of information, some jump to conclusions without building their depth of knowledge. For example, students may have a random fact, but no knowledge of its context, or under what conditions it may or may not be fully true. Returning to the topic of bears, Randy may say that bears sleep in caves. When asked for specifics, he merely says that bears sleep in caves. When probed, Randy cannot qualify or elaborate on that statement to tell whether all bears sleep in caves, or whether some sleep in other places. To support his gaining sufficient depth, go beyond accepting one word, one phrase, or one-sentence reports of what students know, and ask clarifying questions. Let students know you will be excited to see how their insights develop as they build more depth in their knowledge. Then ask, for instance, "Do all bears sleep in caves? What are the implications of finding out that some bears sleep on hillsides or even under houses?" Engaging these more critical forms of questioning alongside "What do you know?" deepens the discussion.

Reframing Inflexible Thinking   Critical thinking also requires flexibility—openness to new ways of doing things, such as changing or adapting ideas. When your students work with subjects similar to something they have done before, but with a new element, they need to apply flexible thinking. Sometimes student inflexibility leads to errors. For example, students may have learned to decipher and calculate word problems requiring them to (a) sum the total cost of various items, then (b) subtract that total from the amount they gave a cashier to determine how much change they would receive. To change the sequence, you might then require them to (a) sum the total of the cost of various items, (b) subtract the cost of the one item returned, and then (c) calculate how much change they would receive. Although you have introduced an additional process, some students may continue with the old or familiar process, thinking they know just what to do rather than stopping and engaging in flexible thinking. They may look at just part of the problem and assume that once they have learned a process they should always apply it.

Some students appear to get "stuck" in inflexible thinking when their strong opinions or past experiences intersect with the topic. For example, Flora reads a math word problem about a girl who buys a plane ticket from Los Angeles to New York, and then returns via Dallas. She is asked to calculate the total miles flown. Flora gets stuck on the idea that a girl wouldn't buy a ticket—her parent would—and does not think further about how to calculate the miles flown. Her experience prevents her from seeing the point of the problem.

Again, adding further critical thinking into your lessons helps build flexibility in thinking and problem solving. Brainstorming and practice with hypothesizing ("what if") help students consider different explanations for events. For instance, "You have just shared your reactions to a man's apparent apathy to his children's misbehavior on a public bus. Let's add some new information. What if the reason for the man's apparent apathy, and perhaps for the children's behavior, was his wife's death that week? How does your thinking change?"

Another method to help build flexibility asks students to re-categorize groups of items or objects by new and different categories. Ask, "How else might these items be categorized—what unique groupings come to mind?" When students become familiar with creating and responding to critical thinking questions, the added depth of their repertoires supports added flexibility. Working with young children to categorize blocks by color or shape provides an additional example of the need for flexible thinking. When asked to categorize and sequence by size, some may produce sets categorized by size but not sequenced. Here you can become playful about adding in new ways to produce categories, first by giving directions, and then having them suggest ideas.

Reframing Your Response to Relational Thinking   Some students use a relational (versus linear) thinking style. Relational thinking may lead students to first "associate" from a prompt rather than going straight to what a linear thinker (perhaps you) might consider "something they know." For example, Ms. Frankin asks Lillian's class to share what they already know about bears. Lillian remarks that she has seen a movie in Vancouver about a bear hibernating among the roots of a tree uprooted by an earthquake. Recognizing your students' use of associations often helps you reframe their statement to share a fact or knowledge you can refer to later. "Ah yes, some bears choose to hibernate under trees, so all bears do not hibernate in caves." Some students come from backgrounds where relational thinking is the norm. Storytelling is a way of teaching lessons in their homes and communities; it may provide the most powerful "answers" to questions. Associations and connections typify conversational and thinking styles rather than right and wrong answers. The listener is expected to associate and infer. If you are able to recognize it, you can build on this skill as an asset. Try having students come up with a story that illustrates a point. Neither way is right nor wrong; each is just different. You want to be sure to walk through and hear out your students' thinking, especially for relational thinkers. In doing so, a wealth of fascinating connections and relationships to your topic may emerge.

When you believe your student brings misinformation into a lesson or unit, you don't want to squash participation, curiosity, or creativity; you want students to re-engage at a deeper level. A few methods for doing that include: (1) setting up your classrooms for openness and support; (2) reframing; and (3) checking for what has been called cultural myopia.

(1) ***Set up your classroom environment for acceptance and openness to alternative or more complex ideas.*** If you use something like a KWL chart, rather than asking "What do you know about [bears]?" add a few qualifiers; for example, "What do you *think you know at this point*?" This allows for expansion and promotes curiosity. Let students know that you will work with and build on all ideas, and then do so by testing their assumptions and checking their validity with multiple sources of information. Discuss ideas in light of conditions under which they are accurate, explanations that help students understand them further, and implications of what you find. Post these conditions so students can easily access and consider them. Often, having students stop, think, and talk with a partner about their idea before contributing to the whole class helps refine their thinking. Provide time to have students practice questioning one another. They may engage in some of the assumption testing and clarifying on their own.

(2) ***Reframe.*** The concept of reframing comes from the idea of "frame" of mind, and how frame of mind colors perceptions of the world. By helping another person "reframe," you help him or her see things from another perspective. Reframing problems as opportunities, or perceived weaknesses as unique features or strengths, are common examples. Fullan and Miles (1992) developed a phrase you may find extremely useful in the classroom: "Problems are our friends." Here is their context:

> It seems perverse to say that problems are our friends, but we cannot develop effective responses to complex situations unless we actively seek and confront real problems that are difficult to solve. Problems are our friends because only through immersing ourselves in problems can we come up with creative solutions. Problems are the route to deeper change and deeper satisfaction. (Fullan & Miles, 1992, p. 745)

Applied to eliciting student knowledge, changing your own frame of reference sometimes helps you help them. In other words, instead of "No—wrong answer," or "Can anyone help Billy?" you might say something like, "You are beginning to think about this. Let's take what you said, and clarify, revise, or expand on it."

Sometimes reframing by offering a slightly altered version of what your students have said allows them to shift thinking, gain flexibility, or even acquire hope. For instance, when a student says, "I just can't understand," reframe that as, "At this moment you may not understand, and expressing that is a good first step. Tell me what you *do* understand, and what else you would like to know." This acknowledges your student's frustration as well as the foundation on which he or she will build a competent response. At the same time, you are giving the student a way to move forward and take more active control of his or her problem solving.

(3) *Self check for cultural myopia.*   Sometimes, rather than jumping to conclusions about misinformation, you may need to check your own belief systems. You might unknowingly be operating from incomplete or incorrect information due to a lack of exposure to a variety of worldviews. Let yourself stop to hypothesize that what seems like an unusual response might be a response from a different worldview and experience.

Some students, when confronted with ideas that they consider unfamiliar or out of the ordinary, may jump to ridicule. For example, students in one middle school classroom are beginning to study iguanas. One student comments, "Yum—they are really good to eat." A second student interjects, "Yuk, you can't eat iguanas, what's wrong with you?!" Several of the students look around wide-eyed. These can become teachable moments, expanding your class's cultural competence for the 21st century as well as their information on the topic. Here are a few examples of what you might say:

- *Sometimes out of ignorance, we jump to conclusions about information that is unfamiliar to us. It sounds like there might be something new to learn today that we didn't expect. Also, we have a new characteristic of iguanas we had not anticipated: source of food in some cultures. Victor, will you tell us more about your experiences with iguanas?*

- *One of the beauties of our class is the rich diversity of experiences and ways of thinking about the world each of you brings. We're going to start a blog on lessons from across the globe as we learn them. Brainstorm with your group about a good name for the blog that will reflect our growing global awareness. Thanks! Now, who would like to get further clarification on something you just heard, so you can post and share?*

- *That's a new idea for me. Let's figure out where we can get more information about that. Who already has ideas, and who would like to get on the Internet and do some research? What other ideas and sources of information might we use?*

III. Mediate Conflicts Between Cultural and School Practices

When conflicts exist across cultural and school practices, it will likely be your students, their parents, or even their communities who feel uncomfortable, misunderstood, or even disregarded. You may not be aware that this situation has occurred if no one raises it directly. Knowing more about the nature of such conflicts can help you respond to or even initiate these conversations. Two critical examples provide a framework for understanding conflicts between cultural and classroom practices: presumptions of deficit and communication styles.

Presumptions of Deficit   Have you ever had students you "knew" right off would have problems—or, on the other hand, ones you "knew" would be academically successful—because of how they spoke? This happens unconsciously, but research demonstrates that if a teacher considers a student's language inadequate, very often that

student ends up having great difficulty or even failing due to *presumptions of their deficits* (Stubbs, 2008). As an example, Stubbs speaks about many Brits regarding the speech characteristic of several large cities as "slovenly and ugly" (p. 77), resulting in perceptions of people from those regions as less intelligent, unambitious, and lacking self-confidence and even reliability! In an example from the United States, Smith (2008) tells about growing up speaking a southern dialect of Ebonics (Black English). When he came into an urban school thousands of miles away, he was labeled as mentally deficient based on others' attitudes and presumptions about his language. His heart-wrenching journey involved being mocked, bullied, and tracked into low-level classes. When he tried to express his frustration, he was again labeled; this time, as a student acting out. Smith went on to become a professor of linguistics, as help from a mentor, who understood the power of language, led to Smith's bridging the divide and becoming empowered. His powerful story portrays a young student affected emotionally, socially, and educationally by linguistic presumptions of deficit. For further insights, we recommend Delpit and Dowdy's (2008) *The Skin That We Speak: Thoughts on Language and Culture in the Classroom*, a powerful collection of stories illustrating the impact of attitudes about language.

Communication Style Differences

Even unconsciously, you may tend to think of ways of communicating as right or wrong, familiar or odd. Interpretation tends to come from experience, and from what is called worldview. Sometimes interpretations incorrectly pair meaning and behavior in the classroom. For instance, one of your students may come from a home culture that uses extremely direct communication, which you might view as confrontational. This can lead to (mis) characterizing the student as disrespectful or aggressive. Students using their second language in school often need extra time to "translate" in their heads or recall the word they want to use. Because of the extra time these students take to pause before answering, their expressive language can be misinterpreted as being cognitively slow. Still other students may come from home cultures in which looking at a teacher directly would be considered confrontational; yet, in the school classroom, *not* looking at the teacher might be (mis) interpreted as disinterested, disrespectful, or evasive. In a classic study, Phillips (1983) documented teachers' (mis) interpretation of long stretches of silence from traditional Navajo students as meaning they were not learning. In reality, these students were highly reflective, learning in a most respectful way that was consistent with their culture.

As a result of these misinterpretations of behavior, some students carry labels, whether overt or covert, and those labels influence how they are treated. Since high expectations (and positive expectations) support students in attaining strong outcomes, using this information to generate hypotheses helps when a hunch might tell you something is wrong.

Cultural Mismatch Between School and Home

If a new student's classroom mirrors his or her home values, behavioral expectations, language, and familiarity of ideas and concepts, that student can build on that familiarity as a "safety zone" from which to take on new challenges. School becomes a structured extension of his or her prior learning and cultural context. These students know how to interpret the verbal and nonverbal signs, signals, and expectations of their teachers—and match their responses to their prior experiences.

However, if that new student does not recognize the social and verbal contexts, he or she has to negotiate three areas: (a) content learning, (b) the new rules of the school culture, and (c) the social-emotional challenges of not having the familiar social-emotional supports that framed his or her prior learning. The demand and complexity are far greater for the student with a cultural "mismatch," increasing not only cognitive but also affective demands.

Students who have "learned how to learn" well within their home contexts, and who have confidence in themselves as learners, bridge this divide most easily. Others often struggle. If your students master this complex double or triple learning, they emerge with complex and powerful outcomes as well. They will have bicultural negotiation skills, and two sets of lenses through which to view and hypothesize about the world. If not mastered or supported, however, the risk of overwhelming the spirit of the learner can be profound.

For some students, the demands of school can become overly complex because their initial learning foundations were not strong. Complexity increases if the number of components increases. Complexity increases again if those components are unfamiliar (whether they are cognitive or social-emotional). Therefore, the complexity of school inter-actions, assignments, and demands will not be the same for all students in your classroom.

Motivation, Mediation, and Meaning in Diverse Classrooms

PD **d** TOOLKIT™

PDToolkit: Video Clip 2.1 demonstrates students connecting their countries of origin to their teacher's introduction of a unit of study on natural disasters.

Coming to know your students' perspectives, drawing out and valuing who they are, and seeing them as unique individuals influences their motivation to engage in the classroom and to learn (Wlodkowski & Ginsberg, 1995). This engagement creates intrinsic rewards, which lead to true and lasting motivation. Wlodkowski and Ginsberg (1995) suggest that establishing inclusion, developing positive attitudes, enhancing meaning, and creating a sense of competence foster meaningful engagement, and thus motivation, in diverse class-rooms. Similarly, MiCOSA's five mediating conversations and interactions facilitate mean-ingful engagement: intent and reciprocity, mediating meaning, bridging thinking, guiding self-regulation, and building competence. The following sections illustrate how MiCOSA weaves these ideas together to support motivation and change in diverse classrooms.

Building a Sense of Inclusion

The sense of belonging is a basic psychological need—a need schools can potentially en-hance (Osterman, 2000). Creating a learning atmosphere of mutual respect and connec-tion fosters a feeling of belonging (Anderman, 2003). This, in turn, leads to openness to learning and to change. With clear intent, you will help students discover their own think-ing skills and processes, which are often embedded within their home cultures. Doing this helps illustrate that you value and respect them as individuals and are there to support them. Seek their willing and reciprocal involvement in developing their thinking skills. Partner with them to uncover their strengths and celebrate their use.

Fostering Positive Attitudes Through Meaningful Engagement

Making learning personally relevant leads to greater engagement and interest, as well as a positive attitude (Bernard, 2010). In MiCOSA, accessing and engaging prior knowledge and cultural grounding help establish a deeper sense of personal relevance, and therefore of meaning. To do this, you need to know why the content area or questions that you explore with your students have meaning.

As teachers explore this question of meaning, their responses move from the concrete to the abstract, and often incorporate critical thinking. For instance, in considering why third graders should study space, one group of teachers moves quickly beyond the value of having students learn concrete facts about the universe their students live in. They want their students to *understand connections and relationships* among natural elements in the world, and to link the notion of human curiosity and exploration with knowing or wanting to know what's in space. In addition, they want students to understand the cost-benefit issues, and the potential of finding new resources: "Sending people into space costs lots of money. What might they find that would justify the expense?" These "higher order meanings" gave teachers the framework to connect more deeply with all their students.

When your instruction incorporates students' cultural practices, histories, or legacies, it begins to close that gap of alienation from school and curriculum for many of them, helping students connect with curriculum, learning, and their own sense of belonging (Delpit, 2008; Kana'iaupuni, Ledward, & Jensen, 2010). It becomes meaningful. Although many textbooks contain culturally relevant content, Gay (2000) explains that to maximize that content, you must know why it is critical and how to use it.

Enriching Meaning Through Connections and Bridges

PD **TOOLKIT™**

PDToolkit:
In Video Clip 2.2 you see Trish demonstrating making personal and cross-cultural connections to student's personal narratives and stories.

Once initial meaning is established, deepen that meaning and engagement through challenging and thoughtful experiences in the classroom. Critical questions and activities, as well as problem- and project-based learning experiences, help students connect their learning to meaningful outcomes. For example, Ms. Appel's class discusses community concerns that a proposed new mine might negatively affect their water supply. Her students do research on hard rock mining and its effects to the watershed. They use multiple sources of information to gather that information, seek connections across their sources, compare the studies they read with their local community, and infer probable implication. They create a website to present their findings, with illustrations, data, and summaries of key issues and links to more extensive sources. In doing so, they use thinking skills of collaboration, precision, accuracy, and incorporation of new concepts. A letter to the editor of the local paper contains a link to the website. Letters go home to their parents and those of others in the school. Making a real difference with a real issue enhances their motivation. Deliberately engaging a number of thinking skills (e.g., *multiple sources, comparing, seeking connections, precision and accuracy*) lays a foundation for using them again on their next project.

In MiCOSA, you will deliberately engage students in thinking about how their learning in one context has applications in new content areas and contexts. You may create these "bridges" from one subject area to another, or to students' lives and future careers. In doing this, you support students' valuing of their own thinking as increasingly meaningful.

Creating a Sense of Competence

To take on increasingly demanding content, students need to believe in their competence as learners. As you challenge them, that sense of competence will sustain their willingness to try more difficult things. As you watch and witness their growing competence, share your observations with them. Encourage them to recognize their growing competencies for themselves, and to be aware of what brought them these successes. To give it another level of meaning, link their growing competence to the use of one or more of MiCOSA's 21 thinking skills. Be specific, so that they build a sense of competence based on believable feedback. For example, you might say, "Sarah, I noticed the critical questions you were asking the group today to clarify your ideas about your election project. When you asked Andy how his candidate's idea on education funding was related to your candidate's position, you made a fascinating *comparison*, and built a *connection and relationship* that helped you both think more deeply. Did you notice that?"

Supporting the Development of Your Own Story

Just as your students carry stories in their heads about themselves as learners, you also carry stories about yourself as a competent and creative teacher. Just as your students' stories are "co-constructed" in part by family, community, and teachers, so your own story will be co-constructed in part by your school community and colleagues. Building support systems that are deliberately structured to celebrate new learning, to pose and problem-solve challenges, and to share resources leads to empowering stories. Ideally, this happens on "school time."

Teachers in Learning Communities

While sometimes the best thinking is done alone, isolation can be a painful way to confront difficulty or challenge. As you encounter times when you feel unsure of yourself on this journey, you don't want those times to lapse into insecurity or negative self-talk. Well-designed teacher support can contradict insecurity and help re-engage with creativity.

Put yourself and your students in a position to build resilience through your own collaborations. Set up a partnership with a colleague to chat over lunch; structure grade-level meetings with a mission to contradict negativity, promote problem-solving, and share successes and new learning. Learn something new once a week, or once a month. Start a study group. Expand your idea of partnering to include your students, their parents, and the community.

Geneva Gay (2010) shares a fascinating way to partner with students in the classroom. She suggests that teachers encourage students to engage in critical dialogue about the conflicts between school and home culture, and to analyze the cultural realities and ideals of different cultural systems for consistencies and inconsistencies. She explains how this benefits the students as well as teachers, who become partners in this process:

> As *cultural mediators*, teachers provide opportunities for students to engage in critical dialogue about conflicts among cultures and to analyze inconsistencies between mainstream cultural ideals/realities and those of different cultural systems. They help students clarify their ethnic identities, honor other cultures, develop positive cross-ethnic and cross-cultural relationships, and avoid perpetuating prejudices, stereotypes and racism. The goal is to create communities of culturally diverse learners who celebrate and affirm one another and work collaboratively for their mutual success, where empowerment replaces powerlessness and oppression. (p. 45)

Students and Parents as Learning Partners

When you truly see yourself as a learner and partner with your students, their parents, and their communities, it lowers your threshold of concern about not knowing everything. Feel free to ask for input, help, feedback, and participation from community mentors. Your interactions become naturally infused with greater respect for your students, parents, and community members. Learning together breaks down the isolation, and it enhances buy-in from the students and communities.

In many communities and cultures, giving respect is central to building any relationship. This extends from parents and elders to youth. In this worldview, adults extend respect to students, rather than demanding it from them. Studies report that giving respect to parents, students, and communities tends to come back twofold in the respect the students and community will show their teachers. To expand your "reach" of what you know and understand, and therefore can truly respect, consider reaching out to and learning about a new group in the school community each month. Sometimes this may be met with caution, or even suspicion at first, but it can be overcome with persistent and respectful connections.

SUMMARY

- Students carry powerful personal narratives about themselves as learners, which influence their motivation, as well as their connection and access to the curriculum. Because their personal stories emerge in part from what they hear about themselves in school, teachers can help support that narrative.

- MiCOSA's components intersect with a framework for culturally responsive teaching. Based on that intersection, three important actions are detailed: (a) activate relevant student knowledge; (b) reframe misinformation from prior knowledge, and (c) mediate conflicts between cultural and school practices.

- Teachers can influence students' motivation and engagement by (a) establishing inclusion and mutual respect; (b) developing positive attitudes by making content personally relevant to students; (c) enhancing meaning by helping students value their own thinking across contexts; and (d) creating a sense of competence by sharing observations about student successes.

- Linking parents and community members as partners helps bridge disconnects between cultures, communities, and schools, and helps teachers identify as learners in the process.

REFERENCES

Aganza, J. (2011). *Encuentros*: Positive results in Vista Unified School District 2009–2010. In V. J. Cook-Morales (Chair), *RtI tiers without tears: Collaboration with your bilingual school psychologist.* Symposium presented at the annual conference of the California Association for Bilingual Education (CABE). Long Beach, CA.

Aganza, J., & Cline, Z. (2009). *Encuentros: A culturally responsive curriculum.* Workshop presented at the Bilingual Special Education Conference, Portland, OR: Portland State University.

Anderman, L. H. (2003). Academic and social perceptions as predictors of change in middle school students' sense of school belonging. *Journal of Experimental Education, 72,* 5–22.

Bernard, S. (2010). *Science shows making lessons relevant really matters.* Retrieved from Edutopia.org

Bransford, J. D., Brown, A. L., & Cocking, R. R. (Eds). (2000). *How people learn: Brain, mind, experience, and school.* Washington, D.C.: National Academy Press.

Delpit, L. (2008). No kinda sense. In L. Delpit & J. K. Dowdy (Eds.), *The skin that we speak: Thoughts on language and culture in the classroom* (pp. 34–57). New York, NY: The New Press.

Delpit, L., & Dowdy, J. K. (Eds.). (2008). *The skin that we speak: Thoughts on language and culture in the classroom.* New York, NY: The New Press.

Freire, P. (1972). *Pedagogy of the oppressed.* Harmondsworth: Penguin.

Freire, P. (1995). *Pedagogy of hope. Reliving pedagogy of the oppressed.* New York: Continuum.

Fullan, M. G., & Miles, M. B. (1992). Getting reform right: What works and what doesn't. *Phi Delta Kappan, 73*(10), 745–752.

Gay, G. (2000). *Culturally responsive teaching: Theory, research and practice.* New York, NY: Teachers College Press.

Gay, G. (2010). *Culturally responsive teaching: Theory, research, & practice* (2nd ed.). New York: Teachers College Press.

Kana'iaupuni, S., Ledward, B., & Jensen, U. (2010). *Culture-based education and its relationship to student outcomes.* Honolulu: Kamehameha Schools, Research & Evaluation. Retrieved from www.ksbe.edu

Nieto, S., & Bode, P. (2008). *Affirming diversity: The sociopolitical context of multicultural education* (5th ed.). Boston, MA: Allyn & Bacon.

Osterman, K. F. (2000). Students' need for belonging in the school community. *Review of Educational Research, 70,* 323–367. doi: 10.3102/00346543070003323

Phillips, S. U. (1983). *The invisible culture: Communication in classroom and community on the Warm Springs Indian Reservation.* New York: Longman.

Reveles, F. (2000). *Encuentros: Hombre a Hombre* (Encounters: Man to Man). Sacramento, CA. California Department of Education.

Rosaldo, R. (1989). *Culture and truth: The remaking of social analysis.* Boston: Beacon.

Smith, E. (2008). Ebonics: A case history. In L. Delpit & J. K. Dowdy (Eds.), *The skin that we speak: Thoughts on language and culture in the classroom* (pp. 16–32). New York, NY: The New Press.

Stubbs, M. (2008). Some basic sociolinguistic concepts. In L. Delpit & J. K. Dowdy (Eds.), *The skin that we speak: Thoughts on language and culture in the classroom* (pp. 74–104). New York, NY: The New Press.

White, M., & Morgan, A. (2006). *Narrative therapy with children and their families.* Adelaide, South Australia: Dulwich Centre Publications.

Winslade, J. M., & Monk, G. (2000). *Narrative mediation: A new approach to conflict resolution.* San Francisco, CA: Jossey-Bass.

Winslade, J. M., & Monk, G. D. (2007). *Narrative counseling in schools: Powerful and brief.* Thousand Oaks, CA: Corwin.

Wlodkowski, R., & Ginsberg, M. (1995). *Diversity and motivation: Culturally responsive teaching.* San Francisco: Jossey-Bass.

Chapter Three

Mediating Conversations for Enhanced Thinking

MiCOSA's mediating conversations distinguish it from most other thinking skill programs because these conversations give you the language to help your students dare to develop new thinking skills, and to learn to apply them across contexts.

Strolling down the aisle of a supermarket provides a colorful array of parent-child interactions. On one end of the breakfast aisle, an exasperated mother snatches the cereal box from her six-year-old son's hand. "Keep your hands off the box!" she reprimands, as she places it firmly back on the shelf. Her son's cries of protest are evidence enough that this was not a mediating conversation! However, further down the aisle a father encourages his son to help choose a cereal for the family breakfast, reminding him they had discussed three important factors: the nutritional value, the price, and the appeal. The boy pulls the Sugar Squiggles off the shelf, and says, "Dad, this one looks great– cool picture, and it's only $2.99 a box!" The father mediates, "You thought about two important things–it looks good and the price is right. That's great. What about nutrition? Let's see what's in this? Ah, this one has way too much sugar. Help me find another cereal that looks tasty, that's good value for the money, and yet is more nutritious." No cries of protest came from this shopping pair!

The first chapter introduced you to the word *mediator* as a kind of "go-between," a great listener and helper, a kind of translator, a facilitator, much like the second parent in the previous scenario. These conversations between parents or other care-taking adults and their children are the earliest opportunities to use mediation. The father in the previous example acts as a "go-between" for the boy and his situation, guiding him to take action to resolve the problem by gathering all the relevant information before making a decision. This way, he supports his son's use of the thinking skill *multiple sources* of information (e.g., nutritional value, reasonable price, appeal) rather than being limited by too little information (the cereal looks good in the picture and the price is right). He uses their shopping excursion as a meaningful context. Within this dialogue, we find illustrations of several of MiCOSA's mediating conversations: the father's *intent* to help his son use the thinking skill, and the son's *reciprocal* response to his dad (his total engagement in the learning); the father's positive guiding comments, supporting his son's developing *competence* in thinking; and finally, the father's mediation of *self-regulation,* evident when he suggests his son go back and re-think before making a final decision. These skills are covered in depth in this chapter.

In a similar way, as a mediator, you will listen very carefully for thinking skills or experiences already embedded within home or cultural contexts and help bring familiarity to new learning. You will place yourself between the students and the new learning, helping build a bridge between the two. You will help your students "own" their personal thinking strengths, and transfer and use those thinking skills again and again to solve challenging new problems.

The MiCOSA acronym, **M**ediation **i**n the **C**lassroom: an **O**pen **S**ystems **A**pproach, emphasizes students as open to, and capable of, change. It is through the mediating conversations that you facilitate that change. You very deliberately structure your conversations to intervene. By doing so, students will gain NEW thinking skills, and make them habits to be used across the curriculum and in life. These conversations require you to forfeit old habits of being the "sage on the stage," and to share your humanness with your students as you partner with them on their journey of learning. Mediating conversations prompt engagement, meaning, response to challenge, a willingness to take risks, self-regulation, and competence.

Five mediating conversations (adapted from the work of Jensen, 2012) effectively support this thinking skill growth in your students:

a. Intent and Reciprocity

b. Mediating Meaning

c. Bridging Thinking

d. Guiding Self-Regulation

e. Building Competence

Intent and Reciprocity

> *Dramatically pulling the jawbone of a shark from a bag, Mrs. Jones asks her students to guess what she is holding. Eagerly they share responses, and as they come closer she uses a swimming motion and then simulates the opening beats of the music from Jaws. Yes—the jaw of a shark! Smiling, she shares her intent for the lesson. "Together we are about to write a report of information. Information about sharks will serve as our model. You will be using an important thinking skill called* systematic search. *Think about those two words,* systematic *and* search. *Now share with your partner what you think this thinking skill means, and how you think you will use it to help you write a report of information." The room begins to hum with activity.*

In this vignette, Mrs. Jones shares her *intent* clearly, that her students will learn the thinking skill of *systematic search* within the context of the standard on writing a report of information. She could have simply said, "Class, today we are going to learn to write reports of information and use the thinking skill of *systematic search*." However, to assure their engagement, their *reciprocity* in the activity, she uses a "hook," pulling the jawbone dramatically from the bag.

Establishing *intent and reciprocity* builds a bond and set of expectations that the interaction or lesson is going to be meaningful, engaging, and successful. You will see your students' reciprocity in their visual engagement, body language, and verbal responses. Pause for a moment to let this mental connection happen, because without reciprocity, no mediation for cognitive change can occur.

You may already ask your students to make connections between their prior knowledge and a subject area. With MiCOSA, you will ask them to make connections between the new thinking skill and their prior knowledge, including culturally based prior knowledge. For example, "The project we are about to do requires us to use the thinking skill of planning. Each of you has probably used that thinking skill at home with your family, community, or friends. Think a minute and get ready to share an example of what you already know about planning. Then we will define it and look at how we can apply it in our work together. How do you and your family use the thinking skill of planning?" This conversation helps establish your *intent*; by connecting to their home experience, you ensure *reciprocity* in the learning relationship.

PDToolkit: In Video Clip 3.1 Marlene and Diandra model using an engaging activity to establish *intent and reciprocity* at the beginning of a lesson.

Although establishing *intent and reciprocity* may seem obvious as a lesson opener, maintain these reciprocal and intentional relationships throughout the lesson to keep learning active. For instance, take a moment for students to share their ideas as a pair-share or on individual whiteboards. This provides an opportunity to check for understanding before transitioning, and also renews reciprocity while maintaining your intent. Use simple acts like pointing to the board to refocus students' attention on the importance of the thinking skill, or use student names to personalize the interaction. These actions support renewed intent and revive reciprocity. Vary the pitch, pace, and tone of your voice and gestures to help give students the "space" to reconnect.

In the following table, you will find examples of engaging activities that can be useful in supporting this mediating conversation. Sample mediating conversations are provided to the right.

Engaging Strategies, Activities, and Mediating Conversations to Support Intent and Reciprocity

ENGAGING STRATEGIES AND ACTIVITIES	MEDIATING CONVERSATIONS SUPPORTING INTENT AND RECIPROCITY
Sensory Connections Connect with students' backgrounds and experiences through the use of sight, sound, and touch. Use music, video clips, reenactments, realia, and readings to introduce your intent and encourage reciprocity.	1. "We have focused this week on using the thinking skill *establishing connections and relationships*. Listen to this concerto by Vivaldi. He titled it one of the four seasons. Close your eyes for a moment and get a picture of each season. Now listen, and as you do, use your thinking skill *establishing connections and relationships* to determine which of the four seasons he is portraying. I'll ask you to share what you hear and what connections you are making to your knowledge of the four seasons." 2. "How many of you turn off the TV or leave the room before the credits come on? Wow, a lot of us do this. What are those credits for? What do they tell you?" *Elicit and acknowledge responses.* "Yes, these lines give credit to all of the people involved in planning and making the video. First, let's look at the credits for Rick Steves' documentary on Venice. Make a list of the different jobs you see as they scroll up the screen." *Students complete the activity.* "Now, let's go to the beginning of the video where Rick Steves introduces the parts of Venice viewers will visit. Look at your list of jobs again, with an eye for how much planning it took to make this movie. After I stop the video, jot down ideas of the planning involved and the jobs they relate to. Next, we will figure out which planning skills we will need as we prepare for our iMovie project."

Quick Writes (Graves & Kittle, 2005) Quick writes ask students to write down their thoughts without concern for grammar or spelling. Use time periods of three to eight minutes, depending on the topic. Quick writes engage prior knowledge and encourage students to summarize, connect, infer, and hypothesize. Graves and Kittle (2005) provide some wonderful ideas for quick writes that encourage students to make rich, personal connections. Quick writes can be used when a new topic is introduced to engage prior knowledge, or after an activity like the "Tea Party" (below).	1. "Today you'll be creating your own math word problems and exchanging them with other groups. The other groups will then solve your problems. When you write a word problem, you use the thinking skill *multiple sources* of information. Let's do a five-minute quick write about *multiple sources.* What ways will you use *multiple sources* to create your problem? What *multiple sources* will you need to solve another group's word problem?" 2. "Yesterday we discussed the story *A Boy Called Slow,* and the themes of responsibility, perseverance, and loyalty. Last night, you interviewed someone at home about examples of those themes in your own family. Now make a quick write to show *connections and relationships* to how your family and the boy's family demonstrate these themes." *Students complete quick writes.* "Now, we'll use the thinking skill of *connections and relationships* again as we share your quick writes and find commonalities across the classroom."
Tea Party (Beers, 2003; Perona, 1989) This can be done online or in person. Each student has a fact (either on paper or in his or her position for the sharing on a wiki). For the in-person version, students circulate the room, sharing a greeting and their fact with as many others as they can in a specific window of time (e.g., six to eight minutes). If they are sharing online, they can be assigned to add their information to blogs or discussion boards by class or by group. What occurs is that everyone comes to the table with a certain background on the subject—a bit more equity of content. Using the blogs, or Google Docs, the teacher and the students have access to the information for future use as well.	1. "I am giving each of you a fact about one of three body systems: the digestive, the respiratory, or the circulatory system. Share and receive as many of these facts as you can within the next six minutes. Afterward, I will ask you to consider how you use the thinking skill of *multiple sources* of information to broaden your initial knowledge base."

(Continued)

ENGAGING STRATEGIES AND ACTIVITIES	MEDIATING CONVERSATIONS SUPPORTING INTENT AND RECIPROCITY
	2. "Each of you has a different example of effective financial literacy. On your discussion board, trade your example with at least eight people."
	Students enter comments on discussion board. "Now, you will use the thinking skill of *establishing connections and relationships* to make at least three more responses. This time connect the information you have just received with three instances in your life in which you would use them."

Mediating Meaning

Working on the theme of exploration, Ms. Gates had set up her room with a large galleon ship. Posters lined the walls, advertising different jobs on the ship (e.g., the cook, the captain, first and second mate, and cabin boy). She asked her students to apply for one of the jobs by presenting their résumés and writing a letter of interest. Corey, normally a competent learner and engaged student, stood frowning with his arms folded. Ms. Gates approached him and asked what was wrong. Corey demanded, "Why are we doing this? It's fake—a fake ship, and fake jobs." Ms. Gates responded, "What a great question, Corey. Think about what connections or relationships there might be for your life after high school graduation and this activity. I am asking you to write persuasively, present yourself appropriately for this job on the galleon ship, and try again if your first application is rejected."

"Oh, I get it!" Corey smiled. "You are helping us get ready for real jobs."

"Absolutely. You've made a great connection, Corey! When you use your thinking skill of establishing connections and relationships, *you can understand a connection between assignments and your life. When you encounter things in your life that don't initially make sense, look for connections and relationships to see what meaning you can make."*

PD **PD** TOOLKIT™

PDToolkit: In Video Clip 3.2 Marissa mediates the meaning of the thinking skill of *cause and effect*; Diandra mediates the meaning of using the skill of *comparing*.

Corey was seeking meaning. As a teacher, you likely already help students in your classroom make meaning of the content you introduce. Meaningful contexts help engage them. In MiCOSA, you will do something a little different, as you mediate the meaning of thinking skills. What does it mean to use a new thinking skill? How does it help your students to access current as well as future content? In the previous example, Ms. Gates *mediated the meaning* of using the thinking skill of *finding connections and relationships* to help Corey establish the meaning of the current activity. She also mediated the meaning of using the thinking skill in that situation and in the future.

Mediators guide students to make meaning and value the relevance of their newly acquired thinking skills. Mediators point out the effectiveness of the thinking skills in context. For instance, in mediating the meaning of using the thinking skill of gathering *multiple sources* of information, you might say, "When you gathered all the information from the directions, your follow-through in completing the assignment went really smoothly because you knew exactly what to do." You share the value and purposes of what you do together. Point out positive consequences of new thinking tools and strategies. Over time, students develop the meanings of their own cognitive change.

In the following table, you will find examples of engaging activities that can be useful in supporting this mediating conversation. Sample mediating conversations are provided to the right.

Engaging Strategies, Activities, and Mediating Conversations Supporting Mediating Meaning

ENGAGING STRATEGIES AND ACTIVITIES	MEDIATING CONVERSATIONS SUPPORTING MEDIATION OF MEANING
Project-Based Learning This is ideal for creating meaning. Projects not only require thinking skills, but collaboration, gathering of content, creativity, and problem-solving. If the projects are meaningful (practical application), students come to see school as relevant to their lives. For many students, requiring student use of technology in their final products, such as websites, PowerPoint/Keynote presentations, or iMovies, enhances their relevance.	"Your group chose a truly worthwhile activity in creating an earthquake preparedness brochure for our school website. It looks like your study of the causes of earthquakes will end up helping the community. How has what you have already done in planning your brochure project helped you organize it?" *Elicit and acknowledge response.* "I can see that using your thinking skill of *planning* has helped you map out the elements you will want to discuss in your brochure. This thinking skill will also help you determine how to plan your time so that you complete the project on schedule."
Jigsaw (Kagan, 1994) Place students in groups. Each group has a content area in which they develop expertise, collaborating with one another and sharing resources. Then each person in that group goes to a group made up of one person from each of the expert groups, so that the expertise can be shared with all others in that second group. Meaning is developed within the responsibility the individuals have to one another, as well as their own levels of expertise.	"As you get together with your expert groups, you'll be acquiring more *sources of information* to share with your home group later on. Have a short discussion with your group about the importance of having more than one source of information." *Students discuss and respond.* "You make some very valid points. I'd agree that when you hear information from several others, it helps you support the point you're trying to make, and serves as a cross check. It also makes your argument richer. Yes, you also have a responsibility to the other group to get accurate information, so these multiple sources help the project assure you will have correct information."

(Continued)

ENGAGING STRATEGIES AND ACTIVITIES	MEDIATING CONVERSATIONS SUPPORTING MEDIATION OF MEANING
Give One, Get One (Kagan, 1994**)** This strategy elicits students' prior knowledge as they share preliminary ideas about a new concept. Students circulate the room and "give one" of their ideas to someone else and "get one" idea from another. They give credit to the contributor(s) when they share their ideas with the whole class. During the discussion time, any misinformation can be clarified. To enhance their knowledge base, use resources such as *SAFARI Montage*, which gives teachers digital media support for building background knowledge.	"As you begin this new unit on exploration, focus on one of its key terms—*exploitation.* Use your thinking skill of *establishing connections and relationships* to help you come up with three examples of what you think this term *exploitation* means. To help you come up with examples, think about other contexts where you have seen or heard this word used. As you *give one* of your ideas and *get one* from a partner, discuss the connections you both found. Now, using your understanding of the word, how do you think it will be used in the context of our unit on exploration?" *Elicit responses.* "Using *connections and relationships* made this concept meaningful."

Bridging Thinking

> *Ms. Starkey compliments her class on the great job they have done on their science experiment, and uses a mediating conversation to bridge the thinking skill hypothesizing from their science work today to yesterday's language arts lesson. "You learned how to hypothesize from learning the scientific process. Hypothesizing is also an important thinking skill you will use in many other subjects and real life situations. For instance, yesterday in language arts you used hypothesizing to help learn the meaning of an unknown word:* hydropower. *You learned from the Greek roots that* hydro *means water, and then hypothesized that* hydropower *would mean power generated by water. You checked in the context of your reading and it made sense. You had correctly hypothesized. What are some other times you use hypothesizing?"*

MiCOSA teachers create learning environments, lessons, and experiences with a vision in mind for how those lessons will still have meaning later in their students' lives. That is, they teach "now," but for the future. Ms. Starkey appreciates that her students will not automatically apply the thinking skills they used today as new contexts arise. Therefore, she uses mediating conversations to help her students bridge those thinking skills across contexts.

You want students to make habits of using thinking skills in a variety of appropriate contexts. Using mediating conversations to bridge thinking helps them begin that journey. To bridge across content areas, you and your students create "bridging principles," or generalizations, in which you strip away the context of the curriculum to isolate and articulate the thinking skill and its purpose(s). You can then help students bridge or transfer this "generic frame," reapplied, to new learning. Sometimes it takes modeling on your part to help the students move from statement of content-bound experience into the more abstract bridging principle. The following example illustrates that process:

> *Initial Questions:*
>
> How did you use multiple sources when you worked on your weather project? What difference did it make? Can you create a bridging principle?
>
> *Student experience:* I needed multiple sources to get all the information for my weather project—I used computer weather links, textbooks, people on the weather channel and at home, and my own experience.
>
> *Initial "Bridge" Attempt (content bound):* When I used multiple sources, I got enough information from different points of view to complete a strong weather project.

This initial bridge attempt is merely a statement of how the thinking skill was useful within the context of the current work. Although a useful statement, it was not a bridging principle, since it was still bounded by the content, and thus could not be transferred to new content. When this occurs, ask your students to think about how the thinking skill can be used with a similar effect but in a new context. Have students try removing the specifics and then refining the statement. Have them try to shift from "I" to "you" to cross check and state the principle in present tense:

> *Second Attempt: Creating a Bridging Principle (transferable).* When I (you) use multiple sources, I (you) gather information from multiple points of view, giving you a broad perspective.

This principle creates the bridge that crosses context and content areas.

Continuing with the previous example, Ms. Starkey suggests:

> *"Let's talk about what a difference using hypothetical thinking made in both those situations." Ms. Starkey prompts, "When I use hypothesizing, I _____."
> The class generates responses together:*
>
> > *When I use hypothesizing, my guess is an educated guess, and has a purpose.
> > When I use hypothesizing, I can imagine several ways to do something.
> > When I use hypothesizing, my ideas can be affected by many variables.*
>
> > *"Great. You have just created what we call bridging principles. These ideas help us bridge the thinking skill from using it in one place to using it in more and more situations."*

As you can see, you can use real student experiences to check and double check the validity of those bridging principles. For example, by using the bridging principle to bridge between home and social situations, Ms. Starkey poses a hypothetical situation to her students: "If you read a blog with clear cyberbullying on it about one of your classmates, what should you do? Use the thinking skill of *hypothesizing* to consider alternatives." This places her students in a potential future situation and creates rehearsal of the thinking skill. In Figure 3.1 you have an example of that bridge, using the thinking skill of *hypothesizing*.

FIGURE 3.1

Bridging the Thinking Skill Hypothesizing

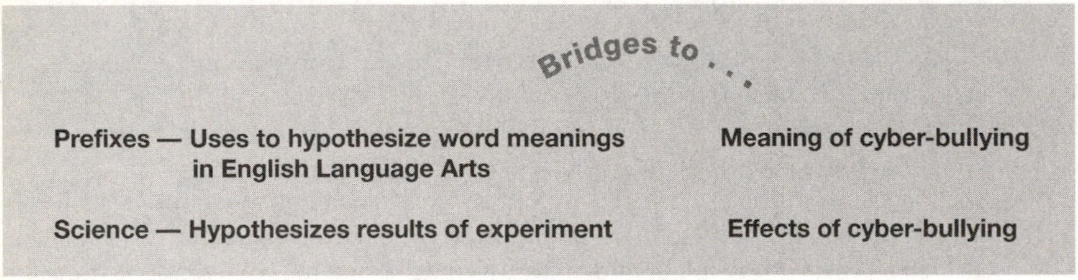

Bridges to . . .

Prefixes — Uses to hypothesize word meanings in English Language Arts

Meaning of cyber-bullying

Science — Hypothesizes results of experiment

Effects of cyber-bullying

Let's synthesize how Ms. Starkey bridges the skill. First, her students learn the thinking skill of *hypothesizing* in an English Language Arts context (Greek and Latin roots). They bridge the skill to a new use in science, and finally to a conversation about a hypothetical, but very real, social situation—cyberbullying. During this process they use the bridging principles they created to help them apply this thinking skill to other learning situations.

FIGURE 3.2

Thinking Skill Card for Cause/Effect - Hypothesizing

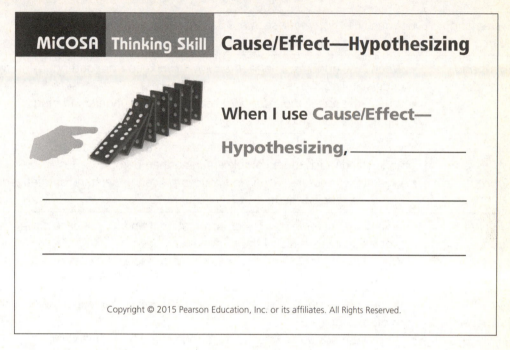

MiCOSA **Thinking Skill**   **Cause/Effect—Hypothesizing**

When I use Cause/Effect—

Hypothesizing,_____

_____

_____

PD **TOOLKIT**™

PDToolkit: Video Clip 3.3 provides two examples. In the first, Lisette helps students bridge the use of visualizing. In the second example, students derive their own bridging principles.

To support you in mediating *bridging thinking*, use one of MiCOSA's 21 thinking skill cards (found in the PDToolkit) to frame students' generalizations. Each of MiCOSA's cards bears the name of the thinking skill and an icon to help deepen meaning. Each has a place for students to meaningfully personalize their own bridging principle. Figure 3.2 shows the card for cause/effect - hypothesizing. Some teachers post large copies of these on the classroom walls to serve as a great reminder. Others have each student create Thinking Skill Journals (paper or electronic), in which students list a bridging principle with examples of using the thinking skill in both their daily life and other academic areas.

To help you begin to conceptualize bridging principles across thinking skills, the table in Figure 3.3 provides examples of bridging principles for each of MiCOSA's 21 thinking skills.

FIGURE 3.3

Examples of Bridging Principles

1. *Systematic Search*	• When I use *systematic search*, I don't miss critical information. • When I use *systematic search*, I find the information I need.
2. *Focus and Attention*	• When I use good *focus and attention*, I can keep from getting lost in my understanding. • When I use *focus and attention*, I can retain and understand bigger chunks of information.
3. *Labels, Words, and Concepts*	• When I learn new *words and concepts* to gather information, I can understand much more complex reading than before. • When I use accurate *words and concepts*, I can understand subtleties in the meaning of the text.
4. *Multiple Sources*	• When I use *multiple sources* of information, I find it's easier to solve problems, since I have all the information I need. • When I use *multiple sources*, I can remember several pieces of relevant information and add them to new information as I solve problems.
5. *Position in Space*	• When I use *position in space* thinking and terms, I can explain what I see to other people. • When I use *position in space*, I can understand how the location of objects and places is related to my own position in space.
6. *Position in Time*	• When I consider my *position in time* and the position in time of what I am studying, I feel connected with it, and can remember it in the future. • When I use *position in time*, it helps me understand what comes after or before. • When I use *position in time*, it helps me in sequencing events.
7. *Precision and Accuracy*	• When I gather information with *precision and accuracy* I don't make foolish mistakes. • When I gather information with precision and accuracy, like looking through a lens, it helps me see greater detail than I would at first notice with a hurried glance.
8. *Goal Setting*	• When I consciously set a goal, it helps me focus and understand where my plan should end. • When I set goals, it gives me a direction and purpose for learning as it helps me understand the knowledge I will personally gain.
9. *Planning*	• When I plan before I do things, I think more about all the processes, and I have a more complete project. • Using planning gives me a map of what is necessary to complete the task so I have a better idea of the time and effort I need to invest in the learning.

10. *Comparing*	• When I use *comparing*, it helps me to be more descriptive, and to consider alternatives. • By *comparing* certain objects or concepts, I am able to understand their attributes, their commonalities with others, and their uniqueness.
11. *Ordering, Grouping and Categorizing*	• When I *group and categorize*, it helps simplify the materials I am looking at, so I can make new connections. • *Grouping and categorizing* helps me file information efficiently in the memory of my brain, so that I can retrieve it later with success and remember the parts.
12. *Finding Connections and Relationships*	• When I *find new connections and relationships*, I feel creative! When I *find connections and relationships*, my work makes more sense to me, too. • They give me my big "a-ha" moments. • Finding them in my learning is like finding another piece to the puzzle that fits and I can better see the whole picture.
13. *Visualizing*	• When I *visualize*, I can make stories come alive, and that helps me describe in writing what I am thinking. • It helps me be more efficient with other thinking tools, also. Making pictures in my head helps me infer, and hypothesize (predict). • It can help keep me safe because I can "play the movie" of a projected outcome in my head before I actually act upon it.
14. *Inferring*	• When I use *inferring*, it helps me analyze information and draw good conclusions. • It helps me "read between the lines" and understand the subtleties of meaning. • It helps me form a bridge to transfer my thinking to new situations.
15. *Cause and Effect— Hypothesizing*	• When I use *hypothesizing*, then I have a way to get "unstuck" in my work, since this gives me new ways to think about something. • It can help stop me from repeating mistakes because it encourages me to stop, think, and change my thinking as a result before I act.
16. *Summarizing*	• When I *summarize*, I know I have understood and can share my ideas easily. • It helps me condense what I have learned so that it is easier to retrieve when I need it later.
17. *Labels, Words, and Concepts*	• When I communicate with *new labels, words, and concepts*, I feel better about being able to say what I have in mind more clearly. • It helps them paint the pictures I have in my head, to share with others. • It helps the reader or listener truly understand what I am trying to say without misunderstandings.

(Continued)

FIGURE 3.3 *(Continued)*

18. *Precision and Accuracy*	• When I communicate with *precision and accuracy*, I think carefully about what I put down, so that I say just what I mean. • It helps stop the reader or listener from making misconceptions or assumptions about what I am trying to say or do. • It ensures that I accurately share my thinking.
19. *Appropriate Pragmatics*	• When I use *appropriate pragmatics* in communicating, it helps others know what I mean in conversations, and I don't get misunderstood. • It encourages others to hear my thinking—my voice.
20. *Feedback for Self-Regulation*	• When I use *feedback for self-regulation*, I appreciate my own observations and feedback from others, and I end up with work I am proud of. • I am able to modify my thinking and actions and I end up with work I am proud of. • I become more skilled at what I do.
21. *Collaboration*	• When I *collaborate* in thinking, my thinking helps others and they help me generate new ideas. • *Collaboration* helps me consider other points of view, take the best from others' strengths that may not be my own, and therefore, as a result, enrich and regulate my own thinking.

In the following table, you will find examples of engaging activities that can be useful in supporting this mediating conversation. Sample mediating conversations are provided to the right.

Engaging Strategies, Activities, and Mediating Conversations Supporting Bridging Thinking

ENGAGING STRATEGIES AND ACTIVITIES	MEDIATING CONVERSATIONS SUPPORTING BRIDGING THINKING
Thinking Skills Journals To foster bridging, use Thinking Skills Journals as a personal record of students' exploration of each thinking skill. Encourage them to build generalizations (e.g., "When I use [thinking skill] I can. . . ."). Now students can apply these generalizations to build their own bridges, both to daily life and to academics.	"As we focus on our thinking skills to help us learn this year, we're going to keep a record of these skills so we can remember how they help us. Today we're going to think about *planning*, because we need this to create a successful project. Talk to someone next to you about when you use planning at home. Now jot that down in your Thinking Skills Journal." *Circulate the room, observing students as they record their responses.* "You came up with great examples of needing planning when you want to save for something you want, or when you plan a party for someone. Good. Now let's bridge those ideas to school.

They record examples in their journals. These entries can be done individually in notebooks, on blogs, as online journals, or as group entries using a wiki.

When do you use *planning* in school? Yes! You plan when you're writing an essay or even when you need to get your homework done and get to soccer practice. Why do you take time to plan? What difference does it make?"

Students offer responses.
"Good. Now let's create a bridging principle so we can remember why planning is important. When I use planning I can. . . ."

Skill Time!

Before introducing the content, prompt, "It's skill time!" Ask the students what thinking skills they might need in order to learn the lesson. Students might generate any of the 21 thinking skills you have focused on. Reinforce how they might be used in the lesson.

In another version, post MiCOSA's 21 thinking skill cards in a pocket chart on a wall in the classroom. Have a student come up and select one he or she thinks will help in the upcoming lesson. Post it clearly up front and ask the student to explain his or her reason for choosing that particular thinking skill. Call on another two students to repeat the process, so that the class understands there are many thinking skills involved in the lesson, even though only one may be selected as a focus.

"We are about to read a new story and discuss the main character's motive in the plot. What is one of the thinking skills will we need?"

Students might generate ideas using the thinking skill establishing connections and relationships, to not only help them connect and relate incidents throughout the story that reveal the character's motives, but to also help them sequence their thinking.
"How has this thinking skill helped us before? How do we anticipate using it now?"

Respond to student ideas, validating specifics, then ask.
"Are there more thinking skills we might need?"

Guiding Self-Regulation

Enter Mr. Zee's fourth grade class. Tina is in a state of frustration and near panic. She has just created her first Keynote presentation, but doesn't know how to return from the program back to her desktop. Her final Keynote picture fills the screen, but with no icons to click she feels at a loss for what to do. Mr. Zee mediates. He does not tell Tina how to solve the problem directly, but guides her to self-discovery. "Tina, explain your problem." (Tina explains). Mr. Zee continues, "Tina, look along the top of your keyboard. See if you can use your thinking to help you solve your problem. What key could you press that might help you? (Tina stares back and forth across the top of the keyboard.) Mr. Zee guides her further, helping her slow her pace by focusing on one option. He points to F12. "Could it be this one?" (Tina smiles and says no because that key increases the volume.) "Good! Now you are using logic and really thinking about your choices. Try another possibility." Very soon, Tina notices the "escape" button and with a sigh of relief presses it, and is able to see how she can return to her desktop. "I got it!" she exclaims. Mr. Zee continues, "When you let yourself slow down and search your options, you have a lot more computer literacy than you thought."

Sometimes students create their own internal barriers that get in the way of accessing thinking. In the previous example, Tina's panic reaction to the technology she did not understand inhibited her *systematic search*. She did not stop and think what she might do, or how she might figure it out. She had given up self-control over the situation and given in to panic. Mr. Zee had a mediating conversation with her, which prompted her to regain control over her behavior and engage in thinking about what to do. He guided her to self-regulate her learning, so that she could use the thinking skills she had at hand. She was empowered.

Students with strong *self-regulation* have a sense of their own control over their learning. They pace themselves and know how and when to call on thinking skills to help them decipher and define problems and problem situations. They use skills and strategies when they get "stuck."

Guiding self-regulation through mediating conversations helps students access those thinking skills and self-control characteristics within themselves. It supports independent thinking. When students begin to gain mastery of *self-regulation*, they gather and process information with greater success.

Self-regulating *pacing* is crucial. Many times, students need you to mediate their pace of learning to help them move more slowly or more rapidly. For instance, to help slow down impulsivity, you might gently place your hand near the student's hand and say, "Let's give your mind a chance here. I see your hand wanting to jump out ahead, so we're missing your thinking. Before you write, let me hear about what you are going to do." Combine this with mediation of meaning: "What a difference I see now that you stopped and considered before writing. What do you think about doing that the next time you are unsure?" In another example, you might help a student pace the task of "drawing for art" versus drawing a "quick sketch" during a science lesson to support understanding. Explaining the different purposes helps the student self-regulate differently. Have your students do the explanation, supporting their emerging independence of thought and action.

When you mediate pacing as a part of self-regulation, be sure that your students then accompany their changed pace with some action, and know what to do after they adjust their pace. Have them articulate a set of thinking skills or a plan. This supports development of self-regulation. Clarify that different tasks require different pacing. Notice and comment verbally, physically, or visually when students use effective pacing and draw attention to its effectiveness. This way, students get the support of external feedback.

Often, students need to learn pacing *in conjunction with* a new thinking skill. When Jon began to struggle with physics, Mr. Montgomery helped mediate different pacing—learning to slow down, in conjunction with different skills—using *systematic search* and locating graphics that would provide cues. Jon learned to differentiate this reading as a unique style, and to invest a different level of effort. Over time, he developed a repertoire of strategies and incorporated them automatically into his newly self-regulated behavior.

Guiding self-regulation also involves helping students develop *flexibility* in their thinking and actions, which is important for all critical thinking. For example, after your students have been studying multiplying fractions, throw in a problem or two that requires subtracting fractions and see if they differentiate and shift to do both kinds of problems. Deciding when and where to use specific thinking and learning skills also requires flexibility of thinking in self-regulation. Give students situations that require both the same and different thinking skills across activities, so they can practice these choices.

PD **pd** TOOLKIT™

PDToolkit: In Video Clip 3.4 Marlene uses questioning to *guide self-regulation.*

Sometimes these opportunities arise from textual material. For instance, a fifth grade science book on volcanoes offers a linear presentation of events leading up to the eruption of Mount St. Helens in Section I; in Section II, it presents types of volcanoes; and in Section III, a discussion ensues of the causes of volcanic eruption. This kind of variety in text offers you the opportunity to introduce and prompt flexible thinking as your students gather and take notes on the information.

The examples in the following table can be useful in supporting this mediating conversation. Sample mediating conversations are provided to the right.

Engaging Strategies, Activities, and Mediating Conversations to Guide Self-Regulation

ENGAGING STRATEGIES AND ACTIVITIES	MEDIATING CONVERSATIONS SUPPORTING GUIDING SELF-REGULATION
GO Choose ("GO" is an acronym for graphic organizer) Present students with two or three of each type of graphic organizer found on one of several websites (c.f., freeology.com; eduplace.com; edhelper.com). Ask them to choose the GO that best matches the task, and explain why. This helps conceptualization, which is central to self-regulation. Giving students a choice helps them conceptualize the use of GOs to build thinking skills, and can be a stepping stone to developing their own. Encourage them to verbalize the choice and *why* it is appropriate, and share that with other students. The ultimate goal is to have students self-regulate their own pacing as they select the most appropriate tools for problem-solving proficiently. GO Choose could be done on Inspiration or Webspiration instead of paper, as a digital option.	"As we're reading about different types of volcanoes, we need to know how to summarize the author's message. Graphic organizers can help us self-regulate our thinking as we summarize information. This section on volcanoes is about the events leading up to the eruption of Mount St. Helens. Which of these graphic organizers (one linear, one with circles, another a T-chart) would help you best summarize the information? Why?" "Yes, this linear representation requires thinking skills of *position in time and sequencing.* The next section is describing types of volcanoes and their characteristics. Which graphic organizer would you choose for this section? Why?" "Great, this GO groups information into categories. This last section discusses the causes of eruptions, so which one might be good to represent that information? Why?" "Yes, the T-chart can help you show cause and effect and also connections and relationships. You've really done some critical thinking in making your choices!"
Charting My Success Students create a graph using a digital spreadsheet (e.g., Excel) with a baseline and weekly progress points to physically watch their progress. A section for self-reflection (what worked well; what will I change) filled out at the end of the week helps them practice self-regulation. The graph can track their progress in content (e.g., books read) or behaviors (e.g., choose to respond positively to friends in class).	"Who likes to be in charge? (*show of hands*) I thought so! You're going to be in charge of tracking your own learning this year in language arts. Students who keep track of their learning learn more. That tracking and reflection helps you continue to master what we have been talking about in self-regulation. I've uploaded a summary of the language arts standards you're responsible for mastering this year. You're going to track your progress throughout the year. In addition, every four weeks you'll write a reflection of how you are doing on the standards you've worked with; what's going well, and how you might want to change some of your study behaviors to do better."

(Continued)

ENGAGING STRATEGIES AND ACTIVITIES	MEDIATING CONVERSATIONS SUPPORTING GUIDING SELF-REGULATION
What's On Your Mind Time Pair students. For one minute each way, one student talks about anything on his or her mind. The second student listens respectfully–he or she offers no comments (this is not easy the first few times). Then the students switch places. This practice in self-regulating listening values students' need to talk to learn. It also "clears the air" for students with something from home or social situations on their minds, and allows them to be able to listen to the lesson more easily.	"Has anyone been looking forward to sharing what's on your mind? Here's your chance to share and be heard. You'll get that chance to talk, as well as listen to your partner when it is his or her turn, without saying much. It's often a difficult skill to just listen! See if you can make a new word by rearranging the letters in listen–yes, silent. To listen well, you have to be silent. You're going to practice self-regulation in this activity by listening very carefully to the other person. It's also thoughtful. This is going to help you later to self-regulate when you collaborate in learning a new lesson or work in pairs or in a group."
Putting It Right With Art (Chancer, 2000) (a) As a *prewriting strategy*, have students draw a picture of the image(s) they want to create with words, to act as a reference as they write. (b) As a *revision strategy*, students pair-share their images and ideas. As they read each other's descriptions, they make a sketch of the images they "see" as they read. The writer places his pre-writing illustration alongside the reader's. They compare pictures. Together, they discuss how to revise the writing pieces so that the reader "sees" what the writer intended. Model this process for the students so that they learn to create positive, yet constructive mediating conversations. This activity helps students self-mediate their pacing and stop to reflect in a collaborative modality.	"Writing is very personal, and to receive feedback from another regarding your writing can be exciting. However, it also holds the potential to hurt feelings. The activity *Putting It Write with Art* will support you in this process, and it will support you in self-regulating your learning. Begin with a positive comment about your peer's writing before you begin to discuss differences of images. Readers, invite your partner writer to read his or her passage aloud, and identify problem area. Try and encourage the writer to come up with any changes rather than having them come directly from you. For example, 'I read your description of the island and your word choice made it sound like a beautiful place to be. When we compare our pictures, the picture that came to me when I read does not match the one you wanted me to have as a writer. Will you read the passage again? As you read, if you pause when you think I should have a certain picture in my head we can both share our visions and discuss why I see it differently. It might help you make changes to the text so that I understand what you are trying to say.'"
Putting the Cart Before the Horse (regulating pacing by using systematic search) When students do not regulate their own learning behavior, you guide self-regulation, in contrast to simply telling. For instance, instead of using a non-mediational prompt such as, "Don't just look randomly for the comparisons, read the text first," help them self-regulate that random, fleeting search by slowing down the pace and engaging in a *systematic search* of the text. In doing so, use the mediation of meaning as well.	"I noticed that sometimes going too fast with your eyes or hands gets in the way of your very capable brain being able to think or find information. This time, try slowing down and using *systematic search* to see if that makes a difference in being able to get the details." *The student tries. You note the success, and follow this with mediation of meaning.* "Fabulous! When you slowed down and looked systematically, you found the right section, and were successful in getting the information you were looking for. Try slowing down and using your *systematic search* with the next comparison and see if it helps again." Allow the student to do this. "I saw a real difference this time too. What did you notice?"

Building Competence

Mr. Phelps pauses to quietly comment on Clyde's highlighting strategy as he searches for pertinent research for his report. "I see you highlighting the key points you will need for your research, Clyde. That's a great strategy to support system-atic search! Well done!" By doing this, Mr. Phelps reinforces Clyde's competence in the context of tasks done or skills demonstrated. He validates Clyde's successful "process" and his use of strategies and thinking skills, as much as the end product.

Taking on increasingly challenging tasks and problems across settings requires a sense of competence, such as Clyde exhibits in the previous example. Students who do not feel competent balk and block. *Building competence* targets students' feeling of being able to succeed at solving new problems and challenges. Their sense of competence comes from experience and self-reflection, as they are able to work with and figure out new challenges. As mediators, you will set the stage for them to believe they have the skills to do the task, based on reality. Competence is different from self-esteem or feeling confident. Competence reflects real skills and success; it is a basis for motivation to work at challenging assignments.

Students who increase their repertoire of efficient thinking skills will be able to more competently approach and engage with new problems and challenging material. They will have the skills that allow them to tackle things they could not do previously. If they have learned the meaning of using those skills as they transfer them, they gain a growing sense of their own competence, and actually ask for more challenging work. For example, Seth used to shrug his shoulders and smile when asked how he would go about planning a writing assignment. After identifying the thinking skills that helped him become more effective (*planning, goal setting, comparing,* and *multiple sources* of information), and practicing bridging them, he later shared with a sense of competence, "Now I know I can do this because I can plan what to do. I can compare and select information I find from multiple sources like books and the Internet, and I can finish my work well and be proud of it!" Seth now says this with confidence in his work years after the initial work with me-diation, so the long-term effect is profound.

Mediators build on prior success to scaffold learners' approaches to more complex tasks. At the early level, comment with authenticity (even warmth) about how well your students used a thinking skill and what success you notice they had from using it. You are "stand-ins" for what you hope they will internalize later, which will reflect their growing competence. Cues such as smiling, a relaxed body posture, speaking directly to students, utilizing humor, and modulating the voice (immediacy behaviors) create psychological or physical closeness, enhancing the interaction (Christophel, 1990; Hostetter & Busch, 2006). Your students' sense of competence will lead to improved learning outcomes, including satisfaction with learning and increased student motivation (Avtgis, 2001; Gorham, 1988).

As a mediator, you will model what eventually will come from *within* your students—they will be able to select and use a set of thinking skills, and to apply that set effectively to whatever problems are presented. As they internalize this, they develop a belief in their own competence as learners. With this sense of competence, sometimes referred to as

PD **d** TOOLKIT™

PDToolkit: Video Clip 3.5 **provides two classroom ex-amples of** *building competence.*

self-efficacy, they know they are *able*. This influences their motivation, perseverance, and often attention. Your ultimate goal is for your students to willingly approach highly challenging tasks and situations with belief in their competence, based on their proven competence in using thinking skills.

In the following table, you will find examples of engaging activities that can be useful in supporting this mediating conversation. Sample mediating conversations are provided to the right.

Engaging Strategies, Activities, and Mediating Conversations Supporting Competence Building

ENGAGING STRATEGIES AND ACTIVITIES	MEDIATING CONVERSATIONS SUPPORTING COMPETENCE BUILDING
Scaffolding Break down a task into manageable segments with students, supported by efficient use of thinking skills. Support their graduated success with increasingly complex segments. Build on small and sequenced successes, so your students gradually build a sense of competence for approaching larger problems.	The following example draws from Greene's (2005) Masterpiece Sentences strategy. "Today, you will develop the thinking skill, *labels, words, and concepts* by creating some wonderful descriptive sentences. This is not easy to do, so we will begin very simply with just a noun and a verb and then build on it, until you have a 'masterpiece.' This picture of the forest will help you. Let me give you an example: The leaves rustled." *To scaffold the development of the sentence, give students green strips of paper to expand the predicate and pink for extension of the subject. Mediate competence building as you circulate the room, quietly commenting on student word choice. For example,* "The owl hooted. Hooted. . . . A brilliant verb choice, Martha! You too, Polly. What a delicious verb—rustled! Your word really helps me hear those leaves moving!" "As I am coming around the class, I am seeing some great word choices. Now let's extend and elaborate on the predicate. Use your green paper now. Ready? Now tell me *how*? *How* did the leaves rustle? *How* did the wind blow?" *Students generate some ideas of word choice.* "Tilly said we could use the word *quietly*; Sian suggested *softly*; and Pippa, *noisily*. Such creativity! What is the name of this part of speech? Yes, Eddie, it is an adverb. Good remembering!"

MiCOSA's Thinking Skill Cards

For students who need to gain competence with specific thinking skills, use the MiCOSA thinking skill cards either on the desk, grouped on paper, as a poster for the room, or on a document that can be downloaded at home if the students frequently do homework on a computer. TS cards, illustrated in Figure 3.2, and found in the MiCOSA Toolkit, list the name of the thinking skill, and carry an icon that represents it. Students generate an example of its use (the bridging principle). These cards provide references for the next steps, or forgotten steps, when the student becomes "stuck."

"Gabi, I noticed you found telling me the sequence of events in the story was much easier when you used the thinking skill *systematic search*. What do you remember about what *systematic search* means?"

Elicit and acknowledge responses; review if necessary.
"Yes, so you can scan the page for the important events in the story instead of skipping around randomly or guessing. Try it here in the story."

Student tries systematic search and teacher is nearby, then comments on her emerging competence.
"Nice job! This time you took your time and read carefully to find all the important parts of the story. I've made a copy of the thinking skill card for *systematic search* for you so it can remind you to scan for the information page by page the next time so you can be successful on your own. Write in your own words what a difference it makes to use *systematic search*, and we'll double check to see how accurate this is in your next activity."

Whiteboard Quick-Checks

When asking students to complete a problem that requires the use of a certain thinking skill, ask them to enumerate and illustrate the use of the thinking skill on their whiteboards.

They develop a sense of competence in applying that thinking skill when you acknowledge their efforts in class.

"Please take out your whiteboards. Now today, rather than asking you to solve this algebraic problem, I want you and your partner to show me how you will use your thinking skill of *planning* to map out the steps you will take to solve it. Remember, at this stage I am not asking you to solve it, but to plan your strategies for solving it. Ready? You have three minutes to make your plan with your partner. Be ready to share your ideas with the class."

When most appear ready, students reveal their plans to the teacher by holding up their whiteboards. The teacher comments on several student plans, emphasizing specific assets.
"What a super job you have done! You have each considered all the steps needed to solve these problems by using planning. Keep them close by so you can refer to them as you work. We will talk about how useful they were following our group work today."

SUMMARY

- Five dynamic mediating conversations support you in helping your students develop and use thinking skills. Each is discussed, with examples from the classroom and sample mediating conversations linked to activities that will support your work.

- Conversations mediating *intent and reciprocity* build a set of expectations that your students will have your support, will succeed, and that their work and engagement will result in enhanced thinking skills. They know they are part of the process.

- Conversations that help *mediate meaning* help students make meaning not only of the content, but also of their newly acquired thinking and learning skills.

- When you guide *bridging thinking*, you help students make connections between what they are doing in class and what they might do in the future. Link their prior knowledge and experience to the tasks as well, so that the relevance of their experiences in school enhances their motivation.

- *Self-regulated* learners pace their work well, and then gather sufficient information to transform and innovate with it. They attend to their products and outcomes with focus and accuracy. They benefit from feedback. Sample mediating conversations illustrate how you will guide and support the development of self-regulation in all your students.

- Many of us as adults question our competence in the face of extremely difficult or challenging new tasks. Our students do so as well. Thus, you will use *building competence* with intention, knowing it will support their approach to difficult or new content areas, as well as their motivation.

REFERENCES

Avtgis, T. A. (2001). Affective learning, teacher clarity, and student motivation as a function of attributional confidence. *Communication Research Reports, 18*, 345–353.

Beers, K. (2003). *When kids can't read: What teachers can do*. New York: Heinemann.

Chancer, J. (2000). Creating Imagery, ELA Professional Development Workshop. Thousand Oaks, CA: Conejo Valley Unified School District.

Christophel, D. M. (1990). The relationships among teacher immediacy behaviors, student motivation, and learning. *Communication Education, 39*, 323–340.

Gorham, J. (1988). The relationships between verbal teacher immediacy behaviors and student learning. *Communication Education, 37*, 40–53.

Graves, D. H., & Kittle, P. (2005). *My quick writes for inside writing*. Portsmouth, NH: Heinemann.

Greene, J. F. (2005). *Language! The comprehensive literacy curriculum*. 4th edition [Unit 5, Masterpiece Sentences]. Longmont, CO: Voyager Learning.

Hostetter, C., & Busch, M. (2006). Measuring up online: The relationship between social presence and student learning satisfaction. *Journal of Scholarship of Teaching and Learning, 6*, 1–12.

Jensen, M. R. (2012). *The mind's ladder: Empowering students in the knowledge economy—Dynamic assessment and classroom learning guidebook 3.0*. Roswell, GA: Cognitive Education Systems.

Kagan, S. (1994). *Kagan Cooperative Learning*. San Clemente: Resources for Teachers.

Perona, S. (1989, Jan/Feb). The tea party: Intro, through, and beyond a piece of literature. *The Writing Notebook*, 30–31.

Chapter Four

Thinking Skills for Gathering Information

In order to create new ideas or solve challenging problems, students must first accurately and thoughtfully gather the information relevant to doing so.

In content- and process-rich classrooms, your students engage with and solve complex problems. To engage at this level, they must first gather sufficient relevant information. Thinking skills needed for gathering information may seem deceptively simple, yet without having them in place, critical thinking will not occur. For students to be able to critically analyze, hypothesize about, or synthesize ideas, they must gather multiple pieces of information, and be able to select what is relevant and accurate from a broad field of options.

Some of your students will gather information with a goal in mind, and will do so thoughtfully and accurately. These students will be ready to work with and transform that information. Being able to do it well can mean the difference between frustration and rising to the challenge. Yet, many of your students may simply neglect to gather enough information to solve a problem. Alternatively, they may gather it impulsively or imprecisely. You will learn to identify and mediate a set of thinking skills for gathering information. These skills prepare the learner to use an additional set of thinking skills to transform information, a second phase of thinking. Finally, students will use a third set of thinking skills to communicate information.

The MiCOSA Model describes seven thinking skills for gathering information: (a) *systematic search;* (b) *focus and attention;* (c) *labels, words, and concepts;* (d) *multiple sources;* (e) *position in space* (size, shape, distance, direction); (f) *position in time* (time, ordering); and (g) *precision and accuracy.*

Your students may already be efficient in some of these skills but not others. In some cases, once students begin to use skills in another phase of learning, such as transforming information, the skills to gather information become solidified rather easily. Often, however, you need to use mediating conversations to facilitate their development.

In this chapter, case examples from real classrooms illustrate each thinking skill, helping the definitions come to life. First, examples of students efficient with the thinking skill are presented to augment definitions. Next, to provide a contrast, examples of students inefficient with the thinking skill help you identify similar students in your own classroom. You will have the opportunity to note a few on your own at this point.

Because MiCOSA stresses using mediation to develop each thinking skill, examples illustrate how a teacher has mediated that skill with the inefficient students in the case studies. Following this, a series of strategies and activities provide additional ways to support you in developing this skill in your classroom. Finally, you will have the opportunity to note some ways you might mediate students in your classroom who struggle with that skill. MiCOSA's thinking skill cards are pictured beside the definitions to remind you of the icons associated with the skill. Your students will use the cards as they learn and become efficient with each skill.

PD **c d** TOOLKIT™

PDToolkit:
See the PDTookit
for downloadable
versions of the
Thinking Skill
Cards.

1. Systematic Search

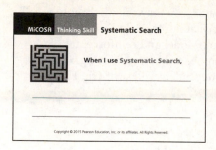

Using *systematic search*, students demonstrate an organized, methodical, and goal-oriented approach to gathering relevant information. For example, in his math lesson, Brandon takes the time to notice that different operational signs and parentheses separate the string of numbers he will work with, indicating that he will perform more than one operation. In reading, to orientate herself well to the task, Melinda surveys the headers, illustrations, captions, graphs, and key questions prior to beginning. At home, when Norma loses her keys, she guides her search by systematically recalling the last three places she visited. If that fails, she systematically explores in another way: she begins on the ground floor and goes systematically from one room to another, searching visually on all exposed surfaces until she makes her find.

Students Inefficient in Systematic Search

Many students do not use *systematic search*. Far too often, you will have some students who do not explore a task sufficiently before beginning; thus, they do not have the information they need to work with the task at hand. You may see this with students who neglect to read directions thoroughly, and then do not seem to know what to do or miss critical steps.

Unlike Brandon, Michael approaches his math problem with pencil in hand, prematurely trying to solve it before systematically searching for all the information about what to do. Unaware of the variety of operations, he misses the signs. Michael performs only half the operations, and he performs these out of order, missing the correct solution. Unlike Melinda, Josie opens the book and begins reading text without scanning, and has no context to guide her understanding. Within five minutes, Josie begins to complain that she does not understand what she is reading about or why it is important. You may have had students who swear they have looked everywhere, yet do not have one of the pieces of material they need for their project. However, when you sit with them to mediate by modeling a *systematic search* for the missing piece, it "astonishingly" appears, previously overlooked by the student's impulsive and non-systematic prior search.

What students in your class might struggle with systematic search?

Mediating Systematic Search with Michael   To help your students strengthen their skills in *systematic search*, first make the issue explicit, then model how it is done. Finally, comment on how using *systematic search* makes a difference in their work. For example, with Michael, you might ask, "Let's look at the problem together. What is it that you have to do?" This identifies the goal and encourages self-regulation, slowing the pace. It models searching for all the pieces before proceeding. You might also have him put the pencil down while "his brain has time to think, keeping the hand out of the way." As a mediator, you may ask Michael to recall a time when he felt successful using *systematic search* at home. Help him bridge this positive experience to his situation in the classroom. Model and reinforce, taking the time to *systematically* gather all the information needed before starting. Often what happens is that in the midst of this process, the student will say, "Oh, I know what to do now!"

Strategies and Activities Supporting Mediation of Systematic Search

Introduce *Start with the Goal in Mind* Ask, "What do you think you will have to do here? How can you tell?" This can be an activity done with the whole class, in pairs, or in small groups, in which defining the problem/goal is the objective. "Write or say your first idea." Then have students systematically gather information that helps them refine the goal. "Write or say your revised idea. How did it change and why?" When students begin by articulating the problem or goal, it helps them have a focus for gathering relevant information. This activity helps them see the relationship between gathering (all the relevant) information and understanding the goal.

Use *Anticipatory Guides* Use anticipatory guides such as giving the students titles, headings, and subheadings to ask questions, such as, "What information do you think you will find under this heading?" "What in the heading makes you think that?" Students record and check their predictions as they enter the text. Discuss explicitly the value of *systematic search*.

As a variation and progression of this activity, list key vocabulary words at the top of the page, above the headings and subheadings. Before reading, ask students to place the selected key words under the header where they think they will find them in the text. Again, as they read, they will check the accuracy of their predictions.

Teach *Skimming and Scanning* Teach your students how to "skim and scan," a strategy you may use yourself. Skimming—quickly glancing at the text, noting headings, subheadings, graphics, and captions—helps students understand what the text is about and assess the amount of energy needed to read the article with understanding. Relate it to gathering information, and specifically to the value of doing it systematically. Scanning helps students locate specific information by doing a systemic visual overview of a physical area, text, or an illustration to locate what is needed.

Demonstrate *Relevancy Matters* Give students a list of 3 to 10 facts about a specific topic. Make some facts relevant and some irrelevant. Working in pairs or groups, ask students to determine which facts would be useful in response to the prompt/topic, and which are not relevant. Have students give rationales for their final selections. Link this to using relevant key words when doing systematic Web-based searches. Follow up by having them use their findings on a search engine.

Practice with *iPad Games*   Many games available on tablets such as iPads can be used to practice *systematic search* in combination with other thinking skills. Most require gathering information systematically prior to trying to play the game. For instance, "Cut the Rope" is an elementary physics-like game in which a mediator can help the player by working with him or her to *systematically search* before moving.

How might you mediate students in your class who struggle with systematic search?

_____

_____

2. Focus and Attention

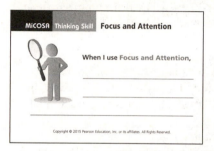

MiCOSA Thinking Skill **Focus and Attention**

When I use Focus and Attention,

Copyright © 2015 Pearson Education, Inc. or its affiliates. All Rights Reserved.

Students must sustain visual or auditory focus long enough to gather relevant information. While teachers might think of *focus and attention* as a singular issue, students actually use different types of *focus and attention* to efficiently gather information. Five kinds of attention are commonly discussed (c.f., Bernstein, 2011; Lee, 2005):

1. First, students must successfully *focus*, or "hone in" on the targeted area so that the correct stimulus for gathering information receives attention. For instance, TJ can focus on the picture of the digestive system on the overhead, as his teacher, Ms. Bryher, begins to explain the path of a cookie through the digestive tract.

2. Students must then *sustain* the focus throughout the duration of time needed to gather all the different bits of information required. TJ sustains that focus on the overhead as Ms. Bryher proceeds through the lesson.

3. Using *selective attention*, TJ also screens out and ignores irrelevant information and focuses only on information pertinent to the task in hand. During the classroom lesson on the digestive system, he ignores the grass being cut, the fly buzzing around the room, or the distraction of the student sitting next to him, and instead chooses to attend to the lesson.

4. Next, students must sometimes be able to *switch*, or *alternate* attention from one task to another without losing focus. Here, in the midst of the lesson, the office may suddenly relay an important message over the intercom. TJ can shift to the message temporarily and then switch back to the lesson. Later in the lesson, he efficiently switches from taking notes to working in a group.

5. Finally, students must sometimes be able to *divide* attention by multitasking while sustaining focus. For instance, TJ concurrently watches the overhead and listens to his teacher's explanations and the classroom commentary while taking copious notes. He *divides* his attention appropriately across tasks.

Students Inefficient with Focus and Attention

Unlike TJ, Tara demonstrates difficulty with *focus and attention* during the same lesson. When Ms. Bryher puts up an outline of work on the overhead, Tara's eyes do not move to that area, "*honing*" her focus. Rather, her eyes flutter from her notebook to her friends. Although Tara finally draws her attention to the overhead, she does not *sustain* that focus, or share her thoughts on the topic when called on. She stumbles verbally and seems bewildered.

Steve's challenge with *selective focus* differs. During a math lesson, he does not screen out irrelevant numbers mentioned in the problem from those needed to successfully complete the task.

Distracted by the pictures and colors on the page, another student, Mary, finds it difficult to *selectively focus* on the print. Her eyes literally dart from picture to picture. Unable to settle into the text, Mary tends to read mechanically, without feeling or meaning.

Switching focus proves extremely problematic for Eric, who seems to perseverate on one task, unable to move back and forth with ease. Jessica's issues with *switching focus* appear during an interruption, which necessitates a shift of focus. She "loses ground" in her work, appears unable to return to where she had left off, and seems forced internally to begin anew with the assignment to regain meaning.

Darrick experiences difficulty in *dividing focus* at home as well as at school. For instance, he cannot watch TV and talk to his friend on the telephone and sustain the thread of both dialogues. Thus, he will ask his friend "what?" or say "I missed that." In school, he has difficulties in collaborative groups when he has to try to track multiple conversations, take notes, and contribute. He simply gets lost trying to *divide his focus* in so many directions.

What students in your class might struggle with focus and attention?

Mediating Focus and Attention with Mary, Tara, and Eric   In helping students strengthen their skills in *focus and attention*, first make the issue explicit and bring your intent to awareness. Then help students use strategies to strengthen the function, and mediate meaning and competence.

In the case of Mary, her problem with *selective focus* has her eyes darting around the work, unable to settle into the text, and losing comprehension as she turns the pages. Her teacher, Mrs. Stevenson, mediates in a two-part strategy. First, she acknowledges Mary's need to take a few seconds before focusing, giving her a moment for self-regulation. She suggests that Mary pause before she begins reading a new page. This provides Mary the opportunity to enjoy skimming the page, and reframes her activity from a deficient and distracting action into a temporary transition. Second, Mrs. Stevenson suggests that Mary now focus on the text, overtly modeling how to *select to focus* and attend. The result is stunning. Mary reads with fluency and comprehension. Her teacher may comment, "When you take the time you need to focus, and get the information you need, you really read beautifully."

Tara's teacher, Ms. Bryher, mediates intent first, verbalizing the need to focus: "Look at the picture on the overhead" (with curiosity, rather than a punitive tone). This helps Tara move her attention to the overhead. With additional cues (e.g., "Look over here") to *sustain the focus,* she can participate. To further assist Tara to *sustain focus,* Ms. Bryher breaks the lesson into smaller segments and uses "pair-share" to build and scaffold her knowledge by sharing. Now Tara can sustain her focus during those shorter periods of time, and process the newly formed information before proceeding further with the lesson.

Eric needs to have his *switching focus* mediated so he can move off a task, so his teacher gives him a signal with a "heads up" that the activity will soon change. Gradually she has him develop his own signal, so that change becomes a more comfortable experience.

Strategies and Activities Supporting Mediation of Focus and Attention

Guide *Focus* Use guided language, such as: "Look at this picture on the screen"; "Put your finger on the directions at the top of the page." Asking what difference this makes (after the fact) can help students continue to practice to focus in multiple situations. It takes time and repetition to create new thinking skill habits.

Support *Sustaining Focus* Elicit from students the processes or procedures that allow them to sustain focus, such as asking: "What is the next step?" Validate students' responses to emphasize why sustaining focus is important.

Improve *Selective Attention* Color code important facts, details, or examples so students learn to identify main ideas and supporting details. Have them do the color-coding next, so they learn how to become active in the process. Then have students explain why they did so to a partner or small group.

Signal *Switching Attention* Give students a signal before interrupting a task. For example, ringing a bell will mean that in one minute they will be asked to change the current activity of reading and do something else. This gives your students time to put closure to one activity before transitioning to the next.

Assist *Divided Attention*   Give study guides (frames/graphic organizers) to assist in note taking while listening to a lecture. Gradually reduce the scaffolding as the student gains more confidence in mastering the skill of dividing his focus.

How might you mediate students in your class who struggle with focus and attention?

_____

_____

3. Labels, Words, and Concepts

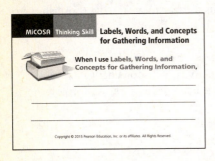

MiCOSA Thinking Skill   **Labels, Words, and Concepts for Gathering Information**

When I use Labels, Words, and Concepts for Gathering Information,

Copyright © 2015 Pearson Education, Inc. or its affiliates. All Rights Reserved.

In order to help students successfully make meaning of the world, establish a repertoire of *words and concepts* relevant to different learning situations students encounter. *Labels* describe or classify words or phrases. They facilitate students' understanding categories, and then help them move to the use of concepts (Lupyan, Rakison, & McClelland, 2007). The National Center for Urban School Transformation (NCUST)'s Johnson and Perez (2010) found that teachers with strong outcomes "pre-identify key academic vocabulary that influences understanding of the lesson content . . . [and that they] provide multiple opportunities for all students to practice using [it] in their own spoken language." Here, students use this critical thinking skill for gathering information. Later, they shift to use *labels, words, and concepts* to communicate their thinking.

Using *labels, words, and concepts*, Kyle discriminates and compares more easily. Adequate *labels, words, and concepts* are needed for such discrimination. For instance, since he has the "label" that identifies the concepts of square and rectangle, discriminating between them becomes fairly easy. Without the concept or label, however, Kyle might fumble with unnecessary verbiage while trying to explain what he is seeing. When processing incoming information, these essential labels assist him in retaining information.

Students Inefficient with Labels, Words, and Concepts

Unlike Kyle, Sarah struggles with *labels, words, and concepts*. She has difficulty working with ideas, because she does not have sufficient vocabulary to form concepts, which simplify the learning. She tends to try to memorize and learn everything as isolated facts, and becomes frustrated when called upon to answer a question because she cannot "find" the words she needs. For example, in a unit of study about weather, she struggles with words and concepts such as *low front*, *high-pressure area*, *precipitation*, and *humidity*. She engages in lengthy attempts to find the right words rather than using concise labels. This prevents her from getting a clear understanding of the development of hurricanes she plans to use to create her podcast on predicting weather in Florida.

What students in your class might struggle with labels, words, and concepts?

PD **d** TOOLKIT™

PDToolkit: See
Video Clip 4.1
for an example of
developing *labels,
words, and con-
cepts*, using total
physical response
(TPR) strate-
gies to support
mediation.

Mediating Labels, Words, and Concepts with Sarah   To support Sarah in her struggle with *labels, words, and concepts*, her teacher elicits Sarah's prior knowledge and uses the Cooperative Learning strategy below, "List, Group, and Label" (Kagan, 1992) to help her categorize. This way she develops the concept, rather than just a vocabulary word. As she gains confidence in naming, grouping, and using her words, her verbal skills become more precise and accurate in the larger classroom setting, and her memory becomes more efficient as well. Her enriched podcast work even impresses her classmates.

Strategies and Activities Supporting Mediation of Labels, Words, and Concepts

Determine *What's My Label?*   Provide the student with the attributes of an object and the objective of trying to name it. For example, "It is a fruit; we can eat it; it is yellow; it is long. What is it?" (*a banana*).

Discover *Cognates in Make a Match*   Many English learners maintain a vast reservoir of vocabulary in their first languages. This game requires some knowledge of words in the student's native language that have English cognates. Write the cognates for certain words of a passage on the board and have your students make a match in the text with the words on the board. *Violá*! Instant meaning and instant smiles.

Create *Word Banks*   Encourage student- or teacher-created word banks as a resource for students.

Introduce *List, Group, and Label*   Before beginning a new unit, tap into students' prior knowledge on the subject or concept. Give each student six strips of paper and ask them to **list** one thing on each strip that they already know about the subject of your lesson (using words or simple phrases, not sentences). Have them place their six words alongside their partner's and **group** the 12 words into categories (create at least three categories). Have them **label** their categories, then share out loud. Build on this prior knowledge and validate its importance as you progress through the unit (Kagan, 1992; Taba, 1988; Tierney & Readence, 2000).

Define by *Concept Drawing*   Encourage students to visualize the meaning of the word or concept. For example, "You hear the word 'democracy' almost daily in the news. What does it mean to you? Draw what you see in your mind." To enhance this activity, have triads share their ideas and pictures (Marzano, Pickering, & Pollack, 2001).

Chart *Figuratively Speaking*   Model using a noun to connect to idiomatic phrases (e.g., *wind–wind*fall, long *winded*, to call someone a *wind*bag). Keep charts on the wall so students can add to the list as they discover new idioms. Discuss the meanings.

Introduce similes, metaphors, and analogies to use while creating poetry or prose. For example, *war*—what verbs can students use to describe war (e.g., destroys, shatters, breaks)? Chancer (2000) suggests that as students write, you ask what other nouns could connect to these verbs and then be used as a comparison, such as glass *shatters*, hearts *break*. Use these as a springboard to create metaphors that link to war. For example,

> War shatters peace into a thousand pieces—
> each shard indiscriminately wounding the flesh of the innocent.
> War breaks the spirit into a million splinters,
> and splatters Earth with its blood.

Play music and identify the figurative language within the song as an additional powerful way to encourage understanding and use of rich language (e.g., Simon and Garfunkel's "Bridge Over Troubled Waters"; Loreena McKennitt's version of Alfred Noyes' song, "The Highwayman").

Practice with *Tech Talk*   Use word games found online to help students strengthen their word banks and word use (c.f., games.com; bigfishgames.com).

How might you mediate students in your class who struggle with labels, words, and concepts?

_____

_____

4. Multiple Sources

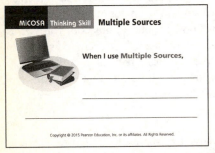

MiCOSA | Thinking Skill | **Multiple Sources**

When I use Multiple Sources,

_____

_____

_____

The capacity to gather and use *multiple sources* enables your students to go beyond the concrete to higher levels of critical thinking. It enables them to move to abstract levels of comparing, contrasting, analyzing, and synthesizing.

All rational thinking requires using at least two sources of information. Your students' decision making and problem solving all necessitate gathering, holding, and using more than one source of information simultaneously, and then processing the information based on those sources. For instance, Thomas gathers and holds information about roles under a feudal system and those in modern democracy so he can then compare and contrast those roles for an assignment in social studies. Rafaela gathers and holds information about the sound-symbol relationship and the context of the text in order to use both sources of information to phonetically blend sounds into words. Daniel gathers and holds information about the numbers in front of him (314×16) and the operation indicated by the sign (x) in order to process the numbers.

Students Inefficient with Multiple Sources

Unlike Thomas, Kevin does not seem to hold two sources of information while he processes the social studies assignment. He can talk about the roles within democracy, but he does not keep the feudal roles in mind simultaneously well enough to form comparisons. In writing a report on sharks, Sarah experiences difficulty referencing more than one source of information; instead, she copies chunks from the text.

What students in your class might struggle with multiple sources?

_____

Mediating Multiple Sources with Sarah and Kevin   By mediating the use of *multiple sources*, you help your students not only gather data, but also learn to organize and "see" how the sources of information relate to one another. For instance, to help Sarah go beyond the replication of the same chunks of data about sharks, use a graphic organizer designed to display the pieces of information in relationship with one another by category, as shown in Figure 4.1. When Sarah understands the meaning of using *multiple sources*, and what a difference it makes in her own work, it is far more likely that *multiple sources* will become a new habit.

Kevin benefits from seeing the meaning of *multiple sources* with a similar graphic organizer as he learns to compare roles in feudal and modern democratic systems. He uses the organizer with pre-established categories (monarch, nobles, knights, and peasants) to allow him to organize his *multiple sources* of information. He can now efficiently match the attributes to the modern democratic system and compare similarities and differences. He describes attributes of the first "source" (monarch) and then, once he establishes the attributes, begins to articulate the same things about the second "source" (president) (Frey & Bower, 2004). Using *multiple sources* now becomes something Kevin finds personally useful—something you can build on to mediate his sense of competence.

FIGURE 4.1

Graphic Organizer Useful with Categorizing Multiple Sources of Information

Category	Source 1	Source 2	Source 3
Characteristics	Multiple rows of teeth p. 26	Cartilage not bone p. 3	Scales like sandpaper p. 12

Strategies and Activities Supporting Mediation of Multiple Sources

Mediate *Reframe for Success*   Use inadequate answers as a springboard for mediation (e.g., "I can see you matched the color, so you are well on your way to gathering *multiple sources*. What else will you need before you can solve the problem? Take a careful look."). You want your students to become active learners, so pause and let them think and speak before telling them what they need. "The shape—good! Now can you select a tile that matches the color *and* shape of the one in front of you? When you stop and consider well, you are good at figuring out the many things you will need in your work. Congratulations." Mediating helps students begin to "own" the thinking skill.

Extend *Thinking Time*

Give students longer exposure to the stimuli. Typically teachers allow only three seconds for a student to answer before they move on. Some students need a longer thinking time. This often is related to thinking style (not ability). Therefore, allow 6 to 10 seconds to improve the odds of a response. After the longer pause time, use language like, "Tell me more. What else do you see? What else do you need to consider?"

Organize *One for All*

Select a content area that can be divided into four categories of information for research. In groups of four, have students choose one of the topics. Students each research one assigned category, and then share and discuss their information with the others. Following the discussion, each student records the information on his or her own four-category graphic organizer. The process continues until each student has all the pieces of information. The group then chooses how to display or share the information with the class. Mediate the meaning of having and using *multiple sources* as you move from group to group. Ask them to identify their *multiple sources*, and then to discuss the meaning of *multiple sources* in the context of the lesson.

How might you mediate students in your class who struggle with multiple sources?

_____

_____

5. Position in Space

Your students' sense of spatial orientation, or *position in space*, helps them build understanding of the relationships of two or more objects in the space around them. It helps them build concepts they will need throughout their lives. Part of what makes this so challenging is that positions in space are all relative. For instance, distance changes; size is completely relative to a second, third, or fourth comparative entity (e.g., an enormous ant; a tiny car). Direction (e.g., in front of, behind) is only stable as long as the points of reference remain unchanged (as in north and south). Therefore, concepts connected to positions in space, such as directionality, distance, size, and shape, become essential components for locating, describing, and visualizing, and eventually for abstract thinking.

Once your students understand how objects relate to each other spatially, they will have the basis for comparative thinking. Thus, they begin to understand and use *position in space* at a concrete level (e.g., bigger, smaller, higher, lower), but developmentally spatial concepts evolve into abstract applications (e.g., comparing and hypothesizing). This transfer of the concrete to an abstract level of thinking enables your students to reason at a much higher level.

Maria, a nine-year-old, has a good sense of left and right and can easily find her way around the school campus. She understands that when you stand in front of her, your right is to her left, a concept that often doesn't form developmentally until around eight years of age. She knows in her culture to read left to right, and top to bottom, and she can copy actions mirrored to her. She can accurately copy letters and visuals from the board or book without reversals.

Students Inefficient with Position in Space

Larry experiences difficulty navigating around the classroom when Mr. Edwards changes his seat. He has not come to understand the relativity of the change. He has to look around to locate things he once found easily, such as the homework box and the pencil sharpener. Larry asks for someone to come with him and show him the way to the office, even though he has been on the campus several months. Another student, Ramesh, finds it hard to follow spatial directions such as putting his name on the top left-hand side of his paper. He writes outside the margins. Ramesh begins solving his math problem in the middle of the paper. Reading graphs or laying out math problems prove equally difficult. Bobby also struggles with *position in space*. He has difficulty packing his backpack, and uses trial and error rather than having a sense of what will and will not fit.

What students in your class might struggle with position in space?

Mediating Position in Space with Larry and Ramesh   To help Larry enhance his *position in space* skills, so that he can navigate his world more successfully, Mr. Edwards first places labels around the room. It is now clear where things belong, so that no matter what Larry's point of reference, those things will remain stable. To mediate Larry's need to develop a sense of *position in space*, Mr. Edwards uses those labels and referents to "play" with the change inherent in so much directionality. For instance, he asks the whole group to face one direction, and then to verbalize names of objects on their left, right, in front of, and behind them. He has them turn a quarter turn and asks, now what is on their left, right, and so on. They talk about this change overtly so that it no longer seems to be such a mystery. Mr. Edwards then takes the class to a more abstract level in using this thinking skill. He asks his students to remain in their seats, close their eyes, and visualize: "If you are facing the whiteboard (or another reference point), picture what will be behind you . . . in front of you . . . to your right . . . to your left."

Following this, Ramesh and a small group of students equally challenged by this skill work on hypothetical situations in which they will take themselves to a particular place in the school (e.g., the library). First, they begin verbalizing the steps and directions, and actually drawing the map, without leaving the classroom. Next, they try to actually follow the "maps." Giggling at their errors, and with the opportunity to make corrections along the way, the activity becomes fun as well as productive. To support Ramesh's skill and confidence building with *position in space*, Mr. Edwards makes sure he has the verbal skills (e.g., up, down, left, right, center). He encourages Ramesh (and others) to verbalize answers to mediating questions such as, "Let's describe in words where you will put your names on the paper. How would you describe it (e.g., upper left-hand corner)? Now, how would you describe in words where you begin each line you write (e.g., on the left margin of the paper where the blue vertical line is)?" Little assists, such as an "L" (for left) found in the outstretched left hand with the thumb at a right angle, help Ramesh temporarily remember the left versus right.

Strategies and Activities Supporting Mediation of Position in Space

Chart *Maps from Memory*   Encourage students to draw a route to a familiar location (e.g., the classroom to the school cafeteria) from memory. Have them follow their memory maps and correct any misconceptions or missteps. Have them draw the next one from their home to a favorite spot they or their families go. At home, they follow their maps to see how accurate they are, and make necessary changes.

Locate by *Techy Toggling*   Bring *Google Earth* up on the smart board and locate the school. Have one of the students illustrate how to toggle to get a 360° view of the building. Assign N, S, E, and W to the locations. Name a place they have to locate nearby and have the students call out what direction they must move. Ask them to talk about how they know, to support those who are still learning this skill.

Identify *Labels for Space*   Using a kinesthetic/tactile approach, real objects, and visuals, help students to understand *prepositions* (i.e., *in, under, over, on, in front of, behind, by, beside*). Model and provide them with the labels they need (I am standing *beside* the chair). You may even use physical touch ("neurological impress") to support their understanding of spatial concepts and directionality. For instance, have them touch their left hand on their right shoulder, their right hand to the right knee, and the right hand on the left ear.

Use *Nonverbal Supports*   Provide the students with grid paper to use in performing math computations. To support better use of spatial concepts when writing, have students use lined paper with margins. Use assists temporarily for remembering right and left, such as the following for right-handed students: "I write with my right." Use the visual of the left hand with the thumb at a right angle forming an "L" to stand for left.

Compare *Active Directions* Practice the relativity of spatial orientation at a physical level with labels. Have each student face in a different direction, and ask: "What is on your left? What is on your right?" Discuss why their answers may be different.

Start *Narrowing the Gap* Some students struggle to visually "transport" words or graphics from a vertical plane (the whiteboard) to the horizontal plane of their desks. This is another form of learning *position in space*. To support these students, first place what they are copying within close range, to limit the distance they must visually transport the image. Experiment by placing the book directly above the students' work or to the left to assist. Gradually extend the distance needed for the "visual transport" as the students experience success.

How might you mediate students in your class who struggle with position in space?

_____

_____

6. Position in Time

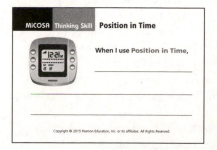

Students efficient with the thinking skill *position in time* understand and differentiate temporal ideas such as past, present, and future; young and old; now and later. The concepts embedded in this thinking skill are critical to using important *transformation* skills such as *sequencing, comparing, contrasting, hypothesizing, cause and effect,* and *ordering and grouping.* For instance, in order to sequence, your students must first be able to order events in time. To understand cause and effect, they must first differentiate but then go beyond "before and after."

Like *position in space, position in time* is also relative and developmental in nature. Understanding the concept of past might involve the past hour, week, month, year, decade, or century. Concepts of old, young, and new are relative; therefore, you will need to consider developmental stages and levels of complexity. Cultural interpretations of time also vary; for instance, in one language, the past tense is not used until a week has passed. Houses still inhabited in Europe may date back to the 16th century; in comparison, 50-year-old houses in California may be perceived as old. In addition, concepts of "on time" vary culturally. Transition words such as *suddenly, after awhile, meanwhile, first, next,* and *finally* signal your students to the temporal shifts needed to gather information. Linked to *position in time*, students use ideas expressed in phrases such as *long ago, two weeks from yesterday, in a fortnight, in a month, historically, ancient,* and *futuristic.* Later, students learn to bridge *position in time* to understanding concepts such as time zones, seasons, why you change the clock for daylight savings time, the temporal relationship of the Earth to its moon (e.g., tides and human cycles), and that the light you receive today from the sun actually began its journey to Earth at the time of Henry VIII! Understanding culturally idiomatic expressions such as killing time, wasting time, cutting time, and saving time all depend on a solid base in temporal orientation, or *position in time*.

Further, a student well grounded in *position in time* has the basis from which to "manage" time. A young student who is efficient in this skill can tell you what happened yesterday, and project when his birthday will occur. For instance, Jasmine knows when recess will come; she knows she has 10 minutes to finish her work. She has the timeframe that allows her to plan homework prior to dinner. In middle school, Karl uses *position in time* to relate a series of events to a timeline and to understand the sequence of the events. Further, he can move forward and backward conceptually as he reads historical texts that jump between different time periods, and use multiple transition words within a short space of text to illustrate the flow of historical concepts. In turn, then, he has the skills to understand the effect of one event on another.

Students Inefficient with Position in Time

Students with inefficient mastery of *position in time* may have difficulty getting a good sense of the amount of time that has passed or is to come, saying such things as: "Isn't it time yet?" Similarly, they may view the three weeks left to do an assignment as a tremendous amount of time, not having the sense that it is finite or that they might break it up effectively. They may use their own age as the primary reference for old and young, long ago or far in the future. One seven-year-old boy was enthusiastically relaying the story of Davy Crockett to his teacher. When she asked when Davy Crockett lived, the boy responded, "A long time ago." When asked a further probe, "How long ago do you think that was?" the boy thought hard, and then responded, "Maybe eight years!" In another example, while going on a trip, Serafina constantly asked her parents, "When will we get there? How long will it take?" She did not comprehend that what she experienced as hours were actually mere minutes.

Byron, on the other hand, regularly comes late to class. When he reads, this challenge actually carries over into his reading as he struggles to answer questions about what occurs before or after any given event. Lani assumes that as she reads from page to page, the events in a novel occur in that same sequence, when in fact the author shifts the order, using flashback and foreshadowing techniques. Lani finds herself quite confused.

What students in your class might struggle with position in time?

Mediating Position in Time with Serafina and Byron   In mediating *position in time*, you want to help students build a sense of time within meaningful contexts. When Serafina complains that surely an hour of the trip has already passed, her parents support this skill by relating the known to the unknown. When she asks, "When are we going to get there?" they relate to the familiar, so that Serafina compares: "You know how long it takes to get to Grandma's house? Well, this will take about the same length of time."

PD **TOOLKIT**™

PDToolkit: In Video Clip 4.2 a teacher illustrates student challenges when *position in time* is embedded in a social studies text.

Relating this skill to Serafina's favorite television shows is another helpful comparison. They might say, "You know how long it takes to watch Power Friends? Well, this will take about the same length of time—a half hour."

To help Byron develop and strengthen his sense of *position in time*, his teacher, Mr. Daniels, examines what Byron does between times and events that make him habitually off schedule. Mr. Daniels mediates a sequence that will allow Byron to enhance efficiency. In reading, Mr. Daniels asks Byron and others in the class to scan a text for "temporal" words such as *first* and *next*. He asks them to place post-it notes to separate the time periods denoted by these types of words. They discuss the content between the post-it note markers and their relationships to the temporal sequences. Mr. Daniels then explores what other words could be substituted, such as *before* and *after*. Bridging to life experiences, he refers to meaningful events in Byron's life, and relates them to *before* and *after* (e.g., "What happened before you went to school . . . after the first day of school? What was one important thing you learned yesterday?").

Strategies and Activities Supporting Mediation of Position in Time

PD TOOLKIT™

PDToolkit: See Video Clip 4.3 for an example of the strategy, *Put Yourself in the Picture*.

Enact *Put Yourself in the Picture*
Project a large image on the screen, making it as near to the ground as possible. It may be a scene from history, or a picture of an event in a story. This strategy can be used in two ways: (a) Ask students to "stand in" the picture and take on the persona of the characters in the picture, acting out what they think is taking place in the "here and now" of that moment; and (b) Ask students, in their groups, to create three enactments; that is, to "step out" of the frame and enact what happened BEFORE this event, DURING the event, and AFTER (Frey & Bower, 2004). This is also an excellent strategy to illustrate and engage students with *cause and effect* relationships.

Construct *Time Tapes*
Relate the unknown to the known. Place a masking tape timeline across the floor. Ask students to stand on the timeline where an anecdote or milestone in their lives occurred. Place concurrent events in history from two or more countries on the timeline to help students understand larger relational concepts.

Identify *Time Cues*
To support students' understanding of the representation of time in books, have them locate transition words such as *finally* and *suddenly*. Look at different kinds of timelines within a textbook (e.g., horizontal, vertical, pictorial). Create an understanding of terms such as "*in the 50s*," or "*during the 1500s*." Help students to see how some textbooks may jump back and forth with time, preferring to order by concept rather than by date. For example, students may learn about Islam from conception to its impact on the world before reversing in time to study early Feudalism which led to the Crusades. The rationale of beginning with Islam may be that, in doing so, students will gain a better understanding of the Muslim point of view of the Crusades versus the Christian viewpoint that is more typical in American schools.

Rearrange *Topic Sentence Time* *Topic Sentence Time* works well with both nonfiction and fiction. Preread the text you will use with your lesson and copy down the topic sentence for each paragraph (choose no more than 10 in a longer passage). Look for cues you can give such as transitions, dates, and before and after events. Rearrange the sentences out of sequence. Partner students to use the cues to help them sequence the events correctly. This helps students look for temporal cues, serves as an anticipatory guide, and provides a summary guide for study purposes after the lesson. The summary guide is particularly helpful for English learners. (based on Sentence Strip Predication, Action Learning Systems, 2003.)

Use *Online Sequencing Games* You will find a variety of engaging sequencing games available online. Each requires a sense of orientation to or *position in time* (c.f., quia.com; thekidzpage.com; languageartsgames.4you4free.com).

Create *Graphic Organizers* Sequence of events and cyclic story maps, hierarchy nets, causality boxes, and herringbone organizers all support your students in organizing their thoughts in an appropriate chronological sequence.

How might you mediate students in your class who struggle with position in time?

_____

_____

7. Precision and Accuracy

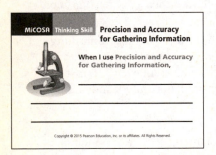

MiCOSA Thinking Skill   **Precision and Accuracy for Gathering Information**

When I use Precision and Accuracy for Gathering Information,

_____

_____

_____

Students who gather information with *precision and accuracy* take care that their information is true, exact, or well defined. *Precision* refers to exactness; for instance, you want to measure with precision before you cut a piece of lumber for the roof. To improve precision, you might ask your students to find more precise words than *really cool* to describe a scene they have witnessed. *Accurate* refers to being correct, error free, or meeting a standard of truth. Accuracy alone may be construed as a generalized "truth" that doesn't need precision. For instance, leaves turn colors in the autumn. Adding precision to the statement, your students might note that in Vermont, the leaves of the sugar maple turn brilliant hues of gold, orange, and red by early October. *Accurate* may require a standard to measure against or compare. For instance, in gathering information from an historical novel, how accurately is the historical context portrayed? Your students would need more than one source of information to make that determination.

Linked with establishing a goal, students efficient with this skill appraise how much or how little to invest in gathering *precise* information and doing so with *accuracy*. Efficiency in this skill helps produce *precise* and *accurate* results, or outcomes. For instance, since Marcella takes the time to gather *precise* information on the train schedule prior to leaving home, she arrives at the station on time. Another student, Tai, *accurately* and *precisely* gathers information on the order of operations for calculating algebraic equations from his book; thus, he successfully performs the operations. Gathering information with *precision and accuracy* often links with its "sister" skill, *precision and accuracy* in communication. However, at each stage of learning the skill has a slightly different meaning and impact.

Students Inefficient with Precision and Accuracy

Without *precisely* or *accurately* gathering information, your students have little to no chance of communicating *precise* or *accurate* information. As a result, you see their imprecise or inaccurate communication in school. These students may invest either too much or too little effort, gathering either too much irrelevant information or too little relevant information. For instance, Levi answered every question, when the teacher had directed students to do every other question.

For example, Mr. Ruffy's student, Zach, tries to locate Mali. He reads his map without accuracy when he finds Maui (Hawaii) and mistakenly thinks Mali is located in Hawaii instead of in West Africa. In Ms. Chapman's math class, Josh goes too fast in copying his problem from the board to the paper, losing precision. He copies the sign for the operation incorrectly (+ instead of −). Sometimes he misaligns the columns, resulting in incorrect results, even though he has a good understanding of the math operation and place value.

Students who have difficulty with *precision and accuracy* may also have difficulties in other skill areas that appear to be issues of *precision and accuracy*. For instance, inefficient use of *focus and attention*, *systematic search* for relevant clues, and gathering information effectively from *multiple sources* may all result in imprecise or inaccurate data gathering. Difficulties with *position in time and space* may make it difficult for your students to transport the *precise or accurate* orientation of an object from the book or smart board to their notebooks.

What students in your class might struggle with precision and accuracy?

Mediating Precision and Accuracy with Levi, Zach, and Josh   Levi rushes through directions because he does not see the need to invest effort in gathering all the information with *precision and accuracy*. Mrs. Allmen, his teacher, uses test directions as an effective way of helping her mediate her students' need for *precision and accuracy*. She shows the whole class a page of a test, but covers the directions and asks them what to do. She elicits and listens to answers, until a demand arises to uncover the directions. At this point, she uncovers only the first part of the directions, and asks, "Now do we know what to do?" This guides Mrs. Allmen's students to discuss the effects of not having sufficient information, and thus the results of not gathering *accurate* or *precise* information from the directions. Another time, to reinforce the need to accurately gather all the information, Mrs. Allmen adds an unexpected direction at the end, such as: "Answer every other question," or "What is the least likely response?"

Zach reads too fast, and is neither *precise* nor *accurate*. He misreads the name of the location he sought, Mali. Zach had valued speed over accuracy, so the similarity of letters (M's, A's, and I's for Maui/Mali) led him to be imprecise and thus inaccurate. To help him learn to differentiate, Mr. Ruffy works with him to mediate self-regulation, slowing down enough to use what Zach knows about attributes to construct meaning. Mr. Ruffy asks, "What do you know from reading about Mali that will help you identify where it is located?" Zach begins to list attributes such as Mali trading with the north across the Sahara. As he does so, he realizes and clarifies where he'd gone wrong, and corrects himself. Now Mr. Ruffy acknowledges him for taking the time to *self-regulate* his pace to make the connection. He points out that sometimes everyone has to take a little more time to acquire *accurate* information. For Zach, Mr. Ruffy shares, "I am impressed with your breadth of knowledge, Zach. When you take the time to be *precise and accurate*, I notice that you put together what you already know with new information very effectively. When it makes sense to you—has meaning—then you are ready to use the information." Mr. Ruffy helps Zach develop meaning through associations and attributes, and mediates competence and meaning for the need for *precision* and *accuracy*. This will help Zach become more efficient in gathering information, as well as communicating it.

Josh struggles with imprecision in math. To mediate, Ms. Chapman involves the whole class. She establishes a goal; then, to achieve that goal, she links it with the thinking skill *precision and accuracy*. "How many of you (in the class) only want to get one of the problems right? How many want to get two? How many want to get them all right?" All hands shoot into the air. "Okay, so we have a class goal for everyone to get all the problems right. What do you need to pay attention to so that you get all the information you need to solve the problems (correct signs, correct numbers, correct alignment)?" "Great! What thinking skill will we need to use to do that?" "Ah! *Precision* and *accuracy*. Who has another example?" Josh adds, "When I slow down, I am more *precise*!"

Strategies and Activities Supporting Mediation of Precision and Accuracy

Draw *Precision from Nature*   As a precursor to gathering *precise and accurate* information, have students gather information from their natural surroundings, uninterrupted, so they come to value how time and attention to detail enhances the "gathering" experience. Ask students to sit quietly outside for a full five minutes observing nature around them. They may notice the ant in the crack in the sidewalk, the bird's feather caught in the chain linked fence, or the squirrel scurrying up the tree, his tail twitching as he pauses en route. Back in the classroom, most will report seeing greater levels of such detail as they discuss their changing observations over time.

Now, working at centers set up with objects from nature (one per student), ask students to draw what they see and make notes about their initial observations. The objects may be a butterfly's wing, a snake's skin, a mushroom, a mealworm, or a plant. Following this, have them use magnifying glasses to examine their objects again, but this time with greater detail and precision. This will lead to a discussion of the appreciation of using time to enhance *precision and accuracy*, as well as meaning and value. Later, when bridging to other content areas, their magnifying glass becomes a symbol of the need for *precision* and *accuracy*.

Introduce *Direction Twist*   Use published worksheets (or create ones) that have a series of directions for the whole class to follow, with a "twist" at the end designed to have them learn the importance of reading all the directions with accuracy. For example, say first: "I am going to give you all a set of directions. It is important to read all the directions before you begin." Then present the list of directions:

1. Write your name in the upper right-hand corner of your paper.
2. Draw three squares in the lower right-hand corner.
3. Raise your hand and shout out: "I am the best reader in the class!"
4. Get up and walk around your desk and then sit back down.
5. Do only number one.

Inevitably, some of the class members will shout out or walk around their desks, not having read to the end. This brings laughter along with learning.

Scaffold *Directed Draw*   Show students a finished picture (e.g., a member of the Mandan tribe hunting buffalo, or something members of your class may connect with culturally). Each student has a blank paper and a box of crayons. Next to the finished picture, the teacher also has a blank piece of paper. Step by step, giving auditory and visual directions, the teacher slowly works with the group to construct the finished picture. For example, "Take your orange crayon and, holding it flat on the paper, lightly make a circle in the middle of the paper. See it on the finished product? It is the head of the hunter. Now, you can see why you have drawn it in the middle of the picture, as well as its shape and size. Now we will work on the neck and shoulders. Feel your own shoulders. Do they go straight out or are they at an angle? . . ." This models work on *precision and accuracy*. Link it with mediating the meaning—the difference it makes to be precise and accurate during such an activity. You might also use the same activity to mediate additional thinking skills such as *multiple sources* of information, position in space, and visual transport (Shuller, 1982).

How might you mediate students in your class who struggle with precision and accuracy?

_____

_____

SUMMARY

- For your students to process thoughtful and effective responses, they must be efficient in gathering information. The MiCOSA Model identifies seven thinking skills critical for gathering such information. Each thinking skill discussion includes classroom examples of efficient and inefficient use, and concludes with many practical classroom strategies.

- To methodically gather information in an organized way, students will use the thinking skill *systematic search*. Five different types of *focus and attention* help sustain visual and auditory focus long enough to efficiently gather this relevant information for processing. *Labels, words, and concepts* help make meaning of the world. However, all rational thought requires the use of at least two sources of information. The thinking skill *multiple sources* enables efficiency of gathering, holding, and using more than one source of information simultaneously.

- *Position in space,* your students' own cognitive GPS, helps them understand the relationships of objects. *Position in time* helps them understand and differentiate temporal ideas such as past, present, and future. It also serves as a prerequisite for many transformation skills such as ordering, grouping, comparing, understanding cause and effect relationships, and hypothesizing.

- Finally, it is essential that students gather information with *precision and accuracy* in order to have the correct information to transform and produce precise and accurate results.

REFERENCES

Action Learning Systems (2003). *The literacy solution: A system for reading comprehension.* Monrovia, CA: Author.

Bernstein, D. (2011). *Essentials of psychology* (5th ed.). Belmont, CA: Wadsworth.

Chancer, J. (2000). Exploring Grammar Creatively, ELA Professional Development Workshop. Thousand Oaks, CA: Conejo Valley Unified School District.

Frey, W., & Bower, B. (2004). *History alive! Medieval world and beyond grade 7.* Rancho Cordova, CA: Teachers Curriculum Institute.

Johnson, J. F., & Perez, L. (2010). *The best teaching in America's best urban schools.* A presentation of the National Center on Urban School Transformation (NCUST) to the faculty at San Diego State University. San Diego, CA.

Kagan, S. (1992). *Cooperative learning.* San Juan Capistrano, CA: Resources for Teachers, Inc.

Lee, S. W. (Ed.). (2005). *Encyclopedia of school psychology.* Thousand Oaks, CA: Sage.

Lupyan, G., Rakison, D. H., & McClelland, J. L. (2007). Language is not just for talking: Redundant labels facilitate learning of novel categories. *Association for Psychological Science, 18*(12), 1077–1083.

Marzano, R. J., Pickering, D. J., & Pollock, J. E. (2001). *Classroom instruction that works: Research-based strategies for increasing student achievement.* Alexandria, VA: Association for Supervision and Curriculum Development.

Shuller, J. (1982). *Using directional draw in the classroom.* A workshop for Conejo Valley Unified School District. Thousand Oaks, CA.

Taba, H. (1988). *Teacher's Handbook for Elementary Social Studies.* Reading, MA: Addison-Wesley.

Tierney, R. J., & Readence, J. E. (2000). *Reading strategies and practices: A compendium* (5th ed.). Boston: Allyn & Bacon.

Chapter Five

Thinking Skills for Transforming Information

Once information has been gathered, students use the more complex thinking skills for transforming information to work critically and creatively with it.

Once your students locate, select, and gather sufficient information, they are ready to critique, create, and problem-solve. In this phase of thinking, they will literally transform information through analyzing, hypothesizing, adding to, or subtracting from it. They will raise new questions, solve new problems, or create ideas in the classroom and in life. They begin to "process" or transform that information using a variety of more complex thinking skills.

Many of these transformation skills equate directly with critical thinking; that is, they support students in the process of making carefully reasoned judgments and decisions. To do so, your students seek evidence, test out hypotheses, seek patterns, analyze and synthesize information, and come to reasoned conclusions. As they transform information, they build new neurological connections. These connections create neural pathways for future memory and retrieval. The more they use the transformation skills, the more those new patterns and pathways build habits of thinking that support greater efficiency and growing expertise.

MiCOSA's nine thinking skills for transforming information, selected in part because of their relevance to standards and curriculum, will have a ring of familiarity to educators: (1) *goal setting;* (2) *planning;* (3) *comparing;* (4) *ordering, grouping, and categorizing;* (5) *finding connections and relationships;* (6) *visualizing;* (7) *inferring;* (8) *cause and effect—hypothesizing;* and (9) *summarizing.*

Students may already be efficient with some of these skills, but not others. Once students begin to use skills to gather information more efficiently, some of the transformation skills emerge rather easily. Often, however, you will need to use mediating conversations to facilitate their development. Although they do not develop in a specific sequence, in some cases, certain thinking skills serve as prerequisites for others. For instance, students need to be able to *compare* in order to *categorize.*

In this chapter, case examples from real classrooms illustrate each thinking skill, helping the definitions come to life. First, examples of students efficient with the thinking skill augment definitions and examples. Next, to provide a contrast, several examples of students inefficient with the thinking skill help you identify similar students in your own classroom. You will have the opportunity to note a few on your own at this point.

Because MiCOSA stresses mediating to develop thinking skills, examples then illustrate how a teacher mediates inefficient skills. Following this, a series of strategies and activities provides additional ways you can develop this skill in your classroom. Finally, you have the opportunity to note some ways you might mediate students in your classroom who struggle with that skill.

Goal Setting

Students who use the thinking skill of *goal setting* establish a direction for their learning. Setting goals guides their collection of information and supports them in establishing plans for accomplishing the goals. Goal-directed behavior becomes purposeful behavior, which is important for the development of independent functioning both in and out of the classroom. It promotes their developing self-initiative and self-directedness. When efficient with *goal setting*, students see the big picture, which motivates goal attainment. For example, Vanessa and Edgar set a goal to create a video using *Animoto*, and to post it on their class website. Once that personal goal is set, it leads to motivation. Vanessa and Edgar then organize the necessary steps, put in the work, and produce their video.

Students Inefficient with Goal Setting

Students inefficient with *goal setting* may seem impulsive, appear to have a fragmented approach to their work, and become easily frustrated. Their goals may be too broad or vague. Thus, they lack the motivation of meaningful engagement, don't find any connection with the learning beyond the teacher-driven assignment, and may become passive. For instance, Beverly's teacher had asked the class to write individual goals for the year. Beverly wrote, "I want to be a better reader." Beverly's goal lacks the specificity to guide her planning, and she has no way to demonstrate whether she has met the goal. In another example, when Alberto's group presents their project to the class, they begin to look around and laugh nervously about half way through. They do not appear to know what comes next. At first, it appears to be a result of inefficient planning. However, it soon becomes clear that the goal itself has never been clearly established or sufficiently refined.

What students in your class might struggle with goal setting?

Mediating Goal Setting with Beverly and Alberto   Students may use the assignment you give, calling that a goal, rather than establishing their own goals. To help them learn to use and make habits of *goal setting*, first mediate by modeling with examples, and then by expectation. Next, ask your students to set goals. If their goals are too broad to effectively guide their planning, provide guiding questions to help them gain insight into the goals. For instance, when Beverly said her goal was to become a better reader, mediating conversations helped her clarify and refine that goal: "Tell me what you mean by becoming a better reader. How will you look or sound? How will we know you have become better? Very clear, Beverly! Now, use what you have said to write a more specific goal. Once you do that, you will know exactly what you want to do, and can develop a plan to get there."

Alberto's group sets a goal to create a presentation about the explorer Cabrillo. This is far too non-specific to guide the process. Again, the mediating conversation helps clarify and refine the goal: "What do you want the class to remember about Cabrillo? Can you come up with three key things about him that you want to have the audience understand?" (For example, what trade route they opened up, the effect of the discoveries on their sponsor country, and the effect on the indigenous group living in that area.) "Great! Now, rewrite the goal so it reflects what you want the audience to know." On a smaller scale, you might set a goal for the class to learn to subtract integers. To mediate *goal setting*, you might ask the students, "Take a few minutes to look at these two pages we will refer to today. Gather some information and then write down your personal goal for this lesson." Student responses may range from "understanding the steps I need to use to subtract integers," to "being sure I ask a question when I don't understand." Then, midway through the instruction, ask, "Now that we have done two problems, how are you doing on your goal? Check back and decide whether you want to modify it." Double-checking the students' self-evaluation toward their goals helps mediate the meaning of using *goal setting*.

Strategies and Activities Supporting Mediation of Goal Setting

Set *Personal Goals*   At the beginning of the year or a unit of study, have your students set personal goals within the context of the classroom goals. Marzano, Pickering, and Pollock (2001) found that having students personalize their own goals is far more effective than enforcing teacher-imposed goals. Provide students with a framework consisting of five elements. First, they should be (a) meaningful, (b) measurable, and (c) have a time frame. Then, students need to (d) carry out the goal they have set and (e) evaluate their performance (celebrate success or revise goal). This can occur throughout the year and at the end of the unit. You will mediate the meaning of *goal setting*, sharing examples of several students' growth due to their setting goals.

Identify a *Goal for the Day*   Share daily goals with your class, letting them know exactly where they will be "headed" and the meaning behind the activities that follow. Daily goals are one critical characteristic of good teaching (Johnson & Perez, 2010). Write goals with specificity, and post them in a place easy to access. The goal should be action-oriented, using words like *summarize*, *describe*, *analyze*, and *create*. Students then personalize the class goal in their own journals; for example, "I will summarize the key reasons of the American Revolution by creating an organizer on Inspiration for the notes"; or "I will end up describing why so few people decided to fight a whole nation." Having students reframe the class goal into a personal one helps make their work meaningful; it guides their collection of information as well as their transformation of it.

Chart Student Progress and *Celebrate Milestones*   Have students chart their progress toward their goals. They celebrate milestones as well as goal attainment. This helps students learn to self-regulate behaviors as well as to achieve academic goals. Provide rubrics for assignments, so they have parameters around which to set their own goals.

How might you mediate students in your class who struggle with goal setting?

_____

_____

Planning

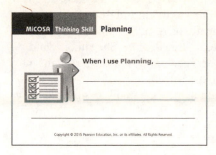

Through *planning*, your students develop roadmaps to reach and achieve their goals. When students *plan*, they have to *consider* and *select* relevant materials and activities, and then sequence those activities and materials into steps needed to attain their goals. *Planning* leads to efficient use of time and resources. For example, Jorge has the goal of writing a multi-paragraph essay. He uses *planning* to determine and sequence the relevant information— the main idea and supporting details—that will support his thesis statement and guide his introduction, supporting paragraphs, and conclusion. *Planning* guides daily interactions and activities. When students set a goal for the day, they gather relevant materials and sequence their work in a manner that scaffolds and supports their own learning, building on success and challenges. Effective *planning* often involves using other thinking skills such as *ordering, grouping, and categorizing; finding connections and relationships;* and *position in time.*

Students Inefficient in Planning

Unlike Jorge, Selena does not spontaneously plan prior to writing. She writes whatever comes to mind related to the topic. Her ideas appear disconnected and lack focus. She struggles to create a thesis sentence or to draw a conclusion from her work since there was no thesis planned. Without a thesis or goal, she selects details randomly, rather than details related to a thesis. When students fail to set goals, they also tend to face challenges with gathering sufficient relevant materials and information. Assignments lack depth, may become fragmented, and can lead to disengaged students.

What students in your class might struggle with planning?

_____

Mediating Planning with Selena   In an era of fast-paced, product-oriented values and habits, you will need to mediate the *need* to plan as well as the process of *planning*. Whether *planning* for writing an essay, creating a PowerPoint, conducting a science experiment, completing a history project, or solving math problems, you begin with an intention about the nature of *planning*—why you and your students do it in life. You will relate how setting a goal leads to gathering information and materials, then to sequencing steps to achieve the goal, as you might see in *planning* for an outing.

You will find it helpful to provide the contrast of what happens when your students don't plan. For example, lack of adequate *planning* can actually become a safety hazard. If you do not plan to put sufficient gas in the car for a trip through the desert where there are no gas stations, nor plan to take water to drink on the journey, you can put your very life in danger. You will "bridge" the ideas to the need and value for *planning* before you have them write essays (or begin science experiments or history projects).

Selena's teacher, Ms. Bee, begins by having her talk about and write the "goal" or thesis statement. This will give focus to her work. Along with the rest of the class, Selena observes and collaborates in creating models for *planning* to write, and in using them to actually complete an essay. She and her peers compare the results of planned and unplanned writing, and discuss what difference it makes to use *planning*. She chooses and uses a graphic organizer for her own work, infusing her "goal" and supporting details into the model. Having had the models, she is now able to move from organizer to essay writing. Although it feels a bit time consuming at first, taking the time to discuss the *planning* process pays off for Selena and several other students.

Strategies and Activities Supporting Mediation of Planning

Introduce *Authentic Planning* Make explicit the need to plan and the value of *planning*. Bridge from home-based and "real life" experiences to school experiences (e.g., *planning* a budget for independent living; *planning* shopping for a party with friends; *planning* trips to visit colleges). Investigate and learn from plans of other people (principals, cafeteria workers, parents). Project (hypothesize) how they think others have to plan (e.g., architects, their teachers, authors they like, businessmen, adventurers, sport or movie celebrities, characters in history). You might have them answer the question, "How would _____ [an expert in an area of interest] *plan* this?"

Elucidate the *Concept of a Plan* Model *planning* and its outcomes, but also model unplanned work and its outcomes. Without the contrast, some students consider *planning* "busywork." This contrast helps students value the importance of *planning*.

Graph a Plan and Plan a Graph Use online or paper graphic organizers to help students learn to *plan*, then move to having students generate their own organizers, tailored to their own needs. This is often far harder than you might think, since students may not understand why a particular graphic organizer makes sense for a particular task. Rather than handing out blank copies of the organizer, have students select one from a choice of two or three organizers and discuss their choice. As an initial scaffold, do this in groups, as group collaboration supports *planning*. To force conceptualization (so they can eventually generate their own organizers), give them an organizer with one error. Have them find the error and report out why that was an error, and then correct it. This forces critical thinking.

Create Opportunities to Use *Project Planning* Incorporate and validate *planning* as an integral part of the next assigned project or assignment. Collect, evaluate, and discuss the group's plans before they proceed further with the actual work. Celebrate good *planning* and encourage more thoughtful plans where necessary. Throughout the project, allow time for students to revisit their initial plan and make modifications to it, if needed.

Use *Rubrics as Planning Guides*   Give students the assessment rubric you have designed right up front, so they know how you are going to assess their work. This rubric then supports their *planning*. For example, if the rubric asks for a well-defined thesis statement and carefully selected details, then they know they must plan to show evidence of these in their essay.

How might you mediate students in your class who struggle with planning?

_____

_____

Comparing

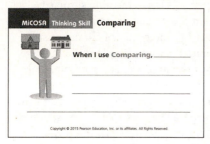

Comparing embraces both similarities and differences. The things students compare can be either tangible or abstract. They may be located in the environment or recalled from memory. For example, at a concrete level, such as choosing between a small or large dessert, students often *compare* spontaneously and happily accept the larger of the two. However, they do not spontaneously generalize how to use comparison. Your students must learn to deliberately compare at conceptual or abstract levels. This skill will support their understanding of the parts of speech from synonyms to metaphors and analogies. It will also support them in *comparing* characteristics of literary characters or historical periods, *comparing* quantities in different-sized containers, or *comparing* data collected over time for a scientific experiment.

   To *compare*, learners need to understand the attributes and characteristics of the things being compared. Students efficient in *comparing* spontaneously assess the characteristics of two or more things. They may *compare* items to determine the best value of a purchase, *compare* a current problem to one they have already solved, and *compare* the shapes of "b" "d" "p" and "q" to form the correct word.

   Furthermore, *comparing* is essential to efficiently using other transforming skills used for critical thinking, such as *finding connections and relationships* or *ordering, grouping, and categorizing*. For example, Diego makes text-to-self connections (Harvey & Goudvis, 2007) within his novel; that is, he makes comparisons between the text and his own life experiences. Liam is able to *compare* math word problems to the ones he has done previously and to the models, building on successful strategies he has seen, modeled, and tried. He also *compares* his current and his prior work, assessing his own progress.

Students Inefficient in Comparing

Students who are inefficient with the thinking skill *comparing* do not spontaneously compare, nor do they seem to notice sets of attributes that would serve as the basis for comparison. In response to, "How are Hamlet and Othello alike?" these students may say,

"I don't know," or "They just are." They have no awareness that they might begin with the phrase, "They both. . . ." English Language Learners and others may not have the *labels, words, and concepts* to express the attributes they see. For instance, Ysenia responds, "I know what I want to say. I know how those two characters are the same, but I don't know the words to explain it."

What students in your class might struggle with comparing?

_____

Mediating Comparing with Ysenia   When you mediate *comparing,* have students deliberately seek how things are alike and different. You can do this at concrete or abstract levels, beginning in early grades *comparing* sizes, shapes, colors, and sounds. You might discuss using models, *comparing* student work with the examples of how to do problems, and using graphic organizers to support the categories of same and different. To mediate, help students identify characteristics they can use to determine similarity and difference, and then mediate meaning or elicit from them what happens when they compare. Graphic organizers can help students pre-identify categories of characteristics helpful in *comparing,* and can build on the ideas generated from a class. In oral language, you can illustrate this thinking skill by engaging in auditory practice. For example, look for similarities and differences in small words with differing middle vowels or same/differing initial or ending consonants by using a mirror for visual feedback, and using an elbowed tube for auditory feedback. Students identify characteristics such as the shape of the mouth, the vibration in the throat, or the sound in the ear to determine similarity and difference. You will want to elicit comparisons from students, rather than providing them. When students are active learners, they are far more likely to remember and use the thinking skill—in this case, comparisons.

    In some cases, you need to dip into skills for *gathering* information to facilitate the comparisons. For instance, Ysenia struggles to find the words to express the similar traits she sees (*comparisons*) between two characters. She doesn't have shades of different meanings for the descriptors like *grotesque, vile, hideous,* or *homely* in her repertoire. To help her express those similarities and differences, mediating conversations support her in finding the *labels, words, and concepts* involved. You may also prompt her to use the resource of character trait lists: "Where might you find some of the words you are looking for? Would they be listed under positive or negative traits? Let's name it, act it out, and add those words to your personal dictionary." In this way, the words become hers.

Strategies and Activities Supporting Mediation of Comparing

Use Models When Students Ask, *Show Me What It Looks Like*   Textbook examples serve as basic ways to help your students use *comparing.* Examples provide models from which the students can *compare* the processes students should use. Some students have no idea why textbooks include those models, and think of them as unnecessary reading that is not central to the text. Often, those same students will also say, "Show me what it looks like," or "Show me what you want." To help these students, mediate why models exist and what use they might be. Ask questions such as, "What in the world is that thing in the grey box on this page? Why do you suppose it might be there? How might you use it? Great, we call these models. What other kinds of models do you find in life that help you compare your work and your processes, so you know how to do things?"

Use *Copy Change*

Using *copy change* (Rasinski & Padak, 2000), first demonstrate a basic structure and its attributes (e.g., haiku and analogy). Then provide a parallel assignment in which students copy the structure but "change" the topic and attributes, using their own examples. As another way to use *copy change*, you first provide a rich description of text from a well-known author. Have your students extract the basic structure from the text, and use it as a model (the "copy" in *copy change*). Then have them "change" the content to fit their own experiences. Mediate or make explicit the meaning and value of *comparing* in this activity. For example, if text reads: "The gentle breeze caressed my cheek, uplifting my spirit," then the copy change might read: "The biting cold wind cut into my flesh like a whetted knife, uplifting my spirit."

Explain the *Concept of an Attribute*

Although you expect students to use attributes in order to compare and contrast, often students do not understand the concept of an attribute and its use in *comparing*. For students to *compare* their work to a model in the text, they must extract the model's attributes and compare them with the attributes of what they have done. You want your students to understand that those attributes are the building blocks of the comparison, so they can also use them to correct errors. Making that relationship explicit (between finding attributes and the thinking skill of *comparing*) helps them make sense of the organizers we use to help them *compare*.

You may have your students list several attributes or characteristics within categories you give them in a topic-related model or organizer. The concept of finding attributes will be critical as they have to compare more complex items and events. Use questioning to elicit their conceptual understanding: "Why would we be listing all these attributes? What happens if we miss some of the attributes when we try to compare or replicate?"

Use *Nonlinguistic Representations*

Use Venn diagrams and graphic organizers to support the differentiation of characteristics (i.e., their similarities and differences). Nonlinguistic representations force your students to conceptualize (Marzano, Pickering, & Pollock, 2001).

Celebrate Our Differences

Have students share differences and similarities in how they solve problems. Students can also share similarities and differences in how they celebrate holidays in the same season, as well as other cultural features.

How might you mediate students in your class who struggle with comparing?

_____

_____

Ordering, Grouping, and Categorizing

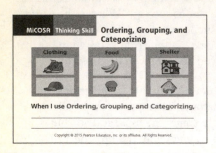

Ordering, grouping, and categorizing helps your students organize and form conceptual sets. When learners can *order, group, and categorize*, they become more efficient thinkers. They can store chunks or categories instead of individual pieces of information. Categorizing information helps students remember more and remember more accurately. This process supports critical thinking. For example, Ms. Polt's class synthesizes their reading on the Lakota into categories of clothing, food, shelter, tools, and cultural practices. Her students remember the information and use it as they discuss how clothing is related to weather or region, allowing them to speak in more abstract terms, and to then draw generalizations. Similarly, when those students need to compare (e.g., Lakota and Navajo or historical and current practices), they organize the information by category, which facilitates their engaging in higher order thinking and discussion.

Ordering (e.g., smallest to largest or first, second, third) is one form of organizing information by attributes. Similarly, *grouping* (such as by colors or shapes) like events is a different way of organizing by attributes. In order to successfully use these skills, students must also integrate the use of *multiple sources* of information with other *transforming* skills, such as *comparing* and *finding connections and relationships*.

Concurrently, using *ordering, grouping, and categorizing* facilitates memory. In math, you order, group, and categorize multiplication tables (e.g., 2's, 5's, 9's) to facilitate recall. Your students use ordering when learning about bones in science. Students learn to read words using groupings such as words that end in *at*. Once they see the pattern (*at, cat, sat, bat*), then their repertoire expands. Immediately they have more words in their memorized word banks. For older students, prefixes and suffixes follow similar patterns (*fresh*: prefix and suffix patterns then expand to *refresh, refreshing, refreshment*).

When you share new knowledge in class, students efficient with *ordering, grouping, and categorizing* can find a "place" to store that new knowledge in memory, *comparing* it with existing sets or groups. For example, in his second grade science class, Jake and his classmates first generate all the information they currently hold about prehistoric mammals. They then develop categories into which they can more efficiently add new information.

By synthesizing information into efficient groups, then labeling it into more abstract levels of categories, you facilitate higher order thinking. Sean compares the differences between World Wars I and II according to the following categories: reasons for the war, countries involved, combat strategies used on both sides, and outcomes. In doing so, he draws on the information he has categorized to develop meaningful interpretations, rather than resorting to reciting lists or examples.

Students Inefficient in Ordering, Grouping, and Categorizing

When your students have fragile thinking skills with *ordering, grouping, and categorizing*, both memory and communication can appear fragmented rather than organized. Students may seem "lost" and nonfocused. In Ms. Polt's class, Mireya does not distinguish the categories from the examples and details while studying Lakota survival. She calls *buffalo* a category, and *source of food* does not appear in her lists or charts. Before mediation, she lists *shelter* as an example rather than a category. Because she does not organize the information, she cannot remember it and cannot share any of the information in a meaningful way.

Your students will find *grouping and categorizing* essential for writing a persuasive multi-paragraph essay. Paragraphs need to be organized by category, with examples. Those categories then become the main ideas, reflected in the topic sentences. When Andrea tries to write a persuasive essay on whether kids should have pets, she comes up with many examples of pet-related activities, ranging from feeding them to walking and taking care of them. She never develops categories. Instead of saying, "You could have a pet to practice and demonstrate responsibility," followed by examples such as feeding, walking, and grooming, her paragraphs said, "You could feed, take care of, and walk a dog." She misses the point of the category of demonstrating responsibility.

Finally, some students may intertwine emotional components with content as they categorize and remember. This can interfere with new categorizing if you do not give them a chance to separate it. For instance, because of his experiences, Marco links guns with *trauma* and *drive-by shootings* rather than with categories of *hunting* or *weapons of war*. Similarly, Jeremy has drawn only from his own sad experiences. He writes that children should not have dogs, because dogs die after only a year. For these reasons, you will want to tap into what your students already "know," or associate and falsely "know," prior to moving deeply into the subject matter.

What students in your class might struggle with ordering, grouping, and categorizing?

Mediating Ordering, Grouping, and Categorizing with Mireya   As you help students strengthen their skills in *ordering, grouping, and categorizing*, broadly speaking, you are helping them learn to organize, draw on prerequisite skills to do so, and learn to see the value in having information synthesized. To mediate the development of groups and categories, begin with areas more clearly "known" to the student and accessible within the immediate environment.

In the case of Mireya, who is not differentiating categories from details, mediating conversations focus on naming categories that have meaning to her. Ms. Polt gives her paper, a pencil, an eraser, and crayons, and asks questions to draw out the category label of *school supplies*. Mediating her initial competence, Ms. Polt points out that Mireya has categorized well this time by finding how things were alike. Following this, Ms. Polt presents her with a range of items that might go into three categories (food, clothing, shelter). To mediate self-regulation and meaning, she tells Mireya, "I see that when you look for similarities, and take the time to let yourself experiment with different possibilities, you have pretty good skills in categorizing. Do you see that too?"

Ms. Polt's mediating conversation then helps Mireya bridge to the academic task. "Now, take a little time again to make and name groups with the information about Lakotas. Use your *comparing* skills to figure out what things go together. Great, Mireya. Now, what label or category will you give each group? Remember that your category label should apply to all of your grouped items."

If your student is unsure how to label the groups, you can suggest examples and have the student(s) test out whether all their items will fit their categories. Use one or two incorrect examples and have them explain why they are incorrect. You can do this with your entire class as well.

Once students understand the notion of categories, they will find predesigned graphic organizers tremendously helpful. To enhance critical thinking skills, have them generate their own graphic organizers. The more students use nonlinguistic systems of representation (e.g., graphic organizers), the more efficiently they will be able to think about and recall knowledge (Marzano, Pickering, & Pollock, 2001, p. 73).

Strategies and Activities Supporting Mediation of Ordering, Grouping, and Categorizing

Begin with the Basics   Begin with basic groups familiar to your students and move toward the complex and abstract. Build from attributes that can be seen and felt, smelled or tasted, and help them learn part to whole (attribute to category) as well as whole to part (category to attribute). Begin with *providing* categories and move to having them *generate* categories. Providing multiple examples assists students in generating categories. If they do not "get" a category with two examples, or three, try five or six. This can be especially helpful across cultures for students with a nonlinear worldview, or with relational or "divergent" thinkers.

Keep the Characters Straight   (Butcher, 2008) While working on a written work with multiple characters (e.g., Shakespeare), students generate categories that represent a number of different relationships between the characters, and assign a color of paper to each category. Depending on the level and sophistication of the students, the number and quality of relationships varies. Students list the characters under each of the categories on the colored paper, the shape of which they could customize (e.g, red triangle represents complex love relationships) and mount on a single piece of construction paper. In this way, using mediation throughout the process, students come to understand complex relationships among the characters and that one character can belong under multiple categories. For example, they may identify family relationships, protagonists, antagonists, those whose love is spurned versus reciprocated, those who seek revenge, and those who use their cunning and wit to solve their problems.

Check for *Prerequisite Words and Concepts*   Be sure young students, or those with difficulties with *ordering, grouping, and categorizing*, understand key words and concepts. For instance, words and concepts such as *big, bigger, biggest*; *first, second, third*; and *shorter* and *longer* are essential to learn ordering. Build in concrete and tactile activities such as packages of varying weights or sizes and timers of various time lengths to reinforce the concepts. Do something similar for grouping and categorizing (e.g., a table full of blue things; things with right angles) and have them participate in creating the "table."

Find *Categories at Home*   Have your students find categories at home; for instance, things that go on certain kitchen shelves, or in top bedroom drawers. Where do all the socks go, or all the glasses? How might they categorize in their own room or space? Why categorize? This makes the thinking skill personally meaningful. You might also ask what would happen if one drawer had socks, a watch, a candy wrapper, pants, papers, dishes, and a stuffed animal in it? With older students, discuss how a supermarket is organized. Why? Look at the receipts from the store. How are columns organized in categories? Link this to our decimal system.

How might you mediate students in your class who struggle with ordering, grouping, and categorizing?

_____

_____

Finding Connections and Relationships

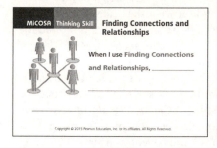

Connections and relationships provide continuity. You see this in families and cultures, in generating ideas, or when seeking and finding the patterns that help solve problems. When students establish *relationships* with efficiency, they find patterns and rules that help them make *connections* between ideas, events, facts, people, or feelings that may have seemed isolated. Those *connections* create meaning. Active and successful learners spontaneously seek *connections and relationships* among events and pieces of information. These students tend to be flexible thinkers and see multiple ways to solve problems. Therefore, finding patterns and relationships becomes central to their developing expertise.

Several types of *connections and relationships* help make your students' work meaningful and expand their understanding. Students might seek linear, causal, parallel, reciprocal, or branching familial relationships. For instance, Susie might seek *parallel relationships* as she tries to *connect* and relate her own prior experiences, insights, and ideas to those of a guest speaker. Jared might discover *causal connections and relationships* when asked to find the impact of the Crusades on trade. Karina uses *mathematical relationships* (e.g., linear, curvilinear, inverse) to find how real and complex numbers relate both arithmetically and graphically. Studying his own family "tree," Felipe sought *branching familial and clan relationships*. Thus, having knowledge of multiple types of relationships opens the world of possibilities to your students. Seeking more than one kind of relationship alongside richness of content supports deeper problem-solving:

> Knowing more means having more conceptual chunks in memory, more relations or features defining each chunk, more interrelations among the chunks and efficient methods for retrieving related chunks and procedures for applying these informational units in problem solving contexts. (Chi et al., 1981)

Many classroom standards overtly address the need to establish *connections and relationships.* You will find that while some standards primarily involve one kind of relationship, more complex standards often require multiple types of relationships. For instance, the Common Core State Standards, Grade 8 Reading Standard III has students analyze how a text makes *connections* among and distinctions between individuals, ideas, or events (e.g., through comparisons, analogies, or categories). Your analysis might draw on temporal, causal, parallel, and spatial relationships. Students can become truly excited when they find more than one kind of relationship. You can enjoy celebrating this kind of "find" with your students, as it characterizes the emergence of what's needed to develop expertise.

Students Inefficient in Finding Connections and Relationships

Students unskilled at making *connections and relationships* tend to be passive as learners. Rather than establish *connections* between ideas, events, facts, people, or feelings, they see and experience the world as disconnected. For example, Mr. Lau asks Pascal how he connects the discussion about Joan of Arc's courage to stand for what she believed in to examples of courage in his own life. He shrugs, responding, "I don't know." He looks around the room, hoping he will be passed over. As an example at a more abstract level, Ms. Williams asks a small group of her students to identify the relationships between the stories *Gleam and Glow* and *I Am Malala.* The students can recount the stories independently, but cannot identify the *connections and relationships*, or the common themes of survival and hope.

The students in Ms. Greene's class articulate the plot of *Caddie Woodlawn* and some characteristics of the main characters such as age, hair, and color, but miss the more abstract character traits such as bullying, inquisitiveness, and adventurousness. Thus, they struggle to generalize and find relationships between the meaning of this story and others.

Another class has worked on numerical progressions; however, when Mr. Baraga asks Kevin to find the pattern and continue the relationships between the numbers 21, 23, 25, 24, 26, 28, 27, _____, _____, and _____, he seems baffled. Kevin responds, "They all have 2's."

What students in your class might struggle with finding connections and relationships?

Mediating Finding Connections and Relationships with Pascal and Kevin   Mediation of *finding connections and relationships* often begins with *connections* between personal experience and that of others. In language arts and social studies, for instance, once students make those relationships between themselves and another person, they then gradually move toward finding relationships between text-to-self, then text-to-text, and finally text-to-world (Harvey & Goudvis, 2007). In mediating, you will move from the concrete to the abstract, such as with concrete traits (brown hair, red dress) to abstract traits (such as kind, brave, or timid). In addition, multiple examples and models (vs. one) at all levels help scaffold the students' generating their own *connections and relationships.*

With Pascal, rather than simply moving to the next student in response to "I don't know," Mr. Lau first allows a discrete six-second pause time. When still unresponsive, Mr. Lau says, "All right, give it a little thought, because I know you'll think of an example, and we will come back to you." Mr. Lau comments to the class, "This is a great opportunity, because I am sure many of us are not sure how our examples from our life might connect with the idea of courage. What is courage?" Defining the abstract trait and its many facets as a class, including what it is NOT (c.f., Frayer, Frederick, & Klausmeier, 1969; Kinsella, 2001), gives an opportunity for all students (including Pascal) to engage and become active. At this point, Mr. Lau offers multiple personal examples: jumping in the deep end of a pool, performing in front of others, admitting to doing something wrong. These multiple examples scaffold the thinking skill development by modeling how students might make their own *connections*. Students then help expand the list, while Mr. Lau writes their examples on the board. Using paired-sharing, students generate further personal experiences, during which Mr. Lau stands near Pascal to make sure he generates an example. He mediates Pascal's sense of competence by simply stating, "That's a good example!"

You often work at a more abstract level when your students seek mathematical relationships. These *connections and relationships* require identifying patterns. Thus, you will want your students to understand the dynamic concepts of patterns and relationships, versus the more static same and different. They must see that patterns repeat, whether they are on fabrics, wallpaper, in nature, in music, or in numerical progressions. Although patterns may be dynamic, the repetition of the pattern lends continuity and predictability to life, as well as to problem solving.

For instance, Mr. Baraga asks Kevin to find the *relationships* within the number sequence, 21, 23, 25, 24, 26, 28, 27, _____, _____, _____. Kevin needs to understand how the relationships between the numbers form patterns. Since his initial response ("they all have 2's") indicates he is not seeking or understanding the idea of a pattern, Mr. Baraga uses questions to check whether he understands the concept. He moves to concrete examples before shifting to the abstract: "Look at these colored blocks. What pattern do you see?" (2 red, 1 blue, 2 red, 1 blue)?" He transfers this to the number pattern, "What happens from one number to the next? Is it getting higher or lower? Good, and the next? Would it be higher or lower?" As Kevin provides the number, Mr. Baraga demonstrates the dynamic flow of the pattern by drawing a series of semicircles looping above the numbers. He then moves to the more precise and accurate relationships by providing space to notate exactly "what happened" between the numbers, as illustrated in Figure 5.1. For instance, if one goes up by two numbers you would notate $+2$; if it goes down by one number, you would use -1.

Once Kevin finds the relationship between each of the numbers, he has to find the pattern, or the larger repeating "chunk." What sequence repeats? Once Kevin finds the $+2+2-1$ pattern, Mr. Baraga asks him to show where it repeated, and then to add the pattern to the chart, concluding by filling in the numbers that followed the pattern.

As before, multiple examples showing different kinds of patterns to Kevin or to his whole class help them generate more possibilities. For instance, a pattern might be that the numbers within the digits are additive, as in Figure 5.2.

FIGURE 5.1

Finding Relationships in Number Patterns

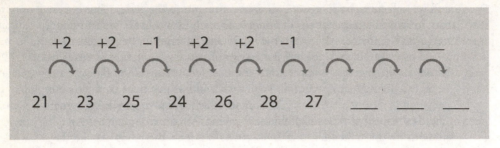

FIGURE 5.2

Example of Number Pattern with Digits as Additive

3	5	8	13	21	34	55	___	___

As you help students "bridge" their skills with this kind of problem to the implications for real life, motivation increases. For instance, Kevin struggles to find patterns—and thus, meaning—in what appears to be otherwise unrelated sets of numbers. As his understanding of patterns and relationships emerges, you will point out the parallels to tackling larger life problems. Often, events or items may seem unrelated or even chaotic. Rather than walking away, Kevin is now prepared to struggle to make *connections* and find meaningful relationships, and perhaps to solve larger real-world problems.

Strategies and Activities Supporting Mediation of Finding Connections and Relationships

Engage Students with *KWHL*   Connect prior knowledge to incoming knowledge by seeking relationships. KWHL charts (c.f., enchantedlearning.com) can facilitate this work. Using the "K" (What do you think you *Know*) allows students to share their prior ideas and conceptions without assuming they are based in fact. This helps you and your students be aware of misconceptions or culturally different constructions of ideas. Continue with the acronym, asking students the "W" (*What* do you want to learn?), the "H" (*How* are you going to find out the information?), and the "L" (What did you *learn* after you did the research?). When your students complete the learning, they go back to their notes and seek *patterns and relationships* between their earlier thinking and the more recent.

Employ Web-Based Programs Like *Inspiration (inspiration.com)* This computer-based mind-mapping or concept-mapping program allows students to map out ideas in a nonlinear form, and find and make *connections* between them. Students write individual ideas and then draw lines between the related ideas. The ideas and relationships initially appear as a mind map full of circles and connecting lines. At the click of a button, the program reorganizes this "map" into a linear outline that the students can easily transfer to a written form. Students with relational thinking and learning styles find this especially useful.

Use *GO Relationships!* Graphic organizers (GO) help students structure relationships. Organizers help them establish initial relationships between key words, concepts, and upcoming assignments.

In literature, social studies, or science, graphic organizers can help students predict categories and elements of a plot or problem (Education Place, 2013). For instance, you might give students a list of key words from one section of a science text, as well as the list of the subheadings. Then ask students to hypothesize under which subheading (e.g., category) each given word or concept belongs. For example, in an article about the usefulness of potatoes, where would the word *inoculate* belong? Does it belong under the heading: The Potato Plant, The Potato Famine of Ireland, or The Use of the Potato in Medicine? By creating this graphic together, you demonstrate the relationships between words and categories in advance of reading the text. Using the thinking skill of *finding connections and relationships*, students have begun their conceptual work on the topic. Now they can dive into the text and see whether their predictions are accurate.

As an alternative, the categories may also be elements of a story, such as character, setting, problem, and solution. Students *establish relationships* between given words and the story elements. You can prompt with such questions as, "How is the word *river* related to setting, problem, or solution? Where does it best fit?" The completed relationship groups allow you to work with your class to predict the whole story, using their graphic organizers. After reading, they compare the two (Action Learning Systems, 2003). Having predicted relationships and meaning prior to engagement not only helps reinforce *connections and relationships,* but also promotes active learning, and can then serve as a study guide.

Stimulate *Free Association* Use association games to promote initial forms of *connections and relationships* (e.g., "If I say *table*, what comes to mind? Which of your ideas are related, and how?"). Have your students articulate relationships that emerge, so they begin to see that *connections and relationships* can lead to the use of categories. Further, they will learn that those categories can be different, depending on the context.

Play *Analogy Games* Use analogy games and activities to promote *connections and relationships*. For example, "Bird is to nest as lion is to _____." Then say why, so others learn from the whole. Have them work in teams to invent analogies for others in the class to guess.

Connect Knowledge   Ask your students to connect what they learned yesterday with what you will introduce today. This helps them gain a sense of continuity. They can refer to their own notes, thoughts, and work, examining and self-evaluating those relationships over time. Connect this to goals your students have set for themselves.

PD ⬤ TOOLKIT™

PDToolkit: See Video Clip 5.2 for an example of making both cognitive and interpersonal *connections* through *Postcards* with a group of educators.

Deepen Connections Using Postcards   Give each student a notecard. Select a book to read aloud that lends itself to your students making personal *connections*. Make an electronic representation (e.g., jpeg, pdf) of a picture from the book, or one related to the content you will read. Display the picture while you read. Pause after reading a few pages, selecting a point in which you feel students can make a strong personal connection. Ask them to take a few minutes to jot down on their "postcard" a personal connection, question, statement, or emotion they have about the text. Now, ask them to trade cards with their partner, read what the other has written, and respond in writing to their connection. Repeat this process again, where the original writer responds to the partner's response. Each writer makes at least two entries on the card before you read on, repeating this strategy of read-stop-respond. Discuss the ways that *connections and relationships* influence one another as well as the understanding of the story. This activity also promotes collaboration, because both writers influence each other; as a result, they alter their thinking, explain more, and think more deeply about their connections (Chancer, 2000).

Introduce For Want of a Nail   This expression comes from the following poem (author unknown):

> For want of a nail, a shoe was lost
> For want of a shoe, a horse was lost
> For want of a horse, a rider was lost
> For want of a rider, a battle was lost
> For want of a battle, a kingdom was lost
> All for the sake of a horseshoe nail

Use this rhyme to introduce the idea of *connections and relationships*, and how even one small thing can connect to a large picture. Refer to the "ripple effect," or the "domino effect." Have students share examples. While this activity can also connect closely to using *cause and effect*, have students discuss the implied relationships. You can do this with pairs or groups, enriching the discussion.

How might you mediate students in your class who struggle with finding connections and relationships?

_____

_____

Visualizing

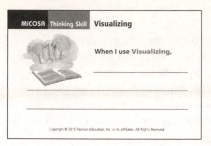

As you observe the world around you, you store images subconsciously as pictures in your mind. What you hear, touch, smell, and feel at the time often gets stored along with those visual images, influencing your memory. Thus, visual memory takes on unique characteristics. *Visualizing* is a powerful thinking skill that can be used to evoke past images or to imagine future ones.

"Visualize your childhood home." This direction asks you to evoke your image from memory. Your "picture" may be of a very large rambling home. The smells of honeysuckle drape the arbor, creating a feeling of warmth you impose onto the image. For some of your students, it may evoke a spot in a country left behind, filled with emotions of loss. Whatever the images, they become part of your students' prior knowledge that you can draw upon to help them create meaningful *connections* to new content. Deliberately evoking visual images supports future learning.

In addition, your students will rely on *visualizing* to project toward the future. They might *imagine* what a future car might look like, given the constraint on oil production, the reality of high gas prices, and the impact of drilling and spillage on the environment. This *visualization* of the future will be key to the creativity needed in the 21st century.

From verbal descriptions and text, Nick builds new visual images, drawing from the ones he had stored in memory. These new visualizations become essential building blocks in his reading comprehension. Because the visualizations draw on his prior knowledge, they provide a motivational and cognitive link to the new information and text. They say a picture is worth a thousand words. In this case, the imagery allows him to synthesize and hold a whole chunk of text with meaning, instead of trying to remember all the words. Because *visualizing* also links feelings and emotions with the chunks of text, the visuals become motivators to move forward with the plot (see also Beers, 2003). As Nick reads a page of text, he stops and forms images that support new information. As he reads on, he readjusts those images to embrace the new content. When Emilia is learning to create imagery in her writing, she carefully considers the language she uses, using words and word combinations that will trigger rich sensory images. For instance, she writes about her aunt's sweet peppermint breath and the rustling of her skirt as she waddles into the kitchen. Visual representations such as graphic organizers help support conceptualization, but they are *not* the same as *visualizing* as a thinking skill. You might think of them as "cousins" to *visualizing*.

Students Inefficient in Visualizing

Some students "overuse" their own prior visual associations, failing to draw sufficiently from verbal cues or text. Because of this, they do not synthesize adequately. For instance, Victor's teacher, Mr. Osetzky, asks him to draw a visual image of the hurricane he reads about in a story. Because of his own prior experience, Victor draws a house with windows boarded up, and concludes that the character Ana feels safe because of the boarded up windows. However, within the story, Ana's house has not had the windows boarded up. Victor has missed that Ana does not feel safe because the windows have not been protected.

For David, forming the image is difficult. He had begun to struggle with reading in third grade, as well as exhibit comprehension problems. By seventh grade, he "hates reading," and seldom finishes a book, even when it is self-selected. He is demonstrating difficulty in understanding the text on the Lewis and Clark expedition, even though he can decode the text fluently. His teacher asks him to draw a picture of what he visualizes in the first section of the reading. His image is sparse, including only a minor detail from the passage, rather than illustrating a main concept.

What students in your class might struggle with visualizing?

_____

Mediating Visualizing with Victor and David   To mediate *visualizing* skills, deliberately stimulate the skill, and give students time to form images by pausing during instruction for that purpose. Ask overt questions such as, "What do you see in your mind's eye?" or share through modeling, "When I read this I can see. . . ." Dim the lights and create a quiet atmosphere by "whisper talking" to reduce external stimuli and help foster your students' focus on the internal.

In the case of Victor, his prior experience detracts from his accuracy in *visualizing.* Mr. Osetzky uses a whole class activity to discuss the importance not only of forming images, but also of changing some of those images as the story progresses. To begin, he reads a story called *FISH* (Regents of the University of California Reading & Literature Project, 2013), designed to support the need to adapt *visualizing* (see Figure 5.3).

Students draw pictures in conjunction with each section of the six segments of the story. Each segment adds a new element requiring students to begin shifting their thinking and *visualizing* to accommodate new information. Some will have great difficulty sticking to their initial image. This indicates that these students may struggle with comprehending text. If their *visualizing* (plus *inference*) skills are efficient, they will have fully made meaning by around the third of six pieces of information. Others, such as Victor, need all six prompts to discover that the story is about a fish.

Victor's teacher then moves to a parallel story, *Park Venture Story* in order to mediate *visualizing* and *inference* skills. He begins by reading the first paragraph and asking students to create an image of what they visualize. This time, however, they overtly discuss how they combine prior experience and current stimulus to create their images. Following the second and subsequent sections and drawings, he highlights the need to shift the image(s) based on new information. Individual examples from other students allow Victor to contribute his experiences and to modify his drawing.

David's teacher, Mr. Nolan, begins to mediate using an exercise seeking direct stimulation of *visualizing.* Drawing the analogy to movies, he asks students to close their eyes while they begin to hear the story of *Lewis and Clark.* They will try to picture and create a movie in their minds as they listen. As they get "pictures," they indicate their success

PD **[PD** TOOLKIT™

PDToolkit:
**Park Venture Story
is found in the
PDToolkit.**

FIGURE 5.3

FISH story

You have never met me, so I'm going to tell you all about me.

I'm not very big, but I'm very active. I have a father and a mother. I have many sisters, brothers, cousins, aunts, and uncles.

Are you wondering what I look like? Use your imagination.

Draw a picture of me in box one. **(Pause)**

After you have heard more of my story, you may change your mind about the way I look.

I have a home. It's a most interesting home. It is very cool and comfortable. My large family and I have plenty of room in our home. It is very big.

Some day you, your mother, father, sisters, brothers, cousins, aunts, and uncles may come to visit me. There will be plenty of room for all of us. Why not bring the neighbors?

Bring all of your school friends, too.

I have heard that some day you and your friends may decide to live in my home. We will not be crowded. But be sure to bring your own oxygen.

Now, do you know where I live? Be careful. Think about what you've heard.

In box two, draw a picture of my home. **(Pause)**

Did you make your best prediction?

I like to play games. Tag is one of my favorite games. My favorite sport is swimming. It seems to me I've been swimming all my life.

In box three, draw a picture of the way you think I look. **(Pause)**

What is your favorite game? What is your favorite sport?

I am sometimes in a school with other boys and girls. My school is quite different from yours. Most of the time we just swim and play tag. Would you like to be in a school like that?

In box four, draw a picture of my school. **(Pause).**

Do you know me now? Keep thinking.

Some plants are very important to me. In fact, I happen to know you use one of the same plants I use. You eat it in ice cream. Do you know the name of the plant we both use?

Now turn your paper over. Draw a picture or write the name of the plant in box five.

I'll tell you the name of the food. Its name is Kelp. It helps make ice cream stay hard and not melt so quickly. It also makes it sm-o-o—o-th! Kelp grows at the bottom of these where I live. Have you changed your mind about the way I look?

Draw my picture in box six. **(Pause)**

---

with a "thumbs up." At the end of the first section, each of them talks about their pictures. Mr. Nolan prompts the group by saying, "Wow, that was amazing that two of you already have a movie started. Let's see how many of you get one with the next section," and then proceeds to section two. A few more, including David, begin to have a "movie" appear in their minds. Mr. Nolan continues, asking students to keep their thumbs up as their "mind movies" stay with them throughout the rest of the story. He asks randomly for one at a time to share a current picture. Intentional moving into the abstract ("mind movies") builds on the fact that some students who appear to struggle at the concrete level actually blossom when given the opportunity to work at a more abstract level.

Strategies Supporting Mediation of Visualizing

Prompt Visualizing with *Imagine That!* Read a story designed to prompt visual images that change with textual change. Ask your students to draw the image that comes to their minds with each prompt. After the first experience (which may be used as an assessment), use that story or a parallel story to highlight the processes of integration of personal experience and textually based content. Change and modify the visual images based on new information. Sample stories and mediation include *FISH* (previously used with Victor) and *Park Venture Story* (in PDToolkit).

Make *Mental Movies* Prompt students to create "mental movies" as you read a text. Avoid showing images or illustrations from the text that might influence students' developing their own images. Encourage them to focus on holding and shifting their "movie" mentally. When proficient, move to pairing mental movies with the texts they read (see the previous example of David).

Create *Storyboards* To help students learn to hold images over time and support comprehension of longer text, use storyboarding. Students draw their images, which represent each chapter, time period, or major event. They share some of those out loud with the class, which fosters gaining the main ideas (e.g., what was important to have drawn about). They sequence those on a "concertina," folded paper or poster paper, so that they can build the sequence of events from their visualization. They can then retell at the end orally, or write from their picture prompts. Students can produce them as iMovies or PowerPoint presentations or post them to TeacherTube or SchoolTube.

Use the Activity *Book Hooks* This strategy encourages students to make book recommendations to their peers. As the recommender shares a portion of the story, it creates a visual "hook" onto which the new student can connect. One at a time, each student talks for an entire minute about the story, attempting to create an image that will "hook" his or her friends on reading it. Using "pair-share," students do this three times (Beers, 2003).

Draw That Tune Use music as a prompt, and elicit student visuals in a variety of modalities (e.g., pencil, oil pastels, collages).

How might you mediate students in your class who struggle with visualizing?

_____

_____

Inferring

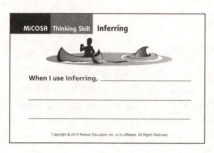

You see a picture of bare trees and snow. Based on your past experiences, you draw the *inference* that the scene occurs in winter. However, without the experience or knowledge of the coldness of snow, or the loss of certain trees' leaves in winter, you cannot *infer* this. The thinking skill of *inferring* involves moving from one piece of information you consider as true to another whose truth you believe follows from the first one. Thus, when you *infer*, you draw conclusions based on information considered true. *Inferring* involves developing insight and helping students "see the light." To *infer* efficiently requires a number of skills. Eduscapes (2009) proposes several of these skills:

- Collecting and analyzing evidence
- Making connections between prior knowledge and new information
- Making predictions
- Drawing conclusions

Visualizing, forming mental images, supports *inferring*. For instance, when you see a picture or develop a mental image of someone wiping water droplets from his or her brow, you may *infer* that the person is hot and feels uncomfortable. When reading, you often consider *inferring* as "reading between the lines" as you make connections between pieces of text, experiences, or information. For example, Joel has a mental picture of the story that he is reading of the single story haunted house, with the main character huddled in the closet of the bedroom near the back door, and the knife-yielding thief barging through the front door. He can *infer* that the boy in the story is afraid. In addition, he may then be able to predict that the boy will attempt to escape, probably through the back door. This evokes a heightened emotional connectedness with the story, and even engages similar emotions in the reader. This creates the need to resolve the fear and, therefore, establish a motivation to continue reading. Thus, in reading, *inferring* also supports students when they *hypothesize* and predict.

Used across the curriculum, *inferring* often refers to drawing logical conclusions. For instance, in a fifth grade science lesson, the teacher has students put a piece of clay on their pulses and insert small straws into the ball of clay, observing what happens (California Science, 2008). As the students observe the movement of the straws at consistent intervals, the teacher prompts, "What can you *infer* from what you observed and from what you knew before from our study of the heart?" They then begin to *infer* that the pumping of blood through the artery causes the movement. She mediates meaning, suggesting that using the thinking skill *inferring* helps them learn to draw conclusions.

Students often must make multiple *inferences* to glean total meaning. Individual *inferences* need to be mentally gathered together, synthesized, and labeled. For instance, to come up with a novel's theme, students must follow more than one set of *inferences* simultaneously, labeling the theme. Thus, students efficient with *inferring* readily identify themes.

Students Inefficient with Inferring

Inferring is key to critical thinking, so it is vital to your students. When inefficient in using inferential thinking, students often have difficulty drawing conclusions or in gathering sufficient information to make decisions. Some of these difficulties may stem from a reading fluency problem. If a student struggles to decode individual words, he or she has little capacity in short-term memory for comprehension. As a result, these students cannot efficiently monitor their own comprehension (i.e., metacognitively). They will be less likely to shift strategies or verify their interpretations of the text's meaning. They may miss the subtleties of the text and lose the *inference*. Building fluency, therefore, is crucial, and supports our students' ability to *infer*.

Inferential thinking is extremely complex. It requires students to collect, analyze, sort, select, and predict from information. Your students may struggle with any one of those components or with related thinking skills, such as gathering and using *multiple sources* of information. Examine some examples of these common errors (Eduscapes.com):

a. Reaching conclusions based on partial information
b. Using insufficient relevant clues
c. Focusing on literal interpretations
d. Over-relying on personal experience
e. Basing conclusions on opinions rather than facts

(a) *Reaching conclusions based on partial information.* Gerardo is reading about Yo-Yo Ma's medical issues and how they influence him when playing the cello (Zimbler, 2009). Having read only part of the sentence, Gerardo wrongly infers that during the time of his issues, Ma could not play the cello. Because he has not gathered and used *multiple sources* of information, Gerardo's *inference* is incorrect.

(b) *Using insufficient relevant clues.* Ian, a seventh grade student, does not pick up sufficient relevant clues to support his *inferences*. In the story *Duffy's Jacket* (eolit.hrw .com), the main character, Duffy, consistently forgets his personal items. Concurrently, the storyline interweaves elements of tension and fear (e.g., fear at the parents' absence; a sign on the cabin wall warning about the Sentinel). Thus, in the end, when a wild looking stranger comes in the night to return Duffy's forgotten jacket, Duffy is terrified that the Sentinel has arrived. Ian fails to note cues throughout the story that foreshadowed the feelings of fear at its climax or the parallel foreshadowing of Duffy's forgetfulness. Thus, Ian cannot begin to *infer* automatically as he reads. He misses the meaning of the climax. When asked to identify the story's foreshadowing, he has no idea.

(c) *Focusing on literal interpretations.* Ms. Begay asks her tenth grade class to *infer* the meaning of a political cartoon in which a military official carries off a large sack of money while Uncle Sam stands by, raising his hands and shrugging his shoulders. Beside Uncle Sam, a woman holds the hand of her child, and asks: "Will there be enough money for education?" (Frey & Bower, 2004). Garrett's difficulty with *inferring* leads to his replying with a literal interpretation: "The military man is taking all the money." He misses the *inference* that excessive military spending creates deficits in social funding, such as education.

(d) *Over-relying on personal experience.* Some students tend to overuse personal experience, missing the subtleties from their texts. In the earlier example (in *visualizing*), Victor relies too heavily on his traumatic prior experience with hurricanes, and *infers* that what would happen to the child in the story will parallel his own experience. Thus, Victor *infers* incorrectly that the child will be evacuated, as had been his experience. He misses the whole point of the child staying in the home and enduring the fury of the hurricane.

(e) *Basing conclusions on opinions rather than facts.* This can distort the interpretation of text, and thus of *inference*. Going back to the political cartoon, Zack does not pull out an *inference*; rather, he so overinvests in his own opinions that all he can say is "The president just doesn't care!" He misses the more general concept of distribution of wealth and prioritizing education and military spending. Such students usually lack the built-in habit of seeking logical evidence as well.

What students in your class might struggle with inferring?

Mediating Inferring with Ian and Garrett

To target mediation of *inferring*, first determine the source of the difficulty. For instance, does your student jump to conclusions based on partial information, overlooking important clues, or focus on literal interpretation? If students are using partial information or overlooking clues, begin by examining their use of *multiple sources, self-regulation* in gathering information, and *finding connections and relationships*. Mediate their self-regulation, so they gather all the information at a useful pace. Graphic organizers can support this, as seeing the relationships and patterns support developing *inference*.

In the case of Ian, who misses relevant clues to Duffy's forgetfulness and fear, you might mediate *finding connections and relationships,* helping him gain competence by using clues to gain the *inference*. Ian sees the potential clues as random acts in the story, rather than cues connected to future events. You can help him seek *connections* between the clues and *relationships* with the ending that predicts it. For instance, begin by asking, "What clues or connections in the story help us know why the stranger appeared frightening to the children?" Follow his response, "Yes, the low light, children being left alone, the isolated cabin, and sign about the Sentinel are all excellent clues." Mediate meaning, "When you begin to make these *connections* and see the *relationships*, then you are starting to make good *inferences*!"

To mediate and strengthen *inferring* in language arts, use well-known stories from your students' cultural backgrounds to enrich the experience and build cross-cultural appreciation. Movies, fairy tales, and legends lend themselves well to developing skills with *inference*. For instance, in *Little Red Riding Hood*, you can model foreshadowing (*inference* for prediction) by stopping at the paragraph in which Red Riding Hood reveals that her grandma lives down "Lonely Lane" far, far away (eolit.hrw.com). Have your students predict or *infer* what will occur to Little Red Riding Hood based on the "clue."

In the case of the political cartoon, Garrett relies too heavily on literal interpretation. To mediate, first acknowledge his literal telling, so that you build reciprocity rather than implying that you must correct him. "Yes, the military is carrying out the money. What might that mean? This can be tricky. You know that no military leader is walking around with a sack of money on his back, so what might that represent, Garrett?" Here, walk the student toward *inferring* that this symbolizes the military as an organization (vs. one man) taking money from the treasury (vs. in a bag). Further, suggest that the symbol of Uncle Sam represents the federal government. This mediation requires your students to use multiple symbols, and helps them connect symbols and *inference*. Here, they need to use *multiple sources* of information and understand symbols, as well as use *inference* to glean the meaning. Often, having small group discussions about multiple examples helps students build this kind of relationship mentally.

Strategies and Activities Supporting Mediation of Inferring

Practice with Quia   A wonderful and playful resource, the Quia website (www.quia .com) helps students practice *inferential thinking*. Multiple choices allow for differentiating *inference* from prior experience or guessing.

Use the *Socratic Seminar*   Students who have read the same text sit in a circle with observers behind them in a concentric circle. The appointed leader introduces a question, and students give their opinions, backing up their opinions with facts from the text. From this question, the leader or another in the group asks a further question (www .socraticseminar.com).

Introduce the *Inference Riddles Website*   The website www.philtuga.com/ riddles provides fun graduated prompts and levels of difficulty for making *inferences* from pre-made riddles. You can extend this activity by having your students create their own riddles, which show off their knowledge in science or social studies.

Employ *Under the Surface Strategies*   *Inferring* means digging mentally "below the surface." Thus, the terms *on the surface* and *under the surface* help students differentiate *literal* from *inference*. Mediating *inferring* may require more focus on understanding signs and symbols. Begin with the familiar to support this work. You will sequence *under the surface* strategies using: (1) signs, (2) symbols, (3) pictures, and then (4) text (Action Learning Systems, 2010).

- *Under the Surface: Signs and Gestures.* Show a familiar sign (e.g., road sign, mathematical signs, gesture from sign language) and ask, "What do you see on the surface?" (yellow pentagon, outline of student). "Now, what is under the surface— what can we *infer* that this means?" (school, students present, proceed with care).

- *Under the Surface: Symbols.* Show symbols (e.g., flag, ring, Statue of Liberty) and ask what they see on the surface, then what it means under the surface. Symbols are greatly influenced by culture; therefore, begin with culturally familiar symbols.

- *Under the Surface: Pictures.* Use pictures to prompt students to generate on the surface and under the surface questions. Begin with a picture that tells a story; for example, an historical picture depicting the Western Movement. Ask students, "What do you see on the surface?" (a woman cooking over a fire, a boy with a bundle of sticks on his back, five men on top of a roof). Expect some students to *infer* immediately, such as, "The woman looks hot," or "She's cooking breakfast." Help them differentiate on and under the surface by asking, "Can you see that in the picture?" Now ask them to look under the surface and see what is *inferred*. Now they can *infer* she's hot and perhaps cooking breakfast, and the child is tired of the burden of carrying the sticks. Repeat this with a couple of pictures to ensure understanding. Norman Rockwell's artwork provides superb examples, as there are always hidden messages beneath his pictures (Action Learning Systems, 2010).

- *Under the Surface: Text.* Display a simple text on a document camera (or overhead). Read together and ask students on the surface questions. When students respond, take a blank piece of paper and "lift" the projected image by moving the paper forward from the wall with their answer from the text on the paper, illustrating that the answer can be found within the text itself. Now ask under the surface questions and students will discover that they cannot lift the answer from the text itself; they must *infer* (Action Learning Systems, 2010).

How might you mediate students in your class who struggle with inferring?

_____

_____

Cause and Effect—Hypothesizing

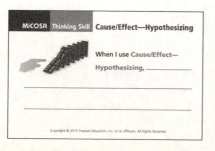

MiCOSA Thinking Skill Cause/Effect—Hypothesizing

When I use Cause/Effect—

Hypothesizing, _____

_____

_____

Cause-effect thinking goes beyond seeking relationships alone, because it seeks *reasons* for these relationships. It identifies the rules or patterns of causation. You find *cause-effect* thinking throughout curriculum; for instance, "What were the major *causes* of the Civil War?" "What are four major *effects* of global warming?" *Cause-effect* relationships tend to deal with past or current situations (WHEN-THEN), and be drawn from factual information in a linear fashion. Key words and phrases that cue *cause-effect* thinking include *because*, *as a result*, *therefore*, and sometimes *why* and *analyze the reasons*.

Although often linked to *cause-effect*, *hypothesizing* asks students to consider "IF-THEN" relationships. You see this within the scientific method. For instance, Carl *hypothesizes* that *if* he plants one tomato plant in sand, one in garden soil, and the third in Miracle Grow, and waters them all once a week, *then* within one month, significant differences between each will occur, with the third tomato plant growing three times as tall as the first. He tests the *hypothesis* with an experiment to generate the evidence.

Hypothesizing is based on situations that are not real, but could be. It helps students test out their worlds, based on educated guesses. *Hypothesizing*, prompted by *"what if . . . pretend . . ."* can also foster imagination and creativity. You might ask, "What if you entered a game show and won $1,000,000 for a charity of your choice? What charity or cause would you donate to? Why did you make the choice you did, and how would you like to see the money used to support the cause?" This allows students to think safely beyond the accepted norm. It helps them test boundaries as well as assumptions. For instance, *"What if I decide to leave home?"* *Hypothesizing* also leads students to engage in prediction.

Students need to become flexible and critical thinkers; thus, practice in developing options, *hypotheses,* and alternatives support this behavior. Students who develop alternatives generate more than one way to do things, more than one plan, or various options when initial plans do not play out as hoped. *Hypothesizing* is at the core of this.

How are *cause-effect and hypothesizing* related? You might see this as a continuum in which *cause-effect* deals with the past or current reality (WHEN-THEN) and *hypothesizing* moves into the abstract or imagined future (IF-THEN). Understanding *cause and effect*, for instance, might lead to the generation of specific *hypothesizing* for the future. For instance, in history, Daniel learns that WHEN economic decline, attacks on borders, excessive military spending, political corruption, and unemployment occurred in ancient Rome, THEN Rome fell (*cause-effect*). From this, he *hypothesizes* that IF the United States has economic decline, attacks on its borders, political corruption, excessive military spending, and unemployment, THEN it may lead to the decline of the United States.

Sometimes *hypothesizing* (IF-THEN) helps students learn prediction. For instance, Ms. Patterson asks her students to *hypothesize* or imagine themselves as the character Pedro in the story *Pedro's Journal,* when Pedro was being goaded into jumping into the water and could not swim. IF they were Pedro, and non-swimmers, THEN what would they do? How would they handle the situation and why (presenting evidence)?

Curriculum standards suggest that students use *hypothesizing* as early as kindergarten. Thus, at an early age you engage students in *hypothesizing*: "What would happen if . . . ?"

Students Inefficient with Cause and Effect—Hypothesizing

Students inefficient with *cause and effect—hypothesizing* often get caught in inflexible modes of behavior, academically as well as socially. They tend not to learn from their errors, and seem to have limited thinking. They often get "stuck" and may appear to block, when in fact they have not learned to generate options ("plans b and c"), generate contingency (alternative) plans, or see causative relationships.

For example, Robbie frequently gets into trouble at recess because he takes the ball away from other students, and then flies into a rage when others want it back. He repeats this behavior daily, and never seems to learn from the previous experience. Robbie does not see his behavior (taking the ball away) as *causative* to the other students' anger, the *effect*. His raging, the secondary *effect*, at times becomes violent. This puts Robbie at risk of expulsion.

One of the issues you may face with students is *flexibility*. For example, Akiva forgets to bring her book to class, and then chooses not to participate. Akiva has become stuck in her one option (no book *causes* no work) and has not generated *hypothetical* options for solving her problem. Frank does not spontaneously consider options while working with his team to generate geographic research on the Civil War. Ms. Bull has asked them to put their findings on a large map of the United States, but they find that the computer lab they work in has no space for the large map. When Frank finds information on the computer, he gets stuck, since he had planned to transfer it immediately to the big map, and the map is not in the room. He looks baffled, and says, "We can't do it now."

Often, students confuse sequences and causation. For example, when asked what *caused* the character Billy in the story to hurry to school that morning, Lionel replies, "He got up, brushed his teeth, ate breakfast, put on his backpack, and ran to school." Lionel sequences the events, rather than responding to the question of *cause*, which had been Billy's excitement about giving out birthday invitations before school started. In another example, students read a story about six people dying in Canada from *E. coli*. Because the story begins with the *effect* (people dying) and next discussed the *cause* (bacteria in the water), several students reported that the *cause* is people dying and the *effect* is the bacteria in the water, because the story presents the events in this sequence. Clearly they confuse *cause-effect* conceptually as well as sequentially. Another problem occurs when students do not realize there can be multiple *causes* and multiple *effects*. *Effects* of one *cause* can become *causes* of a new *effect*.

What students in your class might struggle with cause and effect—hypothesizing?

Mediating Cause and Effect—Hypothesizing with Robbie, Lionel, Akiva, and Frank

Hypothesizing and understanding *causative* behavior goes beyond science and literature, and links well with social behaviors and self-regulation as well. Mediating these skills often helps students come to understand the *causes and effects* of their own behaviors. Your mediation, using bridging, can help them see the relationships and links.

Cause and effect—hypothesizing can help students predict that if they do certain things, then there will be predictable results. Students need to look at multiple potential *causes and effects* of social interactions, for instance, to build flexibility in their actions and responses. Ms. Dranger works with Robbie on the issue of taking balls, first defining the problem and then discussing *cause and effect*. Rather than saying, "The problem with you is . . ." she says, "What IS the problem here?" He has to define his own problem. Rather like *goal setting* sets up the need to gather information, identifying the problem sets up the need to understand *cause and effect*. It also becomes the precursor of *hypothesizing* options to solve the problem. Once Robbie defines the problem (wanting to play with the ball and not having it), then he starts to understand the *effects* of his actions (taking the ball).

Now, he can generate alternate behaviors to get what he wants (e.g., ask when he could use the ball; ask to join the group; seek another ball; select an alternate activity).

In the case of Lionel (who confuses sequence and causation), his teacher first simplifies the language of the concept of *cause* (e.g., what made that happen) and *effect* (e.g., what happened as a result of it). Once he begins to understand the difference between sequence and *causation*, he sees the cause of the character's rush to school in the story. However, you must be cautious of the nature of your simplification. Sometimes teachers inadvertently use language that leads to the sequencing/*causation* confusion. For instance, if you use the words *before* and *after* to simplify the concepts, students can confuse *causation* with sequencing, and tend to think that whatever came before or first *caused* whatever came next in the sequence of the story.

As students learn scientific experimentation, sequence and *causation* become more straightforward, as they often perform experiments in the sequence of "*cause-effect.*" For instance, WHEN they combine vinegar and baking soda underneath the model volcano, THEN it erupts. The *cause,* combining vinegar and baking soda, clearly leads to the *effect,* "eruption" or chemical reaction. In another example, students can observe the *effects* of caffeine on blood pressure by manipulating the *cause* (e.g., drinking or not drinking caffeinated drinks) and measuring the *effect* by taking blood pressure. Thus, as scientists later try to determine *causes* of observed *effects* (e.g., disease), the concept of *causation* is well in hand.

With Akiva, who brings no book to class and has only one *cause-effect* in mind, Mr. Walsh engages multiple *hypotheses* to promote flexibility (plan a, plan b, plan c). *Hypothesizing* leads Akiva to consider alternative possibilities to provide optional behaviors with more positive results. IF I come to class without a book, THEN I will have to find a way to work in class (vs. THEN I can't do anything). This creates an activity from which alternate choices can be brainstormed (e.g., IF I come to class without a book, in order to do my work, THEN I could ask for another book; ask to share someone's book). On the other hand, IF I do NOT think of a good plan, THEN I will not be successful. To mediate, Mr. Walsh has the whole class engage in an activity of creating alternative plans (a, b, c) in challenging circumstances. This supports everyone's flexibility and provides a way to bridge to Akiva's challenge.

When Frank gets stuck with the issue of transferring information from the computer to the large map outside the class, another student offers an option. "IF we print out a small map of the United States and we put it here beside the computer, and mark the information on it, THEN we can later transfer it to our big map." This model of flexible thinking provides his teacher, Ms. Bull, with an opportunity to talk about the value of alternative plans. She validates the idea and encourages the class to think of two other options using *hypothesizing*, and then to choose the best.

PD TOOLKIT™

PDToolkit:
See Video Clip 5.3 for examples of establishing students' prior knowledge about *cause-effect,* finding applications, and bridging their use of *cause-effect* using the strategy *Find Your Match.*
See Video Clip 5.4 for a reflection on using hypothesizing with students.

Strategies and Activities Supporting Mediation of Cause-Effect and Hypothesizing

Graph the Cues   Key words that "cue" *cause* or *effect* can help your students learn to identify and differentiate *cause* from *effect*. However, without understanding that the

FIGURE 5.4

Cue Words When Cause Comes Prior to Effect in Text

Cue Words Indicating Cause (Can be explicit or implied)		Cause from Text	Cue Words Indicating Effect (Can be explicit or implied)		Effect from Text
When *Since* *Because* *Due to* *On account of* *As a result of*	➡	storm clouds formed, Storm clouds formed, storm clouds forming, Storm clouds were forming,	*then* *so* *therefore* *thus* *hence*	➡	it started to rain.

sequence of the *cause and effect* may be interchangeable in sentences, students may still struggle with these concepts, especially English Language Learners. The Graphing the Cues charts support students' efforts in untangling these concepts.

Figure 5.4 illustrates using cue words to identify *cause and effect* when *cause* precedes *effect* in a sentence. When *cause* precedes *effect*, then key *cause* words (e.g., *when, since, because*) come before the cause in text—that is why they are called "cue words." The cue *effect* words precede the actual effects in text. For example, *When* storm clouds formed (*cause*), *then* it started to rain (*effect*). However, when one of the key *cause* words is used, the key *effect* words are not always necessary. Example: *When* storm clouds formed [cause], it started to rain [*effect*]. Conversely, when one of the key *cause* words is not used, the key effect words are necessary. Example: Storm clouds formed [cause]; *therefore,* it started to rain [*effect*].

These words overtly cue *cause and effect*. Learning words that imply *cause and effect* is more challenging. When *effect* precedes *cause* in a sentence, students often get confused. For example, Storm clouds formed *and* it began to rain. Figure 5.5 illustrates the use of the cue words with this "reverse" sequence. When *effect* precedes *cause*, the key *effect* words such as *then, so,* or *therefore* are not used! Example: It started to rain (effect) when storm clouds formed (cause).

You can use these graphic organizers to have students fill in the "blanks" from their own texts, or to model how it works. Practice using them supports enhanced efficiency. For instance, have the students write down as many combinations of sentences using *cause and effect* words as they can. Using the cue word graphic organizer (Figures 5.4 and 5.5), have students create their own cause and effect sentences, and then identify cause in one color and effect in another. For English Language Learners, provide visual support when you can, and have them generate multiple examples, as they are learning both words and concepts.

FIGURE 5.5

Cue Words When the Effect Comes Prior to the Cause in the Text

Key Words Indicating Effect (Not needed in this sequence)	Effect from Text	Key Words Showing Cause		Cause from Text
Then So Therefore Thus Hence	It started to rain	when since because due to as a result of on account of	→	storm clouds formed. storm clouds were forming. storm clouds forming.

Play the *What-If Lunch Bag Game*   At the beginning of the year, share the following rule: All students consider themselves problem-solvers. To practice problem-solving, play the "what if" game. Write typical classroom-based problems (e.g., I forgot my pencil; I saw someone being bullied; I finished my work early) on strips of paper and place them in a bag. Ask one student to pull out one of the problems and pose it to the class. That student asks the group, "What if . . . [I forgot my pencil]?" The class must then generate at least three responses to the *hypothetical* question that match the guidelines. Student guidelines require students to: (a) show active responsibility and (b) generate ideas possible to find within the confines of the classroom. When a response is generated that meets the guidelines, it goes on the board.

Use *Find Your Match (Seen in MiCOSA Video Clip 5.2)*   Create two stacks of colored cards (one color for each stack). The first has *causes* of everyday situations written on it, and the second has *effects* of those situations written. Each student receives either a *cause* or an *effect* card, assuring that the "matches" are all distributed. When the music starts, the students search the room for a "match" to either their *cause or effect* by the time the music stops. When the music stops, each pair reads their *cause-effect* situation.

How might you mediate students in your class who struggle with cause and effect—hypothesizing?

_____

_____

Summarizing

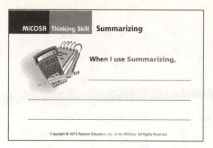

When you *summarize,* you gather together and synthesize key related elements of an experience to help create meaning. This thinking skill requires you to label and use categories of explanation rather than strings of examples. As you establish relationships between categories in text, for example, you come to understand the broader meaning—the main idea. Once you establish the main idea, you can add in relevant details to illustrate the points.

Teachers often connect *summarizing* with language arts instruction, and it *is* critical in that context. A learner efficient in *summarizing* can generate themes and main ideas, and get the "point" or "gist" of lessons in other domains as well, such as math, science, and social studies. Students who summarize efficiently often exhibit strengths in related and prerequisite thinking skills such as *comparing; categorizing;* using *labels, words, and concepts;* and *finding connections and relationships.*

Summarizing, important to critical thinking, supports comprehending the world, regardless of whether the input is visual or auditory. Efficient *summarizing* allows students to store large pieces of information in consolidated "chunks." As students *summarize,* they check for understanding, differentiate main ideas and important details, consolidate that information, and determine what may be taken out without losing meaning.

Students use *summarizing* as a study skill as well. Crucial in note taking, it supports conciseness of thought—necessary to effectively store information. Its brevity aids memory and recall. In addition to written or verbal *summaries,* highly visual learners may create graphic representations, use graphic organizers, or represent concepts with symbols as forms of *summarization* (Harvey & Goudvis, 2007; Marzano, Pickering, & Pollock, 2001).

Freddie demonstrates efficient *summarizing* when taking notes in class by creating a graphic representation to *summarize* what he hears, rather than narratives. He can also verbally *summarize* the essence of a movie or story. He thinks in terms of the gestalt and then uses examples to enrich the telling. Brendan can *summarize* information from *multiple sources* on the impact of the "footprints" from each country, then predict the degree of the need for further conservation of resources in the next five years.

Students Inefficient in Summarizing

Students inefficient in this skill tend to retell instead of *summarize* stories, losing sight of *connections* between events. They struggle to differentiate important versus unimportant details, and get lost on tangents. For example, in response to, "What did we learn yesterday?" Susan shrugs and says, "I don't know." In fact, she does "know." When queried further, however, she relates random facts rather than a synthesized or meaningful whole. Penelope takes notes in biology; however, because she has not *summarized* in chunks along the way, her notes look random. They draw from occasional words said in class, without any sense of main ideas or organizing principles. When asked to explain what she has written, she cannot make sense of it.

Teodoro can read as much as 10 pages of text, but demonstrate no knowledge of what he has read. Thus, he cannot summarize it.

What students in your class might struggle with summarizing?

Mediating Summarizing with Susan and Penelope

Multiple prerequisites support the skill of *summarizing*; thus, you first must check that your students can use those skills (e.g., *comparing; categorizing*; using *labels, words, and concepts; finding connections and relationships*). In helping students understand both the meaning and process of *summarizing,* ask them to use their own words, or even their own visualizations, to make meaning of small chunks of information at a time. Then gradually add in more parts so that the "bigger picture" of *summarizing* can emerge.

Remember back to Susan, who repeatedly selected random facts when asked to *summarize.* To mediate, Ms. Donaldson begins by having her look at the headings, the subheadings, the illustrations, and the graphics. She then covers the text to force Susan away from the details already read. Next, she asks Susan, "Tell me in your own words what you learned on this page, using only one or two sentences at the most." Using Susan's generated sentences, Ms. Donaldson helps her differentiate important ideas from details. When Susan begins to get the idea, Ms. Donaldson mediates meaning, sharing her enthusiastic observation that when Susan uses *summarizing*, she is thinking about what details are important and not important. She is getting the gist of what she reads or hears. Others will enjoy and learn from her summaries. Ms. Donaldson asks Susan to explain how she thinks she summarized so well, mediating competence and meaning. As Susan gives her explanation, the process becomes her own. Susan shares, for example, how skimming and scanning the headings and graphics help her form her *summary*. She grows to value her own thinking.

PD **TOOLKIT™**

PDToolkit:
See Video Clip 5.5
to learn how to
elicit the strategy
"GIST" to engage
a group of
educators learning
summarizing
strategies.

Penelope takes notes without using *summarizing* skills. To mediate, her teacher draws on Marzano, Pickering, and Pollock (2001)'s graphic organizing resource "Student Notes: Combination Technique." Penelope and her classmates take notes on the left-hand side of the organizer while a chunk of text is read aloud to them. Their teacher asks them to pause (mediating self-regulation) and to draw a visual representation of their note-taking in the right-hand column. This forces conceptualization, or meaning-making, as well as active learning. After repeating this process for approximately three chunks of text, students combine these three graphic representations into a one-sentence summary. This three-part process helps Penelope and the others move from the text into their own schema of thought and to learn *summarizing*.

Strategies and Activities Supporting Mediation of Summarizing

Practice the *Combination Technique for Student Notes*   Using a three-part graphic organizer, students take notes on the left side, draw their visual image or representation of those notes on the right, and below create a *summarizing* statement. In sequence, they take notes, draw, take notes, draw, take notes, draw, and then summarize.

As is true for all visual representations, this forces students to hone in and conceptualize the main point rather than to get lost in extraneous details. (Marzano, Pickering, & Pollack, 2001)

Support *Skimming*   In skimming, students look for the gist of the page by focusing on relevant pieces of information. Put up a piece of text on your document camera (or overhead) and give students 30 seconds to skim and scan the page. Have students put their thumbs up when they have found the information. Turn off the doc cam and ask what they learned. Ask those who came up with a *summary* to enumerate how they used their 30 seconds effectively (e.g., they looked at bold areas and titles, pictures, first sentence of the paragraphs).

Scan for Information   In scanning, students "scan" the text for specific information. Prompt the students with something like, "What important river flows through Germany?" Put up the text that contains that information and have them scan or look for the key words like *river* and *Germany*. Have them put their thumbs up when they have found the information. Share out loud.

Leave In Leave Out   Leave In Leave Out supports students in learning to differentiate relevant from irrelevant details in text. Carefully select 26 sentences from a text familiar to your students, listed as facts A to Z (modify number as needed). These facts include 10 important and relevant facts, but also 16 repetitive or minor details intended to be discarded. Student pairs select which 10 facts to "leave in" and which 16 to "leave out" of their summaries. Students make selections and then using transparent strips, cover the sentences that represent the most relevant 10 facts. This encourages flexibility of thinking, as covering allows them to rearrange their thinking. Students discuss the criteria they used to determine the most relevant sentences. Beginning with "A," ask for a show of hands from students who left that fact in. Record an estimate of the number of students raising their hands from none, to a few, to half, to most, to all. Continue doing this from fact "B" to fact "Z." Displaying the results of the survey to the class, point to clusters of items omitted and ask, "Why do you suppose most of you chose to leave OUT these facts?" Generate ideas for reasons students may choose to omit insignificant, irrelevant, or minor details. Do the same with, "Why did you choose to leave IN those facts?" Repeat the same process for sentences where students disagree. At this point, have students take the 10 top "leave in" sentences or facts, and create a coherent summary paragraph. Finally, ask them to *summarize* this paragraph into one or two sentences (Action Learning Systems, 2010).

Generate *GISTs (Generating Interactions between Schemata and Text)*   Show students the first two or three sentences of a paragraph they will read (some 20 words). Ask them to write a *summary* of that portion in only 15 words. Then expose them to the next two sentences, and ask them to maintain the 15-word limit on their *summaries*, but to include any relevant information from the last two sentences. Continue to a third chunk of information, now *summarizing* all three, still using the 15-word limit (Los Angeles County Office of Education, 1998).

PD TOOLKIT™

PDToolkit: GIST is illustrated in Video Clip 5.4, PDToolkit: Trish works with educators to illustrate GIST in Video Clip 5.4.

You can repeat this process with two more paragraphs from the same article. Following the development of all three *summaries*, ask students to create a *summary* of the three *summaries,* using as few words as possible. Students can practice this strategy individually or in groups or teams. In the latter case, use large chart paper and felt markers to complete the summary. Encourage students to mount their summaries on the wall for class analysis and celebrations. This activity can be done by groups using google docs or drive from their electronic devices.

Draw Summaries   Making visual representations of what students read requires them to abstract the key ideas. Thus, having students create storyboards (a sequence of pictures depicting the story) when they read, forces them to focus on the main idea, or to *summarize* the content.

Use *Storymapping*   Storymapping ensures that students include key elements of a story as they retell it in *summary* form. Fetzer's version is particularly useful for English Learners because of its emphasis on oral retell. Create a graphic organizer with the labels of *Setting, Characters*, and *Problem* placed horizontally across the top third of the paper. Across the bottom two-thirds of the paper, make three categories: *Beginning, Middle,* and *End*, also placed horizontally. As you read the story to the students, you model. The students then make graphic representations (quick drawings) *summarizing* the setting, characters, and problem of the story in the linear series of boxes on the top third of the page. Repeat this graphic *summarizing* process for the categories of *Beginning, Middle,* and *End*. Throughout the process, the teacher and students together retell the *summary* up to the point of each newly completed category, somewhat like the neurological impress method. By the end, they will have repeated the story six times and are ready to retell the *summary* of the story on their own, based on visual cues. At this point, they are ready to transfer the oral retell to a written *summarization* (Fetzer, 2010).

How might you mediate students in your class who struggle with summarizing?

_____

_____

SUMMARY

- Students who are efficient with the use of thinking skills to transform information take information they have gathered and create something new. They are better able to make the critical judgments and decisions so needed in the 21st century. Nine powerful thinking skills are discussed, with classroom examples of their efficient and inefficient use and mediation provided. Finally, strategies supporting your work are enumerated.

- *Goal setting* establishes a direction for learning and supports student mastery of objectives. *Planning* helps students select relevant materials and information, and order the steps and processes to efficiently "get there."

- *Comparing* is a process of determining commonalities and differences between two or more things. Students need this as a prerequisite to use another skill: *ordering, grouping, and categorizing*. Students organize and form conceptual sets, helping them store chunks of information rather than individual pieces. As students compare and begin to organize thinking, they seek *connections and relationships* among the isolated parts and can efficiently group them. They look for patterns and rules, and can see multiple ways to solve problems. Students efficient in using this skill tend to be flexible thinkers.

- As students observe their worlds, they store experiences subconsciously in their minds as images, influenced by the interaction with their senses. To do this efficiently, they use the skill of *visualizing,* another important skill for the 21st century. They also use it to help project toward the future. *Visualizing* helps your students *infer*. Using the thinking skill *inferring*, they draw on information from past experiences and apply it to other situations they believe will follow that same pattern. They draw conclusions based on what they believe is true, and as a result develop insight.

- *Cause and effect—hypothesizing* helps students identify rules or patterns of causation. *Cause-effect* relationships tend to be linked to past or current situations (WHEN-THEN), whereas *hypothesizing* is based on situations that are not real, but could be (IF-THEN).

- Students use *summarizing* to gather and synthesize key elements of learning. Summarizing helps students establish relationships between categories of information, store them as chunks, and as a result understand the broader meaning. It is an essential part of critical thinking, because it supports comprehension of their worlds.

REFERENCES

Action Learning Systems. (2003). *The Literacy Solution. A System for Reading Comprehension.* Action Learning Systems Inc: Monrovia, CA.

Action Learning Systems. (2010). *Under the surface strategies.* Retrieved from www.actionlearningsystems.com.

Beers, K. (2003). *When kids can't read: What teachers can do: A guide for teachers 6–12.* Portsmouth, NH: Heinemann.

Butcher, K. (2008, May). Professional Development Training. Los Cerritos Middle School, Thousand Oaks, CA.

California Science. (2008). Grade 5 *Teacher's Edition.* Unit B (p. 124). Boston, MA: Scott Foresman/Pearson Education.

Chancer, J. (2000). Exploring Grammar Creatively. ELA Professional Development Workshop. Thousand Oaks, CA: Conejo Valley Unified School District.

Chi, M. T., Feltovich, P. J., & Glaser, R. (1981). Categorization and representation of physics problems by experts and novices. *Cognitive Science, 5,* 121–152.

Education Place. (2013). Classroom Resources: Graphic Organizers. Houghton Mifflin Harcourt Publishing Company. Retrieved from http://www.eduplace.com/graphicorganizer

Eduscapes. (2009). Inferential thinking across the curriculum. Retrieved from http://eduscapes.com/

Fetzer, N. (2010). *Nancy Fetzer's Reading Curriculum.* Murietta, CA: Literacy Connecions.

Frayer, D., Frederick, W. C., and Klausmeier, H. J. (1969). *A Schema for Testing the Level of Cognitive Mastery*. Madison, WI: Wisconsin Center for Education Research.

Frey, W., & Bower, B. (2004). *History alive! Medieval world and beyond grade 7*. Rancho Cordova, CA: Teachers Curriculum Institute.

Harvey, S., & Goudvis, A. (2007). *Strategies that work: Teaching comprehension for understanding and engagement* (2nd edition). Portland, ME: Stenhouse.

Johnson, J. F., & Perez, L. (2010). *The best teaching in America's best urban schools*. A presentation of the National Center on Urban School Transformation (NCUST) to the faculty at San Diego State University. San Diego, CA.

Kinsella, K. (2001). *Strategies to build a school-wide academic writing program*. Office of the Ventura County Superintendent of Schools. Ventura, CA.

Los Angeles County Office of Education. (1998). *High school reading: Basic to success*. Downey, CA: Author.

Marzano, R. J., Pickering, D. J., & Pollock, J. E. (2001). *Classroom instruction that works: Research-based strategies for increasing student achievement*. Alexandria, VA: Association for Supervision and Curriculum Development.

Rasinski, T., & Padak, N. (2000). *Effective reading strategies* (2nd edition). Upper Saddle River, NJ: Prentice Hall.

Regents of the University of California Reading & Literature Project (2013). *Results Training Manual*. University of California at San Diego: La Jolla, CA: Author.

Zimbler, S. (2009, Feb 27). Make Room for Robots. *TIME for Kids:* New York, New York.

Chapter Six

Thinking Skills for Communicating Information

Five of MiCOSA's 21 thinking skills help enrich the nuances and specificity of your students' multiple modes of communication.

Today's students not only have an abundance of new information to gather; they now have access to a "digital zoo of devices" (Trilling & Fadel, 2009, p. 19) with which to communicate. These devices facilitate both individual and collaborative contributions, not just in one location, but in locations throughout the world. Stanford's Andrea Lunsford concluded from a five-year study of student writing that students now write "more than ever before in history . . . [however], it may not look like the writing of yesterday" (Haven, 2009). They write using social networking, code, e-mails and blogs, poems and songs. They write in college and public school, and they write for classes. But most students' *communication* is not about turning out elegant prose or even persuasive essays; rather, its focus seems to be about instant communication and about audience. That is, writing helps students make connections with one another, something others might say is sorely missing in the era of technology.

Not only is today's writing and social networking "connected," but it is publicly connected with thousands of others (e.g., blogs, websites, Twitter). As a result, some are using *communication* to make a difference way beyond themselves. Perhaps the whole concept of written communication has expanded, rather than deteriorated!

What an exciting and unprecedented time this is to build on students' enthusiasm for new and unique ways of *communicating*! Your challenge is to provide opportunities for students not only to use the information they gather accurately and creatively, but also to deliver their messages in a multitude of ways, from print and graphics to audio, animation, video, and Internet. With the current bombardment of information you access and process daily, your students must carefully consider the accuracy of the opinions they intend to *communicate*. They must learn to carefully analyze their sources when disseminating information, the intent behind what is written, and its truth. Armed with this knowledge, they can begin to evaluate its powerful effect on society, and ultimately their own lives.

Communicating is sometimes confused with knowing. In schools, products of *communication* (e.g., tests, papers, reports) often serve as the only means by which you evaluate students. Likewise, in society, judgments of intellect, wit, and character are made based on *communication* skills. Your students may have *gathered*, *processed*, and *transformed* information successfully, but lack the skills to adequately *communicate* that information. To presume that they do not know, therefore, is potentially erroneous. Likewise, emotional "overlay" often inhibits *communication*, and so may also need to be a target of mediation.

Often without knowing it, you make incorrect assumptions based on cultural differences in *communication* styles. Direct eye contact, a sign of respect and attention in mainstream western cultures, is viewed as disrespectful in others. Questioning the teacher, a "sign" of inquisitiveness in mainstream western cultures, signals ignorance or poor upbringing in others. In some cultures, patting the head can be affectionate, while others view it as extremely inappropriate. A gentle handshake may be seen as "limp or weak" by mainstream western cultures; in some other cultures, however, a firm handshake is viewed as an act of aggression. Thus, *communication* is relative and cultural, steeped in tradition.

Even across cultural contexts, *communication* requires some common skills: (a) *labels, words, and concepts*; (b) *precision and accuracy*; (c) *appropriate pragmatics*; (d) *using feedback for self-regulation*; and (e) *collaboration*. With MiCOSA, you will learn to weave these five skills for *communicating information* into your classroom interactions.

Labels, Words, and Concepts

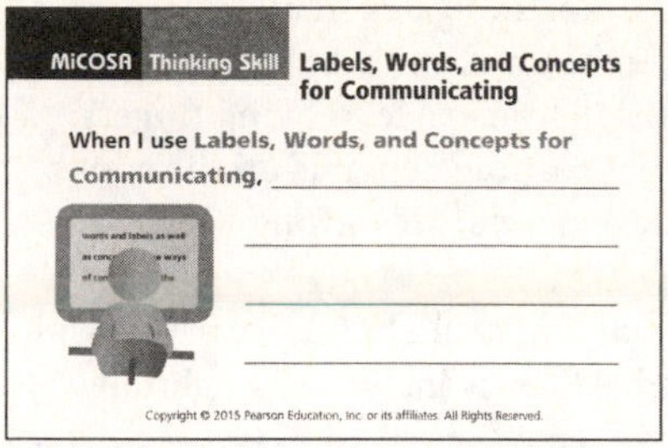

Beyond having a collection of *words*, students also need the *concepts* behind those words so that they become efficient skills for *communicating* information. *Labels* describe or classify *words* or phrases, and support the understanding and use of *concepts*. To have a *word* without a *concept*, or a *concept* with no *label*, does not support your understanding. However, when you link both *labels and concepts*, the *word* becomes meaningful. Meaning facilitates memory; therefore, retention increases as you pair *concepts* and *labels* to create meaningful *words*. Figure 6.1 illustrates these relationships.

In *communicating*, the thinking skill *labels, words, and concepts* allows students to express their thoughts and needs succinctly. When based on common understandings and meanings, *words* and *concepts* create both concise and precise *communication*. However, in today's diverse classrooms, students may not come in with common understandings and meanings. The subtleties of meaning honed by cultural or generational experiences can lead to widely different interpretations of the same *words* (or behaviors on which we place *labels*). Wait until you get to talking about explorers and seamen in middle school! In addition, digital *communication* has created a language of its own, staccatoed with numbers, letters, fragments, or acronyms. You need to keep abreast of this new dimension of language and *communication*, and work with students on when to use what type. Thus, respectfully seek or provide clarification of individual or cultural meanings before assuming that the use of a word is "wrong."

Today, most students use the written language of texting. Here, brevity and rapidity overshadow rich language and *communication*. "For you to see" becomes "4U2C." Although clever, for some students, these abbreviations have become their only written language. Texting and tweeting have become communication genres in their own right, which you want to build on; however, translation to standardized written language may require an introduction to detail and subtlety of meaning.

FIGURE 6.1

Relationships Between Words, Concepts and Labels

Word with No Concept $>$ Concept with No Label $>$ Concept $+$ Label $=$ Meaningful Word

Inefficient _____ **Efficient**

Low Retention   **High Retention**

Sign language presents *labels, words, and concepts* both visually and conceptually. Signs may indicate relationships; for instance, in American Sign Language (ASL), *girl* uses the same sign as *woman,* but the lowered right-hand position indicates smaller stature. Sometimes the sign can be identical, yet indicate a different *word.* In these incidences, understanding both the context and *concept* are essential. For instance, moving fingers that signify flames rising indicate both *fire* and *burn*; the meaning depends on the context. Thus, being able to *communicate* using sign language necessitates strong *words* and *concepts.*

Madison is efficient with *words and concepts* in *communication.* In her conversation with her aunt about political unrest in the Middle East, her verbal fluency includes thoughtfully chosen *words* with *conceptual* clarity within well-developed sentence structures (syntax). Thus, she can engage her aunt in lively and meaningful discussions.

Students Inefficient with Words, Labels, and Concepts

Students with difficulties in this area use imprecise verbal and written language. Frequent use of *words* such as *thing, you know,* and *stuff* may indicate either not having the *word and concept* or not having retrieved it. In addition, not having *words* can lead to displays of anger, frustration, or withdrawal. Using approximations of speech may indicate insufficient effort to retrieve a *word,* incorrect storage of the *word* at the *gathering* stage, or cultural unfamiliarity.

Another form of approximations of speech, malapropisms, often evokes humor. However, they may occur because the student does not have the correct concept of the word. Malapropisms are incorrect uses of *words*, substituting similar sounding *words* with different meanings, usually with comic effect. Malapropisms are based on the dialog from the character Mrs. Malaprop from *The Rivals*, written to poke fun at 18th century aristocracy (Sheridan, 2008/1775). Here are a few examples of malapropisms from that play:

- She's as headstrong as an *allegory* on the banks of the Nile (instead of alligator)
- He is the very *pineapple* of politeness (instead of pinnacle)
- *Illiterate* him quite from your memory (instead of obliterate)

Second Language Learners frequently need to build skills with *labels, words, and concepts*. Second Language Learners acquire basic interpersonal communication skills (BICS) prior to acquiring cognitive academic language proficiency (CALP) (Cummins, 2003). Thus, students still learning a second language may use this more "social" language (BICS level) in school, which lacks the precision, structure, and depth required in much academic communication (CALP). Language level does not equate with intelligence or what the student may actually know. Thus, educators need to take care not to be inappropriately critical, but to correct and instruct so that language learners build deeper *words, concepts, and linguistic* structures.

Some *communication* issues require the expertise of specialists such as speech and language pathologists (SLP). In these cases, the consult of your school's SLP coupled with mediating thinking skills for communication creates a powerful combination.

Richard, a student inefficient with *labels, words, and concepts*, has written a report on Ferraris with outside support and managed to include some helpful precise language. However, when the time arrives to rehearse his oral report, although he uses a poster, he stumbles, using phrases such as: "The thing that sits on the back (with gestures), the wheels, and those two cool things that come out the back (gesturing "round" with his hands)." He struggles to retrieve the more accurate *words*, smiling awkwardly. It turns out that the level of help he had received with his written report provided him with *labels* that he hadn't internalized; therefore, now he cannot adequately *communicate*.

Another student, Elsa, practices her part of the team's science report on the water cycle. She shares their PowerPoint and begins well: "The water cycle has three phases. It starts with evaporation, then there is condensation, and then there is precipitation." She has the *labels*; however, the *concepts* seem to elude her. She continues, "Evaporation is when the water goes up. Condensation is . . . well, I don't remember." She looks at the picture repeatedly, seeking cues. She brightens and concludes, "Oh, and precipitation is when the water comes back down."

What students in your class might struggle with labels, words, and concepts?

Mediating Labels, Words, and Concepts with Richard and Elsa   Richard did
not make use of *labels* in his Ferrari report. Mr. Green remarks, "You have a fascinating topic, and it looks like you have some new terms that would help us get even more from your report. Would you like more time to fully prepare?" On the break, he pulls Richard aside and asks him to read sections of his report to find the *labels* he missed in his oral report. Checking for meaning, he provides the opportunity for Richard to re-describe each *concept,* show where it went, and ask how he might make the poster more useful. Richard concludes that *labeling* the new and difficult parts of the Ferrari might help him and the others. Mr. Green provides an opportunity to practice again with Richard before he re-presents the report the following day. Later, he uses the opportunity with the whole class to discuss *labels* and their use to cue students to remember existing knowledge. He shares how Richard has made a great decision to put *labels* on the poster so that everyone will have a better chance to learn and remember the meanings of spoilers and dual tailpipes. Mr. Green continues to reinforce this thinking skill over the next two weeks by playing attribute games and using *word* banks posted around the room for support.

Elsa has no *conceptual* base developed regarding the water cycle. Reading text, even with pictures to illustrate *concepts,* was insufficient to create meaning for her. Her teacher, Mrs. Storm, acknowledges that the water cycle is a very difficult set of *concepts*. They talk about what happens on the mirror after a hot shower. How did the steam get there? What happens after it hits the mirror? They connect the label of *precipitation* to the water from the shower, and the label *condensation* to the fog on the mirror. In this way, they start to connect Elsa's prior knowledge to help her develop the *concepts* and to mediate meaning. Mrs. Storm writes down each term to provide visual support, then expands it the following day with an experiment for Elsa's whole group, to simulate the processes of evaporation, condensation, and precipitation. She uses a hot plate to boil some water in a pan, representing warm air rising from the land or sea. She asks Elsa to match the new concepts with what occurs. Then, she asks Elsa to hold a pie tin filled with ice, which simulates a cold front of air, and to observe what happens when her "cold front" moves over the pan where hot air is rising. "It's like clouds . . . and then rain," Elsa exclaims, observing the "billowing cloud" forming under the pie tin and the subsequent drip, drip, dripping of water as the cloud water condenses into "rain." "Yes, Elsa, excellent! Now name the parts of the water cycle you just simulated. Why don't you include this experiment in your presentation to the class?"

Following Elsa's group presentation, Mrs. Storm puts the students in roles as weather forecasters. Their jobs are to look for warm and cold fronts and cloud formations daily, and predict what is likely to happen. They will use their iPads to compare their predictions to weather forecasts.

Strategies and Activities Supporting Mediation of Labels, Words, and Concepts

Students who struggle for words at the *communicating* stage may not have them firmly in place at the *gathering* stage. Therefore, you may use similar strategies at both levels.

Provide *Authentic Practice*   Provide ample opportunities for students to speak. For instance, use role-play in which they take the role of someone explaining a topic within their field of knowledge (e.g., scientist, weather person, geologist, mathematician, author). Use other games to enhance fluency such as Pair-Share and Tea Party.

Encourage *Metacognitive Writing*   Encourage students to explain their thinking in writing. For instance, in a math class, give students three algebra problems they solved previously, but in which you have now inserted an error in one of the steps. The students' task is to identify the mistake and then explain the correct answer and steps. This also helps students who are English Language Learners acquire CALP (cognitive academic language proficiency).

Build Fluency with *Choral Reading*   *Choral reading* has either small groups or the whole group read aloud together. Especially with Second Language Learners, choral reading enhances confidence and fluency, and gives them the opportunity to hear and practice communicating. A variation has the teacher reading and pausing every few lines, at which point all students read the next word. This models reading with expression, supports full involvement, and ensures students are following along with the text.

Reduce Anxiety with *Active Hands*   Anxiety inhibits verbal fluency. Researchers (cf. Cleary & Peacock, 1998) have found that having students doing handwork of some kind while they are talking lowers anxiety and facilitates fluency. For example, given a ball of knotted yarn, students begin to pass it slowly through their fingers while they talk. When they come to the knot (every three feet), they stop talking (Everett, 1986). For others, activities like beading or drawing enhance their comfort level in oral *communication*. It takes the emphasis off feelings of awkwardness, as well as off the constant visual contact that is so uncomfortable in many cultures. Culturally specific or culturally relevant activities aid enhanced meaning.

Unblock the Writing Block   Often students say that they have no idea what to write. To help them move forward, engage students in a short conversation about the topic. Lead by asking probing questions to elicit information from your students; this will help them develop their ideas. As they respond, write down on a 3x5 card one-word cues to what they have said. For instance, if a student says, "Last night my brother came over to the house on his motorbike," you write "brother, house, motorbike." When they have generated sufficient information to produce a piece of writing, retell the story to the student. As you do so, point to each key word as it occurs in the story. Then, ask your students to do the same thing. At that point, ask, "Do you think you might be able to write this out now?" Do not leave students until they have begun, since the beginning is usually the point where they block. Say, "How will you start?" "What will your first sentence be?" "Where are you going to put it?" "That sounds great—go ahead, and I'll come back around and see you in a moment" (Bowers, 2000a).

Share the Pen   Even with the support of the prior strategy, some students still block. At this point, use "share the pen." Together, you decide how to begin the story. First, you hold the pen, writing the first sentence, as the student prompts you. Together discuss the second sentence. This time, the student holds the pen and writes. This continues, with the pen moving back and forth between you and student. Spend some time away from the student to encourage independent work (Bowers, 2000b).

Retell with *Story Bags*   Tell a story and put an object in a bag to symbolize something in the story you will ask students to remember later. For instance, for Little Red Riding Hood, you might put a swatch of red cloth in the bag; for a story about the sea, you can place a shell in the bag. This can become a group activity in which students pass around the symbol so that others can contribute after a couple of sentences. Periodically shake up the bag and ask a student to pull out one of the symbols and recall the associated story. The student tells that story in a short form.

Dip into *Noun Bag, Verb Bag, Adjective Bag*   Each bag contains multiple examples within the category (e.g., nouns). One student from each of several groups comes up, selects a word from each category, and places them in a pocket chart. Each group has two minutes to make up a story using their selection of adjective, noun, and verb as a prompt. Students then share their stories with the whole class.

Share with *Tea Party*   In addition to its use to engage intent and reciprocity, Tea Party can quickly provide students with some background knowledge in any given subject, as well as give students a base from which to add to their knowledge. Each student receives a card containing one fact about a topic. Students go around the room, introducing themselves to one another and sharing their facts. The process is repeated for five or six minutes, in which students gather as much information as they can. Here, they build their store of *words, labels, and concepts,* and practice *communication* as well as model it. Encourage students to share their thoughts as Quick Writes, helping them make meaning of the new information (Beers, 2003; Perona, 1989).

Take Turns with *Talking Stick, Pass the Pen, Heart Talks*   Each of these strategies facilitates shared participation and *communication*, and is especially useful for shy students, Second Language Learners, and others reticent to talk. When the student receives the "chip," "stick," or "heart" passed around the classroom, he or she takes a turn to talk. The student then passes on the item to the next person (Dutro, 2004).

Create *Masterpiece Sentences*   This strategy, developed by Jane Fell Greene (2009) as part of her *Language!* program, takes students creatively through the development of a sentence in which a base sentence evolves and becomes a "Masterpiece!" It supports students in developing rich expressive written language. The following description is adapted with permission from Cambium Learning Group (www.cambiumlearning.com).

PD **TOOLKIT™**

PDToolkit: View Video Clip 6.1 **to see a sequence of clips from the engaging and scaffolded strategy** *Masterpiece Sentences.*

Instructions: Each student will need four narrow strips of both pink and green paper: pink for elaborating the subject and green for the predicate.

1. Project an image that will inspire students to write colorfully. It might be a scene of the ocean, mountains, a fairground, a video arcade, or a concert. Ask students to make connections to the picture and write a simple sentence about it using the past tense; i.e., base subject + base predicate (e.g., The snowflake (pink) fell (green). The period at the end needs to be made on its own piece of green paper so that it can be shifted as the sentence develops.)

2. Students put the remaining three pink strips to one side and focus on the predicate (the green). Now, using the remaining three green strips, they answer these questions: How? When? Where?
   How was the snowflake falling? The snowflake fell softly. (adding an adverb)
   When was this happening? The snowflake fell softly in the late afternoon. (adding a prepositional phrase)
   Where was this happening? The snowflake fell softly in the evening on my cheek. (adding a second prepositional phrase)

3. Now students move one of the green pieces BEFORE the subject (but do not move the base predicate). They will need to divide it from the subject with a comma, and make other changes to the conventions.
   In the evening, the snow fell softly on my cheek. or
   Softly, the snow fell in the evening on my cheek.

4. Now elaborate the subject, using the three remaining pink strips. Older students can add an adjectival phrase; others may prefer to add just two adjectives, which will tell us more about the subject. The adjective that tells us "how many?" should always come first. Before they begin to add descriptors, ask them to cut and separate the subject from the definite article.
   In the evening, the lone, silent snowflake with its intricate design, fell softly on my cheek.

5. Students "play" with their sentence, either by changing the words or moving them (and phrases) to paint an even stronger "Masterpiece."

How might you mediate students in your class who struggle with labels, words, and concepts?

_____

_____

Precision and Accuracy

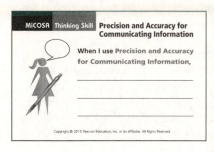

When efficient in using *precision and accuracy* for communication, students gauge the appropriate amount of effort, as well as the *precision and accuracy* necessary to *communicate* their meanings effectively, whether verbally or in writing. This is similar to the thinking skill observed at the *gathering* stage, but involves sharing ideas. What distinguishes *precise* from *accurate* in communicating? Broadly speaking, *accurate* refers to what is true; *precise* refers to exactness. For example: "The park is near my house" is *accurate but not precise*. "The park is 53 meters in front of my house" is both *accurate and precise*. "The park is 50 meters behind my house" is *precise but not accurate*.

In writing, students efficient in *accuracy* choose correct forms of sentence structure, punctuation, capitalization, and verb tenses. For example, Mario makes word choices that say just what he means. He may use *hustle* versus *run*; *amicable* versus *nice*. In science and math, *precision* is critical to *accuracy*—they coexist. Science experiments require *precise* measurements and recordings; otherwise, inaccurate conclusions result. For example, Hans makes meticulous drawings and notes to illustrate his conclusions. Social studies often requires students to demonstrate *accuracy*. *Accuracy* plays a part in finding connections and patterns, or in illustrations of concepts (e.g., in the early 1800s versus 1812). In addition, sometimes *precision* is called for (the War of 1812). Dierdra's timeline assignment comparing events in the space race with events in her family's history allowed personalized connections with her grandmother; her grandmother's precise recollections of John Glenn's orbit of the Earth coincided with her move to the United States.

Students Inefficient with Precision and Accuracy

When this thinking skill is fragile, your student exerts too little or too much effort to *communicate precisely* or *accurately*. Some students will develop so much angst over the *precision* and *accuracy* of their work that they seldom finish on time because of their constant erasing and reworking, trying to perfect every letter. Conversely, fear or expectations of failure may compound other students' habitual lack of accuracy or poor estimate of the time needed. Low expectations, from either the student or that your student perceives coming from you, may also contribute to student "sloppiness," or low-level *precision and accuracy* in communicating information. Much of the literature on closing the achievement gaps between cultural groups stresses the need to enhance expectations that all students truly can communicate with depth, meaning, *precision,* and *accuracy.* Not sustaining your belief in the students' potential places a far greater barrier in their way than any level of poverty or lack of textbooks might. Students can become conditioned to believe their work does not matter, and then meet those low expectations.

Certain content areas highlight student inefficiencies with *precision and accuracy* in *communicating* information. In reading, because of impulsivity or low self-regulation, students jump to use imprecise words. In math and science, when *precision* is lacking, inaccuracy follows, even if the process of obtaining the answer is *accurate*. For instance, Alexis completes a science experiment process *accurately* but writes her answer down inaccurately. Imprecision, as in misalignment of columns or sloppy writing of numbers (3 for 8), can lead to inaccurate conclusions or answers. Misreading signs (e.g., +, −, or ×) (input imprecision) leads to inaccuracy in *communication*.

Aroula and Tom struggle to understand the assignment. They have been asked to integrate history, culture, religion, geography, and political science into one group presentation on the Middle East, using either written or visual media. The first step in the project requires the group to turn in an "abstract" of the project. Aroula and Tom's draft lacks *precision*, and they must rework it with greater detail. Although they have quite a bit of information on each part of the topic, they find themselves at a loss for how to begin to put it together.

Other students demonstrate more straightforward issues in *communicating* with *precision and accuracy*. Drake, for instance, carries a "reputation" as one who doesn't care much about his work, and as a result it generally appears sloppy. He lacks awareness of the need to *communicate precisely*. Even when he has the vocabulary or other requisite skills, his *communication* tends to be choppy and mumbled.

Jasmine, a fourth grader, and her classmates receive an assignment that requires them to write a topic sentence that introduces their readers to their neighborhoods. Jasmine simply writes, "The park near my home is full of pretty trees."

What students in your class might struggle with precision and accuracy?

Mediating Precision and Accuracy with Alexis, Aroula and Tom, and Jasmine

Jasmine's initial topic sentence, "The park near my home is full of pretty trees," lacks interest, detail, and *precision*. Mrs. Robins talks about working with Jasmine's original idea, but with greater *precision*, and prompts her to use additional adjectives, modifiers, and verb changes. Mrs. Robins suggests, "Let's add more *precision* to your description and see what happens." *The park near my home is full of pretty trees* evolves. Jasmine and her teacher are delighted: "The community park a block from my home flourishes with flowering crystal white dogwood trees."

Alexis performs her experiment accurately, but has not used *precision* in communicating her results. Therefore, Mr. Rizinsky mediates self-regulation and the need for *precision* in communication. Rather than pointing out Alexis' errors, he asks her to share her process with him. As she talks through her process step-by-step, he points to notes she made about each step. By slowing down (self-regulating) to check her own *precision* in *communicating* the information, Alexis is able to pick up her own errors and self-correct. Mr. Rizinsky mediates, "When you take a little extra time to focus on the *precision* of your work, you demonstrate how smart you really are." Alexis is thrilled. He asks her to try slowing down and using *precision* again on the next few assignments. If it works again, she will be far more likely to begin using it regularly.

Aroula and Tom approach Ms. Bowen wide-eyed, saying, "We really don't get how to rework our abstract and put all the pieces together." Ms. Bowen realizes that it is not a matter of simply lack of *precision* in *communicating* their ideas, but there also needs to be a far stronger level of scaffolding and mediation to generate those *precise* ideas. Working with the thinking skill of *finding connections and relationships,* she begins with a question that prompts them to generate ideas: "Let's begin by thinking about ways all those pieces might be connected or related. We can brainstorm and then choose one that would make a great project." As they discuss possible connections between history, geography, culture, and political science in the Middle East, the idea of a news broadcast emerges. This provides the organizational structure for the many pieces.

Strategies and Activities Supporting Mediation of Precision and Accuracy in Communication

Provide *Meaningful Contexts for Precision*

Students often need meaningful or novel contexts within which to experience the need for *precision and accuracy*. Some students use great *precision* when writing poetry on self-selected topics meaningful to their lives; yet, in writing teacher-directed essays, that same *precision* does not appear. To facilitate this, use questioning to guide your students toward active participation in generating the topic. For instance, bring in something novel and personalize a prompt from it: "Check out this goldfish I've brought in—this is the best pet in the world. Why do you think I would believe that? Give me some ideas [record brainstorming on board]. What were the strongest three ideas you heard? Take those, and incorporate them into your 'perfect paragraph'" (Kinsella, 2003). Prompts such as, "The school board is proposing that students only need busses when they live over three miles away from school. What is your opinion and precisely why do you believe that?" tap into prior knowledge to create meaning. For instance, as your class begins to learn about different states or countries, plot on a map which students have experience in various places, so that you can call on them as an ongoing resource. Encourage them to go online and write to tourist boards asking for information with enough *precision and accuracy* to get a helpful response. Get students to review other sites and compare their advertising biases. Encourage them to look for patterns that they can emulate as they create a travel brochure. Require two media forms: one "hard copy" brochure for "mailing" purposes, and a short movie/slide show for online advertising.

Meaningful writing is an excellent way to practice *precision and accuracy* in written *communication*. Joining online forums or even blogs can provide meaningful venues. Write to pen pals to emphasize the impact of the letter received. The judgments made about the person based on the *content*, *precision*, and *accuracy* goes two ways, and it's exciting to see students' enhanced investment in the process with this realization. Use resources such as "Things Kids Can Get Free," or environmental issues like "Save the Whales" for additional places to write letters.

Alter *Pacing for Precision*   Having your student slow down can enhance *precision and accuracy*. Do this lovingly and with some way to cue the pace change, such as a gesture; you might consider slowly moving your hands like someone conducting slow music. Draw attention to the time and effort needed for appropriate *precision and accuracy*. Asking students to stop and think whether what they wrote or drew made sense (*using feedback for self-regulation*) helps them pace themselves. Occasionally, ask students to temporarily sit on their hands to get them "out of the way of their brilliant thinking" until the answer is in their head or until they know for sure what to do. Then, ask them to release their hands and proceed. This tends to put the brain back in charge instead of the impulsive action of the hand, which suggests working before thinking.

Foster *Accuracy and Insight*   Produce insight into causes of errors in *precision and accuracy*. Show examples where an error involving *precision or accuracy* exists. For instance, read aloud a sentence in which a word is read incorrectly; show an addition problem in which the person has subtracted. Have students generate ideas about *why* those errors occurred.

Model *Precision and Accuracy*   Call attention to your own modeling of *accurate and precise communication*. From time to time, simulate using inaccurate or imprecise communication, and ask what the thinking skill problem is! For instance, ask, "What would happen if I were to be imprecise in taking lunch roll and left off two names?" "What would happen if I didn't check the timetable for catching the bus home from the beach, *accurately?*" That brings it home, especially to those who feel they could miss out on lunch! Use additional authentic contexts.

 Motivate with *Internet Punctuation Games*   Use resources such as Internet Punctuation Games [gamequarium.com/punctuation] to motivate students to practice enhancing their *precision and accuracy* around punctuation.

How might you mediate students in your class who struggle with precision and accuracy?

_____

_____

Appropriate Pragmatics

MiCOSA Thinking Skill	**Appropriate Pragmatics**
	When I use Appropriate Pragmatics,
	_____
	_____

Today's 21st century world is highly connected socially through technology. Your students will be expected to collaborate with others from diverse cultures, religions, and lifestyles, sharing a spirit of mutual respect as they learn from and work with teams or individuals. You must take care to interpret some of these characteristics within cultural contexts and ensure your pragmatics are appropriate. Do you know what to say, how to say it, and when to say it—and how to "be" with other people? Bowen (2011) helps us answer this, suggesting these helpful indicators of *appropriate pragmatics*, which guide us in our *verbal* interactions:

- Knowing that you have to answer when a question has been asked;
- Being able to participate in a conversation by taking turns with the other speaker;
- Being able to notice and respond to the nonverbal aspects of language (reacting appropriately to the other person's body language and "mood," as well as his or her words);
- Having awareness that you have to introduce a topic of conversation in order for the listener to fully understand;
- Knowing which words or what sort of sentence-type to use when initiating a conversation or responding to something someone has said;
- Maintaining a topic (or changing a topic appropriately, or "interrupting" politely);
- Maintaining appropriate eye contact (not too much staring, and not too much looking away) during a conversation; and
- Distinguishing how to talk and behave toward different communicative partners (formal with some, informal with others).

In addition to knowing and using these appropriate interactions with others, students also need to use *appropriate pragmatics* when they *write*. Inappropriate consideration of audience has led to some extremely hurtful and harmful letters, articles, blogs, and/or chats being posted, some causing irreparable damage. However, in this chapter, the emphasis focuses on *verbal* pragmatics.

Karina typifies the student who efficiently uses *appropriate pragmatics* with her peers as well as adults. She is seen as socially competent and responsive, and gets along well with others. She both listens to and actively participates in conversations with a genuine interest, politeness, warmth, empathy, and, when fitting, humor. This use of *appropriate pragmatics* is part of what is sometimes called "emotional intelligence."

Students Inefficient in Appropriate Pragmatics

Students with pragmatic difficulties have great trouble using language socially in ways that are appropriate or typical of others their age. They often do not understand that you take turns to talk. Students with this difficulty will "talk over the top of you" at times; at other times, they will respond to what you say with inappropriate silences, or in a voice that is too quiet. They may interrupt excessively and talk irrelevantly or about things the listener shows no interest in. Their *communicative* behavior often appears rude and inconsiderate. Students with Asperger's Syndrome will have an especially difficult time in this area.

Others may have a disorder affecting both semantic processing and the *pragmatics* of language use, known as Semantic-Pragmatic Language Disorder (SPLD). Some authorities see SPLD as part of the autism spectrum of disorders while others see it purely as a language disorder. You may want to work with your speech pathologist in these cases, and to distinguish students with autism spectrum disorders. Stroke or brain injury can also underlie problems in semantics and *pragmatics.*

Although isolated examples like the ones following can appear quite amusing and even endearing, these difficulties with word comprehension and social aptitude can be extremely embarrassing, upsetting, and frustrating for the student, and can lead to teasing, criticism, and even bullying. These students often feel that no one likes them and they don't know why; thus, their social isolation is painful.

However, some students may actually be acting with *appropriate pragmatics* within their cultural norms; within the classroom, though, this same behavior may appear inappropriate or inefficient. For example, Dwayne appears not to respond to verbal cues from his teacher, Mrs. Jackson, as he looks away when she asks him a question. After a three-second wait time, which typifies the student-teacher interaction in most classrooms, Mrs. Jackson moves on to another student. However, Dwayne is not ignoring her; he is thinking about the answer. Within his culture, a "wait time" of five to six seconds before responding is not only acceptable, but also typical.

Often, students with inappropriate pragmatics do not check for *prior knowledge* on the part of the listener, and may launch into a long discourse without describing the context in sufficient detail. For example, Alex decides to stay behind after class to discuss an obscure genre from action comic books, launching into a detailed monologue about the characters, sharing it as though Mrs. Hwang knows what he is talking about. At first she tries to relate her confusion by stating, "I am sorry but I don't know this genre," and looks at him puzzled. However, in response, he just increases the detail and intensity of his monologue.

Other students can continue telling stories far too long, and include so much detail that the listener becomes disinterested. Mr. Johnson asks Carlos, a 12-year-old with semantic and pragmatic difficulties, "Tell me all about yourself." Carlos responds, perfectly seriously, with, "It will take a very long time," and makes an immediate start!

The final example of inefficient or inappropriate pragmatics takes place in a sixth grade class working on the *Too Good for Drugs* unit during science class. As Mrs. Velasquez introduces the hazards of alcohol, marijuana, and tobacco, Rose raises her hand and begins a passionate lecture to the class on the ill effects of certain foods on health. She dramatically concludes her speech with the statement, "All kids who eat chips and soda and fried foods are going to get fat, fat, fat, and die young!" Shock and awe strike the room, and eyes turn toward Mrs. Velasquez to see how she will respond to the inappropriate remarks, especially since two students in the class clearly struggle with their weight.

What students in your class might struggle with appropriate pragmatics?

Mediating Appropriate Pragmatics with Dwayne and Rose   From
Dwayne's perspective, Mrs. Jackson's cues were not typical in his culture. Conversely, she misinterpreted his behavior as a "disconnect," and as a result she moved on to another student. While the "checklist" for *appropriate pragmatics* lists appropriate eye contact and knowing that you have to answer when a question is asked, this was not the case

for Dwayne. His lack of eye contact shows respect within his cultural context, as does the pause time he needs to reflect before sharing his answer. Asian cultures, as well as Native American and indigenous Central and South American cultures, often reflect these behaviors. In fact, the tendency for rapid responses may be seen as rude. In these situations, your interactions themselves become the targets of mediation. Following a brief consultation on these issues, Mrs. Jackson begins to approach Dwayne differently. She extends her wait time for the entire class, so that each person has up to five seconds before she prompts a response. Dwayne begins to participate and feels more at ease. Mrs. Jackson celebrates to the whole class the value of thinking before responding, and discontinues the use of the phrase, "Remember to look me in the eye when you talk."

Rose's skill in maintaining a topic, changing the topic appropriately, or "interrupting" politely clearly lacks efficiency. She acts unaware of how to talk and behave toward the class or the teacher. To mediate this example of inefficient pragmatics, Mrs. Velasquez, like Mrs. Jackson, implements a multi-layered approach. She begins with mediating intent and reciprocity, using a brief validation of the core content, "It is true that too much unhealthy food can lead to becoming overweight, which can be dangerous. However, let's return to our current topic. What was it, Rose?" Next, she sets up a meeting with Rose away from the rest of the class. In this meeting, Mrs. Velasquez sets goals with Rose to develop skills in two areas of pragmatics: (a) staying on or maintaining the topic, and (b) building awareness of how to talk and behave toward others. Mrs. Velasquez first explains that staying on the same topic as a class helps everyone have a relationship in the conversation, allowing them to learn together . . . even from one another. She adds, "When someone changes the topic randomly, it causes confusion. The other students don't know where to 'put it in their brains,' and, as a result, may lose the focus of the lesson themselves. That's why sometimes you see your classmates looking irritated when you think you have given them great information. Yes, you may have given them great information, but if it is off topic, they will most likely reject it, and what you wanted them to know will be lost. Let's think of some ways to help you stay on topic, so that your great ideas can be a part of the class, and welcomed." At this point, they discuss what both can do to help. Mrs. Velasquez promises that she will always visibly place the topic under discussion on the board. Before she calls on Rose, she will give her a visual reminder (pointing to the topic for the whole class) to help her stop to think about her response before she makes it. They arrange to check in with each other the next day to celebrate how Rose made this work for her and remain on topic.

The second part of the pragmatics issue addresses how Rose's remarks could be seen as offensive to some students. Mediation focuses on building awareness of how to talk and behave toward others. Mrs. Velasquez begins to frame this part of the discussion by saying, "I have also asked you to come to talk to me today, Rose, because I saw some of the students become very uncomfortable while you were talking about becoming fat and dying." Mrs. Velasquez uses the question, "What effect did you intend to have on your classmates?" in order to help Rose set a goal for more effective *communication* that would lead to others respecting and listening to her. Together, they brainstorm ideas about what produces respect. Rose begins to understand that there needs to be mutual listening and respect of other students' ideas and feelings, and also a consideration of how her words affect others. They make an agreement; Mrs. Velasquez will cue with a subtle thumbs up when she notices Rose practicing respectful communication. This will signal Rose quietly to look around for the response of her classmates. Conversely, Mrs. Velasquez will cue with a tap on her own ear when Rose does something disrespectful. This signals Rose to stop the discourse and reevaluate. Each day before recess Rose quietly gives Mrs. Velasquez an example of one thing she has shared with others that has led to reciprocity.

Strategies and Activities Supporting Mediation of Appropriate Pragmatics

Provide Opportunities for *Role-Playing Appropriate Pragmatics*   Students learn well from appropriate models; thus, role-playing each of the elements (cf. following list) helps build consciousness of the need for *appropriate pragmatics*. Work only on one per day. Doing this early in the year sets the standard for the class and provides a model to refer to later, should it be needed. Select one aspect and role-play a situation that does not demonstrate the *appropriate pragmatics*, followed by what needs to be "fixed" to become appropriate. Assign roles to each of four students, whispering to each so the rest of the class can't hear. For instance, using "learning to take turns in conversation," the topic of discussion might be planning a class party. Three of the students demonstrate *appropriate pragmatics* by taking turns sharing ideas. The fourth student's role is to keep interrupting and talk over the other students. After one minute of role-playing, the teacher tells the actors to "freeze," and asks the class, "What was wrong with that situation?" After the discussion, the same four students take the class suggestions to modify the interrupting behavior, and have another minute of role-playing the discussion using *appropriate pragmatics*. On the classroom wall, post a section on effective *communicating* strategies. Post one effective strategy each time the role-play in completed; in this case, post, "we take turns in conversation." Throughout the day, students and teacher identify and celebrate examples of this *communication* skill as they arise (T A L K, 1977).

The following list is the same list shared earlier (adapted from Bowen, 2011). However, this time, the role of the student using inappropriate pragmatics has been added (listed in italics). That role guides the role-play:

- Knowing that you have to answer when a question has been asked [Adverse Role: *Student ignores the questions or greetings of another*];
- Being able to participate in a conversation by taking turns with the other speaker [Adverse Role: *Student's persistent interruptions and overriding of others*];
- Being able to notice and respond to the nonverbal aspects of language (reacting appropriately to the other person's body language and "mood," as well as his or her words) [Adverse Role: *Student engages in too close proximity, not responding to signals of discomfort of the other such as backing up; or ignoring signals of parent on the phone to indicate please wait to talk*];
- Having awareness that you have to introduce a topic of conversation in order for the listener to fully understand [Adverse Role: *Student comes up to group and begins talking about a scene in a movie with no introduction such as, "Did you see the movie xxx?"*];

- Knowing which words or what sort of sentence-type to use when initiating a conversation or responding to something someone has said [Adverse Role: *Student disagrees with the point being made in the conversation by saying, "That's dumb"*];

- Maintaining a topic (or changing a topic appropriately, or "interrupting" politely) [Adverse role: *Student abruptly changes the topic without a transition*];

- Maintaining appropriate eye contact (not too much staring, and not too much looking away) during a conversation [Adverse role: *Student walks away while they are still talking to him, and responds with his back to his peers*]; and

- Distinguishing how to talk and behave toward different communicative partners (formal with some, informal with others) [Adverse Role: *Student moves from peer group on the playground with informal language and gestures to a conversation with the teacher and does not shift to more formal language*].

Model Correct Pragmatics in Speech   When a student uses incorrect grammar or pronunciation, respond to the intended message rather than correcting the pronunciation or grammar. Provide an appropriate model in your own speech. For example, if a student says, "That's how it doesn't go," respond, "You're right. That's not how it goes."

Use *Authentic Pragmatics*   Take advantage of naturally occurring situations. For example, practice a variety of appropriate greetings at the beginning of a day; practice ways to politely request materials needed to complete a project.

How might you mediate students in your class who struggle with appropriate pragmatics?

_____

_____

Feedback for Self-Regulation

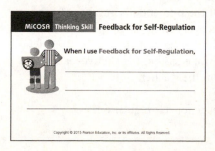

When students notice their mistakes and make the necessary adjustments, they are actually using their own feedback to guide their thinking. These adjustments, or *self-regulations*, can alter both their academic and emotional behaviors. This internal *feedback* might be one of three things: (a) the self-talk that goes on inside the head (i.e., metacognition); (b) the visual check to see if it "looks right"; or (c) the auditory feedback loop, in which saying something out loud creates the auditory signal fed back to the brain to self-check.

  Feedback goes hand in hand with *self-regulation,* since students who use *feedback* well pace themselves (or *self-regulate*) to slow down or ask for clarification when needed. They learn from the results of their own behavior, and grow from it, rarely repeating the same mistakes. How can we help them do this?

Academically, students using *feedback for self-regulation* might use external feedback from teachers or peers to move forward to more complex and creative products. For instance, Mrs. Gonzalez teaches the use of sensory detail in writing. She reads out loud to her students from *James and the Giant Peach* (Dahl, 1996), selecting passages that highlight sensory detail, such as: "his breath was very stale and musty like air from an old cellar." Following the introduction, she asks students to write their own first draft paragraph about a room in a haunted house. Some students in the class produce more sensory detail than others. Mrs. Gonzalez now introduces the ideas of *feedback for self-regulation*. She asks students to go back into their first paragraph, to highlight their own use of sensory detail, and to identify which senses they referenced, using a graphic organizer. Students in her class like Nolan are able to efficiently use this *feedback for self-regulation* and then to go back and create an enriched second draft.

Having strong use of *feedback for self-regulation* is a precursor to future success and autonomy. When students *self-regulate* their work, it becomes more meaningful to them and increases their motivation.

Students Inefficient with Feedback for Self-Regulation

Students who are inefficient using *feedback for self-regulation* seem to be unaware of the effects of their behavior. As a result, they have no reason to *regulate or change* the behavior. Thus, we see low *self-regulation*. For instance, Samantha tends to talk during the lesson while Mr. Waller provides instruction. She appears unaware of other students trying to pay attention, and of those who become distracted by her.

You will want to be cautious not to mistakenly assume that some students simply are not bothering to pay attention to given feedback—that they didn't take the time or care. It may be that they have not understood the meaning of learning to *self-regulate* in their lives. They actually may struggle with how to use *feedback* as a thinking skill, or in knowing what to do with the *feedback* they receive, so their behavior becomes passive.

Adam, for example, needs to hand in a second draft of a sensory detail paragraph he has written, but he has not attended to the feedback embedded in the highlighting and graphic organizers on the first draft. Instead, he busies himself with sharpening his pencils, organizing his desk, checking his backpack, and glancing around the room. Finally, he rewrites his work more neatly, but makes no substantive changes.

Another student, Farid, finds himself staring at the tremendous number of corrections Mrs. Ashby provides. He faithfully recopies everything she has written, but his next paper repeats the same kinds of errors. He has not used *feedback* to *(self)-regulate* his behavior because the nature of the *feedback* did not encourage his active learning; rather, it was unconsciously fostering dependence on the teacher.

What students in your class might struggle with feedback for self-regulation?

Mediating Feedback for Self-Regulation with Samantha, Adam, and Farid   Samantha does not easily *self-regulate* in a large classroom. Mediation begins with

a brief conversation about whether moving her seat somewhere else in the room would help her better *self-regulate*. This makes Samantha active in the process (vs. being told she has to move to right in front of the teacher). Samantha chooses the back because she knows she will not have an "audience" there, whereas in the front of the room she will be tempted to turn around and have all the students' eyes on her. Her teacher, Mr. Waller, lets her know that when he notices Samantha doing especially well with *self-regulation*, he will gently tap on her desk as he walks around the room, in acknowledgement of Samantha's investment of effort. At the end of the period, Mr. Waller comments on her effort and asks, "What differences did you notice as a result of your *self-regulation*?" This allows Samantha to develop meaning in relation to her new behaviors; Mr. Waller supports it with a mediating conversation supporting reciprocity and her growing competence.

Adam sits in passive response to the *feedback* he receives. Lost in thoughts about his problems at home—a rough divorce, which has left everyone fragile—he doesn't see the need to rewrite the paragraph about the haunted house. His internal dialogue shouts, "Who cares?!" Mrs. Gonzalez recognizes she needs to mediate the meaning of why this learning is paramount, not only to Adam, but also to many of her students. She decides to involve the whole class. "Why in the world would we rewrite something that we already wrote?" she asked. Students begin to contribute some ideas. For instance, "We want to do our best work. We can express more than we did before. I am prouder of my work." She then asks, "Okay, when in life might you want to do something over—to use your own feedback or someone else's to do something again?" She then offers a series of prompts to engage the class in "real life" examples of the need for *feedback for self-regulation*, including "re-doing" or "improving on the first attempt." Here are a few of her prompts: Ever play video games more than once for some good reason? Why do that? What was the *feedback* you used? What was the result? How about auto mechanics? Musicians? How might a soccer player use *feedback* to improve his game? Knowing Adam is a skateboarder, she asks, "How about learning to skateboard? What happens the first time you try to do an *ollie*? What *feedback* do you use? Great! It turns out there are lots of times in life you need to pay attention to and use *feedback*—some of it you generate yourself. So what we are doing in class is kind of like practice in using another kind of *feedback*. What *feedback* do you have that you can use on this paragraph? Yes, your teacher's feedback embedded in the graphic organizers and highlighting. Put your revisions in track changes on your next draft, so I can appreciate your attention to the feedback.

Farid feels overwhelmed with the volume of corrections from his teacher, Mrs. Ashby. Fortunately, in discussing Farid's continued problems with another colleague, Mrs. Ashby learns that it is more beneficial to Farid to limit her *feedback* to one or two areas that need improvement. She realizes that including Farid in the process of identifying areas that need to be fixed will help him shift from passive to active learning in the process. She brainstorms on the board a list of the writing issues the class feels are most important to focus on for improvement. They will vote on the top three. Farid (and others) identify one area they struggle with as sentence fragments, so that becomes one of Mrs. Ashby's three areas of focus. The next day, Mrs. Ashby collects samples from students' errors with sentence fragments (with authors' names unidentified) and places them on an overhead screen. She asks the students, "What is the common error in these sentences?" "How do they affect your understanding?" "How can you help the reader get the meaning you intend?" Following this and a short mini-lesson on sentence structure, students work with partners to correct the errors on the overhead and share back with the whole class. Finally, students link this *feedback* to their individual assignments. Mrs. Ashby monitors Farid's *self-regulation* and compliments him on his success.

Strategies and Activities Supporting Mediation of Feedback for Self-Regulation

Use *Binder Reminders*   Some schools require all students to use planners in which they write down homework. Teachers take time at the end of each period (or day) to have students write down their assignments. Some also spend time discussing the meaning of using this information as a means of *feedback* by which they can self-monitor (and *self-regulate*). They discuss examples of parents using planners for work or advanced education, and the use of this source of *feedback* (planners) in business. These applications provide meaning to the assignment, helping to make it a habit.

Encourage *Self-Check Using Feelings*   Encourage students to ask themselves, "If I feel bad, should I use that information to change something?" evoking metacognition.

Practice *Think Aloud*   In reading, sometimes students get stuck. This strategy has them recognize getting stuck as internal feedback, and to use "thinking aloud" about it as a way to move forward. For instance, during paired oral reading, they say out loud, "Oh, what is that word (or something similar)?" and then choose from a group of strategies. They might say, "Let's keep reading and see if the meaning becomes clear from the context," or, "I will try to sound it out" (teachervision.fen.com).

Set *Personal Goals*   Similarly, goals are good benchmarks for self-checking. Creating personal goals allows something to reflect on, using progress toward the goal as the *feedback*.

Keep *Double-Entry Reflective Journals* (www.slideserve.com)   Reflective pieces are a form of *self-feedback*. In any number of subject areas, students might be asked to reflect on their experiences (e.g., reading, science experiment, history project). What helped them be successful? What tools, skills, or strategies supported them? What changes could they make to further improve their work? Following that reflective assignment, students take journal writing to a higher level of metacognition, in which they become aware of using this form of *feedback for self-regulation*. Ask them to write or talk about how their journal entry influenced or changed their thinking or behavior. For example, one student, reflecting after her recent science experiment, felt amazed she could set up, organize, and carry out a meaningful science experiment—and that she liked science! She clamored for more experiences. Her attitude toward science changed.

Create *Rubrics for Self-Regulation*   Well-written rubrics let students know HOW to self-check. Since a clearly written rubric spells out the behavioral indicators for each point of the scale, students can locate their work through comparing what they have done with what is required. Then they use this *feedback* to decide whether to improve or change it. These can be used in a variety of meaningful ways: both teacher and students can create them, students can self-evaluate using rubrics, and student peers can evaluate one another's work.

Use an *Online Coach*   Encourage students to use online sites that give immediate personal feedback for what they are learning.

Putting It Write with Art   Have students write a descriptive piece and draw a picture of what they have written. Students then hide their pictures and give their writing to peers, who draw what they imagine based on what they read. The students then compare drawings and provide *feedback* to each other, comparing levels and numbers of details each imagined the other would see. This strategy also serves as *feedback* to correct misconceptions arising from imprecision of language. Questions such as "Where are the palm trees?" (from the writer) "You didn't tell me in your paper anything about palm trees or their size. If you want them in your description, you need to add that written detail" (from the partner) provide *feedback to self-regulate* in the writing process. This strategy is highly useful with English Language Learners (J. Chancer, 2000).

How might you mediate students in your class who struggle with feedback for self-regulation?

_____

_____

Collaboration

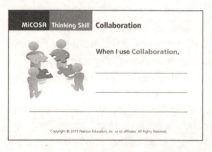

Thinking is not just an individual event; it is also socially constructed and influenced. These collaborative, interpersonal experiences actually enhance thinking. Therefore, *collaboration* is a crucial skill for the 21st century. To engage meaningfully in *collaboration*, your students have to share their thoughts, listen to those of others, and allow themselves to be influenced by another's thinking and ideas. In other words, they don't just do activities like pair-share or reciprocal teaching to share a task or rehearsal, but actually to help move forward their thinking.

When students display efficient collaborative thinking skills, they open their minds as they listen to the thoughts and ideas of peers. *Collaboration* intertwines with other thinking skills from all of the three phases: gathering, transforming, and communicating information. For instance, in a middle school history class, Zach and Spencer pair to *collaborate* on learning about a specific culture in history. They work together in gathering the initial information, each reading and then discussing which categories they might use. Questions to one another (e.g., How did you make that determination? What factors should we use to describe this category?) guide the discovery of how to most effectively categorize their information. Next, they synthesize the information in order to write their own reports. Each has been influenced by the other; each now has stronger learning. Each report is quite unique and reflects use of each boy's own language and sentence structure; yet, the thread of the common, or shared, thinking is apparent in each.

In a fifth grade elementary classroom, the students read the novel *Sign of the Beaver* (Speare, 1984). The theme of the book illustrates how *collaboration* enhances learning. Set in the 1700s, a boy, Matt, has been temporarily left by his father in the wilds of Maine. While adventuring out on his own to hunt, Matt encounters a Penobscot Indian boy about his age, Attean. The two learn essential life skills from one another, each from the other's culture, and out of this develop a friendship. After reading, students work together to make a presentation in the form of a skit to illustrate the *collaboration* in the novel. Brianna, Chandler, and Pedro listen to one another, validate each other's thinking, and then use their initial thoughts as a springboard to brainstorm additional ideas. They continue to actively engage with one another, developing and then performing the skit.

Students Inefficient with Collaboration

Students inefficient or unskilled in *collaborating* fall on two ends of a continuum of participation, yet neither collaborates. The first type is the non-contributor, who may be staring into space or waiting for others to do the thinking—kind of a cognitive loiterer. The second type, the dominant one, either takes charge, sure of having the best thinking in the group, or is "nominated" by others to take charge and/or do the bulk of the work. The "nominees" often consider themselves elite and capable of the "A" grade by themselves, and readily—although often passively—accept the role. These same students often frequently end up resentful of the others. In the case of the dominant volunteer, this student seldom has awareness of the value of others' contributions, and often overtly or covertly demonstrates disrespect for others. This group behavior can either result in discord or result in other members joining the "loiterers" in the background.

Consider the following example of "unused" or "underdeveloped" *collaboration* skills. Mary, Taylor, Eric, and Ian are assigned a *collaborative* project—a report on the Lewis and Clark Expedition. Mary, Eric, and Ian consider Taylor the smartest in the group, so they quickly nominate her to do the work of learning the content. They expect her to parcel out that content to each of the group members on individually made cards in preparation for their presentation. They relegate themselves to poster making, downloading pictures from the Internet, and bringing props. When it comes time for the presentation, the project appears collaborative, although a few of them stumble over some of the words. This is an example of *cooperative* rather than *collaborative* learning. Taylor had taken on the "assignment," not realizing that she could have learned even more or thought differently about the material had the others contributed their thinking to the whole.

In another instance, Darrick, Francisco, Joanne, and Hugh team up to do their science experiment. Darrick initiates the work of the group, taking all the equipment so he can perform the experiment himself. Francisco protests, saying he wants to pour the water into the cylinders. He challenges Darrick as to why he alone should get to do the "fun stuff." Joanne quietly takes her pencil and begins the nonproductive task of copying the instructions into her results booklet, letting the two of them fight it out. Hugh waits and watches. Finally, Darrick declares that Francisco can do parts three and four, giving the appearance of a cooperative experience. At this stage, the others remain passive observers. Following the experimental phase, Darrick then tells Joanne to make the chart. Though Darrick leaves Hugh out of the group project, he finds himself a role in quietly assisting Joanne.

What students in your class might struggle with collaboration?

Mediating Collaboration with Mary, Ian, Taylor, and Eric   In reality, you may not have considered *collaboration* as a way to actually enhance everyone's thinking; thus, you likely have not taught or fostered *collaboration* as a thinking skill. Most teachers tend to think of cooperative groups or strategies as ways to make tasks more efficient, having some "strong" learners help "weaker" learners. At best, perhaps strategies such as pair-share have been used as ways to engage active learning, but they fall short of the potential found in true *collaboration*. Keeping the "sharing" at a level of "I say–you say" misses the opportunity for richer discourse in which students' ideas are modified by one another's thinking. Thus, *collaboration* may become "I say—you say—oh now I say—yes, and what if,—oh well in that case—I never thought of that—wow, now I think—oh!"

In both of the previous inefficient cases, the teachers focus on the *product* of the activity rather than the *process*. In the case of Mary, Ian, Taylor, and Eric's "Lewis and Clark" presentation, Mr. Herrera realizes that his class needs to learn the process of *collaboration*, have it modeled, and understand why it is important. He initiates a new process for the next project. Without calling out names, he shares that he has noticed an imbalance in who did the work on the last projects. He comments that he has seen some of the students taking over with others supporting, but not contributing to the thinking. One or two really did nothing much. Another worked independently, believing he or she had better skills than all the rest of the group.

In overtly discussing *collaboration,* Mr. Herrera points out the value in shared thinking. He shares several examples of how *collaboration* in the work world makes a huge difference (some of the most innovative companies have wonderfully *collaborative* processes). One of the key assets of a high recommendation for a job is "team player" and working with others. College students seek out strong study groups because they are respectful, share ideas and work, and lead to far better results for all the students.

He continues, "To practice learning how to do this, each of you is going to take on a portion of the project that must be shared with the others, and must relate to the work of the others in your group. In fact, you will all rate each other on how respectful you were of others' contributions, how you contributed to the thinking, and how you worked as a team member toward a shared product. Since we are now working on the California Gold Rush, each team will begin by sharing the research." He continues, asking students to brainstorm research topics, find sources of information for the research, and then set deadlines for bringing in their parts to share. He asks specifics, such as how many copies they should bring in and why. In addition, he asks them to talk about the value of establishing these parameters.

The following week they establish new ways to work together (*collaborate*) that will value and integrate each part and create something new out of the whole. First, each person introduces his or her piece, guiding the reading of the others. Each other person in the group asks at least two questions or makes statements in response to the topic, demonstrating their contributions to enrich the learning or making connections with their own research. Following this, they decide on their formats of the reports (e.g., newspaper article, diary entries, website, or PowerPoint) and requirements (e.g., map, timeline, visual, and content). Each student takes charge of one of the requirements and of integrating information from all members for that part.

As a follow-up, groups share what worked for them in *collaboration* and what presented a challenge that they had to work through. Finally, the whole class "visits" each other's presentations (displayed around the classroom) and puts brief constructive feedback on post-it notes on appropriate sections.

PD **pd** TOOLKIT™

PDToolkit: See Video Clip 6.2 for an example of introducing *collaboration* to a class, and students working together to enhance their thinking over time.

Strategies and Activities Supporting Mediation of Collaboration

Stop, Freeze, Collaborate   Model by acting out "not *collaboration*" such as one of the previous scenarios. Then call a "stop freeze" and ask how students can make this collaborative. What is *collaborative*? Then have the students *collaborate* with a partner to generate ideas. Listen to the ideas and then refer to what just happened with their partners—did they share ideas or change any of their own because of what they heard?

Listening Out in the Open   Overtly give information about *collaborative thinking* (as in the previous example). For instance, "When you really listen to someone else's idea, then let yourself respond in your head instead of interrupting, it can change your own thinking, bring you new ideas beyond what they said, or validate what you said before. You have to respect one another's thinking to be changed by it. How do you do that?"

Assign *Jigsaw or Double Jigsaw*   When assigning roles in a jigsaw event, build *collaboration* into the assignment and evaluation (e.g., listened to others, contributed, respectful, helpful to colleagues, integrated ideas of others). Whether with a text or task, each member of the group takes a different part of the whole and teaches his or her part to the other. When you double the jigsaw, each part meets first with others doing the same part, so that they strengthen their knowledge base before returning to their group to share across all parts (Kagan, 1992).

Collaborate Using *Technology Assists*   Web-based word processing programs like Google Docs/Google Drive allow groups to work on the same document from a distance and to see one another's contributions.

Design *Overt Assessment of Collaboration*   Use a rubric in which characteristics of *collaboration* become part of a grade (e.g., contribution to the whole, respect of others' ideas, flow of project). Each student comments about himself or herself and about each other person in the group on each characteristic of your rubric. You can use technology like SurveyMonkey or Qualtrics to have the data set easily available, while filled out anonymously.

Chart *From Seeds to Flowers*   To value each person's contribution to a section of a common document, have each person articulate his or her "bottom lines" in a bulleted or short form (seeds) of what must be there in the final piece—what each student personally considers important. Then have the group look at all pieces together and seek the commonalities and relationships. Out of this, they then build the common document (flower).

Prompt *Collaborative Language*   Raise awareness of using language that represents your student groups' thinking. In preparation for sharing group findings, encourage them to use prompts such as: "We decided that. . . . We believe that. . . . Some of us believe that. . . . Others think that. . . . We came up with several different answers/ solutions. . . . Our ideas are similar to (name group) . . ." (Kinsella, 2001).

How might you mediate students in your class who struggle with collaboration?

_____

_____

SUMMARY

- Communication skills reflect our social nature as people. Today's advanced technology provides an abundance of tools to help your students communicate with others in locations throughout the world. This global communication requires them to understand and respect cultural differences in communication styles. It also requires teachers to provide innovative ways for students to communicate their voices. The MiCOSA Model identifies five common thinking skills that support communication. Each is discussed, with classroom examples of its efficient and inefficient use, as well as strategies and activities to support your work.

- Developing a store of rich *labels, words, and concepts* is an essential skill for communicating information, and is often critical to Second Language Learners. *Labels* describe or classify *words*, and these words, when linked to *concepts*, give communication meaning. To communicate meanings effectively, your students also must have *precision and accuracy,* both verbally and in writing.

- In the 21st century, students are expected to *collaborate* with others from diverse cultures, religions, and lifestyles. They share their thoughts, listen, and allow themselves to be influenced by the thinking and ideas of others. Therefore, it is important that students develop *appropriate pragmatics*, with which they learn to share a mutual respect for each other.

- When students notice their mistakes and make adjustments for improvement, they are using the thinking skill *feedback for self-regulation* to guide their thinking and regulate both academic and emotional behaviors. These students learn from the results of their own behavior and grow from it.

REFERENCES

Beers, K. (2003). *When kids can't read: What teachers can do: A guide for teachers 6–12.* Portsmouth, NH: Heinemann.

Bowen, C. (2011). Information for families: Semantic and pragmantic difficulties. www.speech-language-therapy.com

Bowers, J. (2000a, March). *Little kids can do great things.* Writing Workshop. Ventura, CA: Office of the County Superintendent of Schools.

Bowers, J. (2000b, October). *K-Krew Workshop Series.* Oxnard, CA: Ocean View School District Office.

Chancer, J. (2000). Creating Imagery. ELA Professional Development Workshop. Conejo Valley Unified District Office, Thousand Oaks, CA.

Cleary, L. M., & Peacock, T. D. (1998). *Collected wisdom: American Indian education.* Boston: Allyn & Bacon.

Cummins, J. (2003). BICS and CALP: Origins and rationale for the distinction. In C. B. Paulston & G. R. Tucker (Eds.), *Sociolinguistics: The essential readings* (pp. 322–328). London: Blackwell.

Dahl, R. (1996). *James and the giant peach.* New York, NY: Puffin.

Dutro, S. (2004). *A focused approach to frontloading English language instruction for Houghton Mifflin.* California Reading and Literature Project. La Jolla, CA: University of California San Diego.

Everett, K. (1986). *Bridging language experience into the classroom.* A workshop for Meadows Elementary School, Thousand Oaks, CA.

Greene, J. F. (2009). *Language! A literacy intervention curriculum.* Boston, MA: Sopris West.

Haven, C. (2009, October 12). The new literacy: Stanford study finds richness and complexity in students' writing. *Stanford News Service.* Retrieved from http://news.stanford.edu/pr/2009/pr-lunsford-writing-101209.html

Kagan, S. (1992). *Cooperative learning.* San Juan Capistrano, CA: Resources for Teachers, Inc.

Kinsella, K. (2001). *Strategies to build a school-wide academic writing program.* Office of the Ventura County Superintendent of Schools. Ventura, CA.

Kinsella, K. (2003, March). *Strategies to promote responsible reading and writing in grades 6–12.* Workshop presented to Ventura County Schools. Cowan Center, Camarillo, CA.

Perona, S. (1989, Jan/Feb). The tea party: Intro, through, and beyond a piece of literature. *The Writing Notebook,* 30–31.

Sheridan, R. B. (2008/1775). *The rivals: a comedy.* Gloucester, UK: Dodo Press.

Speare, E. G. (1984). *The sign of the beaver.* Bel Air, CA: Yearling.

T A L K–Teaching Activities for Language Knowledge. (1977). *A project of the National Diffusion Network, Department of Education.* Rockford Public Schools, Rockford, Illinois.

Trilling, B., & Fadel, C. (2009). *21st century skills: Learning for life in our times.* San Francisco, CA: Jossey-Bass.

Chapter Seven

Content, Curriculum, and Standards: Finding the Thinking Skills and Writing Objectives

The thinking skills embedded within content, curriculum, and standards provide catalysts to enhancing both current and future lessons. Similarly, they serve as energizing tools to access and develop the 21 thinking skills.

Remember those "eureka" moments when the "fog clears" and you suddenly "get something"? When I first began learning about mediation and thinking skills, I sometimes felt a bit of that same "fog." I had read about it, knew I was on to something great, but didn't get the full power of it until I began to connect what I had learned to a simple problem: "You are about to board the Santa Maria, bound for the West Indies. Plan the supplies you would need to sustain you on the journey. Explain your reasons."

When I was asked to identify as many thinking skills as I could to complete this assignment, I had one of those "eureka" moments! I began by finding thinking skills that seemed most intuitive: planning, and using multiple sources of information. Then I had to dig deeper. Categorizing would help me organize my lists of supplies. Using hypothesizing helped me consider options. I tried to delve even deeper. I would need goal setting before I could plan. I had to know how many people were going and the duration of the trip (position in time). Finding connections and relationships among the people and the supplies was imperative. How much food could I bring per person? How many days worth do I need? I was "getting it!" Wow! No wonder some of my students struggled when I gave them similar assignments! It had never occurred to me how much thinking went into a task that at first appeared so easy. Now I understood the importance of connecting the thinking skills to the content and standards. I examined problems in different contexts (An elementary teacher).

Across the globe, national and state committees have developed frameworks that outline expectations for student achievement. However, they are named in different ways, from "standards," "academic content standards," and "core curriculum," to "content frameworks." In 2010, the United States crafted common national standards in the areas of language arts and mathematics, called Common Core State Standards (CCSS). For the sake of consistency, in the MiCOSA Model you will see the term *standards* used to refer to all these frameworks.

To begin connecting thinking skills to standards, first you will look for core concepts within the standard you select. The core concepts are the parts of the standard that delineate its major concepts, skills, strategies, or processes. For example, a seventh grade Reading Standard for Literature requires students to "analyze how the author develops and contrasts the points of view of different characters or narrators in text." The core concept of this standard would be to "analyze how the author develops and contrasts different points of view."

The College and Career Readiness Anchor Standards for Writing for grades 6–12 require students to "gather relevant information from multiple print and digital sources, assess the credibility and accuracy of each source, and integrate the information while avoiding plagiarism." One of the core concepts of this standard, and the first, is to "gather relevant information from multiple sources."

Some of the core concepts within standards explicitly link to thinking skills and are easy to identify, while others, which are more subtle and implicit, require analysis. For ease of learning, you will focus on finding one thinking skill at a time, although often more than one is required to teach a standard. You will then use core concepts and thinking skills to design content objectives, Big Ideas, essential questions, and assessments, as well as to guide your teaching.

Locating Explicit Thinking Skills

PDToolkit: See Video Clip 7.1 for an example of educators working together as they locate explicit thinking skills in standards.

Many U.S. Common Core State Standards (CCSS) (2010) use words that explicitly and directly parallel some of MiCOSA's 21 thinking skills. You will find familiar terms such as *compare, connect, infer,* and *order* in CCSS *and* your set of thinking skills. Therefore, you will begin practicing finding these explicit thinking skills within the standards first. For example, the third grade standard in English language arts states, "*Compare* and contrast the themes, settings, and plots of stories written by the same author about the same or similar characters."[1] The verb *compare* points you directly to the thinking skill *comparing,* which implies both comparing and contrasting. In grade seven, the thinking skill *comparing* is being used at a more complex level, "*Compare* and contrast a written story, drama, or poem to its audio, filmed, staged, or multimedia version. . . ."[2] Figure 7.1 illustrates these skills within the CCSS Standards, highlighting explicit thinking skills across content areas and grade levels. Once you identify these thinking skills within the standards, you can use them as your instructional focus to help students better master the standards, and then bridge these skills to other standards throughout the curriculum.

Most teachers are familiar with another explicit thinking skill: understanding and using *cause and effect* relationships. You find *cause and effect* embedded explicitly in a science standard at grade five: "Students know the *causes and effects* of different types of severe weather."[3] In a history example at grade ten, you find, "Students analyze the *causes* and course of the First World War,"[4] and following that, "Students analyze the *effects* of the First World War."[5] Similarly, a less familiar thinking skill, gathering sufficient information using *multiple sources,* appears across grade levels and content areas. Although the exact words *multiple sources* may not appear, the explicit meaning is clear. In grade five, students must "Conduct short research projects that use *several sources* to build knowledge of investigation of different aspects of a topic."[6] Then, in grades nine and ten, they are asked to do a similar task at a higher level, "Conduct . . . research projects to answer a question or solve a problem . . . [and] synthesize *multiple sources* on the subject."[7]

---

[1]Common Core State Standards for English Language Arts (2010), Reading Standards for Literature K–5, Grade 3, Standard 9, p. 12.

[2]CCSS for English Language Arts (2010), Reading Standards for Literature 6–12, Grade 7, Standard 7, p. 37.

[3]Science Content Standards for California Public Schools: Kindergarten Through Grade Twelve (1998), Grade 5, ES4.c.

[4]History Social Science Content Standards for California Public Schools: Kindergarten Through Grade Twelve (1998), Grade 10, 10.5.

[5]CA Standard 5.4.c History Social Science Content Standards for California Public Schools: Kindergarten Through Grade Twelve (1998), Grade 10, 10.6.

[6]CCSS for English Language Arts (2010), Writing Standards K–5, Grade 5, Standard 7, p. 22.

[7]CCSS for English Language Arts (2010), Writing Standards 6–12, Grades 9–10, Standard 7, p. 46.

> **FIGURE 7.1**
>
> **Finding Thinking Skills in Common Core State Standards**
>
> ---
>
> *English Language Arts: Grade 3*
>
> Reading Standards for Literature: 9
> **Compare and contrast** the themes, settings, and plots of stories written by the same author about the same or similar characters.
>
> Reading Standards for Informational Text: 3
> **Describe the relationship** between a series of historical events, scientific ideas or concepts, or steps in a technical procedure in a text, using language that pertains to **time, sequence, and cause/effect.**
>
> Writing Standards: 5
> With guidance and support from peers and adults, develop and strengthen writing as needed by **planning,** revising, and editing.
>
> Listening and Speaking: 1
> Engage effectively in a range of **collaborative discussions** with diverse partners on grade 3 topics and texts, building on each others' ideas and expressing their own clearly.
>
> *English Language Arts: Grades 9–10*
>
> Reading Standards for Literature 6–12: 4
> Determine the **meaning of words and phrases** as they are used in the text, including figurative and connotative meanings.
>
> Reading Standards for Informational Text 6–12: 2
> Determine a central idea of a text and analyze its development over the course of the text; . . . provide an objective **summary** of the text.
>
> Writing Standards 6–12: 2.a
> Introduce a topic; **organize complex ideas,** concepts, and information clearly and accurately to **make important connections** and distinctions.
>
> Speaking and Listening Standards 6–12: 2
> Integrate **multiple sources of information** presented in diverse media or formats (e.g., visually, quantitatively, orally) evaluating the credibility and **accuracy** of each source.

Math Standards: Grade 4

Operations and Algebraic Thinking: 4OA.1
Interpret a multiplication equation as a **comparison,** e.g., interpret $35 = 5 \times 7$ as a statement that 35 is 5 times as many as 7 and 7 times as many as 5.

Number and Operations—Fractions: 4.NF3.c
Add and subtract mixed numbers with like denominators, e.g., by replacing each mixed number with an equivalent fraction, and/or by using properties of operations and the **relationship between addition and subtraction**.

Geometry 4.G.2
Classify two-dimensional figures based on the presence or absence of parallel or perpendicular lines, or the presence or absence of angles of a specified size. **Recognize right triangles as a category,** and identify right triangles.

Math Standards: Grade 7

Statistics and Probability: 7.SP.2
Use data from a random sample to **draw inferences** about a population with an unknown characteristic of interest. Generate **multiple samples** (or simulated samples) of the same size to gauge the variation in estimates or **predictions.**

Math Standards: Grades 9–12 Algebra II

Creating Equations A-CED.2
Create equations in two or more variables to represent **relationships between quantities;** graph equations on coordinate axes with labels and scales.

Math Standards: Grades 9–12 Statistics and Probability

Interpreting Categorical and Quantitative Data: S-ID5.
Summarize categorical data for two **categories** in two-way frequency tables.

Making Inferences and Justifying Conclusions: S-IC1.
Understand statistics as a process for **making inferences** about population parameters based on a random sample from that population.

Try Practice Activity 1 to identify explicit thinking skills in standards.

Explicitly Stated Thinking Skills   Practice Activity 1

Directions: Using the following list of thinking skills, find and underline the words that cue the explicit thinking skill in each of the following standards from Common Core State Standards, and from state standards in California and Florida. <u>Write the name of the thinking skill above each underlined cue.</u>

1. **Math Grade 4.**[8] <u>Compare two fractions</u> with different numerators and different denominators.
2. **Math (K–12).**[9] <u>Attend to precision.</u>
3. **Science Grade 8.**[10] <u>Define a problem from the eighth grade curriculum</u> . . . and carry out investigations of various types, such as systematic observation or experiments.
4. **Writing Grade 1.**[11] [Students] write narratives in which they . . . <u>use temporal words to signal event</u> order.
5. **Math Grade 8.**[12] (Students will) <u>understand the relationship between zeroes and factors</u> of polynomials and <u>make connections among mathematical ideas</u> and to other disciplines.
6. **Speaking and Listening Grade K–2.**[13] (Students will) <u>participate in collaborative conversations</u> with diverse partners about (grade level) topics and texts.
7. **Social Science Kindergarten.**[14] <u>Compare family customs and traditions</u> among cultures.

Gathering Information	Transforming Information	Communicating Information
Systematic Search	Setting Goals	Labels, Words, and Concepts
Focus and Attention	Planning	Precision and Accuracy
Labels, Words, and Concepts	Comparing	Appropriate Pragmatics
Multiple Sources	Ordering, Grouping, and Categorizing	Feedback for Self-Regulation
Position in Space	Finding Connections and Relationships	Collaboration
Position in Time	Visualizing	
Precision and Accuracy	Inferring	
	Cause and Effect—Hypothesizing	
	Summarizing	

Answers: 1. Comparing 2. Precision and Accuracy 3. (a) Setting Goals (b) Systematic Search 4. (a) Position in Time (b) Labels, Words, and Concepts 5. Finding Connections and Relationships 6. Collaboration 7. Comparing

---

[8]CCSS for Mathematics (2010), Grades K–5, Grade 4 Number and Operations, 4.NF2.
[9]CCSS for Mathematics (2010), Mathematics/Standards for Mathematical Practice, Grades K–12, p. 7.
[10]Next Generation Sunshine State Standards (2008–10), Grade 8, SC.8.N.1.1. (www.floridastatestandards.org/Standards/FloridaStateStandardSearch.aspx).
[11]CCSS for English Language Arts (2010), Writing Standards K–5, Grade 1, Standard 3, p. 19.
[12]CCSS for Mathematics (2010), High School–Algebra, A–APR, 2,3.
[13]CCSS for English Language Arts (2010), Speaking and Listening Standards K–5, Standard 1, p. 23.
[14]Tennessee Social Studies Content Curriculum Standards K1.02.d, www.stae.tn./education/curriculum.shtml

Locating Implicit Thinking Skills

PD TOOLKIT™

PDToolKit: See Video Clip 7.2 for an example of a group of educators working together to locate the more challenging implicit thinking skills in standards.

Locating the thinking skills implicit in a standard is a bit more complex; it requires you to analyze the standard and identify the thinking skill or skills necessary to meet it. Frequently, you must identify more than one thinking skill, for two reasons. First, sometimes you may choose to incorporate more than one thinking skill in a lesson. Second, you may identify multiple thinking skills to support students who don't seem to understand a standard because they need help with one of those thinking skills. From the various thinking skills you identify, you will later learn to choose which one(s) to work with or target within your lessons. Look now at a first grade standard from California. First, find one fairly obvious implicit thinking skill. Then "dig deeper" by deconstructing that standard to find other thinking skills.

> **History Social Science, Grade 1: Locate on globes and maps their local community, California, the United States, the seven continents, and the four oceans.**[15]

What might be an implicit thinking skill? How would you find it? Remember, it is often helpful to begin with one of the core concept in the standard: Students will locate the continents. Sometimes you will find it helpful to focus on the verb; in this case, the verb is *locate*.

- To successfully locate the continents, your students will need to use *position in space*. Spatial terms such as *above, below, left, right, top,* and *bottom*, as well as *north, south, east,* and *west,* are key words and concepts that help the students "locate" their own positions in space as well as the positions of other objects. Without adequate spatial orientation, students may flounder, having difficulty following the instructions or modeling from the teacher or peers.

- What other thinking skills might be implicit in the standard? At first glance, *position in space* may appear to be the major thinking skill. However, your students may be efficient with *position in space* but not with other skills that may enhance their learning. In this case, they will need *labels, words, and concepts* so they can learn the names of the places, as well as understand the concept of a continent.

- *Precision and accuracy* in communication helps them accurately pinpoint the locations on maps and globes, or describe the locations.

Now, try finding other implied thinking skills within the following sixth grade standard. It may appear simple on the surface, but actually requires a complex set of thinking skills.

> **Language Arts, Grade 6.**[16] **Present claims and findings . . . [and] use appropriate eye contact, adequate volume, and clear pronunciation.**

---

[15]History Social Science Content Standards for California Public School: Kindergarten Through Grade Twelve (1998), Grade 1, 1.2.1.

[16]Common Core State Standards for English Language Arts and Literacy in History/Science and Technical Subjects 6–12 (2010), Speaking and Listening Standards 6–12, Grade 6.

The core concept of this standard has to do with appropriate ways to enter into a discourse.

- When you think about appropriate eye contact and volume, you tend to think of socially acceptable behavior. This leads you to the skill of *appropriate pragmatics*, which involves the use of language in social contexts and alignment or connection of appropriate verbal and nonverbal cues.
- What else is needed? In gathering information for this task, students must use *labels, words, and concepts* and *multiple sources*. They need to know what volume, eye contact, and pronunciation mean. They need to understand the words *claims* and *findings*.
- Then, they have to hold *multiple sources* as they formulate their oral response.
- Once the information is gathered, they transform it using *comparing*. They compare their speaking and listening with that of peers and models, observing whether the volume and pronunciation are yielding sustained audience attention.
- Finally, in communicating their results, they use *feedback for self-regulation* by observing, listening, or reading explicit feedback on their performance.

If you see different or additional skills needed, we'd probably agree. You may be surprised to see all those thinking skills in one standard. Not to worry! Later you will learn how to choose one or two, and how to integrate them into your lesson. The idea is to find a way to help your students build, use, and transfer new and important thinking skills.

Look at Practice Activity 2 and determine what thinking skills will support this standard. This time you will need to look beyond the verbs, such as *recognize*, *draw*, and *identify*, because

---

Implicit Thinking Skills   Practice Activity 2

Directions: Identify implicit thinking skills that would be needed to help students successfully meet the following standard.

Math Grade 2.[17] Recognize and draw shapes having specified attributes, such as a given number of angles or a given number of equal faces. Identify triangles, quadrilaterals, pentagons, hexagons, and cubes.

Thinking Skills for Gathering Information	Thinking Skills for Transforming Information	Thinking Skills for Communicating Information
Systematic Search	Goal Setting	Labels, Words, and Concepts
Focus and Attention	Planning	Precision and Accuracy
Labels, Words, and Concepts	Comparing	Appropriate Pragmatics
Multiple Sources	Ordering, Grouping, and Categorizing	Feedback for Self-Regulation
Position in Space	Finding Connections and Relationships	Collaboration
Position in Time	Visualizing	
Precision and Accuracy	Inferring	
	Cause and Effect—Hypothesizing	
	Summarizing	

---

[17]Common Core State Standards for Mathematics (2010), Grades K–5, Grade 2, Geometry 2.6.1.

they do little to support finding the implicit skills. Look at the core concept of the standard. It asks your students to identify various geometric forms and know their differences and uniqueness. To do so, students must know their specific physical attributes and given labels.

- Did you think of *ordering, grouping, and categorizing*? This certainly will help. However, in order to "recognize and draw shapes having specific attributes," and "identify [shapes]," your students may also need additional thinking skills.
- First, they will have to use *labels*, *words, and concepts* to understand the meaning of *attribute*, *angle*, *faces*, *triangle*, *pentagon*, *hexagon*, and *cube*.
- The students need to use *attention and focus* and *precision and accuracy*, as they carefully look at the shapes. For example, a pentagon has five sides, and a hexagon has six sides.
- When given shapes of different types, they have to use *multiple sources* (know the attributes of all the shapes) and then *compare* the shapes to correctly *categorize* them.
- Additionally, as the students draw the indicated shapes, correct *position in space* is needed for them to be successful.

As complex as these standards can be, taking them apart is really helpful. For example, take a look at Practice Activity 3, which is associated with World History:

Implicit Thinking Skills   Practice Activity 3

Directions: Identify implicit thinking skills that would be needed to help students successfully meet the following standard.

World History Grade 10.[18] Trace the evolution of work and labor, including the demise of the slave trade and the effect of immigration, mining, manufacturing, division of labor, and the union movement.

_____

_____

_____

Thinking Skills for Gathering Information	**Thinking Skills for Transforming Information**	**Thinking Skills for Communicating Information**
Systematic Search	Goal Setting	Labels, Words, and Concepts
Focus and Attention	Planning	Precision and Accuracy
Labels, Words, and Concepts	Comparing	Appropriate Pragmatics
Multiple Sources	Ordering, Grouping, and Categorizing	Feedback for Self-Regulation
Position in Space	Finding Connections and Relationships	Collaboration
Position in Time	Visualizing	
Precision and Accuracy	Inferring	
	Cause and Effect—Hypothesizing	
	Summarizing	

---

[18]History Social Science Content Standards for California Public Schools: Kindergarten Through Grade Twelve (1998), Grade 10, 10.3.4.

Identify the core concept within this standard. The standard requires students to trace the evolution of work and labor. It also outlines specific areas of focus: (a) the demise of the slave trade; (b) the effect of immigration, mining, manufacturing; (c) division of labor; and (d) the birth of unions. Look for the thinking skills foundational to that core concept and its four areas of focus.

- What helped you identify *cause and effect—hypothesizing*? Did you notice the word *effect* in the standard? What did the word *demise* cue for you? Students must understand what *caused* the demise of the slave trade. But the standard also asks students to attend to the specific *cause and effect* relationships between movements and events like immigration and mining on work and labor.

- Did you think of *position in time*? Great! The use of the word *evolution* suggests something happening over time; therefore, students will need to gather information, using *position in time*, which will help them determine the chronological order of events.

This standard is actually even more complex, and provides you with several other potential areas of thinking skill focus. The intent is not to overwhelm you with a detailed analysis of a single standard, but just to create an awareness of the levels of complexity you might draw on given a complex standard. Once aware, you will be able to identify and mediate thinking skills that prove problematic and stand in the way of a student's understanding of a given standard/concept/idea. Here are a few of the other thinking skills in relation to tracing the evolution of work and labor.

- Students need to gather information about the use of the thinking skill *multiple sources*. Why? Like putting together a complex jigsaw puzzle, this standard asks your students to gather many pieces in order to complete the picture of the evolution of work and labor.

- To do this, they also need to *find connections and relationships* between the events (e.g., demise of the slave trade to the evolution of work and labor).

Yes, this is a lot to take in. However, this highly complex standard was used so that you could see the scope of the connections between standards and thinking skills.

Thinking Skills Underlying Common Terms in Standards

As you scan the standards, you constantly see familiar terms such as *know*, *analyze*, and *describe* that do not explicitly point to using one or two thinking skills. These terms can leave you uncertain as to how to teach them. In addition, their rich depth can be hard to see on first glance. Bloom's Cognitive Process Dimensions strive to order such terms in levels of complexity. Similarly, Webb's Depth of Knowledge model analyzes and levels the expected depth of knowledge required to complete a task. At first glance, you may think that having your students "know" is simple and "analyze" is complex; however, in the context of the standard, it is not that straightforward. Terms such as *describe, determine, evaluate, interpret, generate, decompose* (sounds deadly, but we mean in math!), *delineate*, and *represent* occur frequently and may leave questions as to how to interpret their meaning. Many of these terms are associated with critical thinking, and help your students "sift through" a mass of facts in search of interconnectedness and meaning (Lantos, 2006). This requires considerable use of thinking skills. Therefore, defining these words and analyzing how they are used in the standards helps you locate the thinking skills needed to successfully and critically teach these standards.

Finding the Thinking Skills in "Students Will Know"

Many standards used to require students to "know"; some still do. In addition, you may often want your students to "know things." Dig down a little into the word *know*. Longman's (2000)[19] suggests that to know is to "have information about something, to be sure of something, to be familiar with, to realize something exists or is true, to be skillful or experienced."

In many cases, the term *know* suggests a superficial recognition of facts or base content (e.g., know the times tables; know the 50 states). However, often it is far more complex. Look at the following four social studies standards that ask students to "know" specific content, and locate additional thinking skill(s) that support that knowledge.

1. *Know the history of the decline of Muslim rule in the Iberian peninsula that culminated in the use of kingdoms.*[20] In this particular standard, to "know" with understanding requires several thinking skills. Here are a few. The word "history" and "decline" cue you to use the thinking skill of *position in time* since you need to refer to information over a time period. The Iberian peninsula is mentioned, so the thinking skill of *position in space* is most likely needed since the location is important to the standard. Since there is more than one kingdom, most likely *ordering, grouping, and categorizing* will be necessary.

---

[19]*Longman Advanced American Dictionary* (2000), Essex, England: Pearson Education Limited, pp. 793–794.
[20]History Social Science Content Standards for California Public Schools: Kindergarten Through Grade 12 (1998), Grade 7, 7.6.9.

2. *Know the significance of Hammurabi's Code.*[21] It takes an array of thinking skills to understand why something is significant. First of all, *labels, words, and concepts* define a term for initial understanding. Within that definition, using *cause and effect* helps the student clarify their understanding, since "knowing the significance" can be interpreted as " why is it important?" *Finding connections and relationships* among the events will further deepen the significance of Hammurabi's Code.

3. *Know the great voyages of discovery, the location of the routes, and the influence of cartography in the development of a new European worldview.*[22] In this standard, the use of location suggests the thinking skill *position in space.* Further, the phrase *great voyages* asks students to quantify and sequence voyages of discovery based on which one had more lasting effects. Students need to use *cause and effect, and ordering, grouping and categorizing* to help them make these determinations. Later, they need to *compare* voyages and *find connections and relationships* to see their influence on cartography. These same thinking skills are necessary to then compare cartography with "developing a new European worldview."

Finding the Thinking Skills Required to "Analyze"

In terms of thinking skills, *analyze* is an even more powerful word, central to critical thinking as well as occurring frequently in our standards. What thinking skills will your students need to do that analysis? According to Merriam Webster,[23] *analyze* suggests, "separating or distinguishing the component parts of something (as a substance, a process, a situation) so as to discover its true nature or inner relationships." Longman's[24] adds, "To examine or think about something carefully in order to understand it." Thus, you are both "taking apart" an idea or process, and then thinking about the relationships of those parts to one another or to a broader purpose, in order to seek deeper understanding and meaning. Now take a look at applying that to three standards.

---

[21]History Social Science Content Standards for California Public Schools: Kindergarten Through Grade 12 (1998), Grade 9,9.11.1.
[22]History Social Science Content Standards for California Public Schools: Kindergarten Through Grade 12 (1998), Grade 6,6.6.5.
[23]http://www.merriam-webster.com/dictionary/analyze
[24]*Longman's Advanced American Dictionary* (2000), Essex, England: Pearson Education Limited. p. 45.

(1) *Analyze . . . documents of historical and literary significance, including foundational U.S. documents (e.g., the Declaration of Independence, the Preamble to the Constitution, the Bill of Rights) for their premises, purposes, and structure.*[25]

Knowing the purpose or object of the analysis is critical. That purpose or object often involves complex materials that require categorizing. For instance, in the previous example, students must analyze documents for their premises, purposes, and structures. Begin with the *labels, words, and concepts* behind "premises, purposes, and structures." Not having a firm grasp of those concepts will throw any student off track! Next, move into "taking apart" the documents, and then *categorizing them* into premises, purposes, and structures. Following that, they must find *connections and relationships* among those elements in order to make meaning.

(2) *Analyze in detail how an author's ideas or claims are developed and refined by particular sentences, paragraphs, or larger portions of a text (e.g., a section or chapter).*[26]

Here, analysis requires "breaking down" the standard into the *categories* of the author's ideas, sentences, paragraphs, and larger portions of a text, like sections or chapters. *Finding connections and relationships* between and among those categories leads to understanding how the author's ideas relate to the development of the sentences, paragraphs, and larger chunks of text.

(3) *Analyze to what degree a filmed or live production of a drama or a story stays faithful to or departs from the script or text.*[27]

In this case, analysis requires "breaking down" elements of the production into a continuum in which the *categories* might be: (a) highly faithful; (b) often faithful; (c) seldom faithful; or (d) depart from text. Being able to use *ordering, grouping, and categorizing* is essential. *Comparing* the script and the text helps facilitate that categorizing. Finally, *finding connections and relationships* between and among those categories underlies providing the evidence to substantiate the degree of relationship requested.

Ambiguous High Frequency Terms

Now that you have walked through two ambiguous terms (*know, analyze*), MiCOSA provides a useful table (see Figure 7.2) to help you understand additional high frequency "ambiguous" terms found in the standards, such as *synthesize, interpret,* and *evaluate.* Each of these terms corresponds to several of MiCOSA's 21 thinking skills. In addition, the table indicates which terms link with either critical thinking or creative thinking, both of which are central in 21st century learning.

---

[25]CCSS for English Language Arts and Literacy in History/Science and Technical Subjects 6–12 (2010), Reading Standards for Informational Text, 6–12, Grades 11–12, p. 9.

[26]CCSS for English Language Arts and Literacy in History/Science and Technical Subjects 6–12 (2010), Reading Standards for Informational Text, 6–12. Grade 9–10, p. 5.

[27]CCSS for English Language Arts and Literacy in History/Science and Technical Subjects 6–12 (2010), Reading Standards for Literature 6–12, Grade 8, p. 7.

FIGURE 7.2

Thinking Skills Implied in High Frequency Ambiguous Terms

HIGH FREQUENCY TERM *Denotes frequent association with critical or creative thinking	**DEFINITION**	**MiCOSA THINKING SKILLS REQUIRED**
*Analyze	Separating or distinguishing the component parts of something (as a substance, a process, a situation) so as to discover its true nature or inner relationships (1). To examine or think about something carefully in order to understand it (2).	*Finding Connections and Relationships; Ordering, Grouping and Categorizing; Inferring*
*Interpret	To conceive in the light of individual belief, judgment, or circumstance circumstance (1); to explain or tell the meaning of present in understandable terms (2).	*Labels, Words and Concepts; Multiple Sources; Summarizing; Inferring*
*Evaluate, Assess	To determine the significance, worth or condition by careful appraisal or study (1).	*Comparing; Ordering, Grouping and Categorizing; Multiple Sources; Precision and Accuracy*
*Synthesize	To make something by combining different things into a complete whole; to combine separate things into a complete whole (2).	*Multiple Sources; Ordering, Grouping and Categorizing; Comparing; Finding Connections and Relationships*
Demonstrate, Prove (cf. Math & Science)	To prove or make clear by reasoning, or evidence; to illustrate and explain especially with many examples (1).	*Comparing; Finding Connections and Relationships; Precision and Accuracy; Cause and Effect—Hypothesizing*
Determine, *Decide, Judge	To find out or come to a decision about by investigation, reasoning, or calculation (1). If something determines something else, it directly influences or decides it (2).	*Comparing; Finding Connections and Relationship; Inferring; Cause and Effect—Hypothesizing; Summarizing; Feedback for Self-Regulation*
Distinguish, Differentiate, Discern	To separate into kinds, classes, or categories (1). To recognize the difference between two or more things or people (2).	*Comparing; Multiple Sources; Ordering, Grouping and Categorizing; Precision and Accuracy*

Describe, Delineate, Depict	To represent or give an account of in words (1). To say what something is like by giving details about them (2).	*Labels, Words, and Concepts; Comparing; Finding Connections and Relationships; Visualizing*
*Develop, Elaborate	To set forth or make clear by degrees or in detail (1). To design or make a new idea, product system over a period of time: to grow or change into something bigger, stronger, or more advanced, or to make someone or something do this (2).	*Precision and Accuracy; Planning; Multiple Sources; Cause and Effect—Hypothesizing; Position in Time*
*Integrate, Incorporate	To form, coordinate or blend into a functioning or unified whole (1) combine or work together to create something more effective (2).	*Comparing; Finding Connections and Relationships; Multiple Sources; Summarizing*

(1) Merriam-Webster Dictionary. Online version: www.merriam-webster.com/
(2) *Longman's Advanced American Dictionary* (2000), Essex, England: Pearson Education Limited.

Finding Patterns in Standards

Similarities in standards, presented as patterns across the grade levels, serve as the foundation of the Common Core State Standards (CCSS). Whether those standards are in English, history, social studies, science, math, or technical areas, the CCSS align with broad and cognitively demanding College and Career Readiness (CCR) anchor standards. CCR standards outline 10 criteria for mastery in each subject area. These inform the grade level CCSS, which then outline specificity and increasing complexity at each grade level.

Similarly, you scaffold thinking skills. By looking at the continuum of learning outlined in the CCSS and most other standards, you can determine where you place your students' current level of understanding and plan the journey ahead toward mastery. Figure 7.3 illustrates these relationships, using the CCR "anchor standard" #2 for Reading, and aligning the grade level and reading standard, along with thinking skills needed to teach and learn the reading standard. You teach initial thinking skills from kindergarten on, and build on those each year, increasing the complexity of their use. You also add in additional thinking skills as the content increases in complexity. Italicized thinking skills in the figure represent thinking skills carried over from year to year, and thus provide an illustration on how you can build on prior work.

FIGURE 7.3

Developing Thinking Skills Through the Common Core State Standards

CCR Anchor Standard #2: Determine central ideas or themes of a text and analyze their development; summarize the key supporting details and ideas.[1]

Grade Level	Common Core State Standard	Progression of MiCOSA Thinking Skills Needed
Grade K	With prompting and support, retell familiar stories, including key details.[2]	*Labels, Words, and Concepts* *Precision and Accuracy* *Summarizing* *Position in Time*
Grade 4	Determine a theme of a story, drama, or poem from details in the text; summarize the text.[3]	*Labels, Words, and Concepts* *Precision and Accuracy* *Summarizing* *Position in Time* Additional Skills Needed: *Finding Connections and Relationships, Inferring*
Grade 7	Determine a theme or central idea of a text and analyze its development over the course of the text; provide an objective summary of the text.[4]	*Labels, Word, and Concepts* *Precision and Accuracy* *Summarizing* *Position in Time* *Finding Connections and Relationships* *Inferring* Additional Skills Needed: Ordering, *Grouping, and Categorizing; Planning*
Grades 11–12	Determine two or more themes or central ideas of a text and analyze their development over the course of the text, including how they interact and build on one another to produce a complex account; provide an objective summary of the text.[5]	*Labels, Words, and Concepts* *Precision and Accuracy* *Summarizing* *Position in Time* *Finding Connections and Relationships* *Inferring* *Ordering, Grouping, and Categorizing* *Planning* Here, each thinking skill is used with greater complexity, since the complexity of the task has increased.

[1] P. 10 (see above comment)

[2] #2 K, p.11

[3] P. 12

[4] Lit 6–12 #2, p. 36

[5] P. 38

From Standards to Thinking Skills and Content Objectives

So far, you have identified a variety of examples of specific thinking skills needed to support students learning specific standards. Since standards often represent large concepts to learn, you will need to break them down into manageable objectives. It is within these objectives that you can lay the foundations of your work with the thinking skills—sometimes across several lessons.

Writing Content Objectives with Thinking Skills

Take a look at a standard you worked with earlier in the chapter, which illustrates how you can move from locating the thinking skills in the standards to using those skills to write content and thinking skill objectives. In this first example, the core concepts in the standard are underlined, so you can connect the thinking skills you will need to achieve that learning.

> **Math Grade 2.**[28] <u>Recognize and draw shapes having specified attributes</u>, such as a given number of angles or a given number of equal faces. Identify triangles, quadrilaterals, pentagons, hexagons, and cubes.

The core concept of this standard requires students to recognize specific attributes of shapes (polygons) and to be able to draw them. Earlier you used this main concept to brainstorm a list of implicit thinking skills your students would need: *labels, words, and concepts* to understand the meaning of each term; *focus and attention* and *precision and accuracy* to carefully look at the shapes and draw them; *multiple sources* (know the attributes of all the shapes); and then *compare* the shapes to correctly *categorize* them. In the following example, those thinking skills are embedded within a content objective to overtly demonstrate their role in helping you gain mastery of the content objective.

> *Content Objective:* Students will learn specific attributes of a number of polygons. They will be able to identify, *label, describe,* and *compare* and draw them with *precision and accuracy.*

With the content objective written, now select just one of the identified thinking skills as a focus in a Level I lesson. If you select *labels, words, and concepts,* your objective might look like this:

> *Thinking Skill Objective:* Students will use accurate *labels, words, and concepts* to identify and describe various attributes, ideas, or concepts of a set of objects. As a result, they will be able to verbalize the differences between the attributes.

---

[28]Common Core State Standards for Mathematics (2010), Grades K–5, Grade 2, Geometry 2.6.1.

If you had selected several other thinking skills, the thinking skill objective might then have looked like one of these:

> (a) Students will develop, use, and demonstrate *focus and attention* to help accurately discriminate between two or more attributes, ideas, or concepts.
> (b) Students will use *multiple sources* to describe the attributes of different ideas or concepts.
> (c) Students will *compare* attributes, ideas, or concepts to correctly *categorize* them.
> (d) Students will use *precision and accuracy* to demonstrate their skills of discriminating between attributes.

A second example uses a fifth grade Common Core State Standard (CCSS) for reading, and applies it to a science unit content area.

> **Reading Standard for Informational Text Grade 5.3.** Explain the relationship or interactions between two or more events, ideas, or concepts in a scientific text based on specific information in the text.[29]

The core concept in this standard has students: *Identify the relationship or interactions between two or more events, ideas, or concepts.* Using Natural Disasters (a science unit) as the context, connect the core concept of the standard to the relationships of earthquakes and tsunamis.

What *thinking skills* help students seek and "explain relationships or interactions?" If you look carefully, you will identify many thinking skills at play. *Finding connections and relationships* seems obvious at first; however, when you look at the demands of the content and consider the needs of students, you may modify your selection. Of your many options, you may select *cause and effect* relationships as your primary thinking skill of focus because it is a precursor skill to finding connections and relationships. It is one in which you want your students to have a very strong foundation and it links well with the kinds of relationships you will explore using natural disasters as the context. Therefore, your objective may look like this:

> *Content Objective:* Using the context of natural disasters, students will seek patterns of causation. Through in-depth study, they will explore the *causes and effects* of earthquakes and tsunamis, and understand key elements that support structural integrity.

---

[29]CCSS for English Language Arts and Literacy on History/Science and Technical Subjects K–5 (2010), Reading Standards for Informational Text, Grade 5,3.

When your students are at the beginning stage of learning only one of MiCOSA's 21 thinking skills at a time, that is, Level I, write an objective for the major thinking skill you want to target. In this case, it will be for *cause and effect—hypothesizing.*

> *Thinking Skill Objective:* Students will seek *cause-effect* patterns within various contexts. They will use key words such as *because, as a result of,* and *therefore* as cues for identifying causation within a text. They will also seek connections of this thinking skill to other situations or experiences they encounter in school and beyond.

Often you will need to break a standard down into smaller, more comprehensible parts or lessons. To illustrate this, MiCOSA draws on the work of graduate students from San Diego State University, learning to teach with the MiCOSA Model in a fifth grade class.[30] They broke this standard down into three parts, exploring:

a. Study of the nature of earthquakes and the *relationships* between locations of earthquakes and fault lines to hypothesize their *causes.*

b. In-depth study of tsunamis, a devastating *effect* of earthquakes. They linked this study to the tsunami that had occurred in Japan.

c. *Effects* of earthquakes on structures, structural integrity, and ways to make our schools and homes more earthquake-safe.

The first lesson's objectives, based on "the causes of earthquakes," may look like this:

> Lesson 1: *Content Objective:* After listening to and reading articles on the *causes* of earthquakes, students will *collaborate* with their peers to discuss and *summarize* their understanding of this topic. They will then extend their knowledge through the use of media, technology, seismic graphs, and hands-on activities.

> Lesson 1: *Thinking Skills Objectives:* (a) *Cause and Effect.* Students will identify *cause and effect* relationships. They will use prompting frames of WHEN/THEN to help describe, understand, and communicate these relationships. They will understand that key words such as: *because, as a result of,* and *therefore* are cues for identifying causation; (b) *Summarizing.* Students will summarize their findings to help them understand the key ideas of the text; (c) *Collaboration.* Students will understand that when they collaborate, they are able to enhance their own thinking through sharing their ideas, considering the ideas of others, then revising their original ideas.

---

[30]We appreciate the lesson development contributions of Krsytle Aguilar, Tania Arriaga, Yolanda Barba, Natalia Cardosa, Amy Clarey, Chelsay Jimmie, Nicholas McIntosh, Karen Nunes, Natalie Pontino, Mallory Rachel, Rochelle Telebrico, and Janice Tso.

The second lesson's objectives based on tsunamis, an effect of earthquakes, may look like this:

> Lesson 2: *Content Objective:* After reading informational text, watching a video, and *collaborating* with each other, students will demonstrate an understanding of the *causal relationship* between earthquakes and tsunamis. They will develop an understanding of the *location* and characteristics of tsunamis, and as a result will *hypothesize* where they are most likely to occur.

> Lesson 2: *Thinking Skill Objectives:* (a) *Cause and Effect—Hypothesizing.* Students will identify *cause and effect* relationships and practice making predictions using *hypothesizing.* They will use prompting frames of WHEN/THEN & IF/THEN to help describe, understand, and communicate these relationships; (b) *Position in Space.* Students will plot and understand how one location relates to another. They will understand each location in relationship to their own point of reference; (c) *Collaboration.* Students will understand that when they collaborate, they will enhance their own critical or creative thinking by exchanging ideas with others, reflecting, and revising.

Practicing Writing Content Objectives That Integrate Thinking Skills

Practice Activity 4 provides one thinking skill, *planning,* for the abbreviated content standard. Your job is to link both content and thinking skill objectives.

Content Objectives with Thinking Skills   Practice Activity 4

Directions: Write an objective incorporating the thinking skill of planning. We have underlined the core concepts in the standard segment.

Abbreviated Standard Example: <u>Students will pre-write their ideas</u> for a narrative paragraph.

Thinking Skill: Planning

Content Objective: (Write your content objective and mention the thinking skill, *planning*, too.)

_____

Thinking Skill Objective: ("Pull out" *planning* from the content and write an objective for it that will transfer to other content areas or tasks.)

_____

_____

Sample response: *Thinking Skill: Planning*

Content Objective: Students will *plan* and organize their ideas on a graphic organizer before writing a personal narrative about a childhood event of significance.

Thinking Skill Objective: Students will use *planning* to help them select and gather relevant information and to organize and order the steps and processes they need to take to efficiently reach their goal.

In Practice Activity 5, as in the previous activity, first create related content and thinking skill objectives but this time for *ordering, grouping, and categorizing*. Next, identify another thinking skill that could be used to accomplish the same given standard and write these two related content and thinking skill objectives as well.

Content Objectives with Thinking Skills   Practice Activity 5

Directions: Write a content objective incorporating the thinking skill and its related thinking skill objective.

Abbreviated Standard Example: <u>Follow precisely a multi-step procedure</u> when carrying out experiments, taking measurements, or performing technical tasks.

Thinking Skill: Ordering, Grouping, and Categorizing

Content Objective:
_____

_____

Thinking Skill Objective: Students will use *ordering, grouping, and categorizing.* _____

Now identify a second thinking skill within this same standard, and write a second content objective and its correlating thinking skill objective.

Identified Thinking Skill:
_____

Content Objective:
_____

_____

Thinking Skill Objective:
_____

_____

(continued)

(Continued)

Sample response: *Thinking Skill: Ordering, Grouping, and Categorizing*

Content Objective: Students *will use* their knowledge of *ordering, grouping, and categorizing* to help them follow a multi-step procedure, which will enable them to identify the composition of four different soils. Note: Use your own content.

Thinking Skill Objective: Students will use *ordering, grouping, and categorizing* to help them understand a multi-step task and become more efficient thinkers.

Second sample response: *Identified Thinking Skill: Precision and Accuracy*

Content Objective: Students will demonstrate precision and accuracy in taking all measurements and performing all technical tasks, supporting their identification of the composition of four different soils.

Thinking Skill Objective: Students will use the thinking skill precision and accuracy to help them solve complex problem and become more active and successful learners.

SUMMARY

- The California Common State Standards use words that explicitly parallel some of MiCOSA's 21 thinking skills. Identifying the core concepts of the standards helps locate the explicit thinking skills within them. Examples and practice activities support a deeper understanding.

- Locating implicit thinking skills requires deeper analysis. Again, the identification of the core concepts of the given standard helps provide clues. Examples and practice activities support a deeper understanding.

- Familiar terms, such as *know* and *analyze*, can sometimes be ambiguous. Connections of these terms to the thinking skills begin to emerge as the skills, processes, or concepts embedded in the standard are identified. Examples and a useful analysis chart of these terms support understanding.

- Within the Common Core State Standards, patterns of similarities are now identified and aligned to prepare students for college and career readiness. These standards provide specificity and increasing complexity for each grade level. In a similar way, the thinking skills can be scaffolded. From kindergarten onwards, they are taught and built upon, increasing in complexity as the content becomes more sophisticated.

- Content and thinking skill objectives are first written separately, but when students become more proficient, one powerfully written objective combines thinking skills and content objectives. Sometimes complex standards require their content to be broken down into several objectives. Examples and practice activities support a deeper understanding.

REFERENCES

Lantos, J. (2006, September). Critical thinking is critical. *Los Angeles Times*. Retrieved from http://articles.latimes.com/2006/sep/16/opinion/oe-lantos16

Longman Advanced American Dictionary. (2000). Essex, England: Pearson Education Limited.

Merriam-Webster. (2012). Analyze. Retrieved from www.merriam-webster.com/dictionary/analyze

National Governors Association Center for Best Practices, Council of Chief State School Officers. (2010). *Common core state standards*. Washington, DC: National Governors Association Center for Best Practices, Council of Chief State School Officers.

Chapter Eight

Teaching for Transfer: Getting to the Big Ideas

Teaching for transfer helps students extend their learning beyond the immediate task or subject area to embrace big ideas and transfer critical thinking to new learning situations at school, at home, and in tomorrow's world.

When students leave your classrooms at the end of the year, what will they take out into the world? As you picture your highest goals for them, you may see them using what they have learned to make a difference. They may be constructing new ideas, or generating solutions to pressing social or economic problems. Some of you are fortunate to have witnessed students going on to make important contributions to society. However, this kind of outcome does not result from simply memorizing what you have taught them, or even remembering the fascinating projects they have completed, the elegant reports they may have produced, or compelling books they have read. To achieve such goals they must go beyond what they have learned with you, understand the big idea behind instruction, and transfer their learning to new areas in school as well as to useful contexts and creative applications beyond the classroom.

The process of teaching for transfer links with and builds on students' prior work in locating thinking skills and integrating them with content to develop both thinking skills and content objectives. Those objectives help you establish depth in your lesson, both in critical thinking and in content, so that students can understand bigger ideas and transfer their learning to new contexts.

When you teach for transfer, you are not simply teaching students a collection of facts or even a body of information, but you are teaching them the tools to learn in the future, to transcend or go beyond the immediate. In many ways, teaching for transfer is what education is about (Bransford, Brown, & Cocking, 2000; Martinez, 2010). We want our graduates to be prepared to succeed well beyond the classroom. When students can transfer their learning, they have learned thinking skills and content in sufficient depth to make sense of, and then use or apply, their learning (Anderson & Krathwohl, 2001). When students transfer what they learn, they understand and use new ways to associate and relate to that understanding—to use it to create something new within additional contexts, including future work environments. Through teaching for transfer with MiCOSA, you will use the thinking skills to help your students derive big ideas within your content areas, and then transfer them to new situations. Teaching for transfer prepares them for 21st century careers and for college, to be global citizens prepared to find meaningful careers—a central goal of education. However, transfer is not automatic. It has to be taught, mediated, and practiced.

Differentiating Near and Far Transfer of Learning

In a sense, much of school learning involves some level of transfer. Multiple terms have been used to describe kinds or continua of transfer, ranging from near and far to positive, negative, vertical, horizontal, low road, and high road. Various terms are useful in different ways. Perkins and Salomon (1992) spoke of transfer as developing skills to a level of automaticity, so that the learner could then transfer and use those basic skills in more complex situations. For instance, in learning to play the piano, students practice exercises so that the fingering needed to play in different keys, as well as the ability to use two hands in simultaneous but unique tasks, becomes automatic. The student begins with fairly easy compositions, so that automaticity can be achieved first. Once automatic, the student becomes the pianist, learning to play with feeling and expression. In reading, once the student learns the basic skills of decoding to a level of automaticity, that student becomes a reader, applying the skills to various texts, and free to focus on meaning and other important aspects of reading.

Similarly, in learning critical thinking with MiCOSA, teachers help students learn about, use, and articulate thinking skills. Recall that with teacher support and mediation, students create *bridging principles* that help them overtly *transfer* their use; that is, seek applications of those thinking skills across content. Over time, as students begin to automatize the thinking skills, they become critical thinkers, using thinking skills without the scaffolding of mediation.

In MiCOSA, we find two ideas of transfer most helpful for teachers: *near* and *far* transfer. Near transfer implies that in new learning students apply or transfer what they have just learned to a similar situation. In contrast, far transfer requires the learner to do more manipulation of the original content or processes to fit to the new and more "distant" situation.

In *near transfer*, you transfer learning that is "near" in context. For instance, if you learn to peel a potato, you likely will transfer those skills to peeling a carrot or peeling an apple. Early on, the teaching of arithmetic may occur this way, with one process demonstrated and learned, and then applied in a variety of similar although new problems. Multi-paragraph essay-writing builds on this concept. This kind of instruction focuses on teaching the steps of a task that are applied and transferred to new problems. As students develop depth of understanding through complex content, their skill with near transfer within that content area becomes more sophisticated—critical thinking emerges.

Far transfer, which is more complex, is what you ultimately want for your students. Far transfer leads to a deep level of understanding, enabling students to pull out the key knowledge and skills needed in a new and dissimilar situation—one that involves change. For example, a student of chess may learn the principle of "control of the center," which creates a strategic advantage in the game (Perkins & Salomon, 1988). In chess, controlling the center of the board allows maximum mobility for the pieces, as well as better opportunities to attack or defend. In contrast, huddling in the corner or alongside the edge of the board in an attempt to remain safe actually restricts play and leave pieces vulnerable. Abstracting from that learning, the player then transfers that principle of control of the center for strategic advantage to understand situations far beyond the chessboard. For instance, in political campaigns, candidates often aggressively seek "control" of the center—the voters who may lean either way—to gain strategic advantage from the critical numbers of undecided votes in the "center," thus swaying votes in their direction.

Far transfer works toward big principles that hold the essence of what you want students to know—what they will be able to use and apply beyond the immediate content—so that rather than asking, "Why do I have to learn this?" they participate in answering the question. For most students, far transfer does not occur spontaneously (Oregon Technology in Education Council (OTEC), 2007). It requires critical thought, consciously abstracting the principle from the context so that it can be applied to new contexts (Perkins & Salomon, 1988).

The skills or principles your students abstract and transfer are sometimes called big ideas. Because of their value for transfer, big ideas are said to hold "enduring value beyond the classroom and deal with larger concepts, principles or processes"

(Wiggins & McTighe, 1998, p. 10). These ideas synthesize the important understandings teachers want their students to retain after they may have forgotten the details. Thus, when students reach for and understand those big ideas, they can engage in transfer.

Understanding and Using Big Ideas

Many examples of big ideas are now found in classrooms, workshops, and even textbooks. Often, these examples tend to blur the lines between big ideas and principles that help consolidate ideas and transfer learning *within* a topic or content area, and those ideas and principles that help students transfer to farther reaching areas *beyond* the immediate content. Thus, in MiCOSA, we separate big ideas into Content Big Ideas (CBIs) and Broader Big Ideas (BBIs), and discuss each in some detail, so that you are comfortable in both creating them and guiding instruction toward their discovery. Both are important for transfer and for student learning, but each has unique characteristics and uses.

Content Big Ideas (CBIs): A Basis for Near Transfer

Within specific areas of content, such as literature, science, or math, teachers develop and use Content Big Ideas (CBIs) to summarize the essence of the big ideas of the lesson, and help students focus on areas in which they will use thinking skills to build depth. The CBIs will be useful to students in understanding additional examples or topics within that content area; thus, they help with transfer of learning. Because this transfer occurs *within* the content area, it is linked with near transfer.

For example, a standard within fourth grade Earth science may introduce students to ecosystems of the deserts, tundra, coral reefs, and rainforests. The teacher will create a CBI within that standard; for instance: *Climate, plants, animals, and physical features of ecosystems are interdependent.* To develop depth of content, students will study each characteristic of the ecosystem. Then, using thinking skills such as *finding connections and relationships*, *hypothesizing*, *comparing*, and *summarizing*, they will analyze those inter-relationships to synthesize their findings. The CBI supports rich depth and understanding within the content area of science. It does not attempt to help students transfer beyond science, since the principle is content-embedded; however, the CBI can be effectively transferred within the unit and area of study–in this case, across various ecosystems, from deserts to tundra, oceans, and rainforests.

What Characteristics Help Identify Content Big Ideas (CBIs)?   Content Big Ideas relate to the core concepts of the standards and to the learning you want students to emerge with. Therefore, the first characteristic of a CBI is that it emerges from and summarizes the core concept(s) of the standard. Second, it must provide sufficient depth and detail to convey a meaningful idea. To develop CBIs, most often you must go beyond the words in the language of the standard and think about its content in depth. This will allow your students to consider and then synthesize the big learning ideas involved in the standard. Your CBIs will create the opportunity for students to uncover or construct

FIGURE 8.1

Steps to Constructing a Content Big Idea (CBI)

Steps	Notes
Locate and summarize the core concept of the standard.	Write preliminary statement.
Review content with sufficient depth and detail to determine what Big Ideas will be truly meaningful.	Refine the statement.
Check whether the CBI can facilitate depth of understanding and has further applications within the unit of study.	Refine statement and cross-check characteristics.

the meaning; thus, they are ideal to help guide instruction. Finally, since it will become a basis for near transfer, or transfer within the area of content or study, the CBI must be applicable to other areas within the unit or area of study. Students will come to understand as many as two to four CBIs within a unit, developing depth of content in each.

How to Create Content Big Ideas (CBIs)   Following from these characteristics, Figure 8.1 illustrates three major steps to help you create CBIs, *refining your wording as needed with each step*: (1) Locate and summarize the core concept of the standard; (2) review the content in sufficient depth and detail to determine what big ideas will be truly meaningful; and (3) check whether the CBI can facilitate depth of understanding and has further applications within the unit of study.

Examples and further explanation of each step help model this process:

(1) *Locate and summarize the core concept of the standard.* To create CBIs, begin with your standard, and locate and underline the core concept(s). In math or in science, this may be fairly straightforward; for the ELA Common Core Standards, however, your core concepts will vary with the textual material or subject matter you select. To develop a CBI, you must link these standards to a selected area of content. For instance:

> **Reading Standard for Informational Text Grade 5,3.** Explain the relationship or interactions between two or more individuals, events, ideas, or concepts in an historical, technical, or scientific text based on specific information in the text.[1]

---

[1]CCSS for English Language Arts and Literacy on History/Science and Technical Subjects K–5 (2010), Reading Standards for Informational Text, Grade 5,3.

You might initially read the core concept in this standard without content or context, as: *Identify the relationship or interactions between two or more events, ideas, or concepts.* However, the standard asks you to do this within, for example, a scientific text and based on specific information. Next, you link that core concept with a content area; for example, the study of natural disasters. Using Natural Disasters (a science unit) as the content area, the core concept of the standard might become:

> **Core Concept:** *Explain the relationships or interactions between earthquakes and tsunamis.*

(2) ***Review the content in sufficient depth and detail to determine what big ideas will be truly meaningful.*** What learning do you really consider essential for your students? This requires you to think about or study the content before you refine your initial phrase into a meaningful and useful principle. It is not a matter of rearranging the language of the standard to sound like a useful phrase, although that is often a nice start. For example, with no study or knowledge within the content area, one might come up with the low quality CBI found in Example 1:

> Example 1. Low Quality CBI: Earthquakes cause tsunamis.

Although true at some level, the low quality CBI lacks sufficient specificity and does not reflect any depth of knowledge. However, thinking about the greater depth of content, you may realize that this statement fails to convey that there are multiple potential causes of tsunamis, or that all earthquakes do not cause tsunamis. Finally, while the statement may guide some student study of both earthquakes and tsunamis, it lacks focus and complexity. It is unlikely to provoke a depth of inquiry or critical thinking truly meaningful to students.

As you consider your deeper level of information, refine the statement. A higher quality CBI emerges. It may take a few tries at the language to be sure you say exactly what you intend, and there are several possible ways to go. Example 2 provides one example.

> Example 2. High Quality CBI: Tsunamis are usually caused by underwater seismic events such as earthquakes.

Example 2 builds on the core concept, and conveys sufficient specificity to allow you to guide students into a depth of study in several areas. Specific words help enhance meaning: (a) the term *usually* implies other causes of tsunamis, allowing students to discover the asteroids or landslides that may also cause tsunamis; (b) the phrase *such as* implies that earthquakes are only one example of the underwater seismic events that cause tsunamis—what are others and what is unique about the earthquakes?; (c) the phrase *underwater seismic events* leads to in-depth study of seismic events, how earthquakes can be seismic events, as well as to the question of whether earthquakes experienced on land are similar or different, and have similar or different effects.

(3) ***Check whether the CBI can facilitate depth of understanding and has further applications within the unit of study.*** The primary role of the CBI is to promote depth of knowledge that can be used and remembered; the secondary role is one of near transfer. This step assures that you create a CBI with those characteristics. To cross-check, examine whether the CBI can provide depth, then seek examples of its applicability to other areas within the unit of study. For instance, given the CBI: *Tsunamis are usually caused by underwater seismic events such as earthquakes,* you might ask whether it is consistent with the original core content about understanding complex relationships between two or more things. In this case, yes. Within the unit on natural disasters, students might be asked to explore the relationships of volcanoes to two other natural disasters, and they would be able to discuss underwater volcanoes as seismic events. They would likely seek multiple causes of volcanoes.

In another example of finding a CBI within the previously modeled standard, but using an historical text, the process is the same, but the detail presented is summarized rather than elaborated. As a result, your CBI will look significantly different. For instance, you might select *Indian Captive* as the novel and interweave a fifth grade history standard: *Explain the cooperation and conflict or interactions between American Indian nations and new settlers.* Follow the same three steps:

(1) ***Locate and summarize the core concept of the standard.*** After referring to your standards, with an ELA standard such as the one that follows, link it with an historical text.

Reading Standard for Informational Text Grade 5.3. Explain the relationship or interactions between two or more individuals, events, ideas, or concepts in an historical, technical, or scientific text based on specific information in the text.[2]

Add the Content: History Standard: Explain the cooperation and conflict or interactions between American Indian nations and new settlers.
Text: Social studies textbook, online resources, and non-fiction books.
Summarize the Core Concept: Explain the relationships or interactions between American Indian nations and new settlers.

---

[2]CCSS for English Language Arts and Literacy on History/Science and Technical Subjects K–5 (2010), Reading Standards for Informational Text, Grade 5,3.

(2) *Review the content in sufficient depth and detail to determine what Content Big Ideas will be truly meaningful.* There are several sub-areas of content in this history standard from which to gain specificity or depth; for instance, competition among several American Indian nations, the English, French, and others for control of a land base reflects both the interests and values of the groups involved; cooperation between colonists and American Indians with regard to the fur trade, in agriculture, alliances, treaties, and cultural interchanges represents a different level of trust than the wars—why was that? The role of broken treaties and massacres called into question those values and interests and changed the behaviors; and the resistance of Indian nations to encroachments and assimilation made strong statements—what values drove those decisions? You could create a number of meaningful CBIs from the richness of this content.

Use this opportunity to try Practice Activity 1, creating a CBI that takes students beyond learning "facts" into a meaningful exploration of the issues. A low-level CBI is provided based on the core concept of a standard, so that you can refine it to reflect the previous criteria.

Concept Big Idea (CBI)   Practice Activity 1

Core Concept of Standard: Explain the relationships or interactions between American Indian nations
    and new settlers.
Low-level CBI: Settlers and American Indians both fought and cooperated with one another.

- Review content with sufficient depth and detail to determine what big ideas will be truly meaningful.
- Check whether the CBI can facilitate depth of understanding and has further applications within the unit of study.

Using knowledge of the content and of the criteria, try to create a higher quality CBI:

_____

_____

In checking your response, you may have refined that statement based on some of the following problems inherent in the low-level CBI: First, the true meaning of the standard, involving complex interrelationships based in worldview, economic interests, and disrespect of the sovereignty of indigenous peoples, each evolving over time, is missing altogether. Second, the low quality CBI does nothing to lead the students to seek depth in their explanations (or seek causative factors) for the relationships, but merely leads to naming vague relationships. There are several ways you could create a higher quality CBI, depending on the textual materials you have them read and the directions of insight you hope they will achieve. Perhaps your CBI looks something like one of the two following examples:

CBI 1. Differences in belief systems as well as economic and social interests led to shifting relationships between American Indian nations and settlers over time.

CBI 2. Belief in the right to lie to, subjugate, and even massacre American Indian people led to the breakdown of many initially cooperative relationships with settlers, and to longstanding distrust.

(3) ***Check whether the CBI can facilitate depth of understanding and has further applications within the unit of study.*** CBI 1 facilitates depth of understanding, as it requires students to consider multiple factors—belief system, as well as economic and social interests—and their relationships to sociopolitical outcomes. The harsh realities of the role of economic interests combined with belief systems about the rights of all people can lead to complex thinking and debate. In terms of transfer (to other applications within the unit of study), this CBI can be applied to events from the Trail of Tears to the standoff at Pine Ridge or the takeover of Alcatraz Island. Likewise, CBI 2 facilitates depth of understanding. Students will need to consider the impact of power differences that exist within unequal socioeconomic relationships and the influence of these on the formation of policies. For example, the subjugation of Native Americans as they were forced to build and live on the missions in California can be considered using this CBI.

Broader Big Ideas (BBIs): A Basis for Far Transfer

Once students develop depth within the content, and true understanding of their Content Big Ideas, they are ready to bridge their thinking and understanding to an even broader context—to engage in far transfer using the Broader Big Idea (BBI). The BBI often builds on the CBI. With the BBI, your students' in-depth insights, developed within the CBIs, help them find principles that will apply those insights into new areas of study and thought. The BBI serves as a bridge to transfer from what they already understood to those new areas.

Constructing or deriving a BBI requires multiple thinking skills and clear critical thinking. Building this "bridge" across contexts requires students to gather and hold *multiple sources* of information; to work in the abstract, often using *visualization*; and to seek *comparisons, patterns, and relationships* across content areas. They must be able to use a high level of *feedback* for self-regulation, cross-checking their *hypotheses* for *accuracy*. Your work with them to develop these thinking skills serves them extremely well. When they "see" those connections, students get excited—these are the "ah ha!" moments and insights your students will remember because of their enduring value. These are moments you will treasure.

Consider the prior example of transfer offered by Perkins and Salomon (1988, 1992) in which the learner discovers the power of controlling the center of the chessboard to gain strategic advantage. His or her knight gains four times the situational control from the center of the board than it had safely tucked into its original position. Likewise, other players, from the bishop to the pawn, gain far more control of the chess game by repositioning into the center, where they gain flexibility. Can this lesson be transferred to a new context—distant enough to constitute far transfer and still be meaningful? To create this level of transfer requires "purposeful and conscious analysis, and mindful abstraction of skill from context" (Perkins & Salomon, 1988, p. 25). What Broader Big Ideas (BBIs) might be extracted and abstracted from the chess context and transferred to new contexts?

- Control of the center can enhance control of the total situation.

- Moving away from seemingly safe positions to enhance flexibility can enhance strategic advantage and overall safety.

- Systematically exploring all options—even those that appear risky at first—can lead to repositioning oneself for greater advantage.

Through creating and understanding Broader Big Ideas (BBIs), your students will engage in far transfer. For instance, in what ways do the BBI statements related to controlling the center help students understand another content area outside of chess? How might they apply to business, finance, or military initiatives? In business, Jacob Morgan (2012) writes that effective collaborative organizations must engage with, as well as listen to, a diverse group of key leaders from the center of the organization; this control of the center leads to effective collaboration. In finance, substantial gains have been made through repositioning stock holdings: moving those considered safe but low risk and low reward into diversified higher risk stocks. Likewise, military initiatives cannot be won by staying protected; rather, exploration of the most strategic repositioning yields greatest control of the situation.

What Characteristics Help You Identify Broader Big Ideas (BBIs)?   The Broader Big Idea is an abstract principle or statement that captures the essence of the critical idea behind the CBI or the standard, and is applicable more broadly. Thus, the first characteristic of a Broader Big Idea (BBI) is that it builds on and emerges from a strong Content Big Idea (CBI). Second, the BBI is constructed to lead to depth and insight. This requires you to consider whether the BBI actually facilitates this depth and insight. Using the BBI principles, students should be able to transfer learning from the original area of content to new content areas altogether; thus, testing for transfer is the final step. Because BBIs help transfer learning across content (rather than within), they are linked with far transfer.

How to Construct a Broader Big Idea (BBI)   Using the characteristics of a high quality BBI, four steps support its creation:

1. Begin with a high quality Content Big Idea (CBI) and remove the initial context to form an initial Broader Big Idea (BBI). Beginning with a strong CBI supports the work of developing your BBI most effectively, as you will already have done the challenging work of finding sufficient depth and specificity.
2. Check to see if the BBI has sufficient depth and detail to lead to insight—examine all parts, and use the standard for reference.
3. If insufficient in depth and detail, examine each portion of the CBI and modify or enhance descriptors in your BBI.
4. Determine whether the BBI can be meaningfully applied to other contexts, and modify if needed to assure it can be used for transfer.

Figure 8.2 uses the earlier CBI example from the Indian nations and settlers relationship to walk through each of the four steps to abstract a Broader Big Idea (BBI) from a strong CBI.

FIGURE 8.2	

Creating High Quality Broader Big Ideas (BBIs) from Content Big Ideas (CBIs)

Steps	Examples and Notes
1. Begin with a high-quality CBI and remove the initial context.	**CBI:** *Differences in belief systems as well as economic and social interests led to shifting relationships between American Indian nations and settlers over time.* **Initial BBI:** Differences in belief systems as well as economic and social interests can influence and change relationships.
2. Check to see if the BBI has sufficient depth and detail to lead to insight—examine all parts, and refer to standard if needed.	Sufficient depth and detail? ✓ Use of three intersecting causes is strong. ✓ Lacks sufficient specificity about relationships. ✓ Notion of time lost.
3. If needed, examine each portion of the CBI; modify or enhance descriptors.	**Modified BBI:** Differences in belief systems as well as economic and social interests can influence and change relationships *between people or nations over time.*
4. Determine whether it can be meaningfully applied and transferred to other contexts; modify if needed.	Can it be meaningfully transferred? ✓ Strong application to other historical movements. ✓ Could be applied to current events, and understanding relationship of historical relationships to current events.

Final Broader Big Idea (BBI): Differences in belief systems as well as economic and social interests can influence and change relationships between people or nations over time.

In a second example, illustrated in Figure 8.3, we draw from the second CBI above.

The strength of the CBI in the case of the relationships between Indian nations and settlers made the process of eliciting a strong BBI fairly easy. When your CBI is not as complex, it can be more challenging.

For an example in another discipline, think again about the CCSS standard on reading for informational texts that asks students to *explain relationships or interactions between two or more people, events, ideas, or concepts.* If applied to a science text on natural

FIGURE 8.3

Second Example of Creating the Broader Big Idea (BBI) from the CBI

Steps	Examples and Notes
1. Begin with a high-quality CBI and remove the initial context.	**CBI:** Belief in the right to lie to, subjugate, and even massacre American Indian people led to the breakdown of many initially cooperative relationships with settlers, and to long-standing distrust. **Initial BBI:** Initial relationships of trust can deteriorate and completely reverse if one party displays total disrespect of another.
2. Check to see if the BBI has sufficient depth and detail to lead to insight—examine all parts, and refer to standard if needed.	Sufficient depth and detail? – Actions resulting from beliefs not specified (behavioral component). ✓ Has sufficient specificity about relationships. – Notion of time is lost in BBI.
3. If needed, examine each portion of the CBI; modify or enhance descriptors.	**Modified BBI:** Discriminatory beliefs of one group about another can lead to behaviors that erode previously strong relationships and lead to long-standing distrust.
4. Determine whether it can be meaningfully applied and transferred to other contexts; modify if needed.	Can it be meaningfully transferred? ✓ Strong application to other inter-group relationships and actions. ✓ Could be applied to current events, and understanding relationship of historical relationships to current events. ✓ Relationships between beliefs, actions, and reactions in human interactions can be transferred. ✓ Application to political (e.g., voting trends) and/or educational (e.g., distrust of schools) movements.

Final Broader Big Idea (BBI): Discriminatory beliefs of one group about another can lead to behaviors that erode previously strong relationships and lead to long-standing distrust.

disasters, the teacher might want her students to understand that *natural disasters affect people, places, and economies.*

To derive a BBI, begin by taking out the context-specific language in order to get to the abstract idea. Using this process, an initial idea emerges: *Adverse Actions Affect People.*

1. Begin with a high quality CBI and remove the initial context to form the initial BBI.	**CBI**. Natural disasters lead to complex and interrelated effects on people's lives, their homes, and economies. **Initial BBI**: *Adverse actions affect people.*

Basically, this is a statement of truth and went beyond the immediate context, but it does not guide insight. Principles useful for far transfer should promote insight or govern future actions or reasoning. In that sense, *Adverse Actions Affect People* does not help students gain insight to guide future reasoning or actions.

2. Check to see if the BBI has sufficient depth and detail to lead to insight—examine all parts, and refer to the standard if needed.	– *Adverse actions affect people* is merely a true statement, and not particularly useful because it is obvious. – Currently, it will not lead to insight. – It lacks sufficient depth or detail to provoke critical thought.

Next, modify the initial BBI "*adverse actions, affect people*," so that it will contain sufficient specificity and detail to provoke insight. In this case, the standard and the CBI informed students about the complex interrelationships between the effect of earthquakes or tsunamis on people's lives, their homes, and the economies in which they participated. Several concepts could be included: (a) *complex interactions result from natural disasters;* (b) the word *affect* could be modified to reflect the complex interactions; (c) *people* are the ones affected—also missing from the original statement; and (d) natural disasters are probably more accurately characterized as adverse *conditions* than adverse *actions*. The Modified Broader Big Idea (BBI) in Step 3 considers each of these:

3. If not (useful), examine each portion of the CBI for modifying or enhancing descriptors. Modify.	**Modified BBI**: Adverse conditions lead to multiple effects on people's lives, characterized by complex and often reciprocal interactions.

Finally, Step 4 asks you to determine whether the BBI can be meaningfully applied to other contexts.

| 4. Determine whether it can be meaningfully applied to other contexts and modify if needed. | **BBI**. *Adverse conditions lead to multiple effects on people's lives, characterized by complex and often reciprocal interactions.*

✓ Yes, it can be applied to further contexts; for instance, poverty leads to effects on education, food consumption, nutrition, and health, each of which interacts with one another.

✓ Similarly, it could help students gain insight into why droughts are so powerful—the multiple relationships with food sources, means of production, connection to the land—and to understand how one thing affects another.

✓ It helps students begin to look for potential relationships and interrelationships between events in their world, and to understand that most relationships are not linear, but require complex consideration. For instance, when you consider what kind of car to buy, do you consider that the function of your car might affect the extinction of certain life forms? |

Teaching for Transfer with MiCOSA

In MiCOSA, you will ask your students not only to derive big ideas, but also to apply or transfer them. Content Big Ideas (CBIs) and Broader Big Ideas (BBI) are the foundations for the transfer of learning; they take the form of principles that can be applied. When students create and then apply (or transfer) principles derived from their learning across contexts, they can approach each new problem, subject, or project without feeling like they are always "starting over." This is critical, because when people learn information in multiple contexts they are more likely to use it flexibly in the future.

After your students come to understand or even learn to derive CBIs and BBIs, they will actively engage in using them for near and far transfer. That is, they will use the CBI or BBI as a "bridge" to link what they have previously learned to new areas of content.

Recall that you used a similar process, called bridging, as one of the ways to mediate the thinking skills. With thinking skills, students developed bridging principles, which are similar to the principles you develop as CBIs and BBIs. For example, based on his work with a project in literature, a student might have developed the following thinking skill bridging principle: "When I use hypothesizing, I create many options to consider, and can formulate a better plan." This might be shortened or refined to say, "Using hypothesizing helps create options and leads to better planning." To mediate thinking skill development, you asked students to think of situations beyond the initial one in which their principle would apply. Figure 8.4 shows an example of "bridges," or transfer, to other areas of content using the thinking skill of *hypothesizing*.

PD ToolKit™

PDToolkit: In Video Clip 8.1, the teacher asks students to identify thinking skills they will need for their project, and then to derive bridging principles.

FIGURE 8.4

Example of Transfer Using Bridging Principle for Hypothesizing

Original Context:	Project in literature in which hypothesizing led to thinking of multiple solutions to potential problems in the process of gathering information.
Bridging Principle:	***Using hypothesizing helps create options and leads to better planning.***
Teacher Prompt for Transfer: When else can you use this bridging principle at home?	When I am planning a celebration with my family, I might hypothesize that someone might not arrive on time, so I will look at optional activities for that time period. That way no one will be disappointed.
Teacher Prompt for Transfer: When else can you use this bridging principle at school?	When I do an experiment in science, I have to hypothesize what the result might be and what would cause it. This helps me plan how to do the experiment.

PDToolkit: In Video Clip 8.2, the teacher mediates meaning of a thinking skill, and models bridging or transfer from content to students' current and future lives.

This process (transfer) is not automatic and it requires critical thinking. Thus, you will have worked with your students to develop and use thinking skills alongside their content development. Students' work in bridging thinking skills sets the framework and gives them good practice in using transfer. Similarly, with the CBI or BBI, you also ask students to generate ideas about other areas in which their principle would apply.

Once the CBI or BBI has been established, use the opportunity to engage your students in the critical thinking it will take to transfer the learning from the current content area. Now, using the BBI, deliberately engage them in transfer. The teacher might prompt, "Take a look at your CBI now and generate two or three other ways in which you can use that CBI or principle about natural disasters. As you check for how you can apply your CBI for transfer, consider creating a graphic organizer to support students in brainstorming possibilities for transfer as well." (See an example in Figure 8.5).

FIGURE 8.5

Examples of Transfer of Content Big Idea (CBI)

Content Big Idea (CBI)	Examples of Transfer Within Content Area of Natural Disasters
Tsunamis are usually caused by underwater seismic events such as earthquakes.	• Underwater volcanoes are also seismic events—how many other seismic events exist? • Multiple causes of volcanoes leads to questioning the other causes.

Similarly, with Broader Big Ideas (BBI), you will prompt transfer, but this time you will ask students to consider how their BBI or principle can be used in other content areas. Using the BBI example from the previous study of natural disasters, you might say, "Generate two or three examples of how this principle might apply in new contexts beyond your study of the effects of earthquakes and tsunamis. Work in groups to maximize thinking, and pay attention to all the terms (e.g., *multiple*, *complex*, and *reciprocal*)." This will not be an automatic process, but will require time and critical thinking to consider, test out, and finalize ideas for transfer. Figure 8.6 illustrates this level of transfer.

FIGURE 8.6

Example of Transfer Using Broader Big Idea (BBI)

Broader Big Idea (BBI)	Two Examples of Transfer of BBI to New Contexts Beyond Study of Effects of Earthquakes and Tsunamis.
Adverse conditions lead to multiple effects on people's lives characterized by complex and often reciprocal interactions.	When people live in poverty (adverse condition), it can lead to lowered opportunities to support their education (time, access), as well as fewer resources to support health (affordability of good food and health care). This potentially lowered health and education level feeds back into the poverty cycle.
	War (adverse condition) can lead to multiple psychological effects (e.g., fear, mistrust, PTSD, stereotypes of groups of people), which can influence the future relationships and well-being of groups as well as individuals. Those effects can pre-dispose people to continuing rather than resolving poor relationships.

When students come up with Broader Big Ideas and find ways to apply them, the "ah-ha" happens, and the BBI becomes not only useful, but also memorable. This memory carries over to future learning and creativity, both in school and in the workplace.

SUMMARY

- Teaching for transfer is at the heart of the education process, as this allows students to understand what they have learned with sufficient thought to be able to later apply it.

- Although many terms have been used to characterize transfer, the concepts of near and far transfer are most useful in MiCOSA. Near transfer refers to students using ideas they have learned and applying them to similar situations. In far transfer, however, they abstract the core ideas with sufficient depth and detail to use them in new contexts.

- When teaching for transfer, teachers will develop and then use Big Ideas to guide instruction. Some are "near" in context to the unit of study, and are called Content Big Ideas (CBIs). These facilitate the development of depth within content. The Broader Big Ideas (BBIs) reach across content.

- Once students have understood and can derive the principles inherent in Content Big Ideas and Broader Big Ideas, teachers then ask them to consciously transfer those principles to new areas within or beyond content. This act of transfer requires critical thinking and supports memory.

REFERENCES

Anderson, L. W., & Krathwohl, D. R. (Eds.). (2001). *A taxonomy for learning, teaching, and assessing: A revision of Bloom' taxonomy of educational objectives.* New York: Addison Wesley Longman.

Bransford, J. D., Brown, A. L., & Cocking, R. R. (Eds.). (2000). *How people learn: Brain, mind, experience and school: Expanded version.* Washington, DC: National Academy Press.

Martinez, M. E. (2010). *Learning and cognition: The design of the mind.* Upper Saddle River, NJ: Merrill.

Morgan, J. (2012). *The collaborative organization: A strategic guide to solving your internal business challenges using emerging social and collaborative tools.* Columbus, OH: McGraw-Hill.

Oregon Technology in Education Council (OTEC). (2007). *Learning theories and transfer of learning.* Retrieved from http://otec.uoregon.edu/learning_theory.htm#transfer

Perkins, D. N., & Salomon, G. (1988). Teaching for transfer. *Educational Leadership, 46*(1), 22–32.

Perkins, D. N., & Salomon, G. (1992). *Transfer of learning: Contribution to the International Encyclopedia of Education* (2nd ed.). Oxford, England: Pergamon Press. Retrieved from http://learnweb.harvard.edu/alps/thinking/docs/traencyn.htm

Wiggins, G., & McTighe, J. (1998). *Understanding by design.* Alexandria, VA: Association for Supervision and Curriculum Development.

Chapter Nine

The Power of Assessment

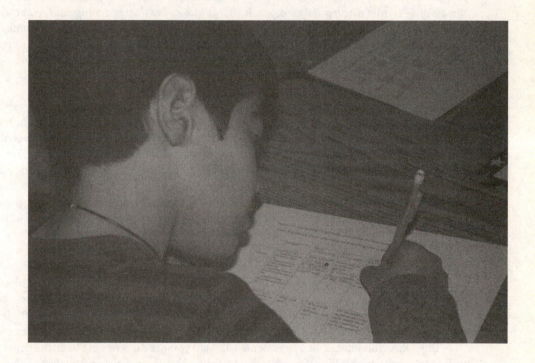

Prior to and throughout instruction, assessments provide constructive feedback to allow students to monitor and regulate their own progress and inform you as to where and when to adjust the steps of instruction to maximize learning.

This year, Mr. Dieter's students are on a pathway to understanding how they think—a pathway where they will come to understand their cognitive strengths and challenges. All assessments this year will provide them with important feedback about their development of the 21 thinking skills, whether from their ability to identify and understand thinking skills needed to complete a task, from their answers to essential questions, or from their ability to form bridging principles for transfer of their learning.

Take a moment and enter his classroom. Mr. Dieter's students are industriously focused on the MiCOSA Thinking Skills Survey in front of them. They look up, as they complete their rating. Mr. Dieter reads aloud the next thinking skill description, "I seek how things are related to each other. I am able to connect my experiences and see patterns and rules." For a moment before they write, they are deep in thought, assessing where they see themselves on a scale of 1–4, from whether they struggle with this to whether they feel competent with this thinking skill and match the description. They know they can be honest in their evaluations, because this survey—this assessment and its feedback—will become the foundation stone on which they will build new knowledge.

At a first glance, the word *assessment* may conjure up negative connotations such as "judgmental," "stressful," or "fixed" results. You may recall tedious hours preparing for tests or anxiously awaiting the results, which may or may not have reflected your true level of understanding. However, when assessment shifts from this viewpoint to a more dynamic one, and informs and guides you and your students to successfully reach the teaching and learning goals, it becomes an empowering experience. Assessment is both formative and summative. While summative assessment (coming at the end to summarize learning) continues to be useful, formative assessment is critical because it informs, shapes, and guides both your teaching and your students' learning.

This dynamic view of assessment, in which feedback from assessment informs and guides instruction, becomes a multi-layered process rather than a singular event. Pre-assessments help focus instruction. Formative assessments, including informal observations, help you make decisions about when to make shifts in instruction. These assessments, including projects, performance activities and performance assessments, become informational stepping-stones on the journey to mastery of learning objectives.

MiCOSA's thinking skills assessments will help you use assessments to examine, as well as to stimulate, thinking. Students will learn to identify, analyze, and evaluate their own thinking skill strengths as well as those they need to enhance. As a result, they engage in metacognition, or thinking about their own thinking and learning. This helps them become active partners in the process of defining their own next steps to gain greater mastery and efficiency.

Essential questions, questions that get at the "essence" of learning, serve as part of the assessment process—to stimulate inquiry and critical thought. Essential questions also guide and inform student understanding of big ideas. When students wrestle with and master these big ideas, they are able to transfer their current learning across contexts and reach autonomy of learning. The students' grand finale in assessment, then, comes when they can independently speak to or even create big ideas, because it affirms that they truly have understood the essential knowledge, and that they will continue to use this knowledge time and time again.

Structuring your assessments in MiCOSA, you will draw on the backward mapping concepts of Wiggins and McTighe (2006). Two guiding questions form the support and structure for the development of the lessons and their assessments:

- What knowledge is essential?
- What assessments inform student understanding?

Determining the essential knowledge within your lesson or unit will inform your assessments. Thus, laying out your standards, target thinking skills, objectives, and big ideas will help you design your methods and targets of assessment. First, you will read and gather information from multiple sources to acquire some depth of content beyond the level of knowledge you expect from your students, so that you can determine what knowledge is essential. Developing meaningful assessments based on this essential knowledge is not achieved by a linear step-by-step approach, but requires a flow back and forth between the steps, modifying and refining ideas along the way. For example, picture yourself planning a lesson on the Underground Railroad. First, you read about this subject in depth. What essential knowledge do you want the students to come away with after the learning? To determine this, you analyze the Social Studies standard to understand which part of it relates to the text. Next, you select a Common Core Standard for Reading Informational text, which will also support this learning. Although many would work, you select a standard that asks students to explain the relationships or interactions between two or more individuals, events, ideas, or concepts in an historical text.[1] This standard is a good match for the content, because the success of the Underground Railroad movement relies heavily on efficient networking. You select *finding connections and relationships* as the thinking skill of focus, because it pairs with the CCSS. Now you know you have successfully identified the essential knowledge of the learning. This becomes transcribed as the lesson objective.

After the essential knowledge has been determined, ask yourself, "How can my students best demonstrate their knowledge of this essential learning at the end of the unit of study? Will it be through their response to the essential questions, some multiple-choice items, or other carefully drafted inquiries? Should I require them to write some short paragraph responses or assess them through a performance; for example, a visual arts performance, a technological presentation, or an essay (Stiggins et al., 2006)? What will that look like?" This becomes the summative assessment.

Once the summative assessment has been established, you can break down the essential knowledge into two or three manageable "chunks"—the big ideas. From these, you will create essential questions that will assess how effectively your students have acquired and understood this essential knowledge. Cumulatively, the concepts of the big ideas should come together and form a complete picture of the essential knowledge (linking to the objective and summative assessment).

Finally, create a bridging principle from the thinking skill you have already identified (in this case, *finding connections and relationships*), reflecting on its role in understanding the essential knowledge. Even though students will create their own bridging principles,

---

[1]Common Core State Standards for English Language Arts Standards (2010) Reading: Informational Text, Grade 5. CCSS.ELA-Literacy RI. 5.3.

it is important that you know what you are asking of them, so that you can guide them toward that end.

By going through this process, you have not only identified essential knowledge you want your students to obtain, but have also begun to determine essential assessments that will help guide and inform you and your students of their mastery of that knowledge.

What Assessments Inform Student Understanding?

Your MiCOSA assessments should measure students' proficiency in:

- Connecting prior knowledge and culture to new learning.
- Using the thinking skills effectively.
- Answering essential questions about the learning throughout the unit of study—revealing an understanding of both Content (CBI) and Broader Big Ideas (BBI).
- Mastering the learning objective(s) and transferring knowledge to new situations.

When you scaffold these assessments as a cumulative process, you form a composite picture of your students' level of mastery of the learning objective(s).

Assessing Students' Use of Thinking Skills

PD **[O** TOOLKIT™

PDToolkit:
Download the
Thinking Skills
Assessment Tools
from PDTookit.

MiCOSA embraces the assessment of thinking skills because they lie at the heart of the learning and are transferable across multiple content areas. Three assessment tools give feedback on the students' current knowledge of the 21 thinking skills: (1) The Student Thinking Skills Survey, (2) The Student Thinking Skills Organizer, and (3) The Teacher and Parent Questionnaires. Review Figure 9.1 for a descriptive overview of each of these surveys. See Appendices B, C, and D for examples of each and download printable copies from PDToolkit.

The Student Thinking Skills Survey   The MiCOSA Student Thinking Skills Survey *Getting to Know Myself as a Learner* asks students to self-assess their level of competence on each of the 21 thinking skills and introduces them to the three phases of learning: *gathering*, *transforming*, and *communicating* information. It helps students build awareness of the skills they will be learning. Here, each thinking skill is intentionally labeled and placed within identified phases of learning. Therefore, do not become overly concerned if some students seem too generous or too harsh with their self-assessment of level of skill. At this beginning stage, the richness lies in the students thinking about their thinking (metacognition), perhaps for the first time. It provides them with an introductory overview of the 21 thinking skills they will be working with throughout the year. This survey also serves as a pre-assessment, helping guide you in selecting thinking skills of focus for your lessons.

FIGURE 9.1

Excerpts from MiCOSA's Three Thinking Skills Assessments

Thinking Skill Assessment	Purpose	Example
1. The Student Thinking Skills Survey: *Getting to Know Myself as a Learner*	* Introduces the student to the 21 thinking skills. * Serves as a pre-assessment. * Feedback supports writing the learning goals and essential questions.	*GATHERING INFORMATION: Think about your learning. When you approach a task and gather information for it, how would you rate yourself on a scale of 1–4 on each of these thinking skills?* *1 = I don't use it or struggle to use it, and 4 = always using this thinking skill* 1. Systematic Search 1 2 3 4 When I am gathering information to begin a task, I look for clues to support me. For example, I read directions and look at headings and graphics.
2. The Student Thinking Skills Organizer	* Supports students in reading and understanding the results of the above survey. * Motivational. Students track and record thinking skills as they are introduced and mastered; students see their own growth over time.	Students use various colors to complete the G.O. depicting their rating. If students rate themselves 1 (on the scale of 1–4), indicating they are struggling with this thinking skill, they color it yellow. If they rate their proficiency as 2, they use orange, 3 is red, and 4 is green.
3. Parent and Teacher Questionnaires	* Parents provide valuable information about their child. * Parent perspectives help teachers understand students. * Introduces parents to thinking skills in home-based contexts, which can augment and support classroom work. * Helps teachers focus objectives.	*You have important expertise about how your child thinks, learns, and solves problems since you have seen him/her learn things important to your family, your community, and his/her development. I would like to ask you about both strengths and struggles in learning. You may not have responses to all these areas, which is fine. Any ideas you can share will be helpful.* Think of something that you have seen him/her learn successfully or well: Think of something you have seen him/her struggle to learn:

The Student Thinking Skills Organizer   Following completion of the student questionnaire, *Getting to Know Myself as a Learner*, students fill out The Student Thinking Skills Organizer. As students transpose their numerical self-ratings from the survey onto this color-coded graphic organizer, both you and they can see patterns of their strengths and thinking skills they need to work on.

Parent and Teacher Questionnaires   Set up as an interview, the *Parent Questionnaire* asks parents to consider their child's thinking in light of activities they do at home. You might discuss this questionnaire at a Back-to-School Night with a larger group, or reformat it as a survey for students of concern. Similarly, you will complete the *Teacher Questionnaire* version only for some students to deepen your understanding for students of concern or to get a general snapshot of your class; you can use this to target your selection of thinking skills along with the student self-assessments.

Answering Essential Questions as Assessments

Essential questions "get to the essence" of content learning and drive student thinking forward. They represent students' critical thinking. When created with careful attention, student answers to essential questions are never "yes-no," or one-line responses. Rather, they require students to respond to deeper, more critical thought; these questions help you think clearly, logically, and deeply (Elder & Paul, 2009). For example, when studying oceans, a meaningful and essential question to check student understanding might ask: How is the depth of the ocean similar to the various strata of the atmosphere?

Essential questions can help you either *analyze* or *evaluate* your thinking. An example of an analysis question may be, "What factors contributed to the tsunami's devastating effect on Japan?" An evaluative question may be, "If I look for a pattern among the *causes* of why I struggle with a particular aspect of my work, will I be able to use this information to change a behavior or perspective to then make the task easier?" Developing powerful essential questions, therefore, is a thoughtful exercise.

Usually it is the teacher who generates the essential questions to intentionally and actively guide, as well as to assess, student thinking. However, students may also begin to generate their own questions as they start to inquire more deeply about the content of an objective. Take, for instance, a study regarding the causes of earthquakes. A student might ask, "I know that the main cause of earthquakes is the movement of Earth's plates, but what causes the plates to shift?" Self-questioning like this motivates students to find answers. Similar authentic inquiry also occurs during the learning. As students begin researching to understand a problem, event, or idea, more questions will start to come to mind. These self-generated questions drive students to extend their thinking and research other sources of information as they seek to find answers. Yet, generating rich, thought-provoking questions does not always occur naturally, so it is important that you set the stage for their development within your classroom.

When you create and use essential questions as part of your instruction and assessment, you foster and evoke critical thinking and a curiosity within your students to *want* to find answers and question further. Moreover, their answers lead to the big ideas of the learning—both the Content Big Ideas (CBIs), which relate to the current unit of study, and the more abstract Broader Big Ideas (BBIs), which are transferable beyond the lesson and unit, spilling into other content areas and making learning connective. Your students especially need the structural guidance that your essential questions offer, so that they can learn how to build and develop depth, and eventually construct meaningful BBIs themselves for transfer. Because of the tremendous value of essential questions, they warrant becoming part of assessment.

Planning for the Use of Essential Questions
Visualize entering Mr. Earl's science classroom and observe how he uses essential questions throughout the learning. He is about to begin a new unit of study that addresses two standards: one related to the reading of expository text (seeking relationships between two or more events, ideas, or concepts), and the other related to causal effects of natural disasters. In preparation for today, he created two learning objectives (one content and one for its related thinking skills) structured around the core concepts of the standards.

> Lesson 1: *Content Objective:* After listening to and reading an article on the *causes* of earthquakes, students will *collaborate* with their peers to discuss and *summarize* their understanding of this topic. They will then extend their knowledge through the use of media, technology, seismic graphs, and hands-on activities.

> Lesson 1: *Thinking Skills Objectives*: (a) *Cause and Effect.* Students will identify *cause and effect* relationships. They will use prompting frames of WHEN/THEN to help describe, understand, and communicate these relationships. They will understand that key words, such as *because, as a result of,* and *therefore,* are cues for identifying causation; (b) *Collaboration.* Students will understand that when they collaborate, they are able to enhance their own thinking through sharing their ideas, considering the ideas of others, and then revising their original ideas.

However, Mr. Earl does not share these objectives with his students immediately. Instead, to establish *intent* for and *reciprocity* with his students, he creates and posts essential questions—using student-friendly language, which he knows will motivate inquiry into the big ideas of both the content and thinking skills.

> **Content Essential Questions (individually posted on colored cardstock)**
> - What are the effects of earthquakes on the environment, people, and economics?
> - What is the relationship of magnitude to effect?
> - How strong is the possibility of earthquakes occurring in my parents' and family's "home" state or country?

Thinking Skill Essential Questions (individually posted on a different colored cardstock)

- Why is it important to learn about *cause and effect* relationships?
- Can a "*cause*" also be an "*effect*" and vice-versa?
- What will help me identify *cause and effect* relationships in other texts or areas of study?
- How does *collaboration* with others affect my thinking and learning?

As Mr. Earl's students enter the classroom, they immediately notice these thought-provoking, yet simply written questions posted on the walls of the classroom. These essential questions act as motivators, enticing students to begin the inquiry and deductive process of understanding what learning is essential.

Mr. Earl transfers one of the questions from the wall to the whiteboard as a focus of inquiry. Selecting the question, "Why is it important to learn about *cause and effect* relationships?" he adds, "Show your understanding by describing a personal experience of an action you made and its effect. How did it change your thinking?" Using this essential question as both a reciprocal "hook" and as a pre-assessment enables Mr. Earl to gain understanding of what his students already know about the thinking skill. This important feedback will help him form a strong foundation on which to build the new learning.

Because their answers will develop and deepen over time, Mr. Earl keeps the essential questions posted on the classroom walls throughout the unit of study, helping students stay focused on their inquiries. He also weaves these questions into his formative assessments, using them as a review for checking for understanding (Ainsworth & Christenson, 1998). Feedback from the students' responses to the questions will inform Mr. Earl where he needs to strengthen understanding, clear up misconceptions, or possibly even re-teach if many experience the same misunderstandings. In addition, he may decide to use them, or at least one of them, again as a summative assessment tool at the close of the unit. This will not only give the students a second opportunity to reflect more deeply on the question, but it will also provide Mr. Earl with feedback on the effectiveness of his earlier suggestions and interventions.

Constructing Essential Questions   Many great educators have written about the power of essential questions, and numerous textbooks now include them to help students focus on the big ideas. Learning to construct them is worth practice. As the answers to the essential questions (EQs) reflect the big ideas of learning, a great way to develop them is to start "backwards," creating the essential questions from "answers." In addition, you may find that some great essential questions will come to mind from natural inquiry versus one of your constructed big ideas; for example, "How do seismic instruments work to graph the magnitude of the earthquake?"

Whichever path you choose, it is important you work through creating both the essential questions and big ideas yourself before you begin the unit. This will help ensure that your EQs (and their answers) have both depth and detail and that the content students learn is worth knowing and understanding. Although it is extremely helpful to generate a number of potential questions to help you better understand a broader scope of inquiry possibilities, narrowing them to only a few helps students focus their learning.

Move from the Big Ideas to Essential Questions

The most effective and efficient way to produce powerful EQs is to start with the CBI and backward plan to create the corresponding question. Chapter 8 guided you through creating CBIs and BBIs, structuring each around each of the following three criteria:

1. Locate and summarize the core concept of the standard (or part of the standard being addressed).
2. Review the content with sufficient depth and detail to determine what big ideas will be truly meaningful.
3. Check whether the CBI can facilitate depth of understanding and has further applications within the unit of study.

Now apply these same criteria to the creation of the essential questions. That is, does the EQ:

1. Connect to the core concept of the standard (or part of the standard being addressed)?
2. Encourage a response of sufficient depth (complexity) and detail to be meaningful?
3. Lead to a statement that can be applied within the unit of study?

As you try to satisfy these three issues of alignment, try to write EQs that evoke curiosity and intrigue. For instance, Mr. Earl's EQ provokes curiosity through engaging students' cultural background: *How strong is the possibility of earthquakes occurring in my parents' and family's "home" state or country?* Once written, make sure you work through how you would like to see your essential questions answered. Create an assessment rubric to evaluate student responses to these questions. In this way, you help students understand the three criteria used to frame the rubric (scale of 1–4) and identify how they will be assessed. Figure 9.2 provides a sample rubric you can use for this purpose.

Broader Big Idea (BBI) criteria provide a similar framework for creating corresponding EQs. Thus, when you use the BBI to generate essential questions, you can use parallel criteria to evaluate student responses: That is, does the EQ:

1. Connect to the CBI, or to the thinking skill connected to the CBI?
2. Encourage a response of sufficient depth (complexity) and detail to convey meaning?
3. Lead to a statement that can be applied to other contexts beyond the unit?

Figure 9.3 provides a sample rubric that may be used to provide feedback on the student's ability to create meaningful BBIs from the essential questions.

FIGURE 9.2

Rubric for Student Response to CBI Essential Questions

	Very Strong	Strong	Adequate	Inadequate
	4	3	2	1
Summarizes Core Concept	The summary of the core concept of the standard is extremely concise and clearly evident in the response to the EQ.	The summary of the core concept of the standard is adequately evident in the response to the EQ and is fairly clearly written.	The summary of the core concept of the standard is only partially evident in the response to the EQ and its meaning unclear.	The summary of the core concept of the standard is neither clear nor identifiable in the response to the EQ.
Includes Depth and Detail	Use of concise language and details clearly reflects an insightful, in-depth understanding of the topic.	Use of clear language and details reflect an understanding of the major points of the topic, but lacks depth.	Simple use of language and inadequate detail reflect a limited understanding of the topic and may reveal some misunderstandings.	Response reveals major misunderstanding of the topic.
Uses Meaningful Application	Response includes a sophisticated example showcasing the writer's ability to apply the big idea(s) of the learning with accuracy.	Response includes an appropriate example demonstrating the writer's ability to apply the big idea(s) of the learning with a fair degree of accuracy.	Response includes an example, but with little connection to the big idea(s) of the learning and with some inaccuracies.	Response omits example or presents an inaccurate one. If it includes an application to the big idea(s) of the learning, then that application is inaccurate.

Move from Content Objectives to Essential Questions   Generating EQs before creating the CBIs is a much harder path to choose. It is not easy to guarantee your questions will generate answers of both depth and detail. In part, this is because you need to have sufficient depth of content to know what essential questions will lead to essential understanding.

However, if you decide to create some of your essential questions from the learning objective, start by refining a basic content-based question, generated from the objective, into more critical questions. For example, from the base question, "What do you *know* about earthquakes?" move to more critical questions such as, "What do you think *causes* earthquakes to occur and why might that be important to know?" or "How can we *predict* when an earthquake will hit?" These questions will guide students to begin to consider the thinking as well as the content.

FIGURE 9.3

Rubric for Student Response to BBI Essential Question

	Very Strong	Strong	Adequate	Inadequate
	4	3	2	1
Links to Content Big Idea (CBI)	Response highly successfully transposes the essence of the CBI into an abstract form by removing all current contextual language. It is correct and masterfully supports transfer.	Response adequately transposes the essence of the CBI into an abstract form by removing most of the current contextual language. It is correct and clearly supports transfer.	Response only partially transposes the essence of the CBI into an abstract form. Some of the contextual language is still present. It is partially correct but is not very effective in supporting transfer.	It unsuccessfully transposes the essence of the CBI into an abstract form. Current contextual language is still evident and the overall meaning is lost. It does not support transfer.
Includes Depth and Detail	Use of concise language and details clearly reflect an insightful, in-depth understanding of the idea or thinking skill.	Use of clear language and details reflect an adequate understanding of the major points of the idea or thinking skill, but lacks depth.	Simple use of language and inadequate detail reflect a limited understanding of the idea or thinking skill and may reveal some misunderstandings.	Response reveals major misunderstandings of the idea or thinking skill.
Uses Meaningful Application	Response includes a sophisticated example showcasing the writer's ability to apply the BBI or bridging principle with accuracy.	Response includes an appropriate example demonstrating the writer's ability to apply the BBI or bridging principle with a fair degree of accuracy.	Response includes an applied example, but with little connection to the BBI or bridging principle and with some inaccuracies.	Response omits an applied example. Alternatively, if it does include one, there is no connection to the BBI or bridging principle. It is inaccurate.

In the early stages of teaching a thinking skill, you create separate thinking skill essential questions. For example, "How will understanding *cause* and *effect* relationships help you *hypothesize* and predict?" These essential questions about thinking skills help students consider how they will use the thinking skills not only in the current assignment, but also in other places. Their answers become *bridging principles* (see Chapter 3), which are a form of Broader Big Ideas, because they support transfer to future learning.

Your additional essential questions will provoke further critical thinking and inquiry. For instance, "Will teaching the *causes and effects* of earthquakes and tsunamis to others help them decide where to live?" or "How can knowing the *causes and effects* of earthquakes and tsunamis help us here in California?" These questions provide a *focus* for what they will come to know and understand, rather than suggesting a passive list of random facts. They invite students to engage in critical thinking.

Measuring Student Mastery of the Learning Objectives and Transfer of Knowledge

To assess student mastery of the learning, provide authentic summative assessments that encourage critical and creative thought as well as opportunities for transfer of learning beyond the unit of study. By asking students to consider next steps, they will develop a mindset that they have not reached "the end" of the learning, but that their newly gained knowledge is only the beginning of future doors of discovery.

PD **TOOLKIT™**

PDToolkit: In Video Clip 9.1 Jackie introduces students to a summative assessment, incorporating reflections on critical thinking used with content and with thinking skills.

Summative Assessment
Summative assessments summarize or "sum up" the learning. As they occur *after* instruction, they are also referred to as post-assessments. The *summative* task, whether a project, performance, essay, or test, should hold no surprises. It is a product to celebrate knowledge gained throughout the lesson from the introduction of the learning objective to its mastery, and it is powerful.

Post-assessments can take many forms. They can be formal or informal, long or short, and there can certainly be more than one. For example, you might ask students to answer the essential questions within the creative context of an essay, presentation, or project; or the assessment may resemble a more traditional test, with multiple-choice and a series of open-ended response questions. However, alongside this you may also require students to write down a *bridging principle* and a "next-step" *essential question*, encouraging transfer of knowledge and further inquiry. Whatever the format, the purpose remains unchanged: you assess in the most authentic way you can to measure the students' proficiency level in understanding the learning objectives, both for content *and* for reasoning or thinking.

As you become more adept at planning for assessment, you will feel comfortable inviting your students to join you in suggesting and selecting ideas for presenting their mastery of the learning objectives. Being active in the creation of the final assessment is highly motivating, relevant, and meaningful to students.

Analyzing an Example of Summative Assessments
Return again to Mr. Earl's class. He knows if he is to write a powerful post-assessment that will give evidence of his students' mastery of the learning objectives, then he must:

- Weave the targeted thinking skill(s), essential content knowledge, and CCSS language arts skill into the assessment.
- Connect to the EQ(s) and big ideas and require a student example (as evidence of understanding and ability to transfer the learning).
- Require students to generate a bridging principle and example beyond the current assignment (as evidence of ability to transfer knowledge of the thinking skill).

Encourage students to pose a "next-step" EQ and to hypothesize a response backed with reasoning (as evidence of their ability to transfer learning). The post-assessment Mr. Earl developed for his students to assess their mastery of the *causes* and *effects* of earthquakes follows. He asks his students to present their knowledge in the form of a newscast. The class will work in four collaborative groups, each assigned to a specific performance task that will contribute to the final newscast. He combines the targeted content and thinking skills together as one summative assessment. Designing it this way, his students will see the link between *content* and *thinking,* and know they will be assessed on their understanding of both. He italicizes the thinking skills being assessed for emphasis.

Lesson 1: *Post-Assessment:* Working in four *collaborative* groups, demonstrate knowledge of key terminology, issues of location, movement in tectonic plates, and basics of seismology as they relate to the *causes* of earthquakes. S*ummarize* this information and share your expertise with the class through a simulated newscast performance. To focus your newscast, select a related essential question and reveal the answer within the presentation. At the end of the newscast, demonstrate your understanding individually by writing one Content Big Idea (CBI) and an example of how it can be used in another situation. Write one *cause* and *effect* bridging principle you have learned, with an example of its use beyond the current assignment.

Notice that Mr. Earl's post-assessment goes beyond the simulated newscast performance. It also asks students to reflect on the big ideas of the learning, both for content and thinking skill. By adding these to the post-assessment planning from the onset of the lesson, students see them as highly valued and not as a less valued afterthought.

Mr. Earl maps out each group's focus for the assessment:

Group 1: The seismologists will answer the question, "What is an earthquake, how is it measured, and how do those different measures affect homes?" This group will study Richter scale levels of earthquakes and their effects on buildings through a simulation experience.

Group 2: The geologists will answer the question, "What are the layers of the Earth and how does its movement cause earthquakes?" This group will make a three-dimensional model to demonstrate their understanding.

Group 3: These are the scientists, who will answer the question, "How does friction of the plates below Earth's surface or the ocean floor cause earthquakes?" This group will create a model to simulate and demonstrate their findings.

Group 4: The explorers will answer two questions. "What are fault lines? Where are they formed?" Using a model they create, they will show the three different types: transform, normal, and reverse fault lines. This group will plot each of the three types of fault lines on a map.

Mr. Earl also poses the thinking skill EQ: "How does *collaboration* with others affect my thinking and learning?" as part of the post-assessment. Finally, he asks his students to pose a "next-step" essential question, such as: "Do scientists around the world *collaborate* to share their hypotheses about possible natural disasters occurring in specific areas? If this is so, how does this happen?" As part of this "next-step" summative assessment, his students will hypothesize a response, supporting their reasoning with as much evidence as they can. For example, they may draw from the development of their newscast experience and discuss how seismologists, geologists, scientists, and explorers from around the world share knowledge.

Finally, Mr. Earl knows it is important to provide opportunities for students to reaffirm and synthesize all they have truly understood about the Content Big Ideas (CBIs) and the Broader Big Ideas (BBIs). He has his students engage in finding examples of transfer for the BBIs he establishes together with them, as this engages their critical thinking and serves as a powerful post-assessment to demonstrate whether or not they can engage in transfer. That act also helps them later use the CBI or BBI in new contexts.

Figure 9.4 synthesizes the big ideas of this chapter's objectives to help conceptualize the relationships between the essential questions, Content Big Ideas, and Broader Big Ideas. They outline knowledge you hope will remain with your students beyond the destination of their journey.

The summative destination is never a clean "goodbye," but a time for reflection. Assessment becomes a supportive part of instruction by encouraging students to create bridges to future learning and the development of an inquiring mind. It is a lifetime, never-ending journey.

Pre-assessing to Connect New Learning to Prior Knowledge and Culture

When your students connect their prior knowledge and cultural understanding to current learning, their readiness to take in new information can be felt in the room! This process of pre-assessing and interpreting prior knowledge before beginning a unit of study provides the "hook" on which to hang new connected knowledge. Feedback from such assessments will inform you about your students' readiness to begin the new topic concept or thinking skill as well as connect them to your lesson. It will guide you in differentiating instruction to better meet the needs, abilities, and interests of each of your students from the start of instruction.

Some pre-assessments may be diagnostic in nature; others will assess prior knowledge of the content, and yet others will inform you about your students' prior knowledge of learning processes, such as how to categorize or understand the main idea. Pre-assessment results may therefore inform you of the need to pre-teach certain vocabulary, concepts, or prerequisite skills to ensure continuous progress in learning. They may show you that some students have already reached a sophisticated level of mastery of the content or thinking skill. This information helps you provide enrichment projects or activities that will encourage a greater depth of learning; that is, you will differentiate instruction rather than expect everyone to begin at a more basic level.

FIGURE 9.4

Example: Synthesizing the Big Ideas and Essential Questions

Content Essential Questions	Content Big Ideas	Broader Big Ideas
1. What is the effect of earthquakes on the environment, people, and economics?	1. Natural disasters lead to complex and interrelated effects on people's lives, characterized by complex and often reciprocal interactions.	1. Adverse conditions lead to multiple effects on people's lives, characterized by complex and often reciprocal interactions.
2. What is the relationship of magnitude to effect?	2. As the magnitude of the earthquake increases, its effect on the Earth's surface increases to a far greater degree.	2. The degree of knowledge of the nature of the magnitude and potential effects of natural disasters influences the ability to prepare for them.
3. How strong is the possibility of earthquakes occurring in my parents' and family's "home" country or countries?	3. The possibility of earthquakes occurring in my family's "home" country or countries increases with the proximity of fault lines to those countries.	3. Looking for patterns among the different variables of natural disasters supports their prediction.

Thinking Skill Essential Question		Generalizing Principle
1. Why is it important to learn about cause and effect relationships?		1. Understanding *cause-effect* relationships encourages me to consider the effect of my actions or thinking before I act upon them and to change my thinking as a result.
2. What will help me identify cause and effect relationships in other texts or areas of study?		2. When I look for cue words such as *because, as a result, or so* within the text, they help me quickly identify causal relationships. When these words are not present I look for places where I can mentally place them in the text.
3. Can a "cause" also be an "effect" and vice-versa?		3. An effect can become a cause and that cause can become an effect of another incident, event, or idea. There can be multiple causes that create an effect and multiple effects stemming from a single cause.
4. How did collaboration affect my thinking?		4. Collaboration helps me consider other points of view, take the best from others' strengths that may not be my own, and, as a result, empower my own thinking.

197

Pre-assessment of prior knowledge and cultural grounding also provides feedback to students. It helps them value their current knowledge and connect it to new information; it anchors them. And, as they consider feedback from their pre-assessment they can start to contemplate their own personal journey toward mastery of the learning objectives. They can consider the skills, processes, ideas, and concepts they will need and the investment of effort they must make to get there successfully.

PD TOOLKIT™

PDToolkit: In Video Clip 9.2 Marissa has her class do an informal pre-assessment, using collaboration to enhance depth of responses.

Creating Meaningful Pre-assessments   Essential questions can make extremely helpful pre-assessment tools. In the earlier example, Mr. Earl used a thinking skill essential question as a pre-assessment, asking: "Why is it important to learn about cause and effect relationships? "Show your understanding by describing a personal experience of an action you made and its effect. How did it change your thinking?" This helped him find out more about his students' understanding of causation, beyond the context of earthquakes. Similarly, you can use content essential questions. For instance, in the case of the earthquake lesson, you might ask whether students can *predict* when and how an earthquake will hit. Feedback from the responses will reveal those students who have begun to understand the causes, and others who have misconceptions. Still others will bring their own personal experiences, and perhaps tragedies, to the question, or they may contribute cultural explanations. As you develop any pre-assessments, you may weave together questions that evoke prior knowledge, cultural grounding, content, and thinking skill experience.

You may find the following, more generic examples useful in assessing students' prior knowledge:

- How does this connect to or differ from your culture? Tell me about it.
- Does this remind you of something you have done before? Tell me about it. How did you feel at that time? Why?
- What does_____(concept word/phrase) mean to you?

By posing these questions, you invite your students to share, to question, and to reflect and connect to their home cultures.

Supporting Student Involvement in Assessment

Students' active partnership in creating assessments empowers them. When they help generate the criteria, they know exactly what they have to do to complete the task successfully and receive a specific score. As a result, they see fairness in the score they receive; there are no surprises. It gives them a sense of control (Ainsworth, 2010). However, you need to lay the groundwork by helping them understand the learning objectives, as well as the essential questions. They must understand the link of essential questions to Content Big Ideas, and to the powerful for the words Broader Big Ideas and bridging principles that help get them there. Encourage students to be part of designing both progress charts and scoring rubrics.

Progress Charts as Self-Assessments

Progress charts can track student progress with reading patterns or mathematical concepts. To design progress charts successfully, the student states the objective and plots his or her progress toward it and its final assessment. When students personalize the objective and write it in their own words, it helps them to conceptualize its true meaning and own it. Figure 9.5 provides an example of a student progress chart with attention to content and thinking skill objectives as well as essential questions.

Design Rubrics to Support Self-Assessments

Rubrics are powerful! They become planning guides for students, analyzing the steps of a task and informing them how they will be assessed. They are an invaluable support for *self-regulation* of learning behaviors. Your students can see where they are, as well as where they need to go to reach a higher level of proficiency. There are no dark corners of ignorance. They *know* the expectations and know how to get there. When you ask students to help participate in the development of the rubric, they become invested in the process and simultaneously learn the requirements in depth. They no longer see assignments just as "what the teacher wants," but far more as a collaborative venture in learning.

You may already create rubrics and student self-assessments to help give and get valuable feedback from your students. Using rubrics to assess your students' skill in critical thinking and reasoning adds in elements such as judgment, analysis, hypothesis, connections, and relationships. For example, do the students not only have a thesis, but also demonstrate skill in judging its credibility or in identifying key components that drove their conclusions and their relationships to the thesis (Brookhart, 2010)? Self-assessments, including well-developed rubrics, assess students' levels of "clarity of reasoning" as they present their evidence (Brookhart, 2010, p. 92). Look for these critical thinking characteristics in the student self-assessment guide shown in Figure 9.6A. This guide, in addition to being numerically scored, also provides spaces for students to create a narrative about their progress. In this respect, it becomes a valuable part of formative assessment.

Figure 9.6B and 9.6C provide completed examples of this self-assessment, based on analyzing the theme of a story. The first relates to a Native American cultural story entitled *A Boy Called Slow* (Figure 9.6B). Figure 9.6C illustrates how students transfer their learning from the critical thinking in class to a home-based example. Students were asked to show their understanding of the lesson in class by analyzing a theme in a story from their own culture. This example relates to the Mexican story *La Llorona*.

FIGURE 9.5

Student Progress Chart Incorporating Critical Thinking into Student Self-Assessment of Content

Name _____ Subject _____ Period _____

Content Standard I Am Learning: CCSS Writing Standards 6–12, Grade 7.4. Produce clear and coherent writing in which the development, organization, and style are appropriate to the task, purpose, and audience.

	My Progress Chart
Content goals: My goals for collecting and using research	• I will use several different resources to research my topic for the information I need to analyze my work. I will check to be sure my sources are reliable. • I will organize my work in a way that others can easily follow and understand.
Thinking skill goals: My goals for using multiple sources and categorizing	• To help me plan my writing, I will write down the categories of information I need to make meaningful connections. • As I read, I will organize the information from different sources into the categories I've set up.
Questions to help me analyze the information in order to reach my learning goals	• Why do I need to use different resources to help me find the information I need? _____ • What do I need to consider about reliability and how will I make judgments about it? _____ • How will categorizing help me in gathering information for my report? How will it help me beyond this report? _____ • How will categorizing help me communicate my ideas as I write my report? _____
Steps to reaching my goals	1. _____ 2. _____ 3. _____ 4. _____ 5. _____
Reflecting on my work	
When could I use these goals in the future?	

Note: Becomes rubric when color coding based on scoring rubric is added.

FIGURE 9.6A

Critical Thinking in Content: Student Self-Assessment (Blank Form)

Assessment Focus	Clarifying Questions	Student Rating	Peer/ Teacher Rating	Student Comments/ Reflections How am I doing? What questions do I still have?
Clearly States & Analyzes the _____ (e.g., Theme, Thesis, Argument, Plot, Point of View)	Have I clearly identified and interpreted what has been asked of me?			
Provides Accurate Supporting Evidence	Did I give (3) accurate examples from the text to support the topic?			
Provides a Clear Explanation of Supporting Evidence	Did I clearly explain *why* I chose the examples I did and *how* they support my analysis of the topic?			
Clearly Expresses Ideas and Thinking in Writing	Do my *ideas, organization,* and *word choices* show clearly what I have learned? Are my *grammar and usage* errors few, so that the reader can still understand what I am trying to say?			

RATING MY WORK: Answer the questions to help you think about your learning. Rate yourself on a scale of 1–4:

4 – ABOVE & BEYOND—I excelled in my response and showed a deep understanding of what was asked of me. I gave strong evidence (examples) to support my analysis. I was able to clearly express my thinking in writing with little or no grammatical or usage errors.

3 – MET TARGET—I understood what to do. I gave reliable, relevant evidence to support my analysis. I was able to clearly express my thinking in writing. Although I had some errors, they do not affect the reader's understanding of what I was trying to say.

2 – GETTING THERE—I understood at a basic level what to do, but found some of the ideas hard to understand. Some of my evidence was missing; some was related to what I was asked, but not all. I had many errors in my written work with the grammar, usage, and organization. This affected the reader's understanding.

1 – GETTING THERE WITH HELP—I was not able to understand the assignment on my own, but began to with help. I needed help finding relevant examples from the text to support my analysis. I had difficulty connecting the examples to my explanation of support. I had many errors with my written work and needed help so that the reader could understand my thinking.

0 – OFF TRACK—I was not able to do this assignment, even with support.

FIGURE 9.6B

Critical Thinking in Content: Student Self-Assessment (Completed Example)

Assessment Focus Story: *A Boy Called Slow*	Clarifying Questions	My Rating	Peer/ Teacher Rating	My Comments/Reflections How am I doing? What questions do I still have?
Clearly States and Analyzes the Theme	Have I identified and interpreted the theme of the story?	4		I know how to figure out a theme. The theme here is: *Respect is earned.* I still wonder if there can be several themes in a story.
Provides Accurate Supporting Evidence	Did I give 3 strong examples from the story to support the theme?	4		This story had lots of examples of Sitting Bull's bravery and talents when he was young. I wonder if you can use more than 3 examples, because I found more.
Provides a Clear Explanation of Supporting Evidence	Did I clearly explain *why* I chose the examples I did and *how* they support my analysis of the theme?	4		I think I explain well how each of the examples relates to being brave and lead to earning respect and a new name.
Clearly Expresses Ideas and Thinking in Writing	*Organization of Ideas:* Does my graphic organizer show clearly what I have learned about the Lakota culture?	3		It was hard to organize what I learned about the Lakota Sioux since all the things I learned were kind of different topics. I listed 5 things I learned. I wonder if there are some ways to think about how to do this better.
	Ideas and Word Choice: Do my ideas and word choices show clearly what I have learned?	3		I used great words like *respectful, powerful,* and *responsible* to describe character traits.
	Grammar & Usage: Are my grammar and usage errors few, so that the reader can still understand what I am trying to say?	3		I messed up with some of my tenses and spelling but you can still understand ok.

RATING MY WORK: Answer the questions to help you think about your learning. Rate yourself on a scale of 1–4:

4 – ABOVE & BEYOND—I excelled in my response and showed a deep understanding of what was asked of me. I gave strong evidence (examples) to support my analysis. I was able to clearly express my thinking in writing with little or no grammatical or usage errors.

3 – MET TARGET—I understood what to do. I gave reliable, relevant evidence to support my analysis. I was able to clearly express my thinking in writing. Although I had some errors, they do not affect the reader's understanding of what I was trying to say.

2 – GETTING THERE—I understood at a basic level what to do, but found some of the ideas hard to understand. Some of my evidence was missing; some was related to what I was asked, but not all. I had many errors in my written work with the grammar, usage, and organization of my work. This affected the reader's understanding.

1 – GETTING THERE WITH HELP—I was not able to understand the assignment on my own, but began to with help. I needed help finding relevant examples from the text to support my analysis. I had difficulty connecting the examples to my explanation of support. I had many errors with my written work and needed help so that the reader could understand my thinking.

FIGURE 9.6C

Critical Thinking in Content: Student Self-Assessment with Transfer of Learning (Completed Example)

Assessment Focus A Story from My Own Culture: La Llorona	Clarifying Questions	My Rating	Peer/ Teacher Rating	My Comments/Reflections How am I doing? What questions do I still have?
Clearly States and Analyzes the Theme	Have I identified and interpreted the theme of the story?	3		I chose this theme: *Using deceit to get what you want often leads to tragedy.* I am not sure if this is the best theme. I could have used one about class differences.
Provides Accurate Supporting Evidence	Did I give 3 strong examples from the story to support the theme?	3		I think I have 3 strong examples. I'm not sure if the examples I chose sound more like a summary when you see them all together.
Provides a Clear Explanation of Supporting Evidence	Did I clearly explain *why* I chose the examples I did and *how they* support my analysis of the theme?	4		I explained how her tricks to get a handsome husband worked, but it all went wrong when she killed her children because he treated her badly. She went loco. I think I get this.
Clearly Expresses Ideas and Thinking in Writing	*Organization of Ideas:* Did I organize the story I retold so that it makes sense?	3		The graphic organizer helped me see the theme and provide the rationale. I could have given more examples.
	Ideas and Word Choice: Did I think carefully about my word choices so that they would say what I mean?	3		I wonder if there are some ways to think about how to do this better. I used words like *vain* and *insecure* to describe the mother. I also think that *deceit* was a great word to describe part of the theme.
	Grammar & Usage: Are my grammar and usage errors few, so that the reader can still understand what I am trying to say?	3		I did pretty well, but still have a few errors, mainly with commas.

RATING MY WORK: Answer the questions to help you think about your learning. Rate yourself on a scale of 1–4:

4 – ABOVE & BEYOND—I excelled in my response and showed a deep understanding of what was asked of me. I gave strong evidence (examples) to support my analysis. I was able to clearly express my thinking in writing with little or no grammatical or usage errors.

3 – MET TARGET—I understood what to do. I gave reliable, relevant evidence to support my analysis. I was able to clearly express my thinking in writing. Although I had some errors, they do not affect the reader's understanding of what I was trying to say.

2 – GETTING THERE—I understood at a basic level what to do, but found some of the ideas hard to understand. Some of my evidence was missing; some was related to what I was asked, but not all. I had many errors in my written work with the grammar, usage, and organization of my work. This affected the reader's understanding.

1 – GETTING THERE WITH HELP—I was not able to understand the assignment on my own, but began to with help. I needed help finding relevant examples from the text to support my analysis. I had difficulty connecting the examples to my explanation of support. I had many errors with my written work and needed help so that the reader could understand my thinking.

FIGURE 9.7

Student Reflection and Self-Assessment of Project-Related Thinking Skills

	Clearly Identifies & Analyzes Thinking Skill Use	Provides Accurate Supporting Evidence	Provides a Clear Explanation of Supporting Evidence	Collaborates Well with Others	My Comments How am I doing? What questions do I still have? How am I self-regulating my learning (pacing; reflecting)?
Gathering Information	Name at least one thinking skill that helped me *gather* information for this assignment:	An example of when I used this thinking skill for this project:	My explanation of *why* and *how* this example uses the thinking skill:	How well did I work with others to *gather* information for this assignment? *(1–2 words):* *Circle all that you did:* – I shared. – I listened. – My thinking was influenced by others.	

	Name at least one thinking skill that helped me **transform** and think more deeply about the information and make it mine:	An example of when I used this thinking skill for this project:	My explanation of *why* and *how* this example uses the thinking skill:	How well did I work with others to **transform** information for this assignment? *(1–2 words):* ***Circle all that you did:*** – I shared. – I listened. – My thinking was influenced by others.	
Transforming Information					
Communicating Information	Name at least one thinking skill that helped me **communicate** what I had learned:	An example of when I used this thinking skill for this project:	My explanation of *why* and *how* this example uses the thinking skill:	How well did I work with others to **communicate** the knowledge I have learned? *(1–2 words):* ***Circle all that you did:*** – I shared. – I listened. – My thinking was influenced by others.	

As you regularly assess your students' use of the 21 thinking skills, a reflection and rubric such as the one in Figure 9.7 helps guide the process. This rubric first allows for student self-assessment, making it quite clear to you what they do and do not understand. You will then follow it up with your own observation record to be shared with the student as a summative or post-assessment.

Using Feedback in Formative Assessment

In the same way you create post- and pre-assessments before you begin to design instruction, you should plan checkpoints to ensure student understanding during the lesson. These formative assessments keep you and your students on track and motivated, and scaffold the student's journey toward depth of understanding, critical thought, and, eventually, transfer. Their feedback helps determine how well students understand the content and thinking goals, and where and how they need guidance to reach them. Wiggins (2012) eloquently sums up the pertinent research on the power of feedback: "by teaching less and providing more feedback, we can produce greater learning" (p. 12).

Feedback informs both the teacher and the student about where they are in their efforts to reach their goals (Wiggins, 2012). Therefore, effective feedback needs to be at or slightly above the student's current level of learning (Hattie, 2012), and must be tied to the learning objectives or goals. It encourages students to go beyond their prior knowledge and to think critically about their learning. If carefully structured and modeled, students will eventually learn to regulate their own learning behaviors as a result of the feedback they receive. Using mediating conversations makes this fairly easy to master. In the following teacher comments, mediation of meaning serves as feedback to support the student's use of self-regulation: "When you slowed down your pace and took time to carefully read each question, and then looked back at the text for key words to help answer them, I noticed you were able to make correct responses. This is a great strategy and you made good use of the thinking skills *feedback for self-regulation* and *precision and accuracy*."

Providing Feedback

With today's pressure to "cover" so much material in so little time, many teachers feel unable to set aside adequate time for meaningful feedback. One way to "find time" to analyze student work is to identify patterns of errors rather than to mark and correct each one. Once uncovered, these error patterns allow you to support multiple students at the same time, as well as have students actively learn to correct the nature of the error. In this way, you can guide them to better understanding (Fisher & Frey, 2012). If you find your feedback is becoming too complex to state simply, or too many students have the same errors, then you should re-teach the information rather than offer lengthy feedback.

Feedback should support students in reaching mastery of the learning objectives. To do this, strive to use student-friendly language, specific comments, and feedback that can be immediately transferred and practiced. Using MiCOSA, you will provide feedback on content, process, and thinking skill development. For example, in a language arts lesson on writing a report of information, you might: (a) comment on the selected topic itself—asking for more details, or to check for accuracy of information (content feedback); (b) suggest the student cluster similar facts together to make the report flow more cohesively (process feedback); or (c) suggest the student revisit how he or she categorized the facts and reflect on how the student could use the thinking skill *comparing* to obtain greater accuracy (thinking skill feedback). This level of specificity allows the student to know how to improve, rather than just feeling judged or graded.

Peer-to-Peer Feedback

You will also want to teach students how to give effective feedback to their peers, so they can support and learn from each other. Help them to understand that "feedback is a two-way street" (Tovani, 2012, p. 48). Students not only receive it, but they can provide you with constructive feedback, too. This gives them the message that their opinion matters, that they have a voice, and that they are an integral part of their own learning development. Finally, feedback not only informs students how they are doing in their efforts to reach their goals, but it informs you how and where to adjust instruction to meet the diverse needs of your students.

Selecting the Right Assessment for Feedback

The kind of feedback you and your students receive will depend on the kind of assessment you use. This chapter earlier mentioned that assessments might range from short answer or multiple-choice questions to more expository written responses, student performance, or oral discussion (Stiggins et al., 2006).

When students are required only to select or make a short response, the feedback you get falls short of offering a picture of *why* the student made that response. However, it is an efficient way to get feedback on a student's mastery of data or patterns of thinking.

If you want to understand how the student thinks, ask him or her to respond to a question posed in a more lengthy written form. This will enable you to reap a far deeper understanding of the student's level of proficiency in reaching your learning objective(s). For example, you might have the student explain his or her use and understanding of the thinking skills *comparing, finding connections and relationships*, or *inferring*, or illustrate and reveal their ability to think critically.

Performance tasks one form of assessment, allow students to apply their learning; therefore, they provide an excellent way to evaluate the student's skills and creative innovations. Although this may involve an actual "performance" from the students, the performance assessment can be as simple as observing a student perform a task: problem solving, inferring, or connecting their thinking.

Asking guiding questions or setting up group discussions are common strategies used in classrooms to elicit feedback on student understanding; these methods work extremely well as formative assessments within the MiCOSA Model. MiCOSA's *mediating conversations* carefully guide your questioning to help deepen or clarify a student's understanding of his or her thinking. Throughout the process, you use the feedback from the student's response to frame the next question. Finally, although setting up interviews or conferences with students may be time consuming, in some circumstances, the investment can clarify any misconceptions you might have formed about a particular student's understanding of the topic, a skill, procedure, or product.

Structuring and Sequencing Formative Assessments

PD TOOLKIT™

PDToolkit: In Video Clip 9.4 Trish has her students respond to their research on great thinkers using a simulation strategy. She elicits their critical thinking as a formative assessment.

Performance tasks and essential questions provide formative assessment opportunities and guide your summative assessments. They are part of an assessment *process*, building from one task to the next and in doing so developing knowledge of the concepts and skills from a foundational level to a higher level of expertise. But how do you structure and sequence these assessments? How do you think through and choose just a few essential questions that you know will be powerful? What tasks are going to help you get from here to there?

First, read your selected content EQs and consider creative ways to get the necessary content across to the students, which actively involve and motivate them to find the answers. What resources can you provide, suggest, or guide the students to find for themselves? Consider your time frame. Determine where to devote extended time to a more complex task, and where to provide short, more transitional activities. If you have more than one thinking skill EQ, try to match each to a section of the content so that students see the content/thinking skill link as well as receive support in bridging their thinking beyond the current lesson. In addition, staggering the EQs throughout the unit of study rather than waiting until the end helps highlight and scaffold each of the important parts of the learning.

Second, consider which task(s) to select. In this chapter, we focus heavily on performance tasks. Ask, "What do I want the task(s) to reveal about my students' understanding?" For example, if you want to be informed of your students' conceptual understanding of the topic or their planning ideas and skills, you may ask students to create a graphic organizer. If you want to understand how capably they can think critically and/or share the learning through collaboration, you can select from an array of tasks, such as essays, skits, oral performances, hands-on activities, collaborative problem-solving, jigsaw activities, project-based activities, and mini-projects.

Provide instruction along the way to support these performance tasks. For example, Performance Task II (following) requires students to identify causal cues within a piece of text. You may present, as a prerequisite, a mini-lesson, modeling for students how to identify key *cause* and *effect* words in text. You may also introduce students to ways they can recognize *cause* and *effect* relationships when the key words are not present in the text.

Connected EQs to Performance Task I

Content EQ: How strong is the possibility of earthquakes occurring in my parents' and family's home country or countries?

Thinking Skill EQ: Why is it important to learn about *cause* and *effect* relationships?

Formative Performance Task I   Students will discuss where they or their parents or grandparents came from. They will then plot these locations on a map and connect them to areas where earthquakes tend to occur. As a result of this exercise, students will interpret and answer the content EQ in collaborative groups, and later share answers in the whole group.

Deepen students' understanding by asking them to respond to the thinking skill EQ. Guide them to respond to the question in their reflective journals, and elaborate their response with a personal connection.

Connected EQs to Performance Task II

Content EQ: What is the relationship of magnitude to *effect* of earthquakes?

Thinking Skill EQ: What will help me identify *cause and effect* relationships in other texts or areas of study?

Formative Performance Task II   After front-loading key vocabulary during instruction to help facilitate meaning, students will read an article on the causes of earthquakes. This task has two parts.

First, during the initial reading, students will make note of concerns they may have about key terminology, issues of location, movement in the tectonic plates, or the basics of seismology (on post-it notes or as electronic comments). They will discuss these concerns with a partner. Any concerns they might still have as a pair will be raised as questions for class discussion and input—either electronically or written clearly on prepared strips and posted visibly at the front of the classroom. If possible, collectively categorize the questions to reduce the number and then address them as a class. Students will respond to the content EQ in their reflective journals.

Second, as they read the text, students will highlight *causal* vocabulary cues, which will support them in identifying cause and effect relationships. They will also identify and highlight the relationships when these vocabulary cues are missing from the text. In pairs, and as a result of this work, students will discuss the thinking skill EQs, recording their understanding and conclusions in their reflective journals.

Connected EQs to Performance Task III

Content EQ: What are the *effects* of earthquakes on the environment, people, and economies?

Thinking Skill EQ: Can a *cause* also be an *effect* and vice-versa?

Formative Performance Task III   Given a model graphic organizer to support summarization, students will collaborate to find the main ideas and important supporting details of the article; that is, the effect of earthquakes on the environment, people, and economies. In their reflective journals, students respond to the thinking skill EQ and give a personal example to support their opinion.

Scaffolding Assessments to Support Instruction and Mastery of the Standard Objective

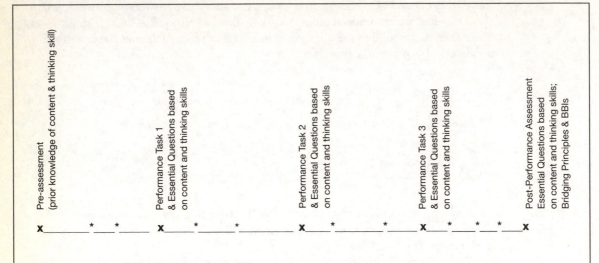

* Ongoing Formative Assessments provide feedback on Performance Tasks/Essential Questions; for example: Informal observations, informal interviews, mediation, quick checks (white boards, thumb up/thumb down), peer assessments, self-assessments, quiz/test, open-ended prompts.

X Performance Tasks include, for example: creating graphic organizers (both conceptual and for planning), essays, skits, oral performance, hands-on activities, collaborative problem-solving, jigsaw activities and mini-projects.

As students complete the performance tasks, move among them observing, questioning, affirming, re-tracking, supporting, and coaching. Note how students work collaboratively. Do they share, and also listen? Do others in the group influence their thinking? From these informal interactions, you can assess students' progress toward meeting the objective requirements as they are presented in the newscast.

Consider the scaffolding presented in Figure 9.8 in relation to this lesson on *causes* and *effects* of earthquakes to see how the key formative assessments—performance tasks–build a foundation for post-assessment. Each piece of feedback you receive affects how you will present the next step of your lesson, and that next part of the lesson will carry your students one step closer to successfully meeting their learning objective(s). It is a cumulative process.

A Synthesis of the Assessment Components

Visit Mr. Lee's fourth grade classroom and see how he uses assessment to guide instruction. Mr. Lee understands that in the 21st century his students must go beyond just *knowing* facts; they must also know how to evaluate and *use* them effectively. He knows that, if they gather information within a meaningful context, then they are far more likely to remember and be able to use and transfer that information. Therefore, his assessments look for integrated understanding.

Step 1: Mr. Lee begins with a Common Core State Standard, which requires students to analyze primary and secondary sources in various texts. He prepares a content objective:

> *Content Objective:* Using primary and secondary sources, students will *compare* the treatment of indigenous people forced to live on reservations and work on the missions in California with the treatment of slaves forced to live and work on the sugar plantations.

He also establishes an objective for the thinking skill, *comparing*:

> *Thinking Skill Objective:* Students will understand that when they *compare* certain concepts, they are able to understand their attributes, their commonalities with others, and their differences.

Mr. Lee conceptualizes the core concepts within the content and thinking skill objectives, and from this he develops relevant CBIs and their corresponding essential questions. He then develops bridging principles for the thinking skill(s) of focus and broadens the scope of the CBIs by creating related BBIs. He knows taking time when planning instruction will provide him an internal "rubric" for guiding students to the highest level of understanding they can reach. He also takes time to answer the essential questions himself before he introduces them to his students. He wants to make sure they are carefully worded questions, which will produce deep and detailed responses. Both his pre- and post-assessments will mirror the big ideas. As part of the post-assessment, the students will work in collaborative groups and return to the essential questions to create BBIs from which they will generalize how these skills, strategies, and processes can support them in the future. His students will also create a bridging principle to support transfer of the thinking skill *comparing* to other contexts.

Step 2: As a pre-assessment, Mr. Lee focuses on the thinking skill *comparing*. He asks the class to brainstorm things we often *compare* in our culture: weather, natural environments (biomes), personal likes and dislikes, political views, faiths, values, material wealth, jobs, fashion, or food. For homework, he asks the class to *compare* two kinds of fruits or vegetables they may eat at home, noting how they are alike and how they are different. He intentionally chooses this apparently simple comparison. However, he encourages his students to go beyond listing comparative attributes such as "they are both round . . . one is orange, one is an apple." He looks to see whether they have included a variety of categories to discuss, such as personal emotions and biases, and the cultural significance of the objects themselves.

Step 3: Along the way, Mr. Lee designs performance tasks that provide feedback and inform him and his students of their progress, as well as where they need to go to gain content knowledge and identify and use the thinking skills. He skillfully weaves both content and thinking skill essential questions into each performance task. He asks groups to research both incidents in history so they can gather multiple sources of information for comparison.

For the first formative assessment and performance task, he asks each group to present a skit that will demonstrate their understanding of four topic areas: (1) life on the missions from Native Americans' point of view; and (2) from the Padres' point of view; and (3) life on the plantations from the slaves' point of view; and (4) from the owners' point of view. He also asks them to respond to the essential question of focus to see if they are beginning to understand one of the big ideas of the learning. Throughout the process of gathering information, planning, and performing the skit, Mr. Lee constantly assesses his students and provides feedback. As they respond to the essential question, he can be seen observing his students as they work—affirming, questioning, or guiding them as he moves quietly from student to student.

A second performance task provides feedback on this student's ability to compare the treatment of the slaves and the Native Americans. The student must select or develop a graphic organizer and show similarities and differences between the two. This formative assessment helps Mr. Lee interpret the depth of comparison he is seeking, and where he needs to adjust his instruction. Again, he asks them to respond to the essential question whose answer will help them summarize the essence of the learning. As before, he observes them through the process and provides feedback.

Finally, as a third performance task, he asks students to submit the plan (outline) of their final presentation. This way he can help troubleshoot problematic areas and offer support. He assesses their needs as they create their plans and provides them with any guidance he feels will support them in being successful. When one group appears to lose some of their depth of content in their planning, he mediates their use of *connections and relationships,* supporting them to incorporate their earlier demonstration of deeper and more accurate factual knowledge. Another group outlines great details of information about the treatment of the slaves, but provides little of the treatment of the Native Americans. Mr. Lee believes that each group's plan must accurately outline the content of their final presentation and their reasoning. He moves from group to group, encouraging them to show depth of understanding in their plans, so that this depth will also be observable in their final performance. He poses a thinking skill essential question related to planning; their responses become bridging principles that will transfer to future learning.

Step 4: As a summative measure, Mr. Lee requires a project in which he asks his students to create a PowerPoint-based presentation showing a comparison between the treatment of the indigenous people, forced to live and work on the missions, and the treatment of slaves forced to live and work on the sugar plantations. He requires students to go far beyond just factual recall, and to compare and contrast these dark periods in history where people were stripped of their cultural backgrounds, suppressed, and forced to work inhumanely for the benefit of others. To ensure his students' investment in the project, Mr. Lee invites them to help him design a scoring rubric after his introduction to the final assessment. What stepping-stones to mastery do they see as relevant? Figure 9.9 demonstrates how this rubric may look.

Step 5: After the final presentation, the post-assessment, Mr. Lee uses the thinking skills rubric to help him check understanding of the pertinent thinking skills. The rubric asks: "What thinking skills helped you gather information for your project? Which helped you in transforming the information? Which skills helped you to communicate your

FIGURE 9.9

Mr. Lee's Rubric for Assessing Thinking Skills and Content Objectives in Context

	4 Exceeds Goal	3 Goal Reached	2 Meets Basic Goal	1 Needs Support to Clarify Goal/Project	Comments/ Questions I Have
PLANNING: • Intent, audience, & form established • Clarity of graphic organizer (G.O.) showing comparisons • Events sequenced	• Intent, audience, & form are established and are very clear • G.O. is clear and shows strong details of comparisons. • Planning guide clearly and thoughtfully shows the sequence.	• Intent, audience, & form are established and are clear. • G.O. is clear and shows details of comparisons. • Planning guide clearly shows the sequence.	• Beginning to establish intent, audience, & form. • G.O. needs more details of comparisons. • The planning guide is beginning to show the sequencing of events clearly.	• Need to establish a clear intent, consider audience & form; further support needed. • G.O. does not clearly show comparisons; needs further support. • Planning guide shows little sequencing; needs further support.	
THINKING SKILL: • Proficiency of use of the thinking skill *comparing*	• Strong examples given of similarities between the two content areas. • Strong examples given of differences.	• Examples show reliable and relevant similarities between the two content areas. • Examples show reliable and relevant differences.	• Similarities between the two content areas are given, but are only at a basic and explicit level and could imply anything. • Examples of differences are given but are only at a basic and explicit level and could imply anything.	• Insufficient examples of similarities given; further support needed. • Insufficient examples of differences given; further support needed.	

	4 Exceeds Goal	3 Goal Reached	2 Meets Basic Goal	1 Needs Support to Clarify Goal/Project	Comments/Questions I Have
CONTENT: • Accuracy and depth of knowledge of treatment of indigenous peoples on the missions and treatment of slaves on the plantations	• Important and insightful material with detailed evidence is provided to support the project thesis. • Material has been carefully selected for its accuracy and relevance. • Excellent sources of information are used.	• Sufficient material and detailed evidence are provided to support the project thesis. • Material is accurate and relevant. • Appropriate sources of information are used.	• Material and detailed evidence are provided to support the project thesis, but it lacks insight and depth. • Some material selected was accurate and relevant, but not all. • The choice of sources provided limited content.	• Inadequate amount of material and detailed evidence provided to support the project thesis. Further support needed. • Much of the material is inaccurate and irrelevant; further support needed. • Sources used are not appropriate; further support needed.	
CRITICAL THINKING: • Reasoning & evidence for both contents	• Information is exceptionally well connected and related to the two topic areas it supports. • Excellent and logical organization of information. • Excellent flow, transitions, & connecting material.	• Information is clearly connected and related to the two topic areas it supports. • Good organization of information. • Good flow, transitions, & connecting material.	• Information is connected and related to the two topic areas it supports, but lacks critical or original thought. • Basic organization of information is evident, but some connections are difficult to find. • There are some disconnected parts and lack of transitions, which interfere with the flow of the piece.	• Information is not clearly connected. Some relationship to two topics, but unclear; further help needed. • Information not well organized—connections hard to find. • Disconnected and difficult to follow; little evidence of transitions & connecting material; further support needed.	

newfound knowledge to us, your audience? How are you working together as collaborative groups?" And finally, "What other questions do you have?"

The information this rubric provides is rich. Mr. Lee can see how comfortable the students are becoming in identifying thinking skills that support their understanding. He can see skills that have not been easily identified, but were important to the learning, guiding his own instruction. He sees from the rubrics that work needs to be done to support collaboration. The groups have made great progress in the last month, but he wants to focus next on helping them become better listeners, so they are able to remember, paraphrase, and connect their own ideas to what they have heard.

As their year together draws to a close, Mr. Lee's students return to the survey they completed as a pre-assessment. Now they complete it again, this time celebrating their growth in understanding their thinking and how well prepared they are becoming for the world beyond.

SUMMARY

- Strong and dynamic assessment begins by determining the essential knowledge in a lesson, project, or unit. Developing and using essential questions, which demand a level of critical thought, stimulate student interest and guide construction of the lesson.

- Assessment should be designed to inform student understanding as well as your understanding of the student. Thus, students and teachers using the MiCOSA Model use assessments of the 21 thinking skills from student and parent perspectives, as well as the classroom. In addition, they conceptualize assessment in a way that provides meaningful feedback, using pre-assessment, formative assessment, and post-assessment to support learning.

- When students are involved in construction of the assessments, engagement rises and students demonstrate more buy-in.

- Formative assessments emerge from the essential questions and are structured to lead the students toward understanding the big ideas of the content, which they will use beyond the time in the classroom.

REFERENCES

Ainsworth, L. (2010). *Rigorous curriculum design.* Englewood, CO: The Lead and Learn Press.

Ainsworth, L., & Christenson, J. (1998). *Student-generated rubrics: Assessment model to help students succeed.* Orangeburg, NY: D Seymour.

Brookhart, S. (2010). *How to assess higher order thinking skills in your classroom.* Alexandria, VA: ASCD.

Elder, L., & Paul, R. (2009). *The art of asking essential questions.* Dillon Beach, CA: The Foundation for Critical Thinking.

Fisher, D., & Frey, N. (2012). Making time for feedback. *Educational Leadership, 70*(1), 42–47: ASCD.

Hattie, J. (2012, September). Know thy impact. *Educational Leadership, 70*(1), 18–23: ASCD.

Stiggins, R., Arter, J., Chappuis, J., & Chappuis, S. (2006). *Classroom assessment for student learning: Doing it right—Using it well.* Boston, MA: Pearson Education.

Tovani, C. (2012). Feedback is a two-way street. *Educational Leadership, 70*(1), 48–51: ASCD.

Wiggins, G. (2012). 7 keys to effective feedback. *Educational Leadership, 70*(1), 10–16: ASCD.

Wiggins, G., & McTighe, J. (2006). *Understanding by design* (expanded 2nd ed.). Upper Saddle River, NJ: Pearson.

Chapter Ten

Lesson Planning:
Pulling It All Together

The MiCOSA Lesson Planning Guide helps you structure and integrate all the elements of the Model you have learned throughout the book. It becomes your personal prompt throughout the delivery of your lesson.

"Have you ever been told stories by a parent, grandparent, aunt, or uncle?" Ms. Inaba asks her class. "Do they come from your background or culture?" As students respond, she continues, "What are some of the reasons these stories are told?" Students then begin to share their ideas. After hearing their replies, Ms. Inaba states, "Some of the reasons you came up with relate to the themes of the stories you have heard or read together at home—the lessons they wanted you to learn. Think for a minute about what a theme is, then write down your initial ideas and hold on to them. You will revisit these ideas and revise your thinking based on new perspectives you gain after we complete our unit on themes in life and literature."

"We are going to read a story about a great Lakota Sioux leader named Sitting Bull. As you read the story, A Boy Called Slow, *look for a theme you believe is central to the story. Find details and evidence to support that theme, and also look for and record insights into Lakota culture. Later you will do similar work, finding themes, evidence, and cultural insights in stories from your own culture, which is also filled with rich ideas and lessons. If you happen to be Lakota, you will choose a story from another culture. Using the thinking skills of* comparing *and* finding connections and relationships, *you will deepen your understanding of themes and of the cultures within our classroom."*

As you begin to develop full lesson plans with the MiCOSA framework, you will integrate all the elements you have learned. Weaving together rich content with your students' prior knowledge and cultural grounding, as Ms. Inaba did in the vignette above, you will use mediating conversations to develop relevant thinking skills. You will bridge those into the big ideas of the standards, assessing for depth of content and transfer of knowledge. MiCOSA's *Planning Instruction* supports the development of your lessons.

MiCOSA's Teacher's Guide to Planning Instruction

MiCOSA helps you integrate critical elements to effective lesson planning. It provides a format that asks you to plan your instruction around thinking skills; use essential questions into rather than to guide inquiry; and encourage discovery of big ideas and transfer of knowledge. In addition, it encourages you to use mediating conversations to support students in moving forward with their thinking and guide them toward autonomy of learning. MiCOSA's format expects you to measure student learning, focusing on assessing students' abilities to answer essential questions that demonstrate their growth in generalizing knowledge across content disciplines, and to support their transfer of learning.

MiCOSA's Teacher's Guide to Planning Instruction (Figure 10.1) creates a framework to pull together all the components of lesson planning to promote critical thinking and to teach for transfer. Each component discussed will become a section of the MiCOSA Lesson Planning Guide. Planning instruction with MiCOSA draws on the backward mapping concepts of Wiggins and McTighe (2006) and follows three guiding questions. The first two form the support structure for the development of lessons:

- What knowledge is essential?
- What assessments inform student understanding?

FIGURE 10.1

MiCOSA's Teacher's Guide to Planning Instruction

I: Determine Learning Goals: What Knowledge is Essential?

Content Standard:
1. Identify content standard and its core concepts
2. Identify the target thinking skill(s).

Develop Lesson Objective(s:)
3. Develop the learning objectives for content and thinking skill(s).
4. Determine the Content Big Idea (CBI) of the objective.
5. Determine a Broader Big Idea (BBI) for the objective.
6. Brainstorm a bridging principle to support transfer of the thinking skill(s).

II: Plan to Measure Learning: What Assessments Inform Student Understanding?

Essential Questions and Post-Assessment Measures
7. Create essential questions for content and thinking skill(s).
8. Design summative assessment measure(s).

Pre-assessment
9. Select pre-assessment measures for both content and thinking skill.

Informal and Ongoing Formative Assessment
10. Identify formative assessment activities linked to post-assessment(s) and EQs.

III: Plan for Instruction: What Methods/Procedures Motivate and Engage Learners and Drive Learning Forward?

11. Develop lesson sequence, integrating the following:
    a. Ground activity in culturally and personally relevant questions and/or events.
    b. Assess prior knowledge and cultural grounding to bridge to new learning.
    c. Develop the thinking skill(s) and bridge to content.
    d. Integrate mediating conversations to monitor and guide understanding.
    e. Use the CBIs and the BBIs to develop the depth of content.
    f. Scaffold strategies and activities to support mastery.
    g. Build formative assessment into these planned strategies and activities.
    h. Use feedback to adjust instruction.
    i. Encourage collaboration.
    j. Integrate summative assessments and transfer of learning. Determine next steps.

The third question leads your planning for instruction and assessment for mastery and transfer:

- What methods/procedures motivate and engage learners and drive learning forward?

Determine Learning Goals: What Knowledge Is Essential?

Instructional planning begins by determining what is worth understanding. What knowledge do you really want your students to learn and understand? Which thinking skills will facilitate that understanding? What materials will you need to use and what daily lessons will accomplish your learning goals? Recall that Chapter 7 outlined how to identify the standard you planned to teach, using it as a focus for teaching the thinking skills and building upon core concepts. Chapter 8 provided background for identifying big ideas, supporting your work in developing content depth. Chapter 9 revealed that determining the essential questions you want students to answer can help you more effectively plan for and measure valuable learning. This chapter shows you how to sequence these steps in your lesson planning. Don't worry if it seems a bit complex at first. Tackle parts of it over to time. As you become more comfortable with teaching thinking skills alongside content knowledge, teaching for transfer (Content Big Ideas and Broader Big Ideas) will come more easily, as will measuring learning based on essential questions. Your teaching will improve and your students will be more successful at learning how to learn—a clear goal for most teachers.

The models from The MICOSA Lesson Planning Guide will help you teach students how to learn. The first model, Figure 10.2, presents sequential processes and sample responses for determining learning goals.

Identify the Content Standard and Its Core Concepts
This step establishes the academic focus of the lesson, detailed in Chapter 7. Within the selected standard, underline the core concepts to help provide a focus for identifying the thinking skills.

Identify the Target Thinking Skill(s)
Locate the thinking skills needed to learn the core concepts. Then, select those you will work with in teaching the standard.

Develop the Learning Objective(s) for Content and Thinking Skill(s)
The objective (detailed in Chapter 7), a manageable chunk of the selected standard, articulates what you intend the students to understand by the end of the lesson. Because you will evaluate this learning in the post-assessment, the content objective should be measurable. For instance, rather than simply saying that students will understand something, speak about their ability to describe, delineate, or demonstrate their learning. Using these "action words" creates a clear link with your assessment. This form of the lesson plan presents the content and thinking skills as two separate objectives, because at first, you will be introducing the thinking skill overtly.

FIGURE 10.2

Determining Learning Goals: What Knowledge Is Essential?

Sequential Steps	Examples
IDENTIFY CONTENT STANDARD and ITS CORE CONCEPTS *(underline core concepts)*	Science Grade 4, LS3.a,b.[1] <u>Living organisms depend on one another and on their environment for survival.</u> As a basis for understanding this concept: a. Students know ecosystems can be characterized by their living and nonliving components. b. Students know that in any particular environment, some kinds of plants and animals survive well, some survive less well, and some cannot survive at all.
IDENTIFY TARGET THINKING SKILL(S) *(highlight or underline focus skills)*	<u>Finding Connections and Relationships</u> Comparing, Multiple Sources of Information, Cause and Effect/ Hypothetical Thinking
DEVELOP CONTENT OBJECTIVE	Students will orally describe and explain in writing their understanding that all living organisms depend on one another and on their environments for survival. They will select and delineate which living and nonliving things belong in four different ecosystems.
DEVELOP THINKING SKILL OBJECTIVE	Using the TS *finding connections and relationships,* students will demonstrate the interrelationships among the environment, plants, and animals within ecosystems. They will also understand how finding these connections and relationships relates to their lives beyond the classroom.
DETERMINE CONTENT BIG IDEA(S) (CBIs)	CBI 1: It is the interrelationships of the elements of an ecosystem that support its survival. CBI 2: When you find the key elements that interrelate in one ecosystem, you can apply those patterns to new ecosystems. CBI 3: In order to survive, the ecosystem's organisms must interact with both the living and nonliving components of their habitat. CBI 4: Plants and animals that can adapt to their environments survive better than poor adapters.

[1] Science Content Standards for California Public Schools: Kindergarten Through Grade Twelve (1998), Grade 4, LS3.a,b.

(Continued)

FIGURE 10.2 *(Continued)*

Sequential Steps	Examples
DETERMINE BROADER BIG IDEA(S) (BBIs)	BBI 1: As humans, we are part of many systems which can include our families, sports teams, religious groups, cultures, and even our town and our world. We rely on and are responsible to each other for survival within each system.
	BBI 2: As humans, we live in communities where we interact with each other and share resources. We must use these resources wisely because our actions impact and change not only our local community, but also the entire world.
	BBI 3: To help us live successfully, we must be ready to adapt and make changes to the way we live our lives.
BRAINSTORM BRIDGING PRINCIPLES *(select one or two for instructional purposes)*	*Thinking Skill Bridging Principles:* When I *find connections and relationships . . .*
	. . . I can begin to understand and identify patterns and trends.
	. . . I learn how different pieces of information are connected and related . . . . then I get a bigger picture of what I'm learning.
	. . . I can make sense of each of the parts and what they are for.
	. . . it helps me remember the parts as well as the meaning.

Determine the Content and Broader Big Ideas   Chapter 8 guided you in how to identify and create *big ideas*, which directly connect to the development of your essential questions (EQs) and lesson plan content. They come in two types:

- Content Big Ideas (CBIs)—ideas transferable within the unit of study itself.
- Broader Big Ideas (BBIs)—transferable, more abstract ideas, often extracted from the CBIs.

Brainstorm Bridging Principles to Support Transfer of Thinking Skills   Chapter 3 demonstrated how to develop bridging principles to help transfer thinking skills across content areas. MiCOSA's emphasis on active learning urges students to create their own bridging principles. However, it is helpful to think about potential bridging principles ahead of time, so that you can guide or provide examples to your students. Student-generated bridging principles help you assess whether your students have grasped the "big picture," the broad meaning, by incorporating new ways of thinking.

Plan to Measure Learning: What Assessments Inform Student Understanding?

Your assessments provide evidence about your students' learning, from their prior knowledge to their advanced understanding. By considering these meaningful outcomes up front, you create a destination on your "map." Chapter 9 detailed the multiple assessments you will use. In planning assessment, it is helpful to begin with the end in mind and then "map backwards" toward the destination. For this reason, you should design your essential questions and summative assessment prior to your pre-assessments. What essential questions do you want the students to answer? List those first; from there, develop summative assessment measures. Then design your pre-assessment measures, making sure they are consistent with MiCOSA's emphasis on prior knowledge and cultural grounding. They should also provide you with information on the student's prior knowledge of the content area and thinking skills. Performance assessments and other formative measures provide critical feedback that will help you adjust instruction along the way. Figure 10.3 outlines the sequence for planning to measure learning and provides examples of assessments within each category.

FIGURE 10.3

Plan to Measure Learning: What Assessments Inform Understanding?

Sequential Steps	Examples
CREATE ESSENTIAL QUESTIONS *Develop Content Essential Questions*	***Content EQs:*** (1) If we transported a plant or animal from one ecosystem to another, how would it affect the organism and how would it affect the environment from which it was removed? (2) What are the relationships between the living and nonliving parts of an ecosystem? (3) How is it that certain plants and animals survive better than others within their habitat?
Develop Thinking Skill Essential Questions *(select one for instructional purposes)*	***Thinking Skill EQs:*** (1) What is the relationship between _____ and _____ ? (2) How are these two items related (connected)? (3) How does finding connections and relationships make a difference for you? (4) How does finding connections and relationships help you understand and remember new knowledge?

(Continued)

FIGURE 10.3   *(Continued)*

DESIGN SUMMATIVE ASSESSMENT MEASURE(S) *(combine content and thinking skill)*	*Post-Assessment:* 1. Students will demonstrate their understanding and application of *finding connections and relationships* by identifying the relationships of living and nonliving components within four different ecosystems. 2. They will write a paragraph response for each of two essential questions (EQs); and 3. will summarize this knowledge by creating two content Big Ideas (CBIs) and one Broader Big Idea (BBI).
SELECT PRE-ASSESSMENT MEASURE(S) Establish prior content knowledge Establish prior thinking skill experience Link with cultural grounding	**Prior Knowledge Content:** Working in collaborative groups, students will hypothesize concerns about what could happen if plants and animals were removed from their natural habitat. To respond, they must construct what they already know about ecosystems, and how its parts are connected and related. An essential question will guide the structure of their response. **Thinking Skill Pre-assessment and Cultural Grounding:** Using pictures they bring from home, students pair-share their *connections and relationships* to a person in the picture. They share a memory of that person, either from personal experience or as a "story" told to them. Working with a partner, they generate multiple examples of connections and relationships between themselves and those in the picture beyond kinship relations.
IDENTIFY FORMATIVE ASSESSMENT MEASURES/ PERFORMANCE TASKS	1. Students will select and categorize living and nonliving things for their ecosystem of focus on a graphic organizer (G.O.) and answer questions designed to elicit their level of understanding of these relationships. 2. Using the cooperative learning strategy Jigsaw, students will take turns teaching others about their ecosystems. Informal formative assessments will include teacher observations and questioning.

Create Essential Questions for Both Content and Thinking Skills   Create essential questions (EQs) for your students that provoke both critical thinking and inquiry. Chapter 9 outlined this process. Content essential questions help students get to the big ideas behind the standards, and thinking skill essential questions support the development and transfer of the thinking skills. Students' answers to these essential questions will allow them to synthesize their knowledge into CBIs, BBIs, and bridging principles, which can be transferred to future learning.

In planning, note a few EQs that will guide the lesson, connecting thinking skills and content. You will use your EQs to guide the students through the transfer process and arrive at a broader understanding. Make sure you have written matching CBIs, BBIs, and bridging principles.

Design Summative Assessment Measures   As a summative assessment, or *post-assessment*, pose tasks that will tell you what students have learned as the *sum* of their experiences. Student responses to the essential questions will help them demonstrate mastery. What big ideas do they have and can they transfer those big ideas? Chapter 9 outlined a variety of post-assessments from oral and visual project presentations to well-developed essay responses. Informal, brief summations and reflections of the day's learning are also useful.

Select Pre-assessment Measures for Both Content and Thinking Skills   Prior knowledge and cultural grounding have several functions. One is *pre-assessment*. Selecting tasks that link with your students' cultures enables you to discover their related experiences, fostering a sense of belonging. You will use this information to create meaningful bridges between their experience and new content.

Develop pre-assessment measures for prior knowledge of content as well as for the thinking skill(s). Introducing the next section of the MiCOSA Lesson Planning Guide, Figure 10.3 illustrates pre-assessment of content and thinking skills with cultural grounding. One pre-assessment rather than two often suffices, because you will be constantly finding further evidence of prior knowledge more informally and authentically throughout the lesson. Intentionally seek these connections with your students' backgrounds and lives.

Identify Formative Assessment Activities Linked to Post-Assessment(s) and EQs   The teaching and learning experiences you design will support student progress toward the objectives. Design formative assessments, including some that serve as benchmarks, and include performance tasks and student self-assessments, along with more informal measures. Provide scoring rubrics. These formative assessment activities will provide you with feedback on student progress toward mastery. Finally, provide opportunities to assess your students' ability to transfer their learning to other situations and contexts. Ask, "Using your bridging principles, create and share ideas about where else you will use these thinking skills."

Plan for Instruction: What Methods/Procedures Motivate and Engage Learners and Drive Learning Forward?

This final section of MiCOSA's Teacher's Guide to Planning Instruction maps out the detailed journey down the instructional road, in which you put together the landmarks and points of reference along the way. The MiCOSA Lesson Planning Guide pulls all the sections of the framework together. The long and short forms below illustrate the final section of the Guide.

MiCOSA Lesson Planning Formats

Once you have determined the learning goals and designed your assessments, you are ready to plan for implementation. To do so, you will use MiCOSA's lesson planning formats to design and script out methods and procedures that will motivate and engage your students and drive their learning forward. This involves coordinating the sequence of your content: you will consider mediating conversations, thinking skill development and critical thinking. Further, you will incorporate essential and guiding questions, formative assessment experiences, and support for transfer of learning. The following checklist will support you in scaffolding student learning as you complete your lesson plan:

a. Ground activities in culturally and personally relevant questions and/or events.

b. Assess prior knowledge and cultural grounding to bridge to new learning.

c. Develop the thinking skill(s) and bridge to content.

d. Integrate mediating conversations to monitor and guide understanding.

e. Use the CBIs and BBIs to develop depth of content.

f. Scaffold strategies and activities to support mastery.

g. Build formative assessments into strategies and activities.

h. Use feedback to adjust instruction.

i. Encourage collaboration.

j. Integrate summative assessments and transfer of learning. Determine the next steps.

MiCOSA offers two formats of the lesson planner—one long and one short. The long form supports your learning process, whereas the short form is for use once the process becomes "second nature."

Using the Long Form of the MiCOSA Lesson Planning Guide

The long form of the lesson planner, designed as a teaching tool, is useful in the learning process. As you plan for implementation, you will physically align the model's instructional components to assure you are interweaving mediating conversations into your thinking skill and content instruction. Writing out a full script, while not something you will do often, allows you to pre-think instructional elements that may be new, such as the introduction of thinking skills, integration of pre-assessment with cultural grounding, and mediation of thinking skills with challenging students to reach for depth of content.

Figure 10.4 provides a scripted lesson using the long version of the planning guide. Understanding ecosystems is the content focus; finding connections and relationships is the target thinking skill. In the lesson, you will see the components you have read about come together as a whole. Looking across the columns, you can double-check the alignment of dialogue, thinking skills, content, and actions. The dialogue you write will support your pre-thinking and alignment of components; it allows you to make adjustments to the plan. You cannot expect to correctly project all student responses, but here you anticipate them. In addition, "teachable moments" will arise that are not in your script; obviously, you will use those to support learning. You can download a blank form of this guide from PDToolkit.

Develop Your Content (Lesson Steps) and Thinking Skills

You will make short notes about the sequence of instruction, with cues indicating when to introduce instructional content, tasks, or activities; you may have already done this in your teaching. With MiCOSA, you will also note when to introduce thinking skills, assessments, essential questions, CBIs, BBIs, bridging principles, and specific ideas for differentiation. The short phrases you insert "highlight" the key parts of your lesson. They become reference checks.

Note the Mediating Conversations

To ensure you are using all five mediating conversations, you will name them in your lesson plan as you use and integrate them alongside the dialogue that introduces or reinforces the thinking skills: (1) *intent and reciprocity*; (2) *mediating meaning*; (3) *bridging thinking*; (4) *guiding self-regulation*; and (5) *building competence*. Recall that these conversations help students integrate these skills into their conceptual repertoires. Note that in Figure 10.4, each of the mediating conversations is used, but not in a numerically linear sequence; rather, you use them where they make sense, guiding the rationale for your interactions at any specific point. For instance, you might want to ensure that what you say brings *meaning* into the lesson, or that you are *bridging* what your students have just learned into a new context. You will note these labels as you create your running dialogue, as the dialogue will integrate the mediating conversations. This also helps you cross-check that you have not omitted any, and allows you to go back later to edit in additional conversations.

Create a Running Dialogue and Integrate Prompting Questions

Creating a running dialogue allows you to really think through your interactions. How will you phrase an introduction, a prompt, or a critical question? Articulating the dialogue allows you to cross-check your plans with the other instructional elements, making sure you do what you intend. For example, if you are introducing a new *thinking skill*, you will first share your *intent* to mediate this thinking skill. Think about the best actions and discourse to use to help foster the students' *reciprocity*, their engagement in the learning, and note *intent and reciprocity* alongside your dialogue that mediates those elements. Similarly, you will create language to help *establish meaning* and guide students to *self-regulate* the pace of their work so they take advantage of their thinking and feedback. What specific language can help you *build competence* and, ultimately, *bridge* that knowledge *for transfer*?

You may prefer to write sections of your proposed dialogue before you complete the rest of your notes on mediating conversations, just to keep the flow of the lesson. After you have written a segment of dialogue, re-read it, then identify and label the mediating conversations you are using. How will you prompt your students to use thinking skills during the lesson? This is an opportunity to go back and revise your dialogue if you have neglected any of the mediation, or if you want to add an activity. To help you develop thinking skill prompts for your students, Figure 10.5 provides an extensive list of examples.

FIGURE 10.4

Long Form Lesson Planner: Excerpt from Lesson, "Finding Connections and Relationships Among Ecosystems."

Plan for Implementation: What Methods/Procedures Will Motivate and Engage Learners and Drive Learning Forward?

CONTENT STEPS and THINKING SKILL FOCUS	MEDIATING CONVERSATIONS	RUNNING DIALOGUE and PROMPTING QUESTIONS	ACTIONS and MATERIALS
DAY 1: Approx. 20 minutes of lesson Begin with Hook Pose Essential Question 1 as Pre-assessment of Prior Knowledge of Ecosystems	Intent and Reciprocity	**DAY 1:** Do we have polar bears living at the beach in San Diego? (Pause for response.) Do we have kangaroos in our mountains in San Diego? (Pause for laughter.) No! Why do you supposed that is?	**DAY 1:** Show picture of a polar bear in its natural habitat and show the beach. Show a kangaroo in its natural habitat; show mountains.
Finding Connections and Relationships	Guiding Self-Regulation	I would like you to really think about this, and then on your whiteboard list at least three problems or issues that you come up with. This EQ (point to it) will help you frame your thinking. Let's read it together, "If we. . . ." Now, first, generate your own thoughts, and then we'll work together. You have three minutes to think and write.	Prior to class, post this essential question up in front of the room: **If we transported a plant or animal from one ecosystem to another, how would it be affected and how would it affect the environment from which it was removed?** Choral read together.
	Building Competence	[Acknowledge their ability to construct ideas from their prior knowledge.] I'm impressed that some of you have some very specific and important ideas you thought of. Some of you have even connected several pieces of information. Thinking about how these ideas connect and relate to each other is something we are going to do a lot, and you already have a start.	Whiteboards: Observe and support students' thinking as they write on their whiteboards.

CONTENT STEPS and THINKING SKILL FOCUS	MEDIATING CONVERSATIONS	RUNNING DIALOGUE and PROMPTING QUESTIONS	ACTIONS and MATERIALS
Collaboration	Intent and Reciprocity	In groups of four, share your ideas. Develop new ones as you talk together, because when we *collaborate*, we often get new ideas. In six minutes, each will choose one of your favorite or most	Provide a note card for each student. Place them in groups of four. Each group will discuss and then orally present key ideas written on cards.
Synthesize Key Concepts	Building Competence (connecting PK to gained knowledge)	interesting ideas from your whiteboard and write it on the card you have been given. Group share your selections. Finally, you will post them so we can build on these ideas you already have.	Circulate/observe/support. Students will post their responses (cards). Whole group shares about six to eight of the strongest responses. Comment on specifics.
	Building Competence	As I was going around the room listening to your group discussions, I heard the term *ecosystems* mentioned. I know it's posted up here on the wall as part of the essential question, but I am impressed that you made that connection. That's what we will be studying: *ecosystems* and their interdependence.	
Labels, Words, and Concepts	Intent and Reciprocity	Here is the definition from your science books. I will post it so that you can use it as a reference to check your understanding as we learn more. Let's read it together. . . . What does it mean, "living and nonliving components"? Discuss it with your partner. (Support their understanding [i.e., living parts = all organisms like plants, animals, bacteria/ nonliving parts = water, sunlight, oxygen, temperature, soil].)	Post the definition: **An ecosystem is a system that has living and nonliving components within an environment. These components are connected in some ways.** Point to the posted EQ as a focus.

(Continued)

FIGURE 10.4 (*Continued*)

CONTENT STEPS and THINKING SKILL FOCUS	MEDIATING CONVERSATIONS	RUNNING DIALOGUE and PROMPTING QUESTIONS	ACTIONS and MATERIALS
	Mediating Meaning	Now let's return to the EQ posted at the beginning of the lesson: **If we transported a plant or animal from one ecosystem to another, how would it affect the organism and how would it affect the environment from which it was removed?** This is actually a pretty complex question, and you won't be able to answer it fully until you have learned more. However, with the knowledge you now have, write down in your journals some of your ideas which will help to answer this essential question. I hope you have some questions about it. What more will you need to know? What do you want to find out? This will be a great starting place for us tomorrow.	Refocus students on posted EQ: **If we transported a plant or animal from one ecosystem to another, how would it affect the organism and how would it affect the environment from which it was removed?** Students write response ideas to the EQ in their journals.
Students Develop Draft of CBI from the Essential Question		At the end of this unit, you will show your understanding of the big ideas of the learning. I have posted two post-assessments here for you so that you can begin to understand how the learning goal will be assessed. Listen carefully while I read them to you. (Read Post-Assessment A & B.) You have already begun to think about one of the essential questions. Tomorrow, you will be introduced to the second. Now I will collect your journals so that I can understand the knowledge you already have and can build on that tomorrow.	Focus on posted **Post-Assessment Part A—(*combined content and thinking skill*)** Students will demonstrate their understanding and application of *finding connections and relationships* by identifying the relationships of living and nonliving components within four different ecosystems.

CONTENT STEPS and THINKING SKILL FOCUS	MEDIATING CONVERSATIONS	RUNNING DIALOGUE and PROMPTING QUESTIONS	ACTIONS and MATERIALS
			Focus on posted **Post-Assessment Part B**— Students will demonstrate their understanding and application of *finding connections and relationships* by writing a paragraph response for each of two presented essential questions related to *Ecosystems and Their Interdependence*. Students will summarize this knowledge by creating two Content Big Ideas (CBIs) and one Broader Big Idea (BBI).
			Collect journals. Use feedback from pre-assessment observations and journal entries to make adjustments as needed in both content and process tomorrow.

DAY 2 SYNOPSIS OF BEGINNING: After reading the students' journal entries, the teacher synthesizes her understanding of the students' prior knowledge of ecosystems. She notes that many are beginning to grasp the big idea that both animals and plants need to be in an environment that meets their needs (e.g., right food/water/temperature/shelter to survive). She refocuses on the second posted EQ: **What is the relationship between living and nonliving parts of an ecosystem?** She also introduces the thinking skill *Finding Connections and Relationships* and defines it as, **"finding out how different pieces of information are related and connected."** Next, she introduces an activity to bridge the thinking skill to the students' personal lives. She models sharing a picture of two women. She shares the *connections and relationships* she has with them. Working in pairs, and with their own family photos, students discover and share *connections and relationships* they enjoy with a person in the picture. To help them further understand *connections and relationships*, the teacher invites them to look at a recipe for making a cake.

(Continued)

FIGURE 10.4 *(Continued)*

CONTENT STEPS and THINKING SKILL FOCUS	MEDIATING CONVERSATIONS	RUNNING DIALOGUE and PROMPTING QUESTIONS	ACTIONS and MATERIALS
Pose Prompting Question that links culture with the thinking skills though analogy.	Bridging Thinking Intent and Reciprocity	Let's look at this recipe for making a *tres leches* cake. Understanding the connections and relationships of making this cake will help you understand *connections and relationships*.	Display picture/recipe and prompting question: **How does making this delicious traditional Mexican cake help us understand the thinking skill *finding connections and relationships?***
Finding Connections and Relationships		Cakes are an important part of many of our cultural celebrations. (Elicit examples from different cultures.) How does making this delicious traditional Mexican cake help us understand the thinking skill *finding connections and relationships?* Go beyond just discussing the ingredients and how they connect. Try and identify how each part or process mentioned in the recipe affects the finished result of the cake. For example, how important is it to have the right temperature to bake the cake? With your partner, discuss this question and then we will hear some of your ideas.	Whiteboards/Pair-Share. Circulate and observe. Look for responses that see connections not only with the ingredients, but in the way it is baked: the type of container used, the position in the oven, the temperature, cooking time, and so on, and how each affects the success of the finished product.
Making a Tres Leches Cake	Guiding Self-Regulation		

CONTENT STEPS and THINKING SKILL FOCUS	MEDIATING CONVERSATIONS	RUNNING DIALOGUE and PROMPTING QUESTIONS	ACTIONS and MATERIALS
	Building Competence	(Share student ideas.) Wow, we heard some really great ideas! You are really beginning to understand how each part of the process of making the cake is important and needs each of the other parts to make the cake a success. If one part is missing, or changes, then the cake will not turn out to be scrumptious, as it should! **The thinking skill *finding connections and relationships* helped us understand how different parts, or pieces, of information are connected and related.** Together, let's create a bridging principle from what we have learned so that we can remember it and use it again and again to help us solve future problems.	Share student ideas.
Bridging Principle			Generate BP with students and post; for example, When I use the thinking skill *finding connections and relationships* I can learn how different parts, or pieces, of information are connected and related.
	Bridging Thinking	Now, in your TS journals write the new bridging principle and give an example of a time when you could use this principle to help you problem solve. Now we are ready to connect the thinking skill to our learning about ecosystems.	TS journals: Students write the principle in their TS journals and give a personal example of transfer of this learning.

SYNOPSIS OF REMAINDER OF DAY 2. The teacher now skillfully bridges the thinking skill to ecosystems. She introduces a collaborative group activity (Jigsaw), asking students to see themselves as scientists who will become experts on each of the four ecosystems: **Desert, Coral Reef, Rainforest,** and **Tundra.** Each group is given directions, research materials on their ecosystem, and a collection of pictures of living and nonliving things of all four ecosystems. After careful reading, each group will decide which pictures (characteristics) belong to their ecosystem. Students organize their findings of the *connections and relationships* they find on a graphic organizer. Now each "expert" shares their findings with "experts" of the other three ecosystems, expanding their knowledge to all four systems. They record this new information on graphic organizers, which become their homework study sheets to prepare them for tomorrow's cube game. While students work in groups, the teacher mediates the thinking skill, Finding Connections and Relationships, using her observations as an informal formative assessment.

(Continued)

FIGURE 10.4 *(Continued)*

CONTENT STEPS and THINKING SKILL FOCUS	MEDIATING CONVERSATIONS	RUNNING DIALOGUE and PROMPTING QUESTIONS	ACTIONS and MATERIALS
DAY 3: Synthesis of Knowledge and Post-Assessment Activities Parts A & B	Intent and Reciprocity	Today we will assess your level of mastery of this work on ecosystems and their interdependence. I am going to give you five minutes to quietly review your questionnaire and your notes/graphic organizer(s) from yesterday before we begin the next activity. Any questions? (Respond to concerns.) Ready, begin.	Collect homework. Hand back marked questionnaires for feedback and to support revision.
Post-Assessment A (Performance Task II)—Checking for Mastery	Mediating Meaning	Now that you have gained knowledge about all four ecosystems, you are going to use your TS *finding connections and relationships* as you look ACROSS ecosystems! Each group has an ecosystems question cube and four index cards, each bearing the name of an ecosystem you have learned about. Each side of the cube has different questions about the relationships within different ecosystems, similar to the ones you answered before. You will take turns and roll the cube and then pick a card, which will inform you of the ecosystem you need to relate your question/ answer to, just like this (model).	Focus on posted **Post-Assessment Part A—(*combined content and thinking skill*). Students will demonstrate their understanding and application of *finding connections and relationships* by identifying the relationships of living and nonliving components within four different ecosystems.** (An interactive cube activity will provide random selection of the questions they will need to answer.)

CONTENT STEPS and THINKING SKILL FOCUS	MEDIATING CONVERSATIONS	RUNNING DIALOGUE and PROMPTING QUESTIONS	ACTIONS and MATERIALS
	Collaboration	To begin, choose a card to inform you of the ecosystem of focus. The person with that expertise will be the one to roll the die. As soon as the die has been rolled, each member of the group will silently record his or her answer on the sheet, using a pen. You will have one minute. Next, you will each share your answers with "the expert." The expert will tell you if you are correct and will help you to elaborate on your answer. Make any revisions to your answers in pencil, so we can see how your thinking changed through collaboration. Those students who are in a group that have two of the same experts on the same ecosystem can share the time.	Provide the cube and four index cards (each bearing the name of one of the four ecosystems) per group. Students record answers, which will be handed in at end of the activity for assessment/feedback.

During activity: Mediate their use of connections and relationships using questions such as: Why did you pick that animal for your ecosystem? How is it related to the temperature and plants? What made you pick that landscape? How did you use seeking relationships to determine that? What is the relationship between plants, the temperature, and animals? |
		Are you ready? Go ahead and share your expert knowledge!!!	
	Building Competence	As I went around the different groups I saw some great *collaboration*. I saw you asking questions of others in the group, answering questions for others, and changing your initial responses to reflect this growing knowledge. Well done! I also heard some great "ah-ha" moments when you were able to come up with a connection between the living and nonliving components that wasn't quite so straightforward.	Collect G.O.s, the questionnaire sheet (from earlier activity), and the answer papers (from the cube activity) as formative assessment/feedback support.
		This part of the post-assessment is in three parts: 1. Respond to the two EQs. 2. Create two CBIs. 3. Create one BBI.	Students need pen and pencil for this task. Observe, monitor, and support.

(Continued)

FIGURE 10.4 (Continued)

CONTENT STEPS and THINKING SKILL FOCUS	MEDIATING CONVERSATIONS	RUNNING DIALOGUE and PROMPTING QUESTIONS	ACTIONS and MATERIALS
Post-Assessment—Creating BBI DAY 3: Synthesis of Knowledge and Post-Assessment Activities Parts A & B	Intent	Let's return to our two posted essential questions. (Refocus students to the two posted EQs.) The first one posted was: **If we transported a plant or animal from one ecosystem to another, how would it affect the organism and how would it affect the environment from which it was removed?** You had started to answer this EQ yesterday, but at that time you did not have the knowledge you now have. Revisit what you wrote yesterday in your TS journals and elaborate on that answer. Also, respond to the second posted EQ: **What are the relationships between living and nonliving parts of an ecosystem?** Your answers will reveal some Big Ideas of the content that are important to remember.	Focus on posted **Post-Assessment Part B—Students will demonstrate their understanding and application of** *finding connections and relationships* **by writing a paragraph response for each of two presented essential questions related to** *Ecosystems and their Interdependence.* **Students will summarize this knowledge by creating two Content Big Ideas (CBIs) and one Broader Big Idea (BBI).**
Summarizing		Write a paragraph on each, but then sum up the essence of what you have to say using one condensed sentence for each. These will be the Content Big Ideas (CBIs). You have a rubric to help you understand how your work will be scored. This will also help you in planning your CBIs.	Revisit the two posted EQs. Provide each student with a scoring rubric for the CBIs and the BBI.

CONTENT STEPS and THINKING SKILL FOCUS	MEDIATING CONVERSATIONS	RUNNING DIALOGUE and PROMPTING QUESTIONS	ACTIONS and MATERIALS
Post-Assessment—Creating BBI		Select one of your CBIs to try to create a BBI. I know you have worked on these before in other content areas, and are becoming familiar with them. Are there any questions you still have about how to create them? (Respond to concerns.) Again, you have the rubric to help you plan. You will have three minutes to work with a partner to share your thinking or to ask questions before you begin. We will discuss your processes of developing the BBIs tomorrow in class.	Students revisit entries in their TS journals and revise and embellish their thinking. Students do not write during the three minutes. At the end of that period, they must work quietly and independently on their work.
Next Steps. Return to the Bridging Principle and connect beyond the unit of study for far transfer.

Bridging for Transfer

Pose Essential Question 3 as homework. | Bridging Thinking | Ok. I'd like you to return your thoughts to the bridging principle we wrote earlier, *when I find connections and relationships, then I learn how different parts, or pieces, of information are connected and related.* How will *finding connections and relationships* help you with other tasks you encounter either at school or at home? Pause to Brainstorm.

As homework, I want to pose this question to you, based on what you have learned so far: **How is it that certain plants and animals survive better than others within their habitat?** Use your new knowledge of both ecosystems and thinking skills to help you answer. | Student responses are recorded on notepaper that can be collected at the end of the period for assessment/feedback purposes.

Write up their brainstorming ideas and celebrate.

HOMEWORK: Introduce the Content Essential Question as homework. |

FIGURE 10.5

Prompts and Prompting Questions for Thinking Skills in the MiCOSA Model

GATHERING INFORMATION	
1. Systematic Search	Let's take a look at all the information so we don't miss anything.
	Let's use a system—where should we start . . . and then?
	What strategy would help us gather the information we need?
	How could we organize the way we gather the information we need?
	What is it that we have to do?
	What do you think we have to do here? How can you tell?
	What clues could help you find what you need?
2. Focus and Attention	Why is it important to focus when we are gathering information?
	Are you ready?
	Can you show me where we will find the information we need?
	Look up here, please.
	What is the next step?
	You have one minute to finish.
	If you clear your desk of what you don't need, do you think that might help you focus a little better?
3. Labels, Words, and Concepts	Let me put the word in the context of another sentence to see if it helps you understand its meaning.
	What word does it remind you of?
	Let's look to see if we can find a part of the word which will give us some meaning (suffix, prefix, root).
4. Multiple Sources	Yes, and what other information here might be helpful?
	What else do we need to consider?
	I can see you did . . . , but you also need to consider. . . .
	Tell me more (or another one).
	What else do you see?
5. Position in Space	Look, or point to (left, right, in front . . .).
	Draw the view from your (right, left, . . .).
	How do these spatial words help us?
	Let's try moving the book over in front of you to help you visually transport the words from the text to your own work.
	Would you return this book to the library? What direction will you go? Can you explain the route to me? What landmarks will help you?

FIGURE 10.5 (*Continued*)

6. Position in Time	Is there an important order we should use to do this (e.g., first, next)?
	You seem to be having difficulty with sequencing what you are reading. Can you put the main ideas of what you are reading on a time line? I think it will help you.
	How do the transition words help us understand the order of the events?
	What event comes after this one? Which one came before?
	How long do you think it will take for you to do this problem? Write down your estimate. We will time you and see how close you were!
7. Precision and Accuracy	Why do we need to be precise when we gather information?
	Let's cover the directions and just show you the first part. What does it ask us to do?
	How can we find out if what we are reading is true (accurate)?
	What answer is the least likely to be correct? Why?
Generic Questions	What do you see here?
	What do you think you have to do?
	What do you think the problem might be? How do you know?
	What is implied here?
	Whose point of view is this?
	What assumptions are we making as we read?
TRANSFORMING INFORMATION	
8. Goal Setting	Let's talk about your goal—what do you want to accomplish?
	OK. A plan needs a goal, steps in order, and an end product. Let's think about that together.
	Why are you doing this?
	What is the purpose of this?
	What are you trying to achieve?
	What problem are you trying to solve?
	Let's chart your progress toward your goal.
	Can you put the class goal (objective) in your own words and tell me what you wish to learn from this lesson?
9. Planning	Do you have a plan? (If not) Let's make one and see what difference it makes.
	How will planning help you reach your goal?
	What graphic organizer will help me plan and organize my thinking?
	Can you show me your plan for organizing your work? How can we make ourselves more efficient at planning?
	Take a moment to close your eyes and think and plan your thinking before you write.

(*Continued*)

FIGURE 10.5 *(Continued)*

10. Comparing	How do you know how it should look?
	Is this like something you have done before? OK, let's compare how it's the same and different and use that information.
	How might we use comparing to help?
	Let's compare our thinking to the model.
	How will comparing help us categorize?
	What are the attributes of (a)? What are the attributes of (b)? How do they compare?
	How are these different? How are they the same?
	What graphic organizer will help us show our understanding of comparisons?
11. Ordering, Grouping, and Categorizing	How would putting the information in categories help you?
	What comes first?
	How could we group these differently? What are their commonalities?
	Under which category does this information (fact) belong?
12. Finding Connections and Relationships	What connection can you make?
	How are _____ and _____ related?
	How does this connect to the problem?
	Does what we say connect to the evidence I present?
	Let me help you connect this new knowledge to something you already know so that you can make better meaning of it.
	How do these parts connect together?
	Have I got all the parts of information I need to solve this problem?
13. Visualizing	Can you picture that?
	What does it look like?
	Stop reading for a moment. Close your eyes and describe what you see in your head. Now read on. Stop. Close your eyes again and describe what you now see. How has the picture in your head changed?
	How can you help put pictures in the head of the reader when you write?
	How can visualizing help you hypothesize?
14. Inferring	Put the clues together. What do you think will happen?
	Can you explain your thinking?
	How did you arrive at that conclusion?
	Is there another conclusion that could be possible?
	What clues helped you come to that conclusion?

FIGURE 10.5 *(Continued)*

15. Cause and Effect—Hypothesizing	What is the cause?
	What is the effect?
	Let's organize our thinking on a graphic organizer to help us understand the causal relationships.
	How can the patterns of causation help us hypothesize?
	As a result of your data, what can you hypothesize?
	Let's use the WHEN-THEN and IF-THEN frames to help us.
	What words will give us cues to causation (*because, if, as a result*)?
16. Summarizing	What are the main ideas?
	As you finish reading this page, take a moment and summarize what you have been reading before you read on. It will help you connect and maintain meaning.
	What did you learn yesterday?
	What were the key ideas of the learning (the Big Ideas)?
	If you draw a symbol next to your note taking, it will help you summarize key points. It will give you the essence of what you have learned.
	Can you record the key points on a graphic organizer?
	What do you conclude?
	What is the gist of this?
Generic Questions	Tell me about your thinking as you do this.
	How are you going to do that?
	You got it—yes, and why is it not _____ (a wrong answer)?
	What is your information based on?
	What experiences made you think that way?
	Do you need to rethink the question?
	What assumptions did you make?
COMMUNICATING INFORMATION	
17. Labels, Words, and Concepts	Can you think of a more exact word for what you want to say?
	Can you draw the word you are trying to say? Sometimes this helps us conceptualize it and you are able to find the right label.
	Think of a word that is an antonym for the word you are seeking to use.
	Can you think of an analogy? Metaphor? And so on?
	Can you use more sensory detail to help me paint a picture in my head?

(Continued)

FIGURE 10.5   *(Continued)*

18. Precision and Accuracy	How accurate do you think this should be?
	Can you give me more details (precision)?
	Can you be more specific (precision)?
	How can you give evidence that your thinking is true?
	Read it back to yourself to see if it is accurate and makes sense.
19. Appropriate Pragmatics	What would you do if . . . ?
	Are you considering others' point of view?
20. Feedback for Self-Regulation	What might you do if someone gave you a suggestion?
	Give yourself a moment to stop and think before you begin. Organize your thoughts first. I think it will help.
	What do you think you could work on to improve this (skill)?
	Let's keep a record of your progress and see why you think your work is improving so much more! What are you doing differently now that you did not do before? Where else could you apply this strategy?
	What do you like about your work? How can understanding what you do well help you improve in other areas you need to work on?
21. Collaboration	How will working with others help you?
	Are you listening to the ideas of others?
	Are you contributing to the ideas of the group?
	Is your thinking changing as a result of your collaboration with others?
Generic Questions	As you finish an assignment, how do you feel about what you have learned?
	What do you think about your performance? Find one thing you are thrilled with and one thing you would like to work on.

Note Actions and Materials   Make notes alongside the dialogue to remind you of specific actions that support student engagement, as well as materials you want to remember to bring into the lesson. For example, you may indicate posting something for the class, organizing students into small groups, informally observing them at work, passing out a set of materials, or writing in electronic journals. This cues you and supports your efforts in delivering the lesson; it also offers enhanced support of student learning. You will want to seek multiple opportunities for students to work collaboratively on projects or short assignments that help them articulate, think through, and connect their learning. Here you will note the configurations of collaborative learning.

Using the Short Form of the MiCOSA Lesson Planning Guide

The second form of the Lesson Planning Guide—the short form—is much quicker and more practical to use over time, once you understand the full, lengthier process. The short form is the "abstract" of the "master"—a simple graphic organizer to support you in jotting down key ideas and concepts, while keeping sight of the big ideas. Figure 10.6 illustrates this short form; the lesson on ecosystems is again used, but this time with the briefer format.

The upper portion of the planning guide—in which you identify your key standards, thinking skills, objectives, Content and Broader Big Ideas, and assessments—remains the same as in the long version. Figure 10.6 illustrates only the portion of the short form in which you previously wrote out the full dialogue and noted all mediating conversations, actions, materials, and cues to your content sequence. With the short form, your content and process sections are abbreviated, but key dialogues, directions, and concepts are left in. If you are using the short version, but become stuck (e.g., how to transition and con-nect a segment of the lesson to the next piece), it may help to revert back to scripting the dialogue in long form. In this way, you can make the length of the lesson plan compatible with your own needs, supporting you as you iron out any difficult segments before you introduce and teach them. Your lesson planner becomes your personal prompt.

Three Lesson Plan Variations on Introducing and Using Thinking Skills

Level I. You will introduce your students to one thinking skill at a time. This helps them develop depth in understanding each thinking skill, deriving meaning and familiarity as they see its connection to their home cultural contexts and prior experience. As you use mediating conversations to help them bridge the thinking skill into content, they begin to develop depth. Using bridging principles to support transfer, they will explore additional content applications of each thinking skill. You may dis-play the poster versions of the thinking skill cards around the room to remind them of what they have already begun to use. An example of a fully scripted lesson using only one thinking skill is provided in PDToolkit.

Level II. After students have demonstrated a working knowledge of four or five key think-ing skills, you can begin to integrate several of these into your lessons simultaneously prior to introducing additional new skills. This will help consolidate their learning, and move them toward a fluid and natural way of integrating multiple thinking skills into their work. Your les-son planner will vary slightly to reflect that change in your thinking skill objective. Figure 10.6 provides an example in which changes from Level I to Level II are indicated in bold.

Content/Thinking Skill Objective: Students will orally describe and explain in writing the *connections and relationships* within an ecosystem. They will identify and *categorize* both living and non-living components of a given ecosystem and make *comparisons* of these components across four different ecosystems using *multiple sources* of information to support their investigation.

FIGURE 10.6

Short Form of The MiCOSA Lesson Planning Guide: Excerpt from "Finding Connections and Relationships Among Ecosystems" and Components

Plan for Implementation: What Methods/Procedures will Motivate and Engage Learners and Drive Learning Forward?

CONTENT STEPS and THINKING SKILL FOCUS	MEDIATING CONVERSATIONS	RUNNING DIALOGUE and PROMPTING QUESTIONS	ACTIONS and MATERIALS
DAY 1 Begin with Hook. Pose Essential Question 1 as Pre-Assessment to Assess Prior Knowledge of Ecosystems	Intent/Reciprocity Mediating Meaning Bridging Thinking Building Competence	Do we have polar bears living on the beach in San Diego? Do we have kangaroos in our mountains? **EQ1: If we transported a plant from one ecosystem to another, how would it be affected and how would it affect the environment from which it was removed?**	Post EQ1 and polar bear/kangaroo pictures. Create groups of four: brainstorm on whiteboards/select one key idea for card. Post and share.
Labels, Words, and Concepts		**Def: An ecosystem is a system that has living and nonliving components within an environment. These components are connected in many ways.**	Post definition and choral read.
Summarizing Thinking		What were the key ideas you came up with?	Students respond to EQ and then record ideas in journals.

DAY 2 Revisit EQ1 and Pose EQ2	Bridging Thinking	Recap yesterday and pose EQ2: **How can we identify an ecosystem by its living and non-living parts?**	Post/choral read EQ2.
Introduce thinking skill: Finding Connections and Relationships	Bridging Thinking	To help us understand more about ecosystems, we are going to learn a new thinking tool. It's called *finding connections and relationships*. **It means finding out how different pieces of information are related and connected.**	
Photo Activity: Link to Thinking Skills	Mediating Meaning	This is a picture of two women I know. We are connected by our friendship . . . by partnership as writers . . . sharing family stories . . . humor. What connections and relationships did you find in my story?	Model picture of friends and connections.
	Guiding Self-Regulation	Now, take out the pictures you brought from home. As you share, try to discover rich connections and relationships. Don't just say, "This is Uncle Fred." Look for as many connections as you can.	Pause to Elicit Responses and Mediate connection to TS. Mediate pair-sharing of pictures, to elicit connections and relationships. Share out in whole group. Post key relationships with arrows ←→. Emphasize relationships.

PD **TOOLKIT**™

PDToolkit: Video Clip 10.2 provides a glimpse of the mediation of multiple thinking skills within one lesson.

Your running dialogue will change as well. Now you can ask students how they might use each skill in a performance task or project they are working on. Using the previous example, prior to a formative performance assessment task, ask them how they will use the thinking skill of *finding connections and relationships* as they approach their ecosystem projects. Have them look at the instructions, think about the task, and write down how they will use *comparisons*, *categorizing,* and *multiple sources* of information.

Level III. When students can use multiple thinking skills fluidly, you can move them into greater autonomy. Your final variation challenges students to critically analyze a task or project, and come up with the thinking skills they will need to perform it. This variation emerges from the second. However, rather than providing students with the thinking skills and asking how a specific thinking skill will help them on the project, you will ask them to consider the nature of the task before them and determine what thinking skills they will need, and why. This is the most complex level of metacognition, or thinking about their thinking. It's truly exciting to see students engaging in this level of thought.

PD **TOOLKIT**™

PDToolkit: Video Clip 10.3 shows multiple components of a Variation III lesson in sequence.

Your lesson planner will still retain most of what you have done previously. However, your thinking skill targets will not be outlined, since your student will be generating them. You may seek more complex bridging principles as your students use them to link your lesson with its big ideas and essential questions. For example, they might say, "*Seeking connections and relationships* enables me to connect current knowledge to past experiences, and as a result gain more meaningful understanding of what I am trying to learn. It also helps me find *causal relationships*, *categorize*, and efficiently *compare* and *contrast*." Your running dialogue will also change to fit this third variation. Figure 10.7 provides an example of the Level III lesson plan, based on a project entitled *Themes in Literature and Life*. Changes from Level II to Level III are indicated in bold. The full lesson plan can be found in PDToolkit.

Self-Evaluation

PD **TOOLKIT**™

PDToolkit: Teachers and graduate students reflect on and discuss their experience and use of The MiCOSA Lesson Planning Guide in Video Clip 10.4.

MiCOSA encourages student self-evaluation, as well as student involvement in the assessment process. Teachers benefit from reflecting on their work as well. A rubric developed for this purpose, titled *A Rubric for Evaluation of Lesson Plans*, is included in PDToolkit. The rubric facilitates self-reflection, or reflection across teams. Both seasoned teachers and graduate students who have developed lessons with the MiCOSA Model have found this rubric for self-evaluation extremely helpful.

FIGURE 10.7

Level III. Lesson Plan Excerpt

Determining Learning Goals: What Knowledge Is Essential?	
IDENTIFY CONTENT STANDARD and ITS CORE CONCEPTS:	CCSS: ELA-LITERACY.RL.5.2.[7] Determine a theme of a story, drama, or poem from details in the text, including how characters in a story or drama respond to challenges or how the speaker of the poem reflects upon a topic; summarize the text.
IDENTIFY THE TARGET THINKING SKILL(S): *(highlight or underline focus skills)*	**Students will critically analyze projects and performance tasks to determine thinking skills needed, and will describe how they can be used.**
DEVELOP CONTENT OBJECTIVE:	Students will define and critically explore the concept of a theme for its use across literature and life stories. They will determine a theme in the story *A Boy Called Slow* (HM text, Grade 5) and support that theme with evidence from the story. Students will then choose a story from their own culture and determine its theme, including the characters' response to challenge; students will include supporting evidence and develop an illustrative presentation to share.
DEVELOP THINKING SKILL OBJECTIVE:	**Students will generate thinking skills appropriate to the project, and describe how they will use them.**
DETERMINE CONTENT BIG IDEA(S) (CBIs):	Themes of stories often reflect the insights and values of the author. They often teach us life lessons.
DETERMINE BROADER BIG IDEA(S) (BBIs):	Themes, whether in literature or across cultures in life, often teach us life lessons, insights, and values of the author's culture. In the case of cultural stories that may have been handed down for generations, that "author" represents a cultural way of seeing the world.
BRAINSTORM BRIDGING PRINCIPLES: *(select one or two for instructional purposes)*	**Students will generate bridging principles from the thinking skills they have identified and selected. Ask: What thinking skill(s) will you use for this project and how will it help you— what difference does it make?**

[7] Common Core State Standards for English Language Arts (2010), Reading Standards for Literature K5,Grade 5, RL 5.2.

(Continued)

FIGURE 10.7   *(Continued)*

Plan to Measure Learning: What Assessments Inform Student Understanding?	
CREATE ESSENTIAL QUESTIONS: *Develop Content Essential Questions* *Develop Thinking Skill Essential Questions:* *(select one for instructional purposes)*	***Content EQs:*** 1. What does the word *theme* mean to you and why is it necessary to learn about them? 2. What themes are in each others' stories? Can we apply those themes to our own lives? How? 3. What evidence will help you connect to the traditions of the Lakota culture? 4. What are values and insights and where do they come from? How are they related to themes? ***Thinking Skill EQs:*** **How will (name of thinking skill) help us with our projects?**
DESIGN SUMMA-TIVE ASSESSMENT MEASURE(S): *(combine content and thinking skill)*	**Post-Assessment**: Students will summarize the Lakota (Sioux) customs, history, language, and traditions in the story relevant to the theme. They will compare those exemplars with those from other cultures within the classroom and make connections. Students will connect their knowledge of theme to a story of their own culture that exemplifies the theme they discovered. They will include the character's response to challenge, clarifying their reasoning with supporting evidence. They will present their stories in written form, and share them with other class members. They will present their stories and themes to the class, supporting their understanding with three pieces of evidence.
SELECT PRE-ASSESSMENT MEASURE(S): *Establish prior content knowledge* *Establish prior thinking skill experience* *Link with cultural grounding*	***Prior Knowledge Content:*** Students define the meaning of the word *theme*. Through a series of critical questions, they will demonstrate their prior understanding of this concept and consider the ideas of others. ***Thinking Skill Pre-assessment and Cultural Grounding:*** 1. Elicit and celebrate the diversity of cultures within the classroom. 2. As a culminating part of the lesson, students will use their own cultural stories to find themes. It may be a story told by parents or other relatives, or a legend, myth, or fairy tale.
IDENTIFY FORMATIVE ASSESSMENTS/ PERFORMANCE TASKS:	1. Students will define the meaning of the word *theme*. 2. They will correctly summarize *A Boy Called Slow*. 3. Students will also correctly summarize their cultural story. 4. They will choose and explain appropriate thinking skill(s) to help them with their projects.

FIGURE 10.7	(*Continued*)

Plan for Implementation: What Methods/Procedures Will Motivate and Engage Learners and Drive Learning Forward.

CONTENT STEPS and THINKING SKILL FOCUS	MEDIATING CONVERSATIONS	RUNNING DIALOGUE and PROMPTING QUESTIONS	ACTIONS and MATERIALS
Elicit thinking skills	Intent and Reciprocity	We've talked a lot about thinking skills and how they've helped us with home and school. **What thinking skills will you need to be successful with this part of the project?**	Students discuss in table groups.
Collaboration	Mediating Meaning Guiding Self-Regulation	Work in your table groups. One person will be the recorder. First brainstorm approximately six to ten thinking skills you think you will use for this part of the project. Collaborate in your groups to come up with three that you think will be most useful to complete this project and indicate why. Prepare to share your ideas with the class.	
		Let's have the groups share. Is there another idea from another group? Is there still another idea from another group?	First group presents one. Acknowledge how it might be used and mediate if it is slightly "off." As groups present, list the thinking skills on the board and be sure to explain why they chose that thinking skill.
	Building Competence	You came up with a lot of important thinking skills we'll be using in our project, but more importantly, you explained why you will be using them. Keep referring to these skills as we work on our project.	

SUMMARY

- MiCOSA's *Teacher's Guide to Planning Instruction* is structured around three questions: The first, "What Knowledge is Essential?" helps teachers develop learning goals, including content and thinking skill objectives and big ideas. The second question, "What assessments inform student understanding?" organizes the planning of essential questions, as well as summative and formative assessments. Finally, the question "What methods/procedures motivate and engage learners and drive learning forward?" helps organize instructional components that will lead to the integration of thinking skills with content on the journey toward mastery and transfer.

- Two forms of the MiCOSA Lesson Planning Guide help teachers structure and script the instruction. The long form, designed as a teaching tool, supports learning. The short form provides a practical format for daily use once you have mastered the process.

- Thinking skills are initially introduced one at a time, allowing students to develop in-depth understanding, and learn to bridge or transfer the skill. In a second variation, teachers introduce multiple thinking skills, and students link them to performance tasks. The third variation challenges students to critically analyze which thinking skills will be needed, and to articulate the transfer.

- A self-assessment rubric for teachers (PDToolkit) provides a tool to use either individually or in groups as lesson plans are developed.

PD **PD** TOOLKIT™

PDToolkit:
The Rubric for
Lesson Plans
is found in the
PDToolkit

REFERENCE

Wiggins, G., & McTighe, J. (2006). *Understanding by design* (expanded 2nd ed.). Upper Saddle River, NJ: Pearson.

Chapter Eleven

Engaging Expectations and Promoting Resilience

Together, the teacher, student, and parent form a powerful triad of positive expectations that combine to boost resilience and improve performance. MiCOSA's mediating framework guides teacher engagement in effective relationships that support these expectations.

Remember your favorite teacher? Why was he or she so special? If your story is like that of many of us, you would tell us your favorite teachers were those who you knew genuinely cared and believed in you. They may have supported you through both academic and emotional challenges. They were teachers you connected with, could trust and confide in, and look up to, and who served as positive role models. You likely found yourself working harder for them and gained a greater confidence in your own abilities through being in their classes. They touched you as they touched most of us, in ways beyond the brilliant analysis or presentation of a topic; they helped us feel connected and capable. As educators now ourselves, we become those positive connections and role models for our students, mirroring that zest and passion for their well-being and success that we appreciated from our favorite teacher when we were the students.

What was it about those inspiring teachers in classic films such as *Dangerous Minds, To Sir With Love, Mr. Holland's Opus,* and *The Miracle Worker* that let you know how powerful teaching can be? The teachers in each of those films not only held high expectations, but also communicated those expectations in a way that their students came to believe they were capable of meeting them . . . and did.

For over a decade, research has demonstrated the value of high expectations (e.g., Achieve, 2009; Benard, 2004; De Jesus & Antrop-Gonzalez, 2006). Believing that your students are capable of deep and critical thinking, problem-solving, or creativity—and communicating that belief—is half the battle to getting them there. To maximize the power of high expectations, two other sources are key: first, when parents and community members hold high expectations, your students gain additional support, which allows them to more easily believe in their own potential; second, when students hold high expectations of themselves, coupled with belief in their ability to learn, their performance improves. When engaged, this powerful triad of expectations (teacher, parent, and student) is foundational to the relationships that help support student success. Each has unique contributions to the whole.

Teacher Expectations and Student Resilience

Sometimes students come to you without the motivation or affective strength to be open to challenging tasks. When you ask them to engage in critical thinking, those affective factors can get in the way. However, motivation and positive affect can be enhanced, and teacher expectations can play a critical role in doing so. Good teachers can actually support and facilitate the development of what is called *resilience* in their students. Resilience helps students build inner strength as they experience their value as thinkers, their flexibility and adaptability as problem-solvers, and their worth as human beings.

For many years in education, students seen as vulnerable were called "students at risk." *Risk factors*, such as coming from single-parent families or experiencing violence in the home, led some to conclude that these students were more likely to fail, and needed more supports. Often these students were financially disadvantaged or from diverse non-mainstream backgrounds (Wlodkowski & Ginsberg, 1995). Yet, despite the challenges in their lives, some of these students today seem to survive and even thrive. How? These are *resilient* students who adapt successfully or even come out stronger under adverse circumstances. They are able to get back up when they fall, to show determination in the face of overwhelming odds, and to problem-solve and learn from mistakes. They have developed a repertoire of strategies to help them cope with the challenges they will face today and throughout their lives. These students feel a sense of commitment to their schooling and look hopefully into the future, a future where they become caring and productive members of their society. Resilient students are more likely to hold positive views of themselves, and to form positive relationships with others.

Knowing what to do helps you maintain high expectations. We now know much more about how teachers can support resilience, which benefits increasing numbers of students. Protective factors, those that protect your students from risk and enhance resilience, are grouped into two categories: those associated with the students' own internal strengths are called *internal protective factors*, while those that support students from the outside—for instance, with support from teachers, parents, and communities—are known as *external protective factors*. Figure 11.1 summarizes the major components of resilience found in research (c.f., Benard, 2004; Resilience Research Center, 2010; Resnick, Ireland, & Borowsky, 2004; Ungar, 2005).

External Protective Factor I: Caring Relationships

When students feel close and connected to their teachers and peers, their academic development improves and risky behaviors decrease (McNeely, Nonemaker, & Blum, 2002). How important are those relationships? A longitudinal study published in the *Journal of the American Medical Association* found that having positive relationships with teachers was more important than class size, amount of teacher training, classroom rules, and school policy in protecting adolescents from destructive behaviors (Resnick et al., 1997).

FIGURE 11.1

Internal and External Protective Factors*

External Protective Factors (Teacher, Parent, Community)	Internal Protective Factors (Within Student)
Caring relationships	Social competence/Positive relationships
High expectations	Self-efficacy/Confident in ability
Meaningful participation	Sense of purpose/Direction in life
	Skilled with problem solving

*Based on work of Benard, 2004; Resilience Research Center, 2010; Resnick, Ireland, & Borowsky, 2004; and Ungar, 2005.

How do you let your students know you care? First, you have to accept that *your* caring matters. Although many students don't "let on" that you matter to them, you do. In fact, often the students most likely to be "at risk" are least likely to believe that you care. Thus, they may act like they don't believe what you say the first time you reach out, or even the second or third time. Many students will test you, and even reject you to see if you abandon them. Keep reaching out anyway.

How do you put a comforting arm around these students, even metaphorically? Although entire books are written on providing support for resilience, here are a few of the ways you can demonstrate a caring relationship right away. Welcome them to class by name and with respect. Find out about their outside activities and hobbies, and ask about them. Let them know that you are aware that their team had a tough game, wish them luck in their upcoming swim meet, or congratulate them on a band contest. Offer your condolences for a loss in their community. In this way, you let them know that they exist for you as a whole person rather than just as a number or a grade. Learn about community events likely to be important to them, and refer to those events in conversation. Show up at their events and cheer. Privately, feel free to tell them what you appreciate about them. Make positive calls to the home, letting parents and guardians know what they have done well in school, even if it's small. Always include positive comments on the work they turn in, rather than just marking errors. Offer to help with homework after school; you can also offer to be a listener if your students have problems, and express empathy.

Provide structured opportunities for modeling and practicing the importance of fostering caring relationships with others. Peer relationships can be extremely valuable.

PD **TOOLKIT**™

PDToolkit: Video Clip 11.1 provides two illustrations of offering caring and support within the context of the classroom.

External Protective Factor II: High Expectations

Many students who have struggled in school for a variety of reasons believe that they are not capable; in addition, they feel that their *teachers* believe that they are incapable, stupid, or lazy. This can become a self-fulfilling prophecy. Your students must know that you believe they can learn and succeed, and that you expect to see them do it. Schools that guarantee their students will graduate and go to college attract vast numbers of students (and their parents), because these students know that the teachers will believe in them and plan to deliver on that belief. Rather than communicate your high expectations as a generic message that "all kids can learn," it is more helpful to use specifics, letting individual students know that you expect them to do well because you have observed them, seen them in action, and believe in them. Prove it by offering support and high expectations. Their emerging belief in their own abilities to meet high expectations becomes a critical protective factor, helping them build traits of resilience: self-efficacy, autonomy, and optimism.

PD **TOOLKIT**™

PDToolkit: Video Clip 11.2 provides an example of a teacher communicating high expectations.

You can do several things right away. For example, take these students seriously. See their potential and teach to that, suggesting that you can help each of them get there. Show them models of others who have gone against all odds to achieve, and dare to offer them something really challenging, because you know they will be excited when they master it.

External Protective Factor III: Meaningful Participation

When students are given responsibility within the school, they form an emotional bond and a sense of pride in their school. Without it, they tend to feel uncommitted and disconnected to their learning environment. Within your school and classroom, you can provide a variety of meaningful activities and opportunities where students are encouraged to think critically, problem-solve, work collaboratively, plan, set goals, and help others (Wehlage, Rutter, Smith, Lesko, & Fernandez, 1989). Create responsibilities for students. Dozens of things need to be done in classrooms. By delegating and sharing responsibility with students, they have a meaningful place in the system. Some teachers have students apply for these jobs.

Meaningful participation occurs at another level when students become part of a democratic community; that is, they have a say in governance and policy (e.g., the class rules). Meaningful participation in the classroom means that their opinions on issues are sought and used. They think together and share ideas (see, for instance, MiCOSA strategies for collaboration). Use critical thinking and dialogue to encourage their meaningful participation in classroom discussions. Project-based learning creates a haven for meaningful involvement. Have students engage in creating evaluation rubrics and other participatory evaluation strategies.

By offering a smorgasbord of choices, you can tap into your students' diverse interests and support their motivation. By facilitating their involvement within groups, and more broadly in school clubs, you help them to connect, belong, experience loyalty and usefulness, and, of course, succeed. Broadening this choice and involvement to community service learning broadens the base of meaning. This in turn strengthens their social competence and self-efficacy, and gives them a sense of purpose and future.

Raising Student Self-Expectations

Resilient students typically demonstrate four internal protective factors: social competence, self-efficacy, sense of purpose, and skill in problem-solving. With MiCOSA, mediating interactions help you communicate your belief in the students; this, in turn, supports their development of belief in themselves. Understanding that potential often lays under the cover of insecurity, self-doubt, or even trauma, you begin with the intent to support and facilitate your students' fullest potential. You seek reciprocity, intending for the students to see that potential as well. This means that interactions designed to hold out high expectations are not just related to thinking; rather, they begin to consider the emotional and motivational aspects of the whole person. Thus, in each of the following cases, MiCOSA's mediating conversations are used to help support students to develop the internal protective factors.

Internal Protective Factor I. Social Competence: Forming Positive Relationships

Students who can establish and maintain positive social relationships pull the best out of others and form positive friendships. They are flexible, empathetic, and genuinely care. Able to laugh at themselves, they find humor in challenging or absurd situations that may face them.

They set academic goals for themselves, as well as social ones, and understand that their academic success is intrinsically linked to goals valued by those around them: the peers that form their various learning groups, and the teacher. Therefore, they understand the relevance in forming positive and considerate relationships with others (Wentzel & Wigfield, 1998).

Michael is an eighth grader. He is new to the school, yet arrives with a confidence and warmth evident from the onset of his appearance at the door. He picks up a book that has dropped on the ground beside him and hands it back with a smile to the owner. He is not "pushy," nor is he reticent to join in when another student strikes up a dialogue. He has already begun to appraise the climate and dynamics of the class. He knows that he may have to prove himself to some of the more assertive members of the class, but not today. He will observe more at first, and understand who to avoid and who among his peers will be open to opportunities for more positive relationships (those who seem to have similar interests and values as his own).

Student Inefficient with Social Competence

On the other hand, Tim arrives as a newcomer to the middle school with a sullen expression, head down, and hands in his pockets. A book falls by his foot and he whirls around, glaring at the "offender," mumbling under his breath. Unlike Michael, Tim is angry at having been sent to a new school, leaving his only friend. He is entrenched in his own emotional world, unable to appraise the climate and dynamics of the class and respond appropriately. He is not in a place to begin to establish positive relationships. Shutting out others and poor social competence will impact his academic development as well as life beyond the classroom. You will want to try to help him turn that around before it escalates.

Mediating Forming Positive Relationships with Tim

All five mediating conversations are integrated into this example. Notice that no specific sequence need occur; in fact, often, mediating conversations occur in tandem with one another.

Intent and Reciprocity

Ms. Sanchez first wants to establish *intent and reciprocity* with Tim. Her intent is to help him engage in positive instead of negative relationships, and to develop a positive enough sense of himself to hold his head up in confidence rather than in defiance. She begins to communicate this intent by modeling a positive relationship for him. "Tim, welcome to the class. I am looking forward to getting to know you." She can assume from his initial negative affect that gaining reciprocity in this relationship will take time, so she reaches out, beginning with, "I'd like to spend five minutes with you after school." During that five minutes, she explains that knowing something about her students helps her tailor the class, so she would like to know what Tim's best learning experiences have been in the past, either in or out of school. She wants to find something to anchor their future "bridge" on—one or two positive experiences in his life where he saw himself responding positively. She uses the time when he is not angry and unsure of himself to begin the conversation, hoping to eventually bridge that knowledge and memory of himself doing well into new situations.

Mediating Meaning

Ms. Sanchez listens to Tim's experiences. Seeking to link into her intent to help him develop positive relationships, she comments, "Tim, I have designed some group learning activities. In addition to helping each other learn, these will be opportunities to have everyone show respect to one other, since we all do better when we are respected, and we all deserve respect (mediating meaning of positive relationships). Most of the class has tried this before, but because you are new, I know it may be a little more challenging. I would like to offer a little help so you can know when you are on track (intent to have him succeed). If it's okay with you, I am going to gently tap the side of your desk as I come by whenever I see you making respectful contributions to those discussions and when I see others being respectful to you (helping guide his self-regulation)." Later, she might notice the effects of his improved behavior, and quietly say to him something like, "Tim, it looks like Sara and Alejandro look forward to working with you on this project. I am happy to see you developing these friendships."

Guiding Self-Regulation and Building Competence   Knowing that change takes time, practice, and repeated use of mediating conversations, Ms. Sanchez first considers that she'll give herself a good six weeks to help Tim make a positive shift. Over time, she seeks ways to help him practice positive relationships and opportunities to mediate the meaning of his changes. Moving from the "gentle tap on the desk" to a more direct conversation, she makes these observations more overt and gives them meaning. She shares thoughts privately with Tim, out of the hearing range of other students. In order not to have Tim feel singled out, she will quietly share positive comments to one or two others in the same group at that time. She might say, for instance: "Tim, I noticed that when you shared your idea on that project, both Mike and Javier seemed to really pick up on it." "I really appreciated your thoughtfulness to Brianna today. I noticed that when you helped her locate her place, she looked relieved. It's good to see you having these positive interactions in class." These whispered moments and quiet gestures that recognize his successes not only show Tim that she noticed his efforts of *self-regulation*, but they also help him *build* a sense of *competence*. This sense of competence enables him to continue building positive interactions on his own initiative.

Bridging Thinking   To assure that Tim will use his new behaviors outside the classroom, Ms. Sanchez looks for ways to help him *bridge and transfer* his positive relationships. For instance, looking for his interests and strengths, she introduces him to the art club and to the faculty sponsor. Enriching environments provide a firm foundation for Tim to continue to practice positive interactions. In addition, she helps "build an audience" for his newfound positive relationships, allowing other key people to hear about him in a different light. She does this in ways ranging from positive calls home when he does something well to sharing positive stories with other teachers. Thus, his reputation begins to change. She builds support for him by building external expectations for more positive behavior.

PD **TOOLKIT**™

PDToolkit:
Additional strate-
gies to support
mediating social
competence
are found in
PDToolkit.

Internal Protective Factor II. Self-Efficacy: Knowing I Can Do It

Students with a strong sense of self-efficacy often have a strong sense of their own identity. They act independently and appear self-disciplined and confident. Socially, they can initiate and maintain relationships with others. Students with strong self-efficacy believe they are capable of achieving goals they set for themselves. They also believe they can have an effect on their surroundings and a certain control over it. They are able to "step back" and distance themselves from personal crises, and get on with tasks at hand. They do not try to blame others for their misfortunes. They believe their own behavior and actions control events that affect them; that is, they have a high internal "locus of control." Finally, these students have autonomy; they make informed and responsible decisions on their own. They have integrity and feel they have a certain amount of control over their own destiny. Picture Garrett, a third grader. He walks into class, then begins taking out his books and organizing his desk. Last night, he sent his homework to the teacher on *Blackboard*, meeting the deadline. While several others around him are talking, Garrett is checking the electronic whiteboard and making updates to his calendar entries for the day. When collaborating on group projects, Garrett is well-prepared and shares with confidence. His peers respect him.

Student Inefficient with Self-Efficacy

Sarah, also a third grader, enters the room, but at first is hard to detect in the group. Ah, there she is, looking up at the "leader" of the group, listening to her every word. Today is similar to many other days. When homework is collected, Sarah approaches the teacher with an excuse for why hers has not been done. Throughout the lesson, Sarah begins any independent work hesitantly. She looks around to see what the others are doing and tries to lean over and ask for help. She sits back in her collaborative group sessions, feeling rather powerless; she is unprepared and contributes little.

Using the Framework to Mediate Developing Self-Efficacy

Ms. Bozeman, Sarah's teacher, extends caring, high expectations, and meaningful participation in the classroom as she applies the framework to her interactions with Sarah.

Intent and Reciprocity

Ms. Bozeman first establishes intent and reciprocity. Her intent is to help address Sarah's sense of powerlessness—to help her begin to understand that she is capable. She wants Sarah to be in control of her situation, rather than having the actions and decisions of others control her. She *intends* to help Sarah develop self-efficacy. Ms. Bozeman begins with Sarah's homework issue, which has impacted her contribution to the group project and her performance overall. Rather than naming and solving Sarah's problem for her, Ms. Bozeman asks for her active involvement, prompting Sarah to identify her problem and its consequences herself. For Sarah, failing to complete her homework in a timely fashion led to coming to school ill-prepared; as a result, her grades did not reflect her true capabilities.

Mediating Meaning

After Sarah identifies her problem, the ongoing dialogue between them goes something like this:

> Ms. BOZEMAN: How do you feel about this, Sarah?
>
> SARAH: Bad . . . but it was not all my fault.
>
> Ms. BOZEMAN: It sounds like you didn't feel you were in control of the time you needed to complete your homework. I know that sometimes you *have* felt in

control and you have handed in your work on time. Tell me about a time when you *did* feel in control of your homework, Sarah? What did you do differently?

SARAH: I did the hard homework first when I was fresh, and later, when I was tired, I only had to worry about the easy work that I enjoyed!

Ms. BOZEMAN: You had a plan! Having a plan is a great strategy, Sarah. How did you feel when you completed your homework on time?

SARAH: Great! I felt good in my group the next day too, because I knew what to say and I knew what the others were talking about.

Ms. BOZEMAN: Good for you, Sarah. I think you are beginning to understand what you need to do to control your homework problem.

Guiding Self-Regulation and Building Competence

Ms. BOZEMAN: OK, Sarah, what are you going to do differently tonight so that you feel in control of completing your homework on time?

SARAH: Do the hard stuff first!

Ms. BOZEMAN: It's great to hear you building on what has worked. Let's use that to make a plan together. First, make a list of tonight's homework and prioritize "the hard stuff" as well as time limits so everything gets done. What do you anticipate may be challenging for you and what do you feel will be easy?

Sarah completes her plan. She now has a strategy to help her be successful.

PD **[O]** TOOLKIT™

PDToolkit:
Additional strategies to support the development of self efficacy are found in PDToolkit.

Bridging Thinking   Ms. Bozeman continues to encourage Sarah to prioritize and verbalize how she will tackle her homework, so that she can continue a successful pattern. Developing a bridging principle together with Sarah, they used the phrase, "When I use a plan to organize my work, I succeed." Ms. Bozeman checks in with her daily on that principle, asking questions like, "Did it work last night to organize your work, and did you succeed again?" She then begins to extend the reach of the bridge by asking Sarah where else planning and organizing her work is making a difference. By having Sarah articulate the results of her newfound self-efficacy, Ms. Bozeman helps Sarah transfer the new behavior to new situations.

Internal Protective Factor III. A Sense of Purpose: Knowing What I Want

Students efficient with a strong sense of purpose know what they want. As with self-efficacy, they feel they have some control over their situations and their success. They do not just see themselves as capable, but are also motivated and determined. Having a strong sense of purpose is very powerful, and predicts a positive future for students. Hopeful, self-motivated, and tenacious, these "goal-setters" set personal goals in order to realize their dreams and aspirations. As they have expectations of high achievement, they are more likely to graduate. In doing so, they resist negative influences such as taking drugs, but they also understand that it is their responsibility to *positively* influence others.

From a young age, Suma dreamed of becoming a veterinarian. She joined the 4H club and attends the lunchtime Connection Builders, a service group for community outreach, where she hopes to raise funds and awareness of animal abuse. She runs in track and field events and sings in the school choir. Suma works diligently at her schoolwork, and always hands her assignments in on time, despite her numerous out-of-school pursuits. In fact, when she knows there will be a conflict with school work and her extracurricular activities, she asks her teacher if she can have access to homework assignments ahead of time, enabling her to project her workload and have it ready in a timely manner. Suma's sense of purpose protects her.

Student Inefficient with Developing a Sense of Purpose   Unlike Suma, Clarissa enters Mr. Ross's English class dragging her feet across the floor to her seat. She slouches at her desk, swinging back in her chair, her body turned sideways as if she wants to avoid even being part of the class. Her homework is not complete. She doesn't even come with a reason why it isn't done. She just shrugs her shoulders, and mutters that this is a boring and stupid class anyway. When work commences, Clarissa remains uncommitted to the task. When asked to begin, she replies that she hasn't got a pen or pencil, and then turns around, disrupting others, as she asks to borrow a pen.

Mr. Ross decides he needs to understand a little more about Clarissa, and turns to her cumulative file. He discovers that for most of her school years, reading has been difficult, and she has experienced a sense of academic failure. As a result, she has "chosen" to opt out and fail on her terms rather than fail through her perceived low ability. She is unable to see a bright future for herself, so she lives each day as a separate entity. She has shut out the fact that today impacts her tomorrow; to consider so would be too painful, as failing today will mean failing in the future. It is far easier to blame the class and the work as stupid, rather than herself.

Mediating a Sense of Purpose with Clarissa
Intent and Reciprocity   Mr. Ross first establishes his *intent* and seeks *reciprocity* with Clarissa. He intends to help Clarissa connect to her class, contribute to the learning, and feel successful. Mr. Ross knows she needs to realize her strengths and have opportunities to share them with others, fostering her peers' respect and acceptance. Only then can she begin to see a positive future for herself.

To understand how he first establishes *intent* by creating a positive learning environment for Clarissa, it is helpful to rewind the "video" of the scenario. Clarissa hasn't reached the classroom door yet. On this take, Mr. Ross is there to greet her, sending a positive message from the onset that he cares about her. When Clarissa states that this is a boring, stupid class, Mr. Ross empathizes with her situation, and reframes her words from *boring* and *stupid* to *challenging*: "It sounds like there are some challenges, and I'd like to see how I can help make a difference. I've seen you come up with some good ideas before, so I think we can tackle this one. Come meet with me during the break today and we'll work together on it." This allows him to be in a position to support her, rather than to feel defensive or defeated. He establishes his *intent* to help her problem-solve her difficulties. Knowing that he cannot meet Clarissa's needs at this moment and in the presence of her peers, Mr. Ross asks to meet with her privately to brainstorm and discuss possible solutions. Respecting her in this way lets Clarissa know that he has heard her voice and that what she says matters. She knows that he is inviting her into the process of problem-solving her concerns (inviting her *reciprocity*).

Mediating Meaning   When Clarissa arrives, Mr. Ross compliments her for showing restraint in class and trying to work quietly even though he knows she was upset. He sees a trace of a smile cross her face, though she still continues to say she finds the class "boring and stupid." He asks Clarissa what her options are to solve this dilemma. She proposes that she might drop the class. Rather than be reactive, Mr. Ross asks what would happen if she chooses this option and drops English. For a moment, Clarissa is silent. She very much wants to graduate, so dropping out of the class is not a true option. She shares her thoughts with Mr. Ross. Gently, he invites Clarissa to share her future dreams. What role will English play in Clarissa reaching her career goals? Once she can answer this, he will help her on the journey to be successful. Clarissa is beginning to get a sense of purpose and future!

Next, Mr. Ross asks Clarissa to provide some ways where he can support her (establishing *intent and reciprocity*). Her challenge with reading surfaces: Clarissa "hates" reading. When Mr. Ross asks if she likes movies (seeking *meaning* for her), Clarissa affirms she does. He assures her that if she enjoys movies she can also come to enjoy reading; it is just that she hasn't found the "right" books yet. Mr. Ross offers to help her find "good" books that he believes she will enjoy, so that she can make those movies in her head. He takes note of her interests so that he can provide suitable high-interest, low-readability books that will appeal to her (Beers, 2003).

Guiding Self-Regulation and Building Competence   With Mr. Ross's help, Clarissa sets realistic personal goals: She commits to reading a book from the suggested "good books" selection for 20 minutes a night. On a reading record sheet, she records the number of pages she has read daily, along with one or two sentences about the content. Each week she hands in her record sheet, sharing with Mr. Ross what she likes or doesn't like about the book and what change she sees in herself as a reader. Mr. Ross also sets up two sessions a week in the after school club, making sure that they work with Clarissa's schedule. Here, she receives reading and homework support, as well as motivation from others to continue her quest for change. Mr. Ross knows that once she begins to experience success she will be more self-motivated to continue without his outside support. He discusses with Clarissa the need to attend the support club for one month even if she initially feels discouraged, so that she can effectively evaluate her progress. During this period, he encourages Clarissa to record her homework daily in her school agenda book, which he checks for accuracy before she leaves class each day.

PD **d** TOOLKIT™

PDToolkit: Additional strategies to support the development of a sense of purpose are found in PDToolkit.

Bridging Thinking   At the end of the month, Clarissa shares written feedback on her accomplishments with Mr. Ross. Together, they evaluate the significance of her investment of time. He guides her to look beyond the immediate moment, and see where this effort supports her in graduating and reaching her career objectives. Mr. Ross uses the *bridging* principle, "When I take ownership of what I really want in the future, I can deal with how to get there." They discuss how taking ownership and being in control worked in this situation and how it could work in the future.

Internal Protective Factor IV. Problem-Solving: Having Ways to Find Solutions

When efficient, students take specific steps to resolve *academic* or *social* problems that confront them. They make judgments, reflect, decide on an action, and eventually provide a solution; that is, they begin to think "critically." As critical thinkers, students make these decisions based on their observations, interpretations, analyses, inferences, and evaluations. They become flexible in their thinking, which enables them to seek and find patterns and connections, and to transfer this new-found knowledge to other problems they want to solve.

Consider Desmond, a tenth grader who had to be absent from school on Tuesday and Wednesday. Not wanting to get "behind" with his class work, Desmond takes matters into his own hands to solve this *academic* problem. First, he checks online for his class assignments. Needing clarification on one of the procedures, he first attempts the problem himself, and then emails a peer to check that he is on the right path. He returns to school Thursday with all assignments completed. Desmond also displays great *social* problem-solving skills. Upon his return, he begins working with a collaborative group on a project entitled *Conservation: Energy-Efficiency in the Automobile Industry*. Desmond quickly assesses that one member of his group, Damien, is not joining in the discussions. Desmond tries to make sure that the group hears Damien's opinions, so that he feels valued and included.

Student Inefficient as a Problem Solver
George is also absent from school and faces the same academic challenge of completing assignments. Unlike Desmond, he makes no attempt to make up the work while away, and returns to school empty-handed. Only after being assigned detention does he attempt his work. However, even with this additional time, he does not complete it by the end of the session. George does not even appear to see there was a problem in the first place. He seems to possess no "self-help" skills when he becomes stuck; no internal "check list" of the steps to take to problem-solve what he needs to do next. He just "gives up" rather than attempt the challenge before him.

Unfortunately, students struggling with *problem-solving* often struggle with *social* skills too, and George is no exception. He constantly gets into confrontations at lunch. For instance, one day he wants to sit on a bench where other boys are already sitting. Rather than waiting to be invited to join them, he pushes himself in between two of them, knocking both boys and papers off balance and killing the upbeat atmosphere. Even though this type of incident usually ends with George being "attacked" by the others, leaving him red-faced and angry, he seems to constantly repeat this "offense." He does not seem to see his role in creating the problem, nor that he has an active role in its resolution. He quickly becomes a social outcast.

Mediating George's Problem-Solving Skills

Intent and Reciprocity   Mr. Dee first establishes intent and reciprocity with George. His intent is to help George identify his problem, its *cause*, and the *effect* on his own life and others. Alongside this, Mr. Dee wants to foster a positive connection with George as his teacher. Eventually this connection will enable George to begin to feel more effective in his life and relationships; it will also help him understand how to take control of his life.

Mediating Meaning   Mr. Dee begins to help mediate meaning for George. He guides George to identify his own problematic areas and invites him into the process of fixing them. What options does he have? What will be the consequences of taking each of those options and which will bring him the results he wants? George begins to understand how his previous behavior has impacted both his *academic* and *social* outcomes.

Guiding Self-Regulation and Building Competence   Mr. Dee chooses to mediate the use of *cause and effect—hypothesizing* to help George develop *self-regulation*. He sees that using these thinking skills will support George with both his *academic* and his *social* development. *Academically*, George has attributed his low grade (*effect*) to a perceived lack of ability rather than seeing that it is *caused* by his failure to complete assignments. Once George has begun to understand the effect his actions have on the outcome and considers his options, Mr. Dee can help him construct a plan to resolve his missing assignment problem.

Reflecting on George's repeated *social* challenges, Mr. Dee sees that George has not understood the *cause* of the problem (his negative behavior) or the *effect* it has on others. Therefore, George cannot project and *hypothesize* options when he feels tempted to repeat the offense. To help George reflect on his *social* problem, Mr. Dee uses the strategy SWBS (Beers, 2003) to "step outside himself" and begin to understand others' points of view and how his behavior impacts them. Here is what it looks like:

Somebody (George) **W**anted_____ **B**ut_____ **S**o_____.
    (George's point of view)

Somebody (the other boys) **W**anted_____ **B**ut_____
    So_____. (Other points of view)

Using this frame, George begins to fill in the blanks. It looks something like this:

GEORGE: "*I wanted* to sit on the table next to Alex, *but* this other kid, Jason, was sitting there, *so* I pushed him over so I could sit there."

Mr. DEE: "Now let's look at it, George, from Jason's point of view. Ready? Jason wanted . . . you finish the SWBS, George."

GEORGE: "*Jason wanted* to sit next to Alex, *but* I pushed him out of the way, *so* he got mad and shouted at me and pushed me back and then the other kids started yelling at me, too."

Mr. DEE: "Good, George. I believe you are beginning to see the problem, the cause and effect of your actions. How could you have prevented Jason and the other kids from getting mad, George? Let's step back in time. It is recess. You are approaching the table and want to sit next to Alex. What could you do differently this time?"

GEORGE: "I could have asked Jason to let me sit there."

Bridging Student Thinking   Although SWBS helps George identify a problem after it occurs, Mr. Dee wants George to bridge his new *cause–effect* skills to additional situations. To support the work, Mr. Dee introduces the strategy *Stop-Look-Reflect-Connect,* asking students to *stop* before they respond, *look* and observe carefully, *reflect* and interpret their observations, then *connect* those reflections to an action. *Stop-Look-Reflect-Connect* guides George to self-regulate negative thoughts before they become actions. As a result, he begins to experience a feeling of competence as he starts to establish positive behaviors with his peers. This competence carries over to his academics, as well. Rather than wait until the problem of late or missing work occurs, George makes plans to organize his workload. He sees the effectiveness and efficiency of this strategy when he is encouraged to *transfer* and project how it will help him solve similar problems in the future. For example, when George visits his grandparents for two months, he will need to plan to collect work from his teachers *before* he goes, and will need to make a plan of action to complete it while away. As the year progresses, George flourishes. George's success is due in part to his ability to identify his problems as well as plan strategies to correct them.

Stop-Look-Reflect-Connect

To encourage a thoughtful and appropriate response to a problem, or to avoid a problem in the first place, ask students to *stop* before they respond, react, or interact and *look* around to observe what they see and hear. Like good detectives, they look and note the *who, what, where, when,* and *how* of the situation. They do not try to make judgments or create solutions at this stage. They just gather the "evidence" before them in a multisensory way. Now encourage them to *reflect* and interpret their observations. What options are available to them to solve this problem? What effect will each option have on themselves and on others? Finally, ask them to *connect* these reflections to a positive and effective action, reaction, or interaction that they will take to rectify the problem.

PDToolkit: Additional strategies to support the development of problem solving are found in PDToolkit.

Expectations of Parents: Re-Thinking Parent Involvement

However differently parents involve themselves with you and your students, high parental *expectations* for their children make a positive difference across all groups. Parents' expectations influence students' expectations, and the students' own expectations of themselves also tend to influence the parents' expectations of them. Likewise, levels of expectation and levels of achievement influence each other (Zhang, Haddad, Torres, & Chen, 2011). How can you work with your students' parents in a way so that they communicate high expectations to their children as well as get involved in meaningful ways?

PDToolkit: In Video Clip 11.3, a school principal talks about the rigorous levels of student engagement, strong results, and high levels of parent involvement resulting from the program.

It is helpful to begin by considering what is meaningful to the parents. Begin by communicating your belief that children begin to learn—both content and thinking skills—at home, through their original cultures and languages. Therefore, you hope to build on and partner with that valuable learning the students bring with them to school.

Parental involvement in your students' education takes a variety of forms when it occurs. Although in some schools, selling wrapping paper, helping with the food drive, and acting as chaperones for field trips counts as "involvement," in general, parental involvement refers to helping with homework, communicating with you as teachers, and participating in school activities. However, it can also mean facilitating "cognitively stimulating activities" (Yamamoto & Holloway, 2010, p. 204). When you partner with parents using MiCOSA, you will build directly on what you know about their roles as initial teachers and mediators of learning. They will become sources of authentic support for thinking skill development.

Parents as Partners in Mediation of Thinking Skills

Thinking skills can be found and practiced in a multitude of contexts in the home and community, from organizing mealtimes to learning traditional dances or understanding the significance of cultural events. You can explain this to parents and give them examples of how they may already develop thinking skills together with their son or daughter at home; for example, when they plan a meal they are using *planning*, or when they prepare for an event, they will use *multiple sources* of information to determine what needs to be done. When simple examples set the tone, parents begin to innovate and even create situations in which they can practice and strengthen thinking skills. This happens powerfully when done in the context of the home culture, using activities they already do together. Parents get excited about having a meaningful role that builds on what they already do, know, and value. In addition, learning to learn, or practicing using thinking skills, can be done in any language—they will transfer into the classroom with bridging. This helps you bridge both linguistic differences and literacy gaps to create new forms of partnerships.

Parent Views of Parent Involvement

Parents view their involvement in their children's education in different ways, especially across cultural groups. Reasons vary from cultural expectations of schools to literacy levels and resources. For instance, parents in some cultures believe strongly that the school's job or "place" is to educate the child, and that too much "involvement" might be seen as interference. These parents may see their jobs as assuring that their children's behavior aligns with traditional roles. In contrast, a teacher may view what a parent perceives as "involvement" as "interference." For example, an African-American mother raised deep concerns that racism from other students in the classroom was interfering with her child's education. In this parent's mind, she saw her raising concerns as a significant form of involvement, while the teacher perceived her concerns as complaining or criticizing. By not reframing the "confrontation" as parent involvement, and factoring in different ways of communicating, the teacher may miss the opportunity to engage with the parent.

Some of your students' parents may not have a high level of English literacy; if direct communication is difficult, they may just stay away. Still others may not have resources for transportation or childcare, making the idea of coming to meetings at the school impossible. On the other hand, you might perceive some parents as having "an abundance" of resources (and a sense of entitlement), yet those parents may believe that parent involvement comes in the form of advocating for their child's "rights." Again, if you can reframe this as a welcome form of parent involvement, then you may be able to circumvent what otherwise may be viewed as pushy and disrespectful behavior that ends up alienating parents and school personnel. This is not to say that parents won't "push your buttons" from time to time. However, as you broaden your views of parent involvement, honoring and respecting differences while maintaining your own self-respect, you further support your students.

PD **TOOLKIT**™

PDToolkit:
A more in-depth discussion of ideas to support inclusion of parents as partners in the learning process is found in PDToolkit.

SUMMARY

- Holding high expectations and communicating those expectations can make a significant difference in student motivation and success. A triad of expectations, from teachers, parents, and the students themselves, forms a powerful foundation for engaged learning.

- Teachers' expectations are best maintained when knowing what to do. Linking teacher actions to the factors that lead to student resilience helps students develop the affective and motivational support to take on challenging work. Based on their students' potential, teachers support resilience through extending caring relationships, specific high expectations with support, and opportunities for meaningful participation.

- Student internal resilience develops when students learn to establish positive relationships, to feel in charge of their own destinies, to have a sense of purpose, and to feel skilled in problem-solving. Teachers can support each of these protective factors using the five mediating conversations.

- Parent and community expectations form the third point of a strong and stable support system for the students. Teachers can support parents to hold high expectations through helping value parent and community contributions to student learning, in content and in thinking skills.

REFERENCES

Achieve. (2009). Closing the expectations gap. American Diploma Project Network. Retrieved from www.achieve.org/files/50-state-2009.pdf

Beers, K. (2003). *When kids can't read: What teachers can do: A guide for teachers 6–12*. Portsmouth, NH: Heineman.

Benard, B., (2004) *Resiliency: What we have learned*. San Francisco, CA: WestED

De Jesus, A. & Antrop-Gonzalez, R. (2006). Instrumental relationships and high expectations: Exploring critical care in two Latino community-based schools. *Intercultural Education, 17*(3), 281–299.

McNeely, C., Nonemaker, J., & Blum, R. (2002). Promoting school connectedness: Evidence from the National Longitudinal Study of Adolescent Health. *Journal of School Health, 72*, 138–146.

Resilience Research Center. (2010). *What is resilience?* Retrieved from www.resilienceproject.org/

Resnick, M. D., Bearman, P. S., Blum, R. W., Bauman, K. E., Harris, K. M., Jones, J., et al. (1997). Protecting adolescents from harm: Findings from the national longitudinal study on adolescent health. *The Journal of the American Medical Association, 278*(10), 823–832. doi: 10.1001/jama.1997.03550100049038

Resnick, M. D., Ireland, M., & Borowsky, I. (2004). Youth violence perpetration: What protects? What predicts? Findings from the National Longitudinal Study of Adolescent Health. *Journal of Adolescent Health, 35*(424), e1–e10.

Ungar, M. (2005). Introduction: Resilience across cultures and contexts. In M. Ungar (Ed.). *Handbook for working with children and youth: Pathways to resilience across cultures and contexts* (pp. xv–xxxix). Thousand Oaks, CA: Sage Publication.

Wehlage, G. G., Rutter, R. A., Smith, G. A., Lesko, N., & Fernandez, R. R. (1989). *Reducing the risk: Schools as communities of support.* New York: Falmer Press.

Wentzel, K. R., & Wigfield, A. (1998). Academic and social motivational influences on students' academic performance. *Educational Psychology Review, 10*, 155–173.

Wlodkowski, R. J., & Ginsberg, M. B. (1995). *A framework for culturally responsive teaching. Educational Leadership, 53*(1), 17–21.

Yamamoto, Y., & Holloway, S. D. (2010). Parental expectations and children's academic performance in sociocultural context. *Educational Psychology Review, 22*, 189–214. doi: 10.1007/s10648-010-9121-z

Zhang, Y., Haddad, E., Torres, B., & Chen, C. (2011). The reciprocal relationship among parents' expectations, adolescents' expectations, and adolescents' achievement: A two-wave longitudinal analysis of the NELS Data. *Journal of Youth and Adolescence, 40*, 479–489. doi: 10.1007/s10964-010-9568-8

Appendix A

List of Strategies That Support the MiCOSA Model

Chapter	Mediating Conversation or Thinking Skill	Strategy and Location in Book	Strategy and Location in PD TOOLKIT™
Chapter 3: Mediating Conversations for Enhancing Thinking			
	Intent and Reciprocity	• Sensory Connections • Quick Writes • Tea Party	
	Mediating Meaning	• Project-Based Learning • Jigsaw • Give One, Get One	
	Bridging Thinking	• Thinking Skills Journals • Skill Time!	
	Guiding Self-Regulation	• GO Choose • Charting My Success • What's on Your Mind Time? • Putting It Write With Art • Putting the Cart Before the Horse	
	Building Competence	• Scaffolding • MiCOSA's Thinking Skills Cards • Whiteboard Quick Checks	
Chapter 4: Thinking Skills for Gathering Information	**Thinking Skills**	**Book**	PD TOOLKIT™
	Systematic Search	• Start with the Goal in Mind • Anticipatory Guides • Skimming and Scanning • Relevancy Matters • iPad Games	• Sherlock Holmes • Treasure Hunt

Chapter	Mediating Conversation or Thinking Skill	Strategy and Location in Book	Strategy and Location in PD TOOLKIT™
	Focus and Attention	• Focus • Sustaining Focus • Selective Attention • Switching Attention • Divided Attention	• Focus: Ready? • Sustaining Focus: Bits • Selective Attention: What's Missing? • Alternating Attention: Book Launch • Divided Attention: Student Notes: Combination Technique
	Labels, Words, and Concepts	• What's My Label? • Make a Match • Word Banks • List, Group, and Label • Concept Drawing • Figuratively Speaking • Tech Talk	• Feeling Bags • Word Previews • Building on Beginnings • Rooting for Words • Concept of a Definition
	Multiple Sources	• Reframe for Success • Thinking Time • One for All	• Nonverbal Supports • Resource Search
	Position in Space	• Maps from Memory • Techy Toggling • Labels for Space • Nonverbal Supports • Active Directions • Narrowing the Gap	• Kinesthetics • Perceptual Work • How Do We Get There? • About How Far? • 3D Models
	Position in Time	• Put Yourself in the Picture • Time Tapes • Time Cues • Topic Sentence Time • Sequencing Games • Graphic Organizers	• Labels for Time • Changes Over Time • Reading Time • Manipulating Time • Back to the Future • What Will Happen Next?

Chapter	Mediating Conversation or Thinking Skill	Strategy and Location in Book	Strategy and Location in PD TOOLKIT™
	Precision and Accuracy	• Precision from Nature • Direction Twist • Directed Draw	• Picturing the Details • Telephone Tree
Chapter 5: Thinking Skills for Transforming Information	**Thinking Skills**	**Book**	PD TOOLKIT™
	Goal Setting	• Personal Goals • Goal for the Day • Celebrate Milestones	• Career Readiness Goals • Goal Post
	Planning	• Authentic Planning • Concept of a Plan • Graph a Plan and Plan a Graph • Project Planning • Rubrics as Planning Guides	• Shady Thinking! • Planning My Future
	Comparing	• Show Me What It Looks Like • Copy Change • Concept of an Attribute • Nonlinguistic Representations • Celebrate Our Differences	• Feeling Bags • Which Doesn't Belong? • Figurative Language • Me We Books
	Ordering, Grouping, and Categorizing	• Begin with the Basics • Keep the Characters Straight • Prerequisite Words and Concepts • Categories at Home	• Topic Sentences • Organizing the Disorganized • Talk Time
	Finding Connections and Relationships	• KWHL • Inspiration • GO Relationships! • Free Association • Analogy Games • Connect Knowledge • Postcards • For Want of a Nail	• Give One, Get One • Keep the Characters Straight • Figurative Language • Text-to-Self, Text-to-Text, Text-to-World

Chapter	Mediating Conversation or Thinking Skill	Strategy and Location in Book	Strategy and Location in PD **id** TOOLKIT™
	Visualizing	• Imagine That! • Mental Movies • Storyboards • Book Hooks • Draw That Tune	• Seeing the Concept • Picture Concepts of a Definition • Adding Landmarks • Mental Movies: The Sequel • Imagine That! Park Venture Story
	Inferring	• Quia Website Practice • Socratic Seminar • Inference Riddles Website • Under the Surface: Signs and Gestures • Under the Surface: Symbols • Under the Surface: Pictures • Under the Surface: Text	• Brain Teasers • Context Clues • Question Answer Response (QAR) • Books That Facilitate Inference Work
	Cause and Effect-Hypothesizing	• Graph the Cues • What-If Lunch Bag Game • Find Your Match	• Ask Me Why and I'll Give You a Cause • Cause or Sequence? • Enriching with Literature • Sentence Flips • The Scientific Method Revisited • SWBS
	Summarizing	• Combination Technique for Student Notes • Skimming • Scan for Information • Leave In Leave Out • GIST • Draw Summaries • Storymapping	• Paraphrasing • Summarizing with Highlighting Strips • Moving from Summarizing to Highlighting • Authentic Summary Practice • Storymapping • SWBS • SHAPE GO! Map

Chapter	Mediating Conversation or Thinking Skill	Strategy and Location in Book	Strategy and Location in PD TOOLKIT™
Chapter 6: Thinking Skills for Communicating Information			
	Labels, Words, and Concepts	• Authentic Practice • Metacognitive Writing • Choral Reading • Active Hands • Unblock the Writing Block • Share the Pen • Story Bags • Noun Bag, Verb Bag, Adjective Bag • Tea Party • Talking Stick, Pass the Pen, Heart Talks • Masterpiece Sentences	• What's My Label? • Feeling Bags • Building on Beginnings • Word Banks • List, Group, and Label • Retell • Storymapping Oral Presentations • Language Experience Approach • Choosing a Graphic Organizer • Copy Change • Talking Chips • Multiple Drafts
	Precision and Accuracy	• Meaningful Contexts for Precision • Pacing for Precision • Accuracy and Insight • Model Precision and Accuracy • Internet Punctuation Games	• Sand Timers • Precision Memory • Precision in Context • Wrong! • The Dear John Letter
	Appropriate Pragmatics	• Role-Playing Appropriate Pragmatics • Model Correct Pragmatics in Speech • Authentic Pragmatics	• Persuasive Sentence Starters • Conversation and Storytelling Skills

Chapter	Mediating Conversation or Thinking Skill	Strategy and Location in Book	Strategy and Location in PD TOOLKIT™
	Feedback for Self-Regulation	• Binder Reminders • Self-Check Using Feelings • Think Aloud • Personal Goals • Double-Entry Reflective Journals • Rubrics for Self-Regulation • Online Coach • Put it Write with Art	• Reading Records • Monitoring Me • Fishbowl • Behavior Charting • Acting on External Feedback • Fix My Feedback
	Collaboration	• Stop, Freeze, Collaborate • Listening Out in the Open • Jigsaw or Double Jigsaw • Technology Assists • Overt Assessment of Collaboration • From Seeds to Flowers • Collaborative Language	• Climate of Collaboration • Results • Give One, Get One • Family Fun
Chapter 11: Engaging Expectations and Promoting Resilience	**Raising Student Self-Expectations**	**Book**	PD TOOLKIT™
	Forming Positive Relationships		• Cooperative Learning Strategies • Jigsaw • Find Someone Who • Pair Check/Pair Compare • Games to Learn Social Skills • SOON Resolved • Strength Building • Each One Teach One • Democratic Debates and Discussions • For Your Ears Only • LOL

Chapter	Mediating Conversation or Thinking Skill	Strategy and Location in Book	Strategy and Location in PD TOOLKIT™
	Developing Self-Efficacy		• Supplies for Hire • Collaborative Learning Experiences • Me vs. The Problem: The Fight Is On! • Strength Building • My Choice • Steps to Success
	Sense of Purpose		• Heroes and Their Inspirations • Guess Who? • Humor Me • Strategies from Developing Self-Efficacy • Goals for Today and Tomorrow • Reframing Your Fame
	Problem-Solving	• SWBS • Stop-Look-Reflect-Connect	• The Scottish Storyline Method for Social Studies • Deep, Wide, and Thought-Provoking • Linking to Scientific Thinking • Stop-Look-Reflect-Connect • SWBS • There Is More Than One Way to Cook an Egg! • Probing Deeper

MiCOSA Student Thinking Skills Survey

Getting to Know Myself as a Learner: Thinking Skills Survey

GATHERING INFORMATION: Think about your learning. When you approach a task and gather information for it, how would you rate yourself on a scale of 1–4 on each of these thinking skills: 1 = I don't use it or struggle to use it, and 4 = always using this thinking skill?

Yellow	Orange	Red	Green
1	2	3	4
I struggle with this.	I am sometimes like this.	I am often like this.	I am always like this.

1. **Systematic Search**   1 2 3 4
   When I am gathering information to begin a task, I look for clues to support me. For example, I read directions and look at headings and graphics.

2. **Focus and Attention**
   a. When it is time to start a new task, I immediately begin to focus.   1 2 3 4
   b. I remain focused until I have gathered all the information I need.   1 2 3 4
   c. I stay focused when there is background noise that could distract me, like the lawn mower or car noise outside the classroom.   1 2 3 4
   d. I shift back to the lesson after a disruption such as a message on the intercom, or someone entering the classroom, or when the teacher stops to share some information with us.   1 2 3 4
   e. I can look at the overhead, listen to the instruction, and take notes without losing my focus and attention.   1 2 3 4

3. **Labels, Words, and Concepts**   1 2 3 4
   I am able to find the word I need to express my thinking, and understand the concepts behind these words. I understand synonyms and antonyms, and that words can have more than one meaning. I am not confused by the meaning of words I have read or heard.

4. **Multiple Sources**   1 2 3 4
   I am able to hold onto two or more pieces of information in my head. I can mentally compare these pieces or put them together as one.

5. **Position in Space**   1 2 3 4
   I am able to compare shapes and sizes. I understand directionality and distance (what is near or far). I do not reverse letters or shapes and know my left from my right.

6. **Position in Time**   1 2 3 4
   I understand concepts of the past (e.g., hour, week, month, year, decade). I understand transition words like *first*, *next*, *suddenly*, and *meanwhile*. I understand timelines and can create time frames to finish my homework on time. I am usually punctual.

7. **Precision and Accuracy**   1 2 3 4
   I gather information with precision and accuracy. For example, I read directions accurately, and correctly copy signs, numbers, letters, and words. In math, my columns are aligned.

TRANSFORMING INFORMATION: When you get into an assignment or task/problem, how do you usually use these skills to help you work through your assignments? How would you rate yourself?

Yellow	Orange	Red	Green
1	2	3	4
I struggle with this.	I am sometimes like this.	I am often like this.	I am always like this.

1. **Goal Setting**
I look for and set my own goals for learning.

   1 2 3 4

2. **Planning**
Once I have gathered the information I need, I sequence the steps I need to take to complete my work or project to enable me to reach my goal successfully.

   1 2 3 4

3. **Comparing**
I compare my current task or problem with models and things I have done before. I understand attributes and characteristics of different things I am comparing. For example, I can compare characters and relationships in stories I have read.

   1 2 3 4

4. **Ordering, Grouping, and Categorizing**
I successfully order, group, and categorize information, objects, ideas, and numbers. This helps me store information in my memory.

   1 2 3 4

5. **Finding Connections and Relationships**
I see how things are related to each other. I am able to connect my experiences with new ideas, and I look for and find patterns and rules.

   1 2 3 4

6. **Visualizing**
I picture things in my mind, like images from stories, or ideas and concepts. I can make changes to those pictures as I learn new information. I can store them in my memory and retrieve them at a later date.

   1 2 3 4

7. **Inferring**
I draw logical conclusions from what I see, hear, or read. I make informed decisions on the information I have been given based on my past experiences.

   1 2 3 4

8. **Cause and Effect**
I look for and understand cause and effect relationships (WHEN/THEN situations). I see the effect of an action or actions.

   1 2 3 4

9. **Hypothesizing**
I think about alternatives in my mind, like "If . . . . were to happen, then . . . . might result" (IF/THEN).

   1 2 3 4

10. **Summarizing**
I summarize easily. I pull information together, synthesize the key points or elements of an experience, and get the "big picture."

   1 2 3 4

COMMUNICATING INFORMATION: Think about your learning. Think about the results when you are ready to talk, write, or show your work or ideas. How would you rate yourself on a scale of 1–4 where 1 = not used or struggling, and 4 = always using this thinking skill?

Yellow	Orange	Red	Green
1	2	3	4
I struggle with this.	I am sometimes like this.	I am often like this.	I am always like this.

1. **Labels, Words, and Concepts**   1 2 3 4
   I have the labels, words, and concepts I need to express my ideas, and am not searching for words I need.
   I can use synonyms rather than be repetitive. I am able to use language that creates meaning for the reader or listener.

2. **Precision and Accuracy**   1 2 3 4
   I am precise and accurate when I need to be. For instance, I make word choices to help me express what I
   mean, and I consider sentence structure and punctuation. I am precise and accurate in math and science.

3. **Appropriate Pragmatics**   1 2 3 4
   I consider what to say and when to say it when I am with other people. I feel others understand what I am trying
   to say, even though they may not agree with me. I keep to the topic being discussed and share the conversation.
   I show feelings/empathy that reflect how the other person feels.

4. **Uses Feedback for Self-Regulation**   1 2 3 4
   I check my own work before I consider it done. I appreciate feedback from peers and teachers. I invest effort to
   correct when I need to. I can adjust my pacing to improve my performance (i.e., slow down/speed up). I ask for
   clarification when I need it.

5. **Collaboration**   1 2 3 4
   I work easily and well in groups or with a partner. I listen to others and share my thinking, which changes as a
   result of what I have learned from others.

Overall Sense of Self as a Learner

1. **Social Competence – Positive Relationships**   1 2 3 4
   I have positive relationships with others, and can sometimes bring the best out in them. I genuinely care about
   others and enjoy collaboration. I use humor to help me through some challenges.

2. **Self Efficacy – Knowing I Can Do It**   1 2 3 4
   I believe I am a capable learner, and I look forward to challenges. I work easily and well by myself, but ask for
   information when I need it. I am self-motivated; I do not relying on the teacher to encourage me to complete my
   project/ assignment.

3. **Sense of Purpose – Direction in Life**   1 2 3 4
   I feel in control of my work and have high expectations for myself. I have goals and dreams, and am motivated
   and determined to reach them.

4. **Skilled with Problem-Solving**   1 2 3 4
   I have ways to find solutions to problems I am given, or that arise from my work or social situations.

Name _____   Date _____

Subject(s) _____

Teacher _____   Period _____

Use The Student Thinking Skills Organizer (Appendix C) to record the results of your Survey. Use the color coding (Yellow, Orange, Red, Green) indicated above to complete Organizer.

Appendix C

Student Thinking Skills Organizer

Directions: Use the color coding from your Survey (Appendix C and PDToolkit) to complete this Organizer. You will use this organizer in the future to record your progress.

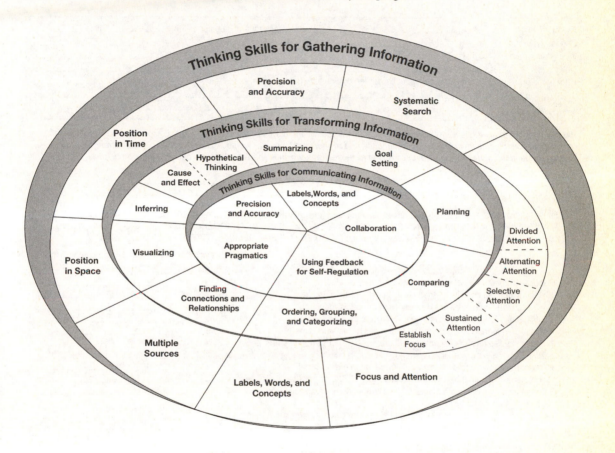

Parent/Teacher Thinking Skills Interview/Questionnaire

Name of Student _____ Gender:_____ Grade:_____ Age: _____

Parent or Teacher _____ Relation to Student:_____

Interviewer (if applicable): _____ Position:_____

Date: _____ Language 1:_____ Language 2:_____

Brief notes on cultural history (e.g., culture of origin, depth of cultural transmission; assimilation)_____
_____
_____

You have important expertise about how your student thinks, learns, and solves problems since you have seen him/her learn things important to your classroom or family, your community, and his/her development. I would like to ask you about both strengths and struggles in learning. You may not have responses to all these areas, which is fine. Any ideas you can share will be helpful.

Think of something that you have seen him/her learn successfully or well: _____

Think of something you have seen him/her struggle to learn: _____

I. THINK ABOUT HIS/HER LEARNING (the skills you listed above). WHEN YOUR STUDENT APPROACHES AND GATHERS INFORMATION FOR A NEW TASK, ON A SCALE OF 1–4 (WITH 1 = HE/SHE STRUGGLES WITH THIS AND 4 = HE/SHE IS STRONG AND CONSISTENT WITH THIS), HOW WOULD YOU SAY HE/SHE DEMONSTRATES THE FOLLOWING:

	Struggles with this				Strong and consistent with this
Reads directions and looks for clues as begins a task	1	2	3	4	_____
Focuses immediately when starts new task	1	2	3	4	_____
Remains focused until he/she gathers all the information needed	1	2	3	4	_____
Stays focused when there are distractions in the background	1	2	3	4	_____
Shifts back to focusing on work after an interruption/distraction	1	2	3	4	_____
Able to listen to/read instructions and take notes at the same time	1	2	3	4	_____
Has sufficient word and concept knowledge to understand what he/she reads or hears—and to express his/her thinking and needs	1	2	3	4	_____
Can hold on to two or more pieces of information in his/her head	1	2	3	4	_____
Understands size, shape, distance, direction (e.g., left/right, near/far)	1	2	3	4	_____
Understands time concepts. Can sequence events & create realistic time frames for completing tasks	1	2	3	4	_____
Gathers information with precision/accuracy (e.g., correctly reads signs, numbers, words, and directions)	1	2	3	4	_____

Notes/Examples: _____
_____
_____
_____
_____

II. ONCE _____ ENGAGES WITH THE TASK/PROBLEM, ON A SCALE OF 1–4 (WITH 1 BEING HE/SHE STRUGGLES WITH THIS AND 4 BEING HE/SHE IS STRONG AND CONSISTENT WITH THIS). HOW WOULD YOU SAY HE/SHE DEMONSTRATES THE FOLLOWING THINKING/LEARNING SKILLS TO WORK THROUGH A TASK OR PROBLEM:

	Struggles with this				Strong and consistent with this
Looks for and sets own goals for learning	1	2	3	4	_____
Plans steps needed to do a project and/or to reach a goal	1	2	3	4	_____
Compares (e.g., uses models and prior information; compares attributes and characteristics)	1	2	3	4	_____
Orders, groups, and categorizes objects, ideas, and numbers	1	2	3	4	_____
Looks for and finds connections, patterns, and rules	1	2	3	4	_____
Forms mental pictures, ideas, or concepts (visualizes)	1	2	3	4	_____
Draws logical conclusions from what he/she sees, hears, or reads (infers)	1	2	3	4	_____
Sees cause-effect relationships (WHEN/THEN situations)	1	2	3	4	_____
Hypothesizes and considers alternatives (IF/THEN)	1	2	3	4	_____
Summarizes easily. Pulls together key points and gets the "big picture"	1	2	3	4	_____

Notes/Examples: _____
_____
_____
_____
_____

III. THINK AGAIN ABOUT _____' S ABILITY TO SHARE HIS/HER THINKING. HOW WELL CAN HE/SHE EXPRESS HIS/HER WORK AND IDEAS ON THE SCALE OF 1–4, HOW MUCH ARE EACH OF THESE LIKE HIM/HER (WITH 1 = HE/SHE STRUGGLES WITH THIS AND 4 = HE/SHE IS STRONG AND CONSISTENT WITH THIS):

	Struggles with this				Strong and consistent with this
Has the words and concepts to express ideas meaningfully, so that the reader or listener understands	1	2	3	4	_____
When needed, is precise and accurate; e.g., in word choice, sentence structure, punctuation, math, or science	1	2	3	4	_____
Considers what to say and how to say it when with others	1	2	3	4	_____
Checks/self-corrects work before he/she considers it finished; values and uses feedback from others	1	2	3	4	_____
Listens to and shares ideas with others when working with others; collaborates	1	2	3	4	_____

Notes/Examples: _____
_____
_____
_____
_____

IV.   OVERALL SENSE OF SELF AS A LEARNER & RESILIENCE

	Struggles with this	Strong and consistent with this
Forms positive relationships with others and can bring the best out in them; he/she genuinely cares about others	1 2 3 4	_____
Sees him/herself as capable as a learner, able to take on challenging tasks; is self-motivated	1 2 3 4	_____
Feels in control of his/her work; has goals, dreams and has high expectations for him/herself	1 2 3 4	_____
Finds solutions to problems encountered at school or in social situations	1 2 3 4	_____

Notes/Examples: _____
_____
_____
_____
_____

V.   WHAT ELSE WOULD YOU LIKE ME TO KNOW ABOUT YOUR CHILD/STUDENT?
_____
_____
_____
_____

Index